KW-484-282

Withdrawn from Stock
Dublin City Public Libraries

THE VOICE OF THE PROVINCES

The Voice of the Provinces

The Regional Press
in Revolutionary Ireland, 1914–1921

CHRISTOPHER DOUGHAN

Leabhar...

16.6.22

Liverpool University Press

First published 2019 by
Liverpool University Press
4 Cambridge Street
Liverpool
L69 7ZU

This paperback edition first published 2022

Copyright © 2019, 2022 Christopher Doughan

The right of Christopher Doughan to be identified as the author of this work
has been asserted by him in accordance with the Copyright, Designs and
Patents Act 1988.

All rights reserved. No part of this book may be reproduced, stored in a retrieval
system, or transmitted, in any form or by any means, electronic, mechanical,
photocopying, recording, or otherwise, without the prior written permission of
the publisher.

British Library Cataloguing-in-Publication data
A British Library CIP record is available

ISBN 978-1-78694-225-8 cased
ISBN 978-1-80085-471-0 paperback

Typeset by Carnegie Book Production, Lancaster
Printed and bound by CPI Group (UK) Ltd, Croydon CR0 4YY

Contents

Acknowledgements

I would like to take this opportunity to thank various people for their help and encouragement during the research and writing of this book. This work is based on my doctoral thesis that I completed in 2015 at the School of Communications at Dublin City University (DCU). Accordingly, I must first and foremost express my gratitude to my thesis supervisor, Dr Mark O'Brien. He had the faith and confidence to take me on as a PhD student in the first place and has kindly provided his advice and guidance at all stages of this project. I would also like to thank the School of Communications at DCU for providing financial assistance during the course of my studies and also for being such a pleasant place in which to study. Additionally, I wish to thank Dr Susan Hegarty of the School of History and Geography at DCU for providing the map that appears in Appendix A of this book.

I would like to thank the staff of the various archives I visited during the course of my research for this book. These include the Military Archives at Cathal Brugha Barracks, University College Dublin Archives, the National Archives of the UK, and particularly the National Library of Ireland. I am especially appreciative of Alison Welsby at Liverpool University Press for her patience and understanding from the time I first made contact with my book proposal.

Finally, I would like to thank my wife, Eileen, for her encouragement and understanding and also her faith in me throughout this project.

Introduction

Irish newspaper history and the regional press

One of the most remarkable developments of the opening two decades of the twenty-first century has been the rapid advent of the internet age and the attendant emergence of social media. This has resulted in the internet becoming a significant conduit in both the social and work lives of a vast amount of people.[1] The arrival of the internet age has led to an almost complete change in the manner in which news is disseminated and consumed, with the internet accounting for an unprecedented level of media proliferation.[2] Whereas only a few decades ago television, radio, and the print media were almost the sole purveyors of news stories, they are now simply just one of the ways in which ordinary citizens may learn of developments in current affairs, business, sport, entertainment, culture, and lifestyle, amongst other topics. However, just over a century ago, the situation could hardly have been more different. In the early twentieth century, it was the print media, predominantly newspapers, on which people relied in order to learn of emerging news stories in the world in which they lived.

At that time newspapers had existed in most countries for at least a century or two, though their physical appearance, 'type on a large sheet of paper that could be, and often was, folded to facilitate carrying or storing',

---

[1] Philip E.N. Howard, Lee Rainie, and Steve Jones, 'Days and nights on the Internet' in Barry Wellman and Caroline Haythornewaite (eds), *The Internet in everyday life* (Oxford, 2002), p. 45.

[2] Xigen Li (ed.), *Internet newspapers: the making of a mainstream medium* (Mahwah, NJ, 2005), p. 2.

had changed little.[3] The two main factors that accounted for the relatively unprecedented popularity of newspapers at the start of the twentieth century were the significant increases in the numbers of the people who could read plus the fact that newspapers had gradually become more affordable. This was a development that manifested itself in Ireland just as much as any other country and it coincided with one of the most critical periods in the nation's history. It was a period that ended with the attainment of self-government though the form of this long-sought autonomy proved both problematic and divisive. Consequently, the inter-relationship between these two relatively simultaneous developments merits serious scrutiny.

This book concentrates very specifically on one key section of the print media in Ireland at this time, the provincial press. It outlines the background of most of Ireland's regional newspapers that were published during the years leading up to independence and it also describes the difficult environment in which such publications had to operate. Furthermore, this book presents case studies of seventeen different provincial titles across Ireland. These case studies provide a succinct overview of the individuals behind these publications and of their experiences during this critical period of Irish history. Perhaps most importantly, though, the editorial commentary of each of these seventeen titles over the eight-year span from 1914 to 1921 is scrutinised and analysed. This includes their reaction to events such as the outbreak of World War I, the Easter Rising of 1916, the dramatic rise of Sinn Féin, the War of Independence, and, finally, the Anglo-Irish Treaty of 1921.

Broadly speaking, the historiography of Irish newspapers is hardly substantial though it has expanded considerably in recent years. A brief overview of the topic illustrates the somewhat sparse but increasing number of publications that document differing facets of Irish newspaper history. Hugh Oram's *The newspaper book: a history of newspapers in Ireland, 1649–1983* is effectively the only text that charts the broader history of Irish newspapers, tracing their origins in Cromwellian times up to the latter part of the twentieth century. There have been histories of individual titles, most notably those of the *Irish Times* by Mark O'Brien and by Dermot James and of the *Irish Examiner* by Des O'Driscoll. Additionally, Mark O'Brien has made valuable contributions to the historiography of Irish newspapers with *De Valera, Fianna Fáil and the Irish Press*, while also co-editing, with Kevin

---

[3]   Shannon E. Martin, 'Newspaper history traditions' in Shannon E. Martin and David A. Copeland (eds), *The function of newspapers in society: a global perspective* (Westport, Conn., 2003), p. 1.

Rafter, *Independent newspapers: a history*, a collection of essays examining various aspects of the history of the *Irish Independent*. Similarly, Felix M. Larkin's numerous articles and essays on the *Freeman's Journal* (which was published between 1763 and 1924) are equally important additions to this previously under-researched area. When it comes to the provincial press, however, the number of equivalent texts is somewhat small.

To date, there has been only one book that comprehensively charts any period in the history of the Irish provincial press. Marie-Louise Legg's *Newspapers and nationalism: the Irish provincial press, 1850–1892* traces the history of provincial newspapers from the immediate aftermath of the Great Famine in the mid-nineteenth century to just after the fall of Charles Stewart Parnell in the early 1890s. More recently, *The Irish regional press, 1892–2018: revival, revolution and republic*, a collection of essays edited by Ian Kenneally and James T. O'Donnell, is a highly notable text that goes some way towards filling this historical gap. Nonetheless, the overall dearth of attention to provincial and regional newspapers highlights the necessity for further critical examination of this strand of the Irish print media. Throughout the twentieth century, the provincial press was a central component of Ireland's media landscape. Through its reportage of local events and provision of local information it fostered a sense of collective identity and played a key role in the lives of its readers and, by extension, in local and national politics.

This book contributes to filling this particular lacuna in the historiography of Irish print media. The primary focus is on the years from 1914 to 1921, sometimes referred to as the revolutionary period of Irish history. While only minimal historical attention has been allotted to this sector, the same cannot be said for other strands of the print media at that time. To date, the most notable study of conventional newspapers during this period of Irish history is Ian Kenneally's *The paper wall: newspapers and propaganda in Ireland, 1919–1921*. This book assesses the role played by the four main Irish national newspapers of the day, namely the *Irish Independent, Irish Times, Freeman's Journal*, and *Cork Examiner* as well as *The Times* of London while also analysing the reporting of the conflict in these publications. Several scholars have focused on the publications of political and cultural organisations while others have concentrated specifically on the related theme of Irish nationalist propaganda. These include historians such as Maurice Walsh, Virginia E. Glandon, Ben Novick, Regina Uí Chollatáin, Patrick Maume, Sonja Tiernan, James Curry, Keiko Inoue, Brian P. Murphy, and Francis Costello.[4]

---

[4] The various texts by all of these authors are listed in the bibliography.

The reasonably substantial scrutiny of other sections of the print media makes the relative inattention to provincial and regional titles all the more puzzling. Numerous historians have been quite happy to cite regional newspapers despite the dearth of historical analysis of such a source. This strange situation is brought into sharp focus during the course of J.J. Lee's seminal work of twentieth-century Irish history, *Ireland 1912–1985: politics and society*. In his assessment of how the broader populace outside Dublin reacted to the Easter Rising, Lee refers to eleven different newspapers across the south and west of Ireland.[5] Apart from labelling Jasper Tully of the *Roscommon Herald* 'a vitriolic anti-Parnellite' and describing the *Clare Champion* as 'strongly Redmondite' there is little elaboration as to the specific sympathies of the newspapers he is citing nor is Lee referring to any body of work to support his observations regarding these papers.[6] This extract is not pinpointed in order to denigrate an eminent historian such as Lee. Nonetheless, it clearly illustrates that even in such a core text of modern Irish history the citation of the provincial press, albeit quite sparingly in this case, is a highly prominent feature despite the paucity of research into this part of the Irish print media.

Scope of research

It is clear, therefore, that there is an obvious void in the historiography of Ireland's print media. The aforementioned imbalance in relation to the 1914–21 period only serves to underscore this undoubted gap. Nevertheless, this gap alone is not sufficient to justify a study such as this. It is also necessary to pose some pertinent and relevant research questions. These questions are framed with the intention of gaining an understanding of the complex interrelationship between provincial papers and their readers and to what extent such papers were simply following events or attempting to play a part in shaping them.

The first of these research questions seeks to determine the nature of the relationship between the provincial press and society. In this respect this study investigates the extent of the involvement of the provincial

---

5 J.J. Lee, *Ireland 1912–1985: politics and society* (Cambridge, 1989), pp 32–5. Three of these titles, the *Kerryman*, *Kilkenny People*, and *Roscommon Herald* are the subject of case studies in this book. The remaining eight titles are the *Clare Champion*, *Connacht Tribune*, *Cork Examiner*, *Leinster Leader*, *Limerick Leader*, *Tipperary Star*, and *Wicklow People*.

6 Ibid., pp 33–5.

press and its personnel in numerous aspects of social life. Such aspects embrace organisations and institutions such as the Gaelic League, the Gaelic Athletic Association (GAA), and the Catholic Church. To date, historical analysis of such bodies has not recorded, or has possibly overlooked, the involvement or influence of Ireland's regional newspapers in the emergence of the latter two institutions as such dominant forces in twentieth-century Ireland. This research question additionally investigates involvement of the provincial press in broader elements of Irish society such as agriculture, trade, commerce, and politics.

The second research question aims to establish the characteristics of the proprietors, editors, and reporters who constituted the senior ranks of the provincial print media. Accordingly, the backgrounds of the people who owned, managed, edited, and wrote for the provincial press are examined. By extension, this study further considers whether the provincial press was divided into two homogeneous nationalist and unionist camps, or whether a wider spectrum of opinion existed. This includes identifying those newspaper editors and proprietors who played an active part in politics, scrutinising the nature of their political activity, and establishing if their allegiances shifted during the course of these years. It also evaluates whether such allegiances fully dictated their coverage of events, if their papers remained reasonably impartial in their commentary, or if a more partisan tone was adopted.

The third research question that is comprehensively addressed is how the relationship between provincial newspapers and the British authorities manifested itself. Tackling such a question requires an examination of the broader subject of wartime propaganda and it also demands close scrutiny of the imposition of censorship of Irish newspapers between 1914 and 1921. In addressing this question this study also considers whether the application of such censorship produced a unified reaction from the provincial press or if it provoked a variety of responses depending on local conditions. Such censorship came into force at the start of World War I but became a far more relevant issue following the 1916 Rising and the ensuing rise of Sinn Féin.

The fourth and final research question seeks to determine how the provincial press responded to the many critical developments that took place in Ireland during the 1914–21 period and the effects they had on provincial newspapers and their personnel. This encompasses a number of attendant issues such as how the provincial press responded to World War I and the thorny question of Irish support for the British war effort, but more specifically recruitment to the British Army and ultimately conscription. It also appraises the response of the provincial press to the

1916 Rising and seeks to establish whether and to what extent it may have radicalised some nationalist titles.

In a similar vein, this question also considers the unionist response to the Rising and the increasingly militant situation in Ireland that ensued. It assesses whether unionist titles simply reacted with a predictable and singular sense of revulsion or if the growing violence generated any sense of fear that the British government might accede to nationalist demands. Also considered is whether this led to an even further hardening of attitudes or whether the rise of Sinn Féin resulted in any reappraisal of Irish nationalism within unionist circles. Additionally, in answering this question, this study closely scrutinises how the provincial press and its personnel responded to the rise of Sinn Féin in the aftermath of Easter 1916 and determines whether there was any uniformity in that response. Furthermore, it seeks to establish if the Irish electorate's rapid and dramatic transfer of allegiance to Sinn Féin was in any way foreseen or predicted by provincial newspapers. Effectively, this question investigates whether any such titles illustrated a sense of prescience and basically saw 'the writing on the wall' or were they simply reacting to developments. This research question also scrutinises the response of provincial newspapers to the War of Independence from 1919 to 1921 and the subsequent Anglo-Irish Treaty of December 1921. In this respect, particular attention is devoted to determining how the political beliefs of editors and journalists, as well as the activities of the British government, the British military, Sinn Féin, and the Irish Republican Army (IRA) shaped the coverage of the conflict. Finally, this research question also seeks to identify the extent to which, if at all, nationalist newspapers articulated the view that social change, radical or otherwise, should accompany the ultimate goal of Irish self-government.

In addressing these questions, an overview of the various titles in each of the four Irish provinces is provided. Additionally, this book presents case studies of specific publications, both nationalist and unionist, and also independent, to map the characteristics of the provincial press, its personnel, and its coverage of events during the revolutionary period to shed light on this heretofore rather neglected aspect of Irish media history. In so doing it concentrates predominantly on the editorial response of individual newspapers as this reflected the sympathies and affiliations, and possibly even the prejudices, of those in control of such newspapers. The editorial comment that is scrutinised and analysed largely relates to the key issues that dominated Irish politics during these years from the introduction of home rule in 1914 to the Anglo-Irish Treaty of 1921.

The editorial response of each of these newspapers is accompanied by a brief description of the advertisements that regularly appeared. In some cases, notably the *Cork Constitution*, *Impartial Reporter*, and *Londonderry Sentinel*, such advertisements help to provide a reasonable idea of the readership of the newspaper. However, in the majority of cases it is simply not possible to provide such an indication despite qualitative analysis. While some subtle differences between newspapers were discernible, there is scarcely enough evidence to make any accurate assessment of the readerships. Indeed, the most noticeable feature was that there was a similar staple of advertisements across the majority of newspapers. These consisted principally of advertisements for local department stores, agricultural machinery and supplies, motor cars and bicycles, various types of flour, assorted foodstuffs, medications, and, occasionally, professional services such as dentistry and auctioneering. Such difficulties in gauging the readership of newspapers does not render scrutiny of their editorial commentary any less appropriate.

Close scrutiny of editorial commentary is actually all the more relevant since the vast majority of provincial papers were published on a weekly basis. Accordingly, most provincial titles published more than fifty editorials per year (with the exception of those that experienced periods of suppression). Other titles were published more frequently, such as the *Londonderry Sentinel* (three times a week), and the *Cork Constitution* (daily except Sundays), which meant they contained a far greater amount of editorial comment. Nonetheless, these two titles, similar to the majority of the other papers examined in this study, concentrated their editorial focus principally on national issues. There were some exceptions to this amongst the newspapers examined but they only account for a small minority. The weekly, rather than daily, editorial output of the clear majority of provincial titles allowed them to reflect critically on national events and consequently (unlike national newspapers) they had more time to deliver a considered rather than an immediate reaction to events. Accordingly, a detailed analysis of the contemporary response to the many critical developments that took place between 1914 and 1921 is provided that, to date, have been largely overlooked.

Carrying out research into senior figures of the provincial press who composed these editorials is no easy task. Few political and military figures of this era left personal papers, with even less of them deciding to write memoirs. Personalities such as Tom Barry, Dan Breen, and Ernie O'Malley proved an exception to this general trend. Newspapermen, however, left virtually nothing in the form of personal papers much less published memoirs or autobiographies. This dearth of source material is compounded by the fact that 'newspapers refrain, as a rule, from discussing their affairs in their own columns', as one prominent Ulster title put it on the occasion of its centenary in 1929.[7] The scarcity of primary source material becomes even clearer when examining some of the personal papers of the very few journalists who left some form of documentation. Ernest Blythe, a senior Sinn Féin figure during the Anglo-Irish War and a minister in the first Free State Government, was originally a journalist by trade. However, despite providing a substantial witness statement to the Bureau of Military History in Dublin, Blythe only made passing reference to his time as editor of the *Southern Star* in Skibbereen between 1918 and 1919. The statements of two other working journalists to the same body further underline the reticence of such people to reveal their profession. Frank Necy was a member of the Irish Volunteers and was imprisoned in Wales following the 1916 Rising yet he made no mention of the fact that he was working as a reporter for the *Dundalk Democrat* at the time. Even on the fiftieth anniversary of the Rising, in 1966, Necy only wrote anonymously of his experiences and made no mention of his reporting job at the time.[8] William Myles, a member of the Irish Volunteers while simultaneously working as a reporter for the *Clonmel Nationalist*, only made passing reference to his journalistic work in his statement to the Bureau of Military History.

The paucity of journalistic recollections simply means that other avenues must be explored. One of the first of these alternative channels of investigation is the somewhat morbid pursuit of seeking out the obituaries of such journalists. In the past this may well have been a thankless task but the emergence of online archives with their attendant search facilities renders this a considerably less fraught avenue of research. Nonetheless, such an approach must be treated with some caution as obituaries tend to be quite subjective, avoiding any inclination to 'speak ill of the dead'. Although such obituaries often appeared in national papers, they are predominantly drawn from provincial titles which are also the provider of another important form of source material. Centenary editions or commemorative issues of such publications frequently contain historical information pertaining to the particular title that is simply not available elsewhere. Similar to obituaries, however, there is a need to be somewhat

---

7 *Londonderry Sentinel*, 29 Sept. 1929.
8 *Dundalk Democrat*, 9 Apr. 1966. Necy's obituary in the same paper in 1970 revealed that he had only identified himself as 'No. 1468', the prison number allocated to him, when describing his involvement in the Easter Rising and his subsequent imprisonment.

circumspect with this source material as newspapers will generally adopt an uncritical view of themselves and their history.

Aside from directly drawing from provincial newspapers, a variety of other sources are utilised. These include repositories such as the Bureau of Military History in Dublin, the National Library of Ireland (NLI), and the archives of University College Dublin (UCD). These repositories, which hold the personal papers of senior political figures such as John Redmond, Desmond Fitzgerald, Erskine Childers, and Piaras Béaslaí, amongst others, contain numerous highly pertinent documents. These include items such as memoranda relating to dealing with the press, instructions to local branches of the Sinn Féin party, and general guidelines as to the most effective use of propaganda. Nonetheless, some of the most important primary sources cited in this study are held in the National Archives (United Kingdom) and the National Archives of Ireland.

The Colonial Office files of the UK National Archives contain documents relating to what was termed 'seditious literature' plus the regular press censorship reports that were issued by Lord Decies, the Press Censor for Ireland at the time. Both the UK National Archives and the National Archives of Ireland also hold circulars that were regularly sent by Decies to the broader print media at the time in addition to correspondence with specific provincial titles. Such material is invaluable to a study such as this and helps to provide a portrayal of the media environment in which newspapers were compelled to operate.

Structure of the book

The main body of this work is divided into five sections. The first of these sections (Chapter 1) provides a broad overview of the provincial press at the start of the period in question. This overview considers the difficulties and challenges that manifested themselves during these turbulent times. This includes a brief examination of relatively simple matters such as the day-to-day life of the provincial journalist to the more pressing issues of how a variety of external parties sought to exert as much influence and control as possible over the print media in the provinces. These external parties initially took the form of political organisations such as the Irish Parliamentary Party and later Sinn Féin. The outbreak of World War I, but more particularly the Easter Rising of 1916, resulted in the external pressure taking the form of censorship, the threat of suppression, and ultimately the actual suppression of many provincial titles and in some cases serious attacks on newspaper offices. Accordingly, this opening chapter also scrutinises the relevant legislation under which such censorship took place and the way it was applied.

The subsequent chapters examine in detail the provincial press in the respective provinces. This includes specific and detailed focus on four or five titles from each province, though Dublin and Belfast newspapers are excluded as they were comprised principally of national titles or titles that were aimed at significantly larger readerships than most provincial papers. Examination of an equal amount of papers from each province facilitates a reasonable geographical balance. Some titles are chosen arising from the fact that they came into considerable conflict with the authorities and were forcibly suppressed, while others have been selected because they traditionally represented a more moderate form of nationalism. Several other titles are chosen because they can be unambiguously categorised as unionist organs and accordingly this lends a political balance to this study. Such organs were principally located in Ulster but not restricted to that province.

This examination of individual newspaper titles necessitates a slight diversion from a chronological narrative of events between 1914 and 1921. This is required in order to provide the historical background of each of the titles profiled in this book. It is only in this manner that the reaction of these newspapers to developments in Ireland between 1914 and 1921 can be viewed in context. Exploration of this period of Irish history on a local, county, or provincial basis has become quite common in recent years. This is illustrated by the works of historians such as David Fitzpatrick, Peter Hart, John Borgonovo, Marie Coleman, and Michael Farry, amongst others. Their studies have specifically focused on Clare (Fitzpatrick), Cork (Hart and Borgonovo), Longford (Coleman), and Sligo (Farry). This localised approach is further evident in texts by historians such as Gemma Clark and Joost Augusteijn.[9] While the structure of this book shares some common features with these works, it does not follow precisely the same path. Instead, it offers a universal all-Ireland analysis that is segmented by the local case studies of individual newspapers. These local case studies are contained in four separate chapters that examine provincial titles based in Leinster, Connacht, Munster, and Ulster respectively. In addition to facilitating a reasonable geographical spread of newspapers there are many valid reasons for organising such case studies on a province-by-province basis.

The provinces of Ireland, unlike the counties, are the oldest territorial divisions.[10] Indeed, as one historian has pointed out, 'the division of

---

[9]   The various titles by all of these authors are listed in the bibliography.

[10]   Maurice Craig, *The personality of Leinster* (Dublin, 1961), p. 7.

Ireland into counties was entirely an English innovation'.[11] Furthermore, this historical division of Ireland dates back to pre-Christian times to the extent that the province had evolved as the 'essential political unit' by the twelfth century.[12] Ancient Irish legend also endorses this more traditional composition with figures such as Cúchulainn (Ulster) and Queen Maedhbh (Connacht) indisputably associated with their provinces. Even in the more modern era this provincial identification has remained strong. Familiar phrases from Irish history such as 'To hell or to Connacht', 'Ulster says no', 'Ulster will fight and Ulster will be right', and even the 'Munster Republic' reaffirms this longstanding recognition of the province as a badge of identity in the Irish psyche. In the sporting arena, the most prominent and oldest organisation, the GAA, has operated for over a century on provincial structures while its provincial championships have retained their popularity for an equivalent period of time. Such structures have been reinforced in the sport of rugby where the advent of professionalism in the 1990s has led to rivalries between the four Irish provinces receiving a new lease of life.

This undoubted sense of provincial identity provokes the question as to whether newspapers in the four separate provinces reacted differently to events in Ireland between 1914 and 1921. Similarly, it also necessitates an investigation of the experiences of newspaper editors and proprietors in the four provinces and, more importantly, if those experiences varied significantly. With this in mind, this study covers a spectrum of positions and perspectives across the provincial press. The case studies of individual newspapers were strategically selected to ensure a fully inclusive representation of political outlook whilst also maintaining a geographical balance. This included titles that were considered early supporters of Sinn Féin, titles that remained loyal (or somewhat loyal) to the Irish Parliamentary Party, titles representing the unionist viewpoint, titles that were suppressed, titles that were predominantly associated with a specific personality, and, finally, titles that maintained a somewhat distanced stance on events in Ireland during these years.

In Leinster, all the newspapers considered were unequivocally nationalist and found themselves incurring the wrath of the British authorities at one time or another. The titles in question are the *Enniscorthy Echo*, *Kilkenny People*, *Midland Tribune*, and *Meath Chronicle*. To give voice to the southern unionist view of developments, the *Cork Constitution* is one of the Munster publications to be examined. Also,

[11] Richard Hayward, *Munster and the city of Cork* (London, 1964), p. 4.
[12] Marianne Elliot, *The Catholics of Ulster* (London, 2000), pp 8, 17.

from County Cork, the *Skibbereen Eagle*, a paper with quite a chequered history, is subjected to similar scrutiny. Also, undergoing detailed scrutiny is the *Clonmel Chronicle*, a paper that sought to follow a neutral line under the editorship of Arthur Ross Burns, a northern Presbyterian. The two remaining Munster newspapers to come in for detailed analysis are titles that arguably suffered the greatest disruption within the period covered by this study. The *Southern Star* of Skibbereen and the *Kerryman* based in Tralee both experienced suppression, forcible closure (in the case of the *Kerryman*), and the imprisonment of their editors. Consequently, any history of the Irish provincial press would be glaringly incomplete without affording them comprehensive attention.

Connacht is the only one of the four provinces that did not feature a unionist title of major significance, but it renders the story of its provincial newspapers no less important or interesting. The editor–proprietors of two of the Connacht titles examined in this study endured terms of imprisonment similar to the experience of the editors of the *Southern Star* and *Kerryman*. Patrick Joseph (P.J.) Doris of the *Mayo News* and Patrick Dunne of the *Leitrim Observer* were incarcerated because of their journalistic endeavours so it would be historically remiss to overlook the cases of both their publications. The other two Connacht titles, the *Tuam Herald* and the *Roscommon Herald*, unlike most of the other nationalist organs featuring in this study, were established prior to 1880 and traditionally represented a more constitutional brand of nationalism than that espoused by Doris and Dunne.

Unsurprisingly, there were far more unionist newspapers in Ulster than in the other three provinces combined. This study focuses specifically on two of them, the *Impartial Reporter* of Enniskillen and the *Londonderry Sentinel*. These differed not alone in political sympathy from most of the contemporary nationalist titles but also because they were well-established and were very much family businesses. By the second decade of the twentieth century, each title had been inextricably linked with several generations of the same family for close on a century. The *Impartial Reporter*, although almost one hundred years old by this time, was under the proprietorship of only its third owner, William Copeland Trimble, his father having served as first editor of the paper following its establishment in 1825. The *Londonderry Sentinel*, meanwhile, founded only four years after the Enniskillen paper, was owned by James Colhoun, whose father and grandfather had preceded him as owners of the paper.[13] By complete contrast, one of the other Ulster newspapers

---

[13] *Londonderry Sentinel*, 29 Sept. 1929.

profiled was not only unreservedly nationalist but also newly arrived on the scene. The *Donegal Democrat*, first published in 1919, was established by John Downey and Cecil A. Stephens in the aftermath of Sinn Féin's decisive victory at the general election of December 1918.[14] The Irish Parliamentary Party, which was all but decimated at this election, was closely associated with the remaining Ulster newspaper that is the focus of this chapter. The *Anglo-Celt* of Cavan, whose managing-director, John F. (J.F.) O'Hanlon, was the unsuccessful Irish Parliamentary Party candidate in the East Cavan by-election of 1918, was another of the older group of nationalist titles founded prior to 1880.

The adoption of such a structure facilitates a balanced but comprehensive portrayal of the provincial press and the lives of its proprietors, editors, and journalists during this crucial period of Irish history. Titles representing not just both sides of the political divide but also the competing strands of Irish nationalism are scrupulously analysed. The journalistic voice of unionism is also the subject of comprehensive and thorough analysis, but this analysis is not confined to titles located in Ulster. It is neither feasible nor practical to examine in minute detail newspapers from every corner of Ireland but a representative sample of regional journals from Cork, Kerry, Tipperary, Wexford, Offaly, Kilkenny, Meath, Mayo, Galway, Roscommon, Leitrim, Cavan, Donegal, Derry, and Fermanagh ensures there is no geographical bias. It is in such a manner that this historical gap can be filled, and justice done to this long-overlooked aspect of Irish history.

---

[14] Hugh Oram, *The newspaper book: a history of newspapers in Ireland, 1649–1983* (Dublin, 1983), p. 140.

1

Provincial Newspapers: Politics and Censorship

The emergence of the provincial press

Provincial newspapers only began to emerge as a significant feature of the Irish media landscape from around 1880 onwards. Between 1880 and the foundation of the Irish Free State in 1922 a considerable number of (principally nationalist) titles were launched that outstripped any previous developments in this sector. However, the emergence of the provincial press in Ireland came at a relatively late stage by comparison with some other countries. By this time in Britain the leading provincial newspapers had already come together to form the Press Association in 1868 in order to represent their interests. The relatively advanced state of development of the provincial press in Britain was illustrated by the fact that the Press Association proceeded to enter into an agreement with Reuters news agency (which had set up an office in London in 1851) under which the latter organisation provided international news to the provincial press in exchange for domestic news.[1] Seventy-eight daily newspapers were established between 1855 and 1870 in British provincial cities, principally in Lancashire and Yorkshire. Amongst these titles were papers such as the *Birmingham Daily Post*, the *Sheffield Daily Telegraph*, and the *Liverpool Daily Post* while other newspapers that had first appeared earlier in the century, such as the *Manchester*

---

[1] Martin Conboy, *Journalism: a critical history* (London, 2004), pp 124–5; Donald Read, *The power of news: the history of Reuters* (2nd ed., Oxford, 1999), p. 48; Kevin Williams, *International journalism* (London, 2011), pp 52–4.

Guardian, *Glasgow Herald*, and the *Scotsman*, commenced publication on a daily basis.[2]

Despite such undoubted developments, provincial newspapers in Britain still lagged behind their counterparts in the USA. This was partially due to the influence attained by US regional newspapers that resulted from their sterling contributions to the coverage of the Civil War. However, one of the main reasons for the remarkable strength of the American regional press was that it benefited significantly from being the earliest purveyor of news due to the vast distances to major cities. Wiener makes the point that in Britain provincial newspapers had at best a five-hour advantage over the nationals in London in disseminating local news while in the USA such an advantage could be as much as twenty-five hours.[3]

Such geographical and time factors obviously did not apply to Ireland. Similarly, the country's smaller population and significantly lesser number of major regional cities meant that the large amount of titles established in Britain was not mirrored in Ireland. Nonetheless, in the late nineteenth and early twentieth centuries the Irish provincial press developed to an extent that had not been witnessed theretofore. Such development was plainly evident during the 1914–21 period when sixty-eight of the 135 provincial newspapers being published in Ireland during these years had been established between 1880 and 1914 (see Appendix B). Despite such noteworthy advances there has been only one published text specifically chronicling any period in the history of this section of the print media in Ireland. Marie-Louise Legg's *Newspapers and nationalism: the Irish provincial press, 1850–1892* assesses the development of the provincial press in Ireland from the end of the Great Famine up to the demise of Charles Stewart Parnell. The burgeoning nationalism that had begun to manifest itself in the fifteen years or so up to the end of the period covered by Legg was marked by well-documented events such as the Land War and the emergence, in the form of the Irish Parliamentary Party under the leadership of Parnell, of a serious force in Irish constitutional nationalism. It was also a period that witnessed the establishment of a host of provincial titles, almost all strongly nationalist in sympathy. It was a trend that continued right up to the period that is the primary focus of this study.

Legg traces the genesis of this trend to 1876, a year that witnessed the first provincial titles identifying themselves as 'nationalist' being

---

[2] Joel H. Wiener, *The Americanization of the British press, 1830s–1914: speed in the age of transatlantic journalism* (New York, 2011), p. 103.

[3] Ibid., pp 103–4.

established. The titles in question were the *Western News* (Ballinasloe), *The Celt* (Waterford), and the *People's Advocate* (Monaghan).[4] The decades that followed witnessed the establishment of substantial numbers of provincial titles whose longevity is illustrated by their continued existence right up to the second decade of the twenty-first century. The 1880s marked the appearance of nationalist titles such as the *Leinster Leader* (1880), *Midland Tribune* (1881), *Westmeath Examiner* (1882), the *Nationalist and Leinster Times* (sometimes referred to as the *Carlow Nationalist*) and *Western People* in 1883, *Drogheda Independent* (1884), and the *Limerick Leader* and *Enniscorthy Guardian* in 1889. The *Southern Star* in Skibbereen, the *Clonmel Nationalist*, and the *Leitrim Observer* were first published in 1890 while the last decade of the nineteenth century was also notable for the founding of the *Mayo News* (1892), *Kilkenny People* (1893), and the *Longford Leader* and *Meath Chronicle* in 1897. There was little indication of a decline in this process in the first decade of the twentieth century as the *Fermanagh Herald* and *Enniscorthy Echo* arrived on the scene in 1902 followed by the *Clare Champion* in 1903, the *Kerryman* in 1904, and the *Tipperary Star* and *Connacht Tribune* in 1909.

The *Dungarvan Observer* and *Donegal Democrat*, first published in 1912 and 1919 respectively, are the only extant provincial newspapers established between 1910 and the founding of the Irish Free State in 1922. Nonetheless, several other titles emerged during these years that remained in existence for considerable periods of time. These include the *East Galway Democrat* (1910–49), *Strokestown Democrat* (1913–48), and the *Weekly Observer* published in Newcastle West, County Limerick between 1915 and 1927. Indeed, in the thirty years after 1880 many other titles also went to press for the first time, which, although no longer in existence, lasted for close on a half a century or more. Categorised in this grouping are the *Galway Observer* (1881–1966), *Wexford Free Press* (1888–1966), *Donegal Vindicator* (1889–1956), *Westmeath Nationalist* (1891–1939), and the *Frontier Sentinel*, another nationalist title, published in Newry between 1904 and 1972. Nonetheless, this study is not just an examination of the emergent nationalist press of this period. Also coming under scrutiny are other newspapers, although similarly nationalist in their sympathies, which had their origins in an earlier era.

In this respect, publications such as the *Tuam Herald* (launched in 1837), the *Anglo-Celt* (established in 1846), and the *Roscommon Herald* (founded in 1859) are the subject of intense analysis. Such scrutiny and

---

[4] Marie-Louise Legg, *Newspapers and nationalism: the Irish provincial press, 1850–1892* (Dublin, 1998), p. 80.

analysis is not limited to openly nationalist titles. This is a study of the provincial press in all four provinces and consequently newspapers that can unambiguously be categorised as unionist in their sympathies are also considered. With such a consideration in mind, the *Impartial Reporter* (established in 1825) of Enniskillen and the *Londonderry Sentinel* (established in 1829) come in for specific scrutiny. Another unionist title, the *Cork Constitution*, is also considered, in addition to the *Skibbereen Eagle* and the *Clonmel Chronicle*. The latter two papers were independent organs though the *Skibbereen Eagle* has sometimes been referred to as a unionist title. Detailed analysis and examination of such a broad range of newspapers ensures that as comprehensive a portrait as possible of the provincial press is provided. However, it is crucial to bear in mind that this work is not merely an assessment of such titles, whether nationalist or unionist, as faceless entities. Their coverage of events between 1914 and 1921 will undoubtedly figure prominently but the people behind these papers are, for almost the first time, afforded historical recognition in their own right.

The cast of characters, be they reporters, editors, or proprietors, fully merit this recognition. The body of pressmen (for they were almost entirely men) that constituted the provincial press corps during these years included an array of individuals who between them reported on close on a century of Irish history. They were a cohort that collectively lived through the Land War, the Home Rule campaign, the Easter Rising of 1916, the War of Independence and Civil War, two World Wars, and (in some cases) the advent of the Northern Ireland conflict in the 1960s and 1970s. They were a body of individuals who have, up to now, only received passing attention from historians. Amongst their number are figures such as William Copeland Trimble, editor–proprietor of the *Impartial Reporter* of Enniskillen. Trimble, though trenchantly unionist in his sympathies and only a reluctant supporter of the Land League, agitated strongly for land reform and the fairer treatment of tenant-farmers in his native County Fermanagh.[5] On the other hand, William Doris, co-founder of the *Mayo News*, attended the first Land League meeting at Irishtown, County Mayo, in 1879, was one of the founding members of the first branch of the League in the county, and became an MP a number of years later.[6] Michael A. Casey, who took over as editor of the *Drogheda Independent* at the request of William O'Brien MP, was also a friend and confidant of Charles Stewart Parnell

[5] *Impartial Reporter*, 27 Nov. 1941.
[6] *Connaught Telegraph*, 18 Sept. 1926.

and Michael Davitt.[7] Jasper Tully, long-time editor–proprietor of the *Roscommon Herald*, was MP for South Leitrim from 1892 to 1906 and was among those imprisoned along with Parnell in Kilmainham Gaol.[8] John F. O'Hanlon, managing-director of Cavan's *Anglo-Celt* newspaper for over sixty years, was a close ally of John Redmond. He contested the East Cavan by-election in 1918 as the Irish Parliamentary Party candidate in opposition to Arthur Griffith and though defeated on that occasion he was elected to Dáil Éireann as an independent representative ten years later.[9]

In the west of Ireland, Thomas J.W. Kenny, who co-founded the *Connacht Tribune*, was the first journalist to greet aviators Alcock and Brown when they landed in Connemara in 1919 following their first trans-Atlantic flight.[10] J.A. Power, a successor to Kenny as editor of the *Connacht Tribune* is credited with coining the phrase 'Black and Tans' to describe the British force deployed in Ireland during the War of Independence.[11] Patrick Quinn was best-known as political correspondent of the *Irish Independent* for over thirty-five years. However, prior to that he worked as a journalist with the *Clare Champion* and *Galway Observer* and was on the scene on Dublin's Talbot Street within minutes of the shooting dead of Tipperary IRA leader, Seán Treacy. He was also one of the last civilians to see Michael Collins alive after speaking to him at Bandon Barracks the day before the latter's death at Béal na Blath.[12] Tommy O'Brien is best-remembered as a popular radio broadcaster, presenting an opera music programme on Radio Teilifís Éireann for almost forty years right up to the late 1980s. Yet O'Brien was originally a journalist, as a cub reporter he ran dispatches for the IRA in South Tipperary and was a friend of Dan Breen and Seán Treacy. Working initially for the *Clonmel Chronicle* he later spent several years as editor of the *Clonmel Nationalist*.[13]

This very small sample of individuals, who earned their livelihood in the newspaper business in Ireland during these years, provide ample

---

[7] *Drogheda Independent*, 25 Mar. 1938.

[8] *Roscommon Herald*, 17 Sept. 1938.

[9] *Anglo-Celt*, 29 Dec. 1956.

[10] *Connacht Tribune*, 11 May 1940.

[11] *Connacht Sentinel*, 24 Apr. 1951. Power is credited with coining the phrase while working as a sub-editor with the *Freeman's Journal*. He became editor of the *Connacht Tribune* in 1940.

[12] *Irish Independent*, 25 Aug. 1964.

[13] *Irish Times*, 25 Feb. 1988.

evidence of a substantial group of journalists who are more than worthy of detailed attention. This will become abundantly clear in subsequent sections of this study as additional figures such as Edward Thomas Keane, James Pike, and William Sears are the subject of close historical scrutiny for the first time. Nonetheless, the necessity for such scrutiny would not exist but for the developments in communication, commerce, the journalistic profession itself, and, most notably, education, that took place in the second half of the nineteenth century and the early twentieth century.

Professional and educational advances

The combination of such factors led to a significantly increased proportion of the population possessing the ability to read newspapers. It is a development not lost on Legg who noted in her study of the Irish provincial press that this was an era when 'the habit of reading a newspaper was entering its golden age'. It was an age when the ability to read 'was no longer just a skill to keep a man from drink' but 'an important passport to entry into the modern world'.[14] However, as with any such development, it did not happen purely by accident. The increasing engagement of the broader populace with the print media can be attributed to three distinct factors. The first of these was the considerable improvement in communication and distribution systems that began to take effect in the closing decades of the nineteenth century. The second related to developments within the journalistic profession itself. Thirdly, and probably most importantly, was the significant increase in the levels of literacy throughout the country. All three factors have been commented upon by a variety of historians.

Legg contended that as far back as 1850 the development of the provincial press 'was stimulated by increased urbanisation, by fiscal reforms and by improved transport links'.[15] Her contention is supported by O'Brien who specifically cites 'the development of towns along the railway routes' as further aiding the growth of the provincial press in the second half of the nineteenth century.[16] Nonetheless, the abolition

---

[14]   Legg, *Newspapers and nationalism*, p. 175.

[15]   Ibid., p. 29.

[16]   Mark O'Brien, 'Journalism in Ireland: the evolution of a discipline' in Kevin Rafter (ed.), *Irish journalism before independence: more a disease than a profession* (Manchester, 2011), p. 16.

of taxes on newspapers after 1855 can be regarded as the principal catalyst in the rise of the provincial press, not only in Ireland but also in Britain.[17] This was one of the main factors in the aforementioned surge in the number of British provincial titles after 1855 and the subsequent formation of the Press Association in 1868. Improvements in telegraph and telephone systems further enhanced this process while from the 1870s onwards press clubs were established 'for the purposes of socialising and exchange of intelligence among journalists'. This led to the formation of the National Association of Journalists in 1884, an organisation that was later to become the Institute of Journalists.[18] Such journalistic solidarity proved more difficult to achieve in Ireland. The Association of Irish Journalists was established in 1887 but, as outlined by O'Brien, it was beset by divisions that were characteristic of 'the partisanship of nineteenth century Irish journalism'. Ultimately, this organisation was unsuccessful in its attempts 'to unite journalists of strongly diverging political views'.[19] Nonetheless, the Telegraph Act of 1868, which granted newspapers concession rates for the transmission of their printed material, provided a considerable impetus to the newspaper trade in Ireland.[20] This facilitated significant reductions in the price of newspapers that in turn created the incentive for the launch of many provincial titles in the late 1800s and early 1900s. The appearance of these newly established titles, however, did not lead to any significant embracing of the 'new journalism' that had begun to manifest itself within the British print media.

The most famous proponent of the 'new journalism' (a phrase coined by Mathew Arnold in 1888) was W.T. Stead of the *Pall Mall Gazette*. Bingham and Conboy detail Stead's contribution to this departure as including the introduction into the British market of 'innovative American techniques in interviewing, cross-head layout, and aggressive self-promotion'. It also included the running of 'sensational campaigns, most notoriously the "Maiden Tribute of Modern Babylon" series of 1885 investigating child prostitution' which ultimately resulted in Stead serving a prison sentence.[21] There is scant evidence of any such dramatic

[17] Legg, *Newspapers and nationalism*, p. 172.

[18] Conboy, *Journalism*, p. 126.

[19] Mark O'Brien, 'Journalism and emerging professionalism in Ireland' in *Journalism practice*, 10, no. 1 (2016), pp 109–22.

[20] D. George Boyce, *Nineteenth-century Ireland: the search for stability* (rev. ed., Dublin, 2005), p. 275.

[21] Adrian Bingham and Martin Conboy, *Tabloid century: the popular press in Britain, 1896 to the present* (Oxford, 2015), p. 6. Bingham and Conboy identify Irish

departures within the Irish newspaper trade during this period though there were some instances of the 'new journalism'. The most notable of these, as detailed by Larkin, was the 'Christmas on the Galtees' series of 1878 in the *Freeman's Journal* dealing with the plight of tenants on an estate in County Tipperary.[22] However, it was not a departure that was embraced to any significant degree in Ireland. Indeed, many Irish newspapers of this time, as Larkin also notes, 'tended to be unashamedly partisan' in their politics, leaving little likelihood of any major journalistic innovation.[23] Nonetheless, Irish journalism was not devoid of a certain element of progression during these years.

This was illustrated, as noted by Foley, in improvements in shorthand skills, an adherence to impartiality, and an awareness of new methods, such as the interview, an innovation that was becoming considerably popular as a tool of the trade.[24] Such relative advances were accompanied by a significant increase in the number of people involved in journalism. Census figures indicate that those earning their livelihood in the profession stood at 259 in 1861.[25] By 1901, this figure had increased dramatically to 909 and by 1911 there was a further increase to 1,102.[26] Such developments, however, would be rendered far less significant without the substantial advances in literacy levels that were taking place almost simultaneously.

The advances in this regard from around 1850 onwards were quite marked. The literacy rate of those aged five and upwards rose from 47 per cent in 1841 to 75 per cent in 1881. This rise was greatly aided by 'the establishment of a network of Catholic secondary schools around the

journalist T.P. O'Connor, founder and editor of the *Star* newspaper in Britain, as one of the other major exponents of the 'new journalism'. O'Connor also served as an Irish nationalist MP for Liverpool.

[22] Felix M. Larkin, 'Green shoots of the new journalism in the *Freeman's Journal*, 1877–1890' in Karen Steele and Michael de Nie (eds), *Ireland and the new journalism* (New York, 2014), p. 39.

[23] Felix M. Larkin, 'Keeping an eye on Youghal: The *Freeman's Journal* and the Plan of Campaign in East Cork 1886–1892' in *Irish Communications Review*, vol. 13, p. 27.

[24] Michael Foley, 'How journalism became a profession' in Rafter, *Irish journalism before independence*, p. 30.

[25] Boyce, *Nineteenth-century Ireland*, p. 275.

[26] Census of Ireland 1901/1911 (www.census.nationalarchives.ie/). The figures from 1901 and 1911 are estimated based on those who described themselves as either newspaper proprietors, editors, reporters, journalists, authors, or generally employed in the newspaper business.

country'.[27] By 1901, the percentage of those without the ability to read or write had dropped to 14 per cent.[28] This had fallen to about 12 per cent by 1911 and was principally confined to remote rural districts. The downward trend in illiteracy was further assisted by the increased number of teachers; even though the overall population was declining there was a rise in the number of teachers, from 8,000 in 1867 to 13,500 in 1914.[29] Consequently, provincial newspapers began to cater for an increasingly literate populace who had started to move away from predominantly labouring jobs towards employment requiring a degree of literacy such as serving in shops and clerking in offices.[30]

The combined effect of fiscal reforms, improved transport links, a relative increase in the level of professionalism within the newspaper business, and, perhaps most notably, the steadily rising rates of literacy meant that the print media now occupied a previously unknown position of prominence and influence. By the end of the second decade of the twentieth century, these developments in technology, communications, and education had led to what Boyce describes as 'a print-based world'.[31] The relevance of such a societal change is fully recognised by Walsh who states that 'the Irish Revolution coincided with the birth of mass democracy, in an age when the press was perceived to be a decisive factor in shaping the political world'.[32] At a provincial level such journalistic influence was recognised by the nascent Sinn Féin party at a very early stage. As early as 1907 it had spent £250 on the launch and publication of the *Leitrim Guardian* in Manorhamilton.[33] In the years before World War I, however, newspapers still had no experience of the censorship restrictions that came into effect during the 1914–18 period under the Defence of the Realm Act.

---

[27] O'Brien, 'Journalism in Ireland', p. 17.

[28] Ciara Meehan, '"The prose of logic and of scorn": Arthur Griffith and Sinn Féin, 1906–1914' in Rafter, *Irish journalism before independence*, p. 191.

[29] Boyce, *Nineteenth-century Ireland*, p. 275.

[30] Legg, *Newspapers and nationalism*, p. 120.

[31] Boyce, *Nineteenth-century Ireland*, p. 275.

[32] Maurice Walsh, *The news from Ireland: foreign correspondents and the Irish Revolution* (London, 2008), p. 180.

[33] Richard P. Davis, *Arthur Griffith and non-violent Sinn Féin* (Dublin, 1974), p. 43.

The Irish newspaper business in the early 1900s

During the decade or so prior to the outbreak of World War I, most aspects of the Irish newspaper industry differed little from those of Britain and many other countries. Reporters filed their copy anonymously and the author's name almost never appeared with their articles. The conditions under which journalists plied their trade during the period under consideration in this study are starkly outlined by Walsh who comments that they 'filled the columns of their newspapers anonymously in a literary endeavour barely removed from the industrial discipline of the factory'.[34] The industrial revolution era working conditions notwithstanding, Irish journalism, according to a contemporary historian of the Fourth Estate, had attained a position of some considerable stature by the early 1900s. In his 1911 book, *Masters of English journalism*, T.H.S. Escott noted the extent to which the 'Irish genius' had 'so widely permeated the English press'. Not alone did Escott recognise the impact of Irish journalists working in England but he also acknowledged the achievement of 'authority and success' that 'made him a power in his native land from [the] Giant's Causeway to Cape Clear'.[35] Escott's geographical emphasis would certainly suggest that provincial newspapers shared equally in what he clearly believed to be the burgeoning success of the broader print media in Ireland.

Within the country itself the national press and the provincial press enjoyed a symbiotic relationship, the precise nature of which is difficult to map and is, for reasons of space, beyond the scope of this work. While it is likely that this relationship may warrant its own study, such an undertaking would be fraught with difficulty. While national titles such as the *Freeman's Journal*, the *Irish Independent*, and the *Irish Times* produced weekly digests of their titles (the *Weekly Freeman*, the *Weekly Irish Independent*, and the *Weekly Irish Times* respectively) aimed at the provincial market, these titles consisted of digests of national and international news, not regional or local news. As no circulation figures exist for the period under consideration it is near impossible to gauge the competition between the national and provincial press. Similarly, by-lines were a rarity, so it is impossible to adjudicate whether provincial journalists contributed to national titles or whether those titles simply lifted content and reproduced it without attribution. While teasing out these issues may

---

[34] Walsh, *The news from Ireland*, p. 22.
[35] T.H.S. Escott, *Master of English journalism: a study of personal forces* (London, 1911), pp 305–6.

well be interesting in its own right, the answers would still, ultimately, remain a matter of speculation and are beyond the scope of this work.

The task of classifying those who controlled Ireland's provincial newspapers into a small number of homogeneous groups is slightly less onerous though still somewhat problematic. Nonetheless, a division into two general categories can provide a reasonably broad overview of the proprietorship–editorship of the Irish provincial press during this period. The first category comprised slightly longer-established titles whose ownership (and frequently editorship) had transferred through one or more generations of the same family. The second category consisted of many of those (principally nationalist) titles that had only been established relatively recently and were essentially still only finding their feet as the turbulent 1914–21 period approached. The former category incorporates unionist and nationalist publications such as the *Tuam Herald*, *Anglo-Celt*, *Impartial Reporter*, and *Londonderry Sentinel* (as will be seen in later chapters) plus titles such as the *Leinster Express*, *Sligo Champion*, and *Banbridge Chronicle*.[36] The latter category covers papers including the *Leitrim Observer*, *Kerryman*, and *Enniscorthy Echo* (as will also be detailed in later chapters) and, amongst others, the *Connacht Tribune* and *Tipperary Star*.[37]

The dearth of journalistic memoirs and autobiographies referred to in the introduction renders it difficult to describe the challenges faced by these editors and proprietors (and indeed the reporters who were employed by them) while working in the newspaper business during these years. There is one source, however, which does shed some light in this regard. The Irish Journalists Association was an organisation formed in 1909 that sought to address the concerns of working journalists and bring about improved working conditions where it was deemed necessary. Although labelling this body a trade union might be an overstatement it did strive to address issues such as reporters' salaries, though with very limited success as the Association went out of existence within two

---

[36] *Leinster Express*, 7 Aug. 1943; *Sligo Champion*, 14 Jan. 1966; *Banbridge Chronicle*, 2 June 1951. Michael Charles Carey succeeded his father as editor–proprietor of the *Leinster Express* in 1903; Alfred McHugh took over ownership of the *Sligo Champion* after the death of his father, P.A. McHugh MP, in 1909; Arthur Waldo Emerson became owner of the *Banbridge Chronicle* following the death of his father in May 1912.

[37] *Connacht Tribune*, 11 May 1940; *Tipperary Star*, 7 Nov. 1925. Thomas J.W. Kenny founded the *Connacht Tribune* in 1909; Edward Long established the *Tipperary Star* also in 1909.

years of the foundation of the Free State. Nevertheless, its short-lived monthly newsletter, the *Irish Journalist*, featured several contributions from newspapermen that document, albeit to a limited extent, the experience of working as a journalist in Ireland at that time.

In a representative organisation comprised principally of ordinary employees, the employer could be perceived as one of the main barriers to its objectives. Accordingly, contributions from editors or proprietors were extremely scarce. Nonetheless, the November 1915 issue of the *Irish Journalist* featured an article entitled 'Sidelights – On editing a provincial paper'. The author was T.J.W. Kenny, editor of the *Connacht Tribune*. Kenny's writing tended to be overly colourful at times, but he did provide some insight into the challenges of running a provincial newspaper. He argued that it was 'not a mere local paper'; neither was it 'a one-horse show' whose contents 'never embrace anything outside the rural district of the demesne walls'. Kenny recognised that it was the editor's duty to 'see to it that the paper is made of general as well as local interest' and also to understand 'that its readers know something of the existence of the telegraph, the railway train, the Atlantic liner – or the war'. The *Connacht Tribune* editor further asserted that it was the specific function of a provincial newspaper to 'take a political character' but should not sink to the status of being a mere mouthpiece of a particular political party.[38] Unfortunately, Kenny did not broach the subject of censorship though this may well have been purely due to space limitations.[39] Regardless of the non-discussion of censorship, Kenny's article does at least provide some indication of the mindset of the provincial editor.

It is regrettable that the views of other provincial editors were not similarly documented but fortunately the *Irish Journalist* did bequeath the opinions of a few reporters that shed some light on the concerns of the ordinary journalist working in the provinces. It is probably of little surprise that foremost of those concerns was the matter of salary. In December 1914, a provincial reporter (only identifying himself as 'Ogánach') claimed that the maximum wage a journalist in his position could expect to earn was in the region of thirty-five shillings per week. In almost time-honoured fashion this state of affairs was attributed to the perennial city versus country conflict. The needs of the journalist working

---

[38] *Irish Journalist*, vol. 1, no. 13 (Nov. 1915).

[39] Kenny may not have mentioned censorship because it only became a far more pressing issue for provincial papers in the aftermath of the Easter Rising even though restrictions on the reporting of military operations had been in effect since the start of World War I.

outside the capital (the Irish Journalists Association was a Dublin-based organisation) was 'little understood by his metropolitan confrère'. The anonymous contributor further berated 'the indifference of the Dublin journalist for his country cousin', an indifference that was 'begotten of ignorance'.[40]

The antipathy and sense of injustice felt by this member of the provincial press corps is quite intriguing in light of an article that appeared in the previous month's issue of the same newsletter. This contribution bemoaned the failure of journalists in the provinces to form local committees 'to discuss their own local grievances and to deal promptly with any matters that might arise affecting their interests'. The same contribution referred to a weekend meeting organised in a large provincial centre at which 'not a single pressman in that centre put in an appearance'. It added that some of these pressmen stated afterwards that 'it would be more than their positions were worth to join the Association'. In a scathing conclusion, the same pressmen were lambasted for their 'hopeless apathy' and for being 'past masters in the art of criticising the efforts of those who are honestly trying to do something to improve their conditions, but when it comes to a question of doing anything for themselves they are as helpless as the infant in arms'.[41]

The stinging criticism was not wholly unjustified, if the views of another anonymous provincial reporter from a few months later are to be believed. This writer contended that some pressmen in the provinces could earn up to £3 per week though not from salary alone. He detailed how profit from travel expenses (earned primarily in his case from cycling to wherever his job took him but being allowed to claim a train fare) plus other incidental expenses could raise the weekly income to this amount. Nonetheless, this journalist stated categorically that it was up to provincial pressmen 'to make themselves worth more money'. Such amelioration in pay and conditions could best be achieved by joining the Irish Journalists Association 'in large numbers'. Failure to do so meant that provincial pressmen would 'have only themselves to blame for getting badly paid for their work'.[42] It seems, however, that such urgings fell on deaf ears, as almost eighteen months later the *Irish Journalist* (in one of its final issues) was still lamenting 'the failure of our provincial members to form County Committees'.[43]

[40] *Irish Journalist*, vol. 1, no. 3 (Dec. 1914).
[41] *Irish Journalist*, vol. 1, no. 2 (Nov. 1914).
[42] *Irish Journalist*, vol. 1, no. 7 (Apr. 1915).
[43] *Irish Journalist*, vol. 2, no. 6 (Sept.–Oct. 1916).

The mindset of individual journalists (albeit a small number of them) is at least discernible to some extent from the pages of the *Irish Journalist*. The political leanings of the individual provincial titles that employed these journalists can be determined from the *Newspaper press directory and advertisers' guide*. In its own words this annual publication contained 'particulars of every newspaper, magazine, review, and periodical published in the United Kingdom and the British Isles'.[44] The directory was in essence the trade journal for the print media in Britain and Ireland and effectively the 'bible' for advertisers. In addition to providing brief but descriptive listings for almost all newspapers, both national and local, it also carried advertisements placed by selected newspapers that were directed at potential advertisers. Such listings and advertisements reveal much about the nature of the Irish newspaper business at the time.

In most cases, the *Newspaper press directory* stated the broad political sympathy of individual titles. The collation of such political sympathies from the 1917 edition of the directory, plus numerous aspects of the research carried out for this study, reveal the following breakdown of political allegiance during the 1914–21 period:

Nationalist	69
Unionist/Conservative	43
Independent	12
Neutral	5
Political sympathy not stated	6

These figures do not include every Irish publication listed in the *Newspaper press directory*; rather, the data has been extracted to include only provincial titles.[45]

---

[44] *Newspaper press directory and advertisers' guide 1917.*

[45] The figures exclude the main national newspapers plus other newspapers whose chief circulation was in the three major cities of Dublin, Cork, or Belfast. Also excluded are magazines and periodicals plus titles which were effectively localised editions of other newspapers. For example, the *Fermanagh News* (Enniskillen) and *Donegal Independent* (Letterkenny) were local editions of the *Donegal Vindicator* (Ballyshannon), while the *Monaghan Democrat* was the local edition of the *Dundalk Democrat*. Also, these figures take into account some obvious errors and omissions relating to the *Newspaper press directory*; for example, titles such as the *Longford Leader*, *Enniscorthy Echo*, and *Western News* (Ballinasloe) were listed as independent organs even though their sympathies were clearly nationalist. The directory also did not include a listing for the *Kerryman* or the *Southern Star* (Skibbereen), both papers being unambiguously nationalist organs.

While most unionist titles were understandably concentrated in Ulster, it is important to note that there were also unionist papers published in many other parts of the country. These were spread over numerous different counties and included titles such as the *Carlow Sentinel, Kilkenny Moderator, Wicklow Newsletter, Waterford Conservative Gazette, Midland Counties Advertiser, King's County Chronicle* (Offaly), *Limerick Chronicle, Longford Journal, Meath Herald, Sligo Independent*, and *Westmeath Guardian*.[46] Unfortunately, accurate circulation figures are not available for any provincial newspapers so it can only be speculated that these titles may have been catering for a small readership by comparison with their nationalist counterparts.[47] Indeed, many titles were quite happy to promote themselves as the only paper of a specific political persuasion in a certain region.

The *Ulster Herald*, for example claimed to be 'the only nationalist weekly paper for mid and west Ulster' while the *Waterford Standard* asserted that it was 'the only unionist paper in the city and county'.[48] On the other hand some provincial papers laid claim to a readership well beyond their natural catchment area, sometimes even outside the country. The *Northern Standard*, a unionist organ from Monaghan, stated that its circulation encompassed not only its county of publication but extended 'throughout the north of Ireland'. The *Tyrone Constitution* made the significantly more grandiose assertion that it had 'a considerable circulation in America, India, and the colonies'. Not to be outdone, the *Connaught Telegraph* believed that its readership was spread not only 'throughout the province of Connaught' but also extended to the United Kingdom and America.[49]

It was also not unusual for newspapers to declare some form of religious affiliation. The *Fermanagh Times* was a 'thorough Protestant and conservative paper' while the *Longford Journal* advocated 'the

---

[46] Appendix A shows the geographical location of each provincial title while Appendix B provides an overview of the political sympathies/orientation, publication dates, and key figures at each individual provincial newspaper during the 1914–21 period.

[47] The *Newspaper press directory* did not supply circulation figures for individual titles and they were not published during this period. Nonetheless, newspapers were the only existing mass medium so it can reasonably be concluded that they circulated widely considering the attention afforded to them by the British authorities in terms of regulation and censorship.

[48] *Newspaper press directory and advertisers' guide 1917*, pp 215–16.

[49] Ibid., pp 209–15.

interests of all sects of Protestants'. The *Ulster Gazette* (Armagh) simply advocated 'sound Protestant principles' and supported the Church of Ireland, and in a somewhat similar manner the *King's County Chronicle* (Offaly) merely stated that it was 'attached to the reformed churches of Ireland, England, and Scotland'.[50] Nationalist titles, whose religious sympathies obviously lay predominantly with the Catholic Church, were notably less forthright in declaring the religious creed to which they subscribed. One of the very few nationalist papers to make any assertion in this respect was the *Kilkenny Journal*; it described itself inoffensively as a 'defender of Roman Catholic principles' rather than 'the impugner of other men's creeds'.[51]

Perhaps even more revelatory were the advertisements placed by some publications in the *Newspaper press directory*. Numerous titles wished to convey a specialised appeal to potential advertisers. The *Cork Weekly Free Press* was one such example as it portrayed its readership as being comprised extensively of 'the farming and commercial classes'. Others, such as the *Nenagh News*, 'read by all classes – the peer and the peasant', wished to depict themselves as having a more universal and egalitarian appeal. However, many other papers promoted themselves in a manner that may seem extremely supercilious over a century later. Dublin's *Daily Express* (not to be confused with British publication of the same name) declared to potential advertisers that it was 'the financial and society paper' that was 'read by all the best people'. The *Cork Constitution* boasted that it was read 'by people representing a greater purchasing power than the readers of all the other papers published in Munster'. The *Irish Times* followed a similar line when contending that it was 'the organ of the moneyed community' while its weekly edition, the *Weekly Irish Times*, was read 'throughout the land in all well-to-do families'.[52]

Expressions of political sympathies tended not to appear in advertisements though there were some exceptions. The *Ulster Gazette* declared itself the 'official organ of the mid-Armagh Conservative Association and the County Grand Orange Lodge of Armagh'. The *Londonderry Sentinel* clearly wanted potential advertisers to know that it was 'opposed to Home Rule or any legislation tending to sever the Union between England and Ireland'.[53] Nonetheless, outright statements of political affiliations were not typical of most provincial papers. In

---

[50]   Ibid., pp 207–9.
[51]   Ibid., p. 213.
[52]   Ibid., pp 206, 547, 583–4.
[53]   Ibid., pp 84–5.

general, such detail appeared under the newspaper's listing rather than in an advertisement (not all papers ran advertisements). As with religious outlook, unionist titles tended to articulate their political allegiances in a somewhat more overt manner than their nationalist counterparts. While most nationalist papers merely described themselves as 'nationalist', their unionist counterparts tended to be rather more effusive in this regard. The *Ballymena Observer*, for example, unambiguously advocated 'loyalty to the throne and the maintenance of the Union' while the *Strabane Weekly News* was 'a staunch supporter of the Unionist party'. The *Belfast Newsletter* adopted a slightly more moderate tone, simply supporting 'unionist principles', while the aforementioned *Daily Express* sought to 'maintain intact the imperial union'.[54]

Nationalist titles were slightly more tentative in revealing their politics. The *Western People* (Ballina) merely stated its support for 'sound national principles'. The *Enniscorthy Guardian* was only slightly more assertive in claiming to act 'in the interests of "Peasant Proprietors" and was also "for home rule"'. The *King's County Independent* was slightly more vocal, declaring itself 'a strong advocate of the national cause' that also devoted 'much space to political and general affairs affecting the welfare of Ireland'. Other nationalist papers were not only more forceful in asserting their nationalist credentials but were equally happy to publicise their allegiance to the principal force of Irish nationalism at the time, the Irish Parliamentary Party. The *Fermanagh Herald* was 'a thorough nationalist paper' that supported 'all the movements of the party', while the *Galway Observer* identified itself as 'the recognised organ of the national party' but equally advocated 'freedom for all classes'.[55]

The links between provincial newspapers and the Irish Parliamentary Party, and indeed the Unionist Party, was not something that happened by accident. Nor was it a situation that came about because several MPs also happened to be newspaper proprietors or editors. It was a scenario that evolved as politicians (not only in Ireland) came to realise the increasingly influential position occupied by the print media. Accordingly, they recognised the necessity to cultivate this relationship to ensure that as many newspapers as possible were sympathetic to their aims and aspirations. This may have involved financial support for newspapers where feasible or indeed playing a role in their initial establishment. The relationship could occasionally be mutually beneficial as many newspapermen moved into the political arena on the strength of their journalistic

---

[54] Ibid., pp 207–8, 215.
[55] Ibid., pp 207–15.

experience. This was a noticeable feature of the Irish Parliamentary Party during its time as the dominant force in Irish nationalism. Its successor in this position, the Sinn Féin party, held radically different ideas as to how Irish self-government should be achieved. However, Sinn Féin differed little from its predecessor in its desire to exert as much influence as possible on the press, both national and local, and the party spared little effort to fulfil that desire.

Politics and the print media

The British Government's desire to negate such an influence was evident as far back as the 1860s. As Legg observed, even at such an early stage the authorities at Westminster were already becoming concerned that Irish newspapers were exerting a subversive influence on 'a population thought ignorant and easily led'.[56] The supercilious attitude of the British authorities notwithstanding, their fear was justified as to the influence of the print media. Michael Foley asserts that even as early as 1880 approximately 'one third of the provincial press had declared themselves as nationalist'.[57] Allied to the aforementioned spate of provincial titles launched from 1880 onwards the claim that the provincial press 'performed an essential role in the development of the idea of the nation' seems wholly valid.[58] It should, however, be noted that newspapers were not the only means by which Irish nationalist aspirations were promoted.

In this respect pamphlets and posters played an important role and complemented other printed outlets although they were somewhat more propagandist in nature. The publication of pamphlets had long been common in Irish history stretching back to the time of Jonathan Swift, who was one of the most noted exponents of this medium. This method of advancing the nationalist cause was still quite prevalent by the late nineteenth and early twentieth centuries. Some of the most fitting examples of this include Arthur Griffith's 'The Home Rule bill examined' (1912), James Connolly's 'The re-conquest of Ireland' (1915), and 'Military rule in Ireland' (1920), written by Erskine Childers.[59]

---

[56] Legg, *Newspapers and nationalism*, p. 76.
[57] Foley, 'How journalism became a profession', p. 25.
[58] Legg, *Newspapers and nationalism*, p. 174.
[59] The pamphlets and posters referred to in this section of the text can be accessed at Trinity College Dublin Library Digital Collections (http://digital collections.tcd.ie/home/).

Posters were an equally popular form of propagating the Irish nationalist cause during this period. They were used to great effect at the height of the Land League campaign of the early 1880s. As Frank Rynne notes, posters were used to advance the aims of the organisation in the remotest parts of Ireland and contained phrases such as 'Down with the oligarchy', 'Proclaim to the world your undying detestation of that foul feudalism that robs and ruins', and 'Protest against landlord injustice, tyranny and oppression'.[60] By the early stages of World War I, posters were figuring prominently in the recruiting campaign in Ireland. This was not only a feature of the campaign by the British authorities but also of the Irish Parliamentary Party's support for the war effort. One such poster highlighted the case of Stephen Gwynn, an Irish Parliamentary Party MP who had enlisted, and encouraged 'every decent Irishman' to 'follow Private Gwynn's example and join the Irish brigade today'. Other posters featured senior party figures such as Joseph Devlin and John Dillon urging Irishmen to join an Irish brigade or regiment.

As the more republican form of nationalism came to the fore in the aftermath of the Easter Rising, Sinn Féin also utilised posters in equal measure and perhaps more emotively. One poster was emblazoned with the heading 'Roger Casement's last message' that was 'written in Pentonville before his execution' while the bottom of the poster encouraged the electorate to 'vote for Sinn Féin and freedom for Ireland'. Another poster contained one of the most well-known slogans to emerge during this time. It relates to the South Longford by-election of 1917 in which the Sinn Féin candidate was Joseph McGuinness, who was imprisoned in England at the time. The poster depicts McGuinness in prison garb, against the backdrop of an Irish tricolour, accompanied by the slogan, 'Put him in to get him out'.

There is little doubt that both pamphlets and posters continued to be a popular form of propagating the aims of a broad range of Irish nationalists in the decades prior to independence. Nonetheless, they did not really constitute any specific element of the mainstream media. Within the mainstream media the growing volume of provincial titles that began to emerge from the early 1880s signified a highly notable development. These new titles were predominantly nationalist which is hardly surprising as many of their owners and editors were actively involved in nationalist politics. Several commentators have remarked on

---

[60] Frank Rynne, 'This extra-parliamentary propaganda: Land League posters' in *History Ireland*, 16, no. 6 (The Fenians: 150th anniversary) (Nov.–Dec. 2008), pp 240–1.

the involvement of such owners and editors (principally as members of the Irish Parliamentary Party) that began to manifest itself in the last two decades of the nineteenth century.

Felix M. Larkin traces the connection between Irish nationalist politics and the print media back to *United Ireland* (established by Charles Stewart Parnell), the *Freeman's Journal* (which had longstanding ties to the Irish Parliamentary Party), and, in later years, the *Irish Independent*.[61] Larkin actually identifies thirty-eight MPs with some form of journalistic connection.[62] Mark O'Brien notes the central role played by the press in the development of the Land League and the campaign for land reform. This was a process, he states, aided 'by the fact that many newspaper proprietors and editors were senior Irish Parliamentary Party politicians'.[63] The involvement of press personnel in the broader nationalist movement is also noted by Foley who comments that 'the number of journalists engaged in politics was substantial'.[64] Such political engagement is quantified by Legg who confirmed that 'between 1880 and 1910, fourteen proprietors/editors stood for parliament, all of them advocating varieties of nationalism'. All but two of the fourteen who went forward as candidates were elected.[65]

The journalistic dimension to Irish nationalist politics also draws comment from Patrick Maume, who contends that newspapermen such as the aforementioned Jasper Tully of the *Roscommon Herald*, James P. (J.P.) Farrell of the *Longford Leader*, and the Doris brothers (William and P.J.) of the *Mayo News* 'became significant political figures in their own right'.[66] Maume's contention could also apply to other MPs drawn from the ranks of the provincial press such as James Laurence (J.L.) Carew, proprietor of the *Leinster Leader*, editor–proprietors John Patrick

---

[61] Felix M. Larkin, 'Parnell, politics and the press in Ireland, 1875–1924' in Pauric Travers and Donal McCartney (eds), *Parnell reconsidered* (Dublin, 2013), pp 76–9. Larkin comments on the reluctance of the *Irish Independent* to acknowledge Parnell as its founder. He details how the Parnellite *Irish Daily Independent* was launched in 1891 and was purchased by William Martin Murphy in 1900 and subsequently relaunched as the *Irish Independent* in 1905.

[62] Felix M. Larkin, 'Double helix: two elites in politics and journalism in Ireland, 1870–1918' in Ciaran O'Neill (ed.), *Irish elites in the nineteenth century* (Dublin, 2012), p. 129.

[63] O'Brien, 'Journalism in Ireland', p. 17.

[64] Foley, 'How journalism became a profession', p. 31.

[65] Legg, *Newspapers and nationalism*, p. 138.

[66] Patrick Maume, *The long gestation: Irish nationalist life, 1891–1928* (Dublin, 1999), p. 7.

(J.P.) Hayden (*Westmeath Examiner*) and Patrick Aloysius (P.A.) McHugh (*Sligo Champion*), Daniel David (D.D.) Sheehan (editor of the *Southern Star* in Skibbereen prior to his election to Westminster), and Sir Thomas Esmonde, founding shareholder and one of the main financial backers of the *Enniscorthy Echo*. This substantial journalistic aspect to the movement for Irish self-rule gave rise to a situation in which the broader populace ceased being 'the passive, God-fearing, providence-accepting victims of the natural disaster of the Great Famine'. Instead, they were 'now addressed by newspaper editors and other vociferous individuals ready and willing to create and lead political mobilisation'.[67]

This burgeoning nationalist assertiveness was stoked not only by mainstream newspapers. In addition to the steady flow of newly established provincial titles, the closing decades of the nineteenth century and the first two decades of the twentieth century also witnessed the emergence of many 'advanced-nationalist' publications. Such publications stridently challenged the status quo in Ireland at the time and provide further evidence of the increasing journalistic presence in Irish society. They included organs not only of political organisations such as Sinn Féin but also of institutions of cultural nationalism (sometimes referred to as the 'Irish Ireland' movement), labour and trade union organisations, the suffrage movement, and the more militant wings of Irish nationalism. The most prominent of these were titles such as *An Claidheamh Soluis, The Leader, Irish Worker, Bean na hÉireann,* and the *Irish Volunteer*.[68]

Political parties and Irish newspapers

These advanced-nationalist publications represent only a small sample of the overall number of such titles that were founded in the period from 1890 to 1920. Their readership, circulation, and longevity varied widely from one organ to another. The proliferation of these titles, allied to the amount of newly established provincial papers that appeared on the scene during the same period, provide ample evidence of the fast-increasing popularity and prominence of the broader print media. Nonetheless, from an Irish perspective possibly the most relevant aspect of the rise of the popular press in the late nineteenth and early twentieth centuries was

---

[67] Boyce, *Nineteenth-century Ireland*, p. 178.

[68] Many of these titles are examined in Mark O'Brien and Felix M. Larkin (eds), *Periodicals and journalism in twentieth century Ireland: writing against the grain* (Dublin, 2014).

that it coincided with the predominance of the Irish Parliamentary Party as the main force of Irish nationalism. Hence it is no great surprise that their paths should have crossed with considerable regularity during these years. The *Freeman's Journal*, which became 'the foremost nationalist newspaper in Ireland in the nineteenth century', had extremely strong links with the party from the early 1880s onwards. The paper's owner, Edmund Dwyer Gray, was a Home Rule MP who initially opposed Parnell but as the latter assumed an almost unassailable position as leader of the Irish Parliamentary Party Gray lent him his support.[69] Parnell himself was fully cognisant of the benefits of a supportive newspaper as he launched his own publication, *United Ireland*, in 1881, under the editorship of William O'Brien (formerly a reporter with the *Freeman's Journal* and yet another journalist who subsequently became an MP).[70] This deep-rooted engagement with the popular press has been remarked upon by a number of historians. Boyce believes the development of the party during Parnell's time as the 'most modern of political movements' was attributable not only to 'its strict pledge of loyalty' but also to 'its use of the popular press'.[71] The use of the popular press referred to by Boyce was not limited to national publications. As early as 1880, Parnell was consulting with Edward Walsh, the editor of the *Wexford People*, regarding the candidature of Timothy Healy in the upcoming election to the House of Commons.[72]

The Parnell split of 1890–91 came at a time when the provincial press was still amid its evolution as a predominantly nationalist force. At the time, many of what were to become the most significant organs within the sector, such as the *Limerick Leader*, *Kilkenny People*, *Clare Champion*, and *Connacht Tribune*, were either in their infancy or had not even been established. Consequently, any analysis of how the broader provincial press responded to the split is of rather limited value. This perhaps explains why historians who have documented this specific episode in Irish history, such as Frank Callanan, Roy Foster, and F.S.L. Lyons, afford minimal attention to the response of provincial newspapers to the split. Callanan notes the fiercely anti-Parnellite sentiment of Jasper Tully's *Roscommon*

---

[69] Felix M. Larkin, 'Gray, Edmund William Dwyer' in James McGuire and James Quinn (eds), *Dictionary of Irish biography* (Cambridge, 2009).

[70] Felix M. Larkin, 'A Great Daily Organ': *The Freeman's Journal*, 1763–1924' in *History Ireland*, 14, no. 3 (May–June 2006), p. 45.

[71] Boyce, *Nineteenth-century Ireland*, p. 271.

[72] Parnell to Walsh, 5 Nov. 1880 (National Library of Ireland, John Redmond papers, MS 15,220/1).

Herald while Lyons merely comments that Edward Harrington of the *Kerry Sentinel* was one of Parnell's most prominent supporters.[73] Foster, meanwhile, records the strange situation in Parnell's native County Wicklow where the nationalist *Wicklow People* assumed an anti-Parnellite position while the conservative-unionist *Wicklow Newsletter* defended Parnell. The latter publication's defence was rather reluctant, however, and arose from Parnell's position as a 'local benefactor' in addition to his 'efforts on behalf of the county's ports, and his largesse as an employer'.[74] Marie-Louise Legg, whose aforementioned study of the Irish provincial press covers the period up to and including the Parnell split, did not discuss how it was received by provincial newspapers. It is, nonetheless, interesting to note that some of those titles that went on to become the most significant Sinn Féin supporters, such as the *Mayo News*, *Meath Chronicle*, *Enniscorthy Echo*, and the *Kerryman*, were only launched after the fall of Parnell. However, such an observation should be regarded with some caution, as at least two of these papers (*Mayo News* and *Enniscorthy Echo*) had strong links to the Irish Parliamentary Party in their early years. Indeed, the links between that party and the provincial press grew even stronger following the death of Parnell.

Senior party figures, such as the aforementioned William O'Brien, enjoyed what Paul Bew describes as 'a specially warm relationship with a wide range of important provincial newspapers'. This relationship embraced an impressive geographical spread that included titles in each of the four provinces.[75] The close ties between the Irish Parliamentary Party and the provincial press drew further critical analysis from historians. Legg made the point that the involvement of so many newspaper proprietors in active politics meant that 'political parties gained a more subtle understanding of the way the press could be used' as such proprietors possessed 'an intimate understanding of the working of politics in practice'.[76] Boyce

---

[73] Frank Callanan, *The Parnell split, 1890–91* (Cork, 1992), p. 162; F.S.L. Lyons, *The fall of Parnell, 1890–91* (London, 1960), p. 119.

[74] R.F. Foster, *Charles Stewart Parnell: the man and his family* (Atlantic Highlands, NJ, 1976), p. 210.

[75] Paul Bew, *Conflict and conciliation in Ireland 1890–1910: Parnellites and radical agrarians* (Oxford, 1987), p. 113. O'Brien enjoyed this 'warm relationship' with provincial titles such as the *Connaught Telegraph* (Castlebar), *Mayo News* (Westport), *Kerry People* (Tralee), *Killarney Echo*, *Sligo Champion*, *Roscommon Messenger*, *Limerick Leader*, *Midland Tribune* (Birr), *Southern Star* (Skibbereen), *Westmeath Independent* (Athlone), and *Anglo-Celt* (Cavan).

[76] Legg, *Newspapers and nationalism*, p. 173.

articulates a similar view in stating that the Dublin-based papers 'did not possess the special local knowledge and intimacy that the editors and writers of the provincial newspapers enjoyed'. These circumstances allowed 'able and talented journalists' like James Daly of the *Connaught Telegraph* and Tim Harrington of the *Kerry Sentinel* to become 'local – and in some cases national – political leaders as well'.[77]

The increasingly intimate relationship between the party and the provincial print media occasionally resulted in sympathetic newspapers seeking the assistance of the party. In October 1905, David Sheehy, MP for South Meath, wrote to party leader John Redmond requesting that some financial support be allocated to the *Drogheda Independent* (the paper had got itself into debt as a result of a libel action). Sheehy urged that generous help be provided to the editor, Michael A. Casey, as the paper had 'a great circulation in Louth, Meath, and North Dublin' and was 'a very influential supporter of our movement'.[78] In a similar manner, John Dillon, deputy leader of the party, wrote to Redmond concerning urgent appeals for financial assistance he had received from the *Connaught Leader*.[79] The close engagement with the provincial press also extended to involvement in the establishment of newspapers. In March 1901, John Muldoon, MP for North Donegal (and later East Wicklow and East Cork), introduced John Redmond to 'two Omagh gentlemen' (Mr Lynch and Mr O'Connor) at the House of Commons who were seeking the party's help 'in the project of establishing in that town a nationalist newspaper for Tyrone and Fermanagh'. Muldoon urged Redmond's endorsement of the project and merely asked that he write to Lynch and O'Connor saying that he had heard of the possibility of the establishment of a nationalist newspaper in Omagh and that he hoped it would be 'entirely successful'.[80] The 'Mr Lynch' referred to by Muldoon was in fact Michael Lynch who subsequently was central to the foundation of the *Ulster Herald* in Omagh later the same year.[81]

The ties between the provincial press and the Irish Parliamentary Party have received significant attention from historians but links to Sinn Féin have drawn far less analysis. In many respects this is quite understandable; Sinn Féin's victory at the 1918 general election sounded the death knell

---

[77]   D. George Boyce, *Nationalism in Ireland* (3rd ed., Dublin, 1995), p. 205.

[78]   Sheehy to Redmond, 25 Oct. 1905, MS 15,228/1.

[79]   Dillon to Redmond, 25 Sept. 1905, MS 15,182/7; *Connaught Leader* was a provincial title published in Ballinasloe between 1885 and 1907.

[80]   Muldoon to Redmond, 27 Mar. 1901, MS 15,208.

[81]   *Ulster Herald*, 20 Apr. 1935.

for the constitutional party but Sinn Féin's time as the major force in Irish politics effectively lasted only four years (1917–21). On the other hand, the party founded by Isaac Butt in 1873 occupied this position for over four decades. Allied to this is the fact that following its 1918 election victory Sinn Féin placed great emphasis on gaining favourable publicity in the foreign press. The distribution list for the *Irish Bulletin* (the newsletter of Dáil Éireann referred to in the introduction) provides firm evidence of this concentration of attention on the foreign media.[82] This aspect of Sinn Féin strategy is dealt with comprehensively by Maurice Walsh but it should not mask the fact that the party's desire to enjoy the benefits of a supportive and sympathetic provincial press was just as strong as that of the party it had vanquished at the polls in December 1918.

Guidelines issued to local party organisers in May 1917 stressed the need to 'take steps to bring all possible influence to bear' not only on 'members of public boards and other persons of importance in their districts' but also 'on the local press to secure support for the policy of Sinn Féin'.[83] Further instructions assumed a decidedly more menacing tone as those organising local branches were bluntly told that 'the influencing of local newspapers' was to be secured by sending:

> deputations to the editor or proprietor, before whom the prospect of support or its opposite should be intelligently and candidly put. If local 'Nationalist' papers will not express local opinion on national subjects there is no use for them.

The party's apparently ambivalent attitude towards the maintenance of a free press in the country was further indicated by the instruction that:

> articles and letters on Sinn Féin should be sent to the press, and their insertion demanded if necessary.[84]

This hard-line attitude towards provincial newspapers did not always translate into actual intimidation. Apart from County Cork, where the *Cork Examiner*, *Cork Constitution*, and *Skibbereen Eagle* attracted the

---

[82] Names and addresses of recipients of *Irish Bulletin* (daily list) as at end of July 1921 (Bureau of Military History, Mary Alden Childers collection, CD6/9/16k). In addition to being sent to recipients in Ireland, Britain, and the USA, the proscribed newsletter was sent to press outlets in several European countries and also to Australian, Canadian, and Japanese press representatives.

[83] Official instructions for the organisation of Sinn Féin clubs, 16 May 1917, CD6/6/3.

[84] How to form Sinn Féin clubs, CD6/9/4.

undesired attention of the IRA, there is little evidence of republicans threatening any other provincial newspapers. Nevertheless, there is little doubt that Sinn Féin regarded this section of the print media as a crucially important medium for their publicity. From around the middle of 1918, the party's propaganda department (the forerunner of the Department of Publicity set up by Dáil Éireann) commenced a series 'of weekly notes, written from the national point of view and sent out to the provincial press'. These notes were sent to 'upwards of 40 newspapers in all parts of the country' that 'received and in the majority of cases used these notes'. The person in charge of Sinn Féin's propaganda department at this time was Robert Brennan, formerly a provincial journalist himself, having worked at the *Enniscorthy Echo*.[85] The Department of Publicity, headed initially by Lawrence Ginnell and then by Desmond FitzGerald, that superseded the department headed by Brennan, was similarly focused in its intent to influence, to the greatest extent possible, both national and local press coverage of the unfolding situation in Ireland. To this end, it included among its tasks not only the 'daily supervision of the press' but also, where possible, 'a daily supply of news to the press', 'the provision for the press of suitable articles', and the 'indirect influencing of the editorial policy of the press'. With this is mind daily interviews were to be held with the Dublin press allied to correspondence with the provincial press. However, if possible, a representative of the department 'should be free to travel to the provinces to interview editors of the provincial papers'.[86]

Irish republicans continued in their endeavours to dictate the nature of the press coverage of the increasingly hostile situation in the country right up to the closing stages of the Anglo-Irish War. As late as May 1921, Erskine Childers, who had succeeded Desmond Fitzgerald as head of the Department of Publicity, reported that 'constant efforts are being made to influence the Irish press to present news in a form more favourable to the National movement'.[87] However, by this stage the more militant side of Irish republicanism had begun to display a concerted interest in ensuring favourable newspaper coverage. In May 1921, the IRA issued a set of directives to local brigade commanders that clearly illustrated this desire. A general order was sent to local IRA units stating that brigade commandants were to 'be held responsible for the prompt

---

[85] The Department of publicity, history and progress, Aug. 1921, CD6/9/6h.

[86] Some notes on general principles of propaganda, MS 33,913/9.

[87] Report from the Department of Publicity 16 Mar.–7 May 1921 (University College Dublin, Desmond Fitzgerald papers, P80/14/16).

transmission to GHQ [General Headquarters] of reports of conflicts, ambushes, attacks, execution of spies, and enemy outrages in their district'. If a written report could not be sent without undue delay the brigade commandant was to 'immediately send a suitable man to GHQ to report verbally to the Director of Publicity'.[88] This instruction, seeking to ensure the swift documenting of the IRA's version of events, was accompanied by a memo requesting specific information regarding local newspaper correspondents. Brigade commandants were required to divide local newspapers or their correspondents into four different categories: 'friendly', 'friendly but intimidated', 'neutral', and 'hostile'.[89] Those local journalists classified as 'friendly' were to be supplied regularly and promptly 'with all information with regard to military activities which it was desirable to make public'. However, the recommended method for dealing with newspapers or their correspondents that fell into any of the other three categories took on a decidedly more sinister tone. Those categorised as 'hostile', 'neutral', and even 'friendly but intimidated' were to be 'regularly supplied with information, and pressure brought to bear on them to publish it'. Where such 'pressure' did not produce the desired result then 'drastic action' could be taken.[90]

Regrettably little is known of the response of individual IRA units to this directive from GHQ. This may well be primarily because a truce was called less than two months after its issuance. Fortunately, one response that was documented was from the Cork No. 1 Brigade which operated in an area that witnessed a greater amount of hostilities during the War of Independence than almost any other area of the country. The brigade provided GHQ with the names of almost fifty local journalists working in County Cork plus areas of Kerry, Limerick, and Waterford. Also included in its response was the classification for a number of newspapers as had been requested of them, in addition to a number of comments regarding certain titles. The *Cork Examiner* was considered 'the most dangerous rag in Ireland', pretending 'to express moderate opinion', but 'actually hostile' to republican aims. The *Cork Constitution* was also regarded as 'openly hostile' but did not arouse any similarly derogatory comment, evidently because it circulated 'only to confirmed Unionists'.

---

[88] General Orders, No. 25, 4 May 1921 (National Library of Ireland, Florence O'Donoghue papers, MS 31,208).

[89] Newspapers to be classified as 'friendly but intimidated' were defined as those that were 'so intimidated by the enemy as to be afraid to use or publish information unfavourable to the enemy'.

[90] Publicity memo No. 1, 4 May 1921, MS 31,208.

The *Waterford News* was classified as 'friendly but intimidated' but the *Waterford Star*, *Waterford Standard*, and *Munster Express* were all viewed as 'hostile' and doing harm to the republican cause.[91]

The IRA's antagonism toward the *Cork Examiner* resulted in the paper's offices being attacked in December 1920 (following repeated condemnations of IRA violence) with its printing machinery sustaining serious damage. This antipathy for the Cork newspaper was shared by elected Sinn Féin representatives. In an exchange with Piaras Béaslaí (TD for Kerry East) in Dáil Éireann in March 1921, Seán Hayes (TD for Cork West who had a significant connection to the *Southern Star* newspaper in Skibbereen as detailed in Chapter 4) bemoaned how 'provincial papers, such as the *Cork Examiner*', were 'hampering the work of the Republic'.[92] Criticism of IRA actions had also resulted in the offices of the *Irish Independent* being raided by armed republicans in December 1919 following the attempted assassination of Lord French, Lord Lieutenant of Ireland, at Ashtown, County Dublin. Dan Breen, the Tipperary IRA leader stated how he and his comrades who took part in the operation took umbrage at the tone of the paper's reporting of the attack.[93] Indeed, it was not unknown for newspapers that disagreed with the policies or tactics of Irish republicans to suffer attacks on their offices or staff. Peter Hart, while accepting that 'both sides tried to suppress hostile newspapers' points to the cases of the *Cork Examiner*, *Cork Constitution*, and *Skibbereen Eagle*, all of which 'had their employees and premises attacked and their papers seized and burned by the rebels'.[94]

It is important to note Hart's qualification that attempts to suppress newspapers were not limited to the Irish republican side. There were numerous instances of the British military raiding the offices of provincial newspapers; these occurrences are examined in detail in later chapters that document the experiences of individual newspapers. Most of these incidents occurred from early 1920 onwards. Prior to that, censorship had been in effect, as it had been since the start of World War I. The introduction of wartime censorship in Britain and Ireland coincided

---

[91] Schedule No. 1 – Newspapers, MS 31,208.

[92] Dáil Éireann debates, 1st Dáil, vol. F, no. 20, 11 Mar. 1921 (Houses of the Oireachtas, https://www.oireachtas.ie/en/debates/debate/dail/1921-03-11/).

[93] Dan Breen, *My fight for Irish freedom* (Dublin, 1981), p. 105. Breen took part in the attack at Ashtown but not in the raid on the *Irish Independent* as he had been injured in the earlier operation.

[94] Peter Hart, *The IRA and its enemies: violence and community in Cork, 1916–1923* (Oxford, 1998), p. 103.

with the British authorities launching a massive propaganda campaign that involved them seeking to control the output of the print media to an extent previously unknown. This aspect of British policy and the subsequent continuation of censorship in Ireland (after it had been discontinued in Britain at the end of the war) are considered in the next two sections.

Press–State relations in the early 1900s

Although the newspaper business had attained a position of considerable influence by the time of the outbreak of the Great War, the succeeding four years saw its independence severely challenged as the British Government sought to exert control of the reporting of their military campaigns. The desire to exercise such control was evident during the Boer War (1899–1902) when several of the war correspondents of British newspapers in South Africa felt aggrieved at the way censorship was applied.[95] By the end of World War I, however, there was a sense that newspapers had been overly acquiescent to the wishes of the British authorities. Consequently, a notion had taken hold 'that the reputation of the press had been tarnished by collaboration with the Government'.[96] It was a notion that almost all elements within the press were eager to dispel. As Walsh notes, 'no longer could all the correspondents be counted on to be simple imperialists'.[97] The Anglo-Irish conflict of 1919–21 provided one of the first opportunities to banish any suggestion of compliance with the government. Consequently, if these correspondents of British newspapers were determined to challenge British policy in Ireland where they saw fit then correspondents of the (predominantly nationalist) Irish provincial press were hardly likely to assume any less belligerent a position.

Thus, the scene was set for, if not a showdown, then a serious clash of priorities between the British Government and the broader print media. In the decade prior to the commencement of the Irish War of Independence, the British Government had displayed little hesitation in acting against publications that incurred its disapproval. Initially it was organs from the advanced-nationalist stable such as *Scissors and Paste* and *An Claidheamh Soluis* that attracted such attention, but this extended to

[95] Jacqueline Beaumont, 'The British press and censorship during the South African War 1899–1902' in *South African Historical Journal* 41, no. 1 (Nov. 1999), pp 271–2.

[96] Walsh, *The news from Ireland*, p. 181.

[97] Ibid., p. 30.

several provincial titles as their numbers increased and their tone grew more stridently nationalistic. Consequently, in the wake of the Easter Rising in 1916, several provincial newspapermen were arrested and interned by the British authorities despite having played no active part in the Rising. Unsurprisingly those imprisoned were from papers that were perceived as strong supporters of the Sinn Féin cause. These included P.J. Doris, co-founder and editor of the *Mayo News*, Maurice Griffin, one of the three co-founders of the *Kerryman*, and the founder and editor of the *Enniscorthy Echo*, William Sears.[98] With the success of Sinn Féin at the 1918 general election and the subsequent establishment of Dáil Éireann in 1919 the number of newspapers that came into conflict with the British authorities increased significantly.

Doris, Sears, and Griffin represented newspapers that were openly supportive of Sinn Féin policies well before the latter's electoral success in December 1918. However, as Ian Kenneally claims, the majority of the Irish press in 1918 was controlled by proprietors who were hostile to Sinn Féin.[99] Despite this, the intriguing situation existed that even within publications that were no friends of Sinn Féin, journalists whose political sympathies clearly lay with that party's brand of separatist nationalism were employed. Such a scenario existed in the case of the *Dundalk Democrat*. Journalist Frank Necy, whose limited involvement in the Easter Rising led to his imprisonment, had worked with the County Louth paper since about 1905 and later edited it for almost twenty years.[100] Yet Necy's editor at the time was Thomas F. McGahon, a staunch supporter of John Redmond and the Irish Parliamentary Party who was deeply distrustful of the newly emergent political force in Ireland.[101] This situation was mirrored at the *Anglo-Celt* in Cavan. The managing-director of the paper, the aforementioned John F. O'Hanlon, stood as the candidate of John Redmond's party in opposition to Arthur Griffith in the East Cavan by-election of 1918. However, on the editorial staff of the paper at the same time was Thomas K. Walsh, a strong Sinn Féin supporter who was involved in the foundation of the party in County Cavan.[102] Even at newspapers supportive of Sinn Féin, such as those owned by Doris and Sears, similar anomalies existed.

---

98   *Mayo News*, 27 Feb. 1937; *Kerryman*, 7 Apr. 1928; *Enniscorthy Echo*, 30 Mar. 1929.
99   Ian Kenneally, 'Truce to Treaty: Irish journalists and the 1920–21 peace process' in Rafter, *Irish journalism before independence*, p. 223.
100   *Dundalk Democrat*, 7 Mar. 1970.
101   *Dundalk Democrat*, 25 Jan. 1941.
102   *Anglo-Celt*, 15 Apr. 1950.

P.J. Doris had founded the *Mayo News* with his older brother William in 1892. William Doris was one of the many newspaper proprietors who also became an MP. While William's loyalty remained solidly with his parliamentary colleagues, the outlook of his younger brother grew irrevocably more militant. P.J. Doris befriended Arthur Griffith at an early stage and wholeheartedly espoused the separatist policies advocated by the Sinn Féin founder.[103] This led to an estrangement of the two brothers that was not resolved within their lifetimes.[104] When William Sears launched the *Enniscorthy Echo* in 1902 one of the main financial backers was Sir Thomas Esmonde MP. While Sears supported the Irish Parliamentary Party at the time of the paper's establishment his allegiance shifted to Sinn Féin very soon after that party's foundation in 1905.[105] Esmonde meanwhile appeared to follow the lead of Sears when he joined Sinn Féin in 1907 and withdrew from Westminster, though he did not resign his seat. He returned to the Irish Parliamentary Party in 1909, however, as a 'gesture of national reconciliation' and distanced himself from the paper thereafter.[106]

These conflicting loyalties within many newspapers were not only reflective of similar conflicts of loyalties that had evolved throughout the broader populace but also a precursor to the developing conflict between the broader print media and the British authorities. In his history of Irish newspapers from their origins in Cromwellian times up to the 1980s, Hugh Oram makes the reasonable claim that from Easter 1916 to the end of the Civil War 'the newspaper industry of Ireland endured the most hazardous and difficult period of its entire existence'.[107] This was not solely due to the level of violence that prevailed in the country during these years. While the intensely militant conditions certainly exacerbated the difficulties for Irish newspapers, it was the imposition of military censorship at the start of World War I that laid the foundation for such a treacherous period in Irish newspaper history.

---

[103] *Mayo News*, 27 Feb. 1937.
[104] Owen McGee, 'Doris, William' in McGuire and Quinn, *Dictionary of Irish biography*.
[105] *Enniscorthy Echo*, 30 Mar. 1929.
[106] Patrick Maume, 'Esmonde, Sir Thomas Henry Grattan' in McGuire and Quinn, *Dictionary of Irish biography*.
[107] Oram, *The newspaper book*, p. 123.

British wartime propaganda and Irish censorship

The limited number of texts that document this period of Irish print media history make only passing reference to censorship regulations and even less to the British Government's dealings with the print media during World War I. It is necessary, however, to consider both issues for two reasons. First, it is important to understand the experience that the British Government had gained during the war in dictating newspaper coverage of the conflict. Secondly, it is essential to appreciate the restrictions under which Irish newspapers had to operate, particularly after the Easter Rising, when the situation in Ireland began to grow increasingly militant.

The British Government's desire to exert its influence over the print media was borne out of the realisation that 'this war would require propaganda of unprecedented sophistication and scope'. To this end, even prominent authors such as Thomas Hardy, James Barrie, John Galsworthy, Arthur Conan Doyle, H.G. Wells, and John Buchan were recruited to serve the cause.[108] Britain also seized a massive advantage in the forthcoming propaganda war when one of its cable ships, *Telconia*, cut the direct undersea cables linking Germany with the USA. This left the British in almost total control of the news flow across the Atlantic which was a crucial factor in winning the sympathy of the American public.[109] The British Government also realised from an early stage that 'the ideal recruiting ground for propagandists was from among the most powerful newspaper proprietors and editors'. Such proprietors were generally happy to co-operate for the simple reason that 'war was good business for newspapers'.[110]

The Prime Minister, David Lloyd George, was foremost among those at the highest level of the British Government to have an enthusiastic appetite for the war of words. Lloyd George is described by historians as 'being fascinated by the revolutionary expansion of the popular press' and of having a passionate interest in propaganda.[111] Therefore, the press was

---

[108] Adam Hochschild, *To end all wars: a story of protest and patriotism in the First World War* (London, 2012), pp 147–8.

[109] Philip M. Taylor, *Munitions of the mind: a history of propaganda from the ancient world to the present era* (3rd ed., New York, 2003), pp 177–8.

[110] Phillip Knightley, *The first casualty: from the Crimea to Vietnam: the war correspondent as hero, propagandist, and myth maker* (3rd ed., New York, 2003), p. 69.

[111] James Margach, *The abuse of power: the war between Downing Street and the media from Lloyd George to Callaghan* (London, 1978), p. 17; Taylor, *Munitions of the mind*, p. 187.

seen as a potential ally in the pursuit of war aims which possibly goes some way to explaining what is generally perceived as British success in this regard during World War I. Even though strict censorship of the reporting of military operations had been in effect since the early days of the war, British newspapers were generally happy to co-operate as many editors saw themselves as willing partners 'in the government's effort to win the war'.[112] Most importantly, however, was the assistance of newspaper proprietors and they were duly rewarded with 'knighthoods and lordships' that 'were generously distributed among the press and, finally, prestigious posts in government itself'.[113] As another historian comments, 'this was Lloyd George's way of thanking the "press lords" for their loyal service'.[114] The complicity of major sections of the press had a downside, however.

The failure to report anything that even remotely portrayed the actual horrors of war led to resentment for the war correspondent amongst those ordinary soldiers serving at the front.[115] The totally illusory nature of newspaper reports of military activity was even acknowledged by Lloyd George, who admitted privately in December 1917 that 'if the people really knew, the war would be stopped tomorrow. But of course, they don't – and can't know. The correspondents don't write and the censorship would not pass the truth'.[116]

The war correspondent even incurred the wrath of one of the greatest of the war poets, Siegfried Sassoon. In his poem 'Fight to a Finish', Sassoon derides the 'Yellow-Pressmen' whom he visualises being bayoneted by 'the boys' during their victory march through London.[117] This loss of credibility in those reporting from war zones had a knock-on effect in Ireland. As Maurice Walsh points out, the ensuing conflict in Ireland afforded journalists 'who had been under attack for their collusion with government propaganda during the First World War' the opportunity 'to reassert their identity as truth tellers'.[118] The effort to

---

[112] Alice Goldfarb, 'Propaganda in Britain and Germany during the First World War' in *Journal of Contemporary History*, 13, no. 3 (July 1978), p. 478.

[113] Ibid., p. 486.

[114] Niall Ferguson, *The pity of war* (London, 1998), p. 214; The most notable recipients of such posts were Lord Northcliffe of *The Times* and *Daily Mail*, Sir Max Aitken (later Lord Beaverbrook) of the *Daily Express*, and Sir George Riddell of the *News of the World*.

[115] Hochschild, *To end all wars*, pp 223–4.

[116] Ferguson, *The pity of war*, p. 213.

[117] Paul Fussell, *The Great War and modern memory* (London, 1981), p. 86.

[118] Walsh, *The news from Ireland*, p. 188.

regain lost credibility resulted in prominent British newspapers such as *The Times*, *Daily Mail*, *Daily News*, and *Manchester Guardian* displaying little hesitancy in being highly critical both of the actions of British armed forces in Ireland and of British Government lethargy in finding a resolution to the Irish situation.[119]

Despite the massive propaganda campaign waged by Britain during World War I, very few resources were deployed during the Anglo-Irish War to ensure victory in this aspect of the conflict. This may have been because the British Government believed there was little necessity to engage in propaganda on what was, for them, a purely domestic issue. It was September 1920 before former Fleet Street journalist Basil Clarke was recruited for such a purpose. His time in Ireland, however, was not marked by any great success. As Michael Hopkinson observes, 'he was soon associated with the failure to counter in any coherent way the wave of propaganda resulting from the deaths of Terence MacSwiney and Kevin Barry'.[120] Effectively this left military censorship as the only tool employed by the British authorities to control the output of Irish newspapers.

The Press Censor's office in Dublin comprised the Chief Press Censor plus eleven other staff, three of whom were army personnel.[121] Since the outbreak of World War I, press censorship had been enforced by the Press Bureau in London and the Irish press was subject to the same regulations as British newspapers. However, in the wake of Easter 1916, the decision was made to establish a press censorship office specifically for Ireland though it would still be complementary to the Press Bureau's operation in London.[122] In early June 1916, General Sir John Maxwell wrote to the Irish press to inform them of this development and of the appointment

---

[119] Christopher Doughan, 'What the papers said: portrayals of the Irish War of Independence in the British and Irish print media' (MA thesis, NUI Maynooth, 2011), pp 34–5.

[120] Michael Hopkinson, *The Irish War of Independence* (Dublin, 2002), p. 45; Hopkinson further notes that by this stage 'both the military and political leadership' in Dublin Castle had become 'obsessed with the hostile coverage by Irish newspapers'. Efforts to boost their own propaganda campaign were seriously hampered by the fact that 'lines of communication between the various publicity agencies were confused and often overlapped'.

[121] *Irish Independent, Freeman's Journal*, 5 June 1918.

[122] Donal Ó Drisceoil, 'Keeping disloyalty within bounds? British media control in Ireland, 1914–19' in *Irish Historical Studies*, 38, no. 149 ('Power the state and institutions in Ireland') (May 2012), pp 54–6.

of Lieutenant-Colonel Lord Decies as Chief Press Censor. Maxwell also requested that each title 'be good enough to forward a copy of your daily or weekly paper directly after issue' to the newly established office for examination, and added that he felt sure he could 'rely on your support and assistance in not publishing in your papers any matter that might be of inflammatory nature'.[123] The Office of the Press Censor initially operated out of military headquarters, Parkgate, Dublin but moved to Ely Place in August 1919 before transferring to 85 Grafton Street three months later where it remained until the closure of the office in August 1919.[124]

Lord Decies (born John Graham Beresford) held the position of Chief Press Censor from 1916 to April 1919. Entering the British Army in 1887, he served throughout the Boer War and accompanied General Sir John Maxwell to Ireland during the Easter Rising of 1916.[125] Decies was assisted by Major Bryan Cooper who succeeded to the post following the former's resignation in April 1919. Cooper had previously been elected as a Unionist MP for South County Dublin in 1910.[126] Little is known of others who worked in the Press Censor's office, but the few who have been traced, although Irish-born, held a firm allegiance to Britain.[127]

There is no sense that Lord Decies was the tyrannical symbol of British power that Irish republicans would probably have wished him portrayed. Indeed, the little that is known of the Chief Press Censor from 1916 to 1919 suggests that he was a reasonable and honest individual. One provincial newspaper, although disagreeing with the nature of the censorship in Ireland, described him as a 'courteous, affable, and capable gentleman, with whom it was easy to arrange matters on a reasonable and satisfactory basis'.[128] On his resignation from the post, another nationalist

---

[123] Press Censorship Records 1916–1919, National Archives of Ireland, 3/722/15-128, 1 June 1916.

[124] Press Censorship Records 1919–1919, 3/722/15-128, 1 Aug. and 20 Nov. 1916.

[125] *Irish Independent*, *Irish Times*, 2 Feb. 1944; *Irish Press*, 3 Feb. 1944.

[126] *Irish Times*, 12 July 1930. Cooper was subsequently elected to Dáil Éireann in 1923 as an independent member and was again elected four years later but this time as a Cumann na nGaedheal member.

[127] *Irish Independent*, *Freeman's Journal*, 1 Aug. 1919; *Irish Times*, 26 Aug. 1919. Two of those who have been identified were a Captain Shaw and W.R. Williamson who held positions as senior assistants to Lord Decies. Shaw had served during the Gallipoli campaign and was formerly honorary secretary of the Irish Unionist Alliance. Williamson, a Derry native, had seen service for over a year on the Western Front with the Inniskilling Fusiliers.

[128] *Killarney Echo*, 17 June 1916.

provincial title commented that 'Lord Decies acted all through in a most courteous and tolerant manner' and felt 'certain that all sections of the Irish press regret his departure'.[129] Indeed, Decies himself was also willing to acknowledge the talents of those diametrically opposed to the government he represented. In one of his regular press censorship reports he conceded that the Sinn Féin organ *Nationality* was 'extremely well written and edited' by Arthur Griffith, adding that 'much that is written is undesirable but extremely difficult to censor'.[130] Decies's sense of fair-mindedness was further illustrated in October 1921 when he wrote to the *Freeman's Journal* criticising the British authorities for the continuing internment of Irish political prisoners.[131] Major Bryan Cooper, who succeeded Decies as Press Censor in 1919, also exhibited a similar sense of respect for Irish newspapers. Upon the closure of the Press Censor's Office in August 1919, Cooper wrote to the Irish press on how he had 'received the greatest kindness and courtesy' from 'journalists of all parties' and of his appreciation of the 'skill and labour' required in the production of a newspaper.[132]

Even though both Decies and Cooper were clearly honourable and upright personalities they still had the difficult task of enforcing censorship. The censorship they had to impose was, understandably, to prove unpopular with those in charge of Irish newspapers. Nonetheless, censorship was hardly a new phenomenon in Irish journalism. As far back as the 1870s, the British Government introduced 'measures to limit the freedom of the press to claim to speak on behalf of a separate Irish people'.[133] Even before the situation in Ireland grew increasingly tense following the Easter Rising the wartime censorship had come in for harsh criticism. Regulations that had been instigated at the start of the war to limit what could be published were described as 'probably the strictest, most rigid, and most autocratic the press of these countries has ever experienced'.[134] To make matters worse the censorship had been conducted in an 'arbitrary and high-handed' manner, 'strongly marked by egregious incompetency and ridiculous absurdity'.[135]

---

[129] *Nationalist and Leinster Times*, 3 May 1919.
[130] Press Censorship Report, Sept. 1917, Colonial Office, National Archives, Kew, CO904/166/1.
[131] *Freeman's Journal*, 8 Oct. 1921.
[132] Press Censorship Records 1916–1919, 3/722/21-71, 29 Aug. 1919.
[133] Legg, *Newspapers and nationalism*, p. 107.
[134] *Irish Journalist*, vol. 1, no. 1, Oct. 1914.
[135] *Irish Journalist*, vol. 1, no. 2, Nov. 1914.

Press censorship was originally incorporated in the Defence of the Realm Act (DORA) and subsequently renewed in the Restoration of Order in Ireland Act (ROIA) though there was little difference between the applicable regulations in both acts. Between 1916 and 1919, Decies issued a plethora of circulars to the Irish press reminding them of their obligations under the legislation. Several of these were reasonably understandable and were hardly likely to cause any great difficulty for Irish newspapers. They included guidelines regarding the publication of reports relating to shipping losses or fatalities, the arrival or departure of hospital ships, the location of wireless stations, and instances of telegraphic or cable breakdown.[136] However, it was the majority of the remaining instructions issued by Decies that were to prove most problematic for Irish newspapers. These included directives with regard to the publication of speeches made at meetings of boards of guardians, political meetings, and election rallies. Such directives additionally related to the printing of posters and election literature, publication of letters from arrested prisoners, and mention of the 'late rebellion' of Easter 1916.

The first instance of the Press Censor indicating that the publication of political speeches or resolutions might be subject to censorship came as early as August 1916. Decies advised newspaper editors that 'resolutions or speeches passed or made at the meetings of corporations, county, urban or rural district councils should be most carefully considered before publication'. The same circular also stated that 'criticism of the government or its administration which is directly the cause of disaffection is not permitted'.[137] Similar directives became a regular feature during the following three years as Sinn Féin won a series of by-elections and ultimately emerged triumphant at the general election of December 1918. Prior to the North-Roscommon by-election of February 1917, Decies reminded editors that 'reports of speeches or other political propaganda' in connection with the upcoming election was fully subject to censorship regulations.[138] Shortly before the Kilkenny by-election of August 1917, the press was warned 'that the publication of reports of seditious speeches, articles or other matter which is intended or likely to cause disaffection is forbidden by the Defence of the Realm Regulations'.[139] Only a few weeks before the 1918 general election

---

[136] Press Censorship Records 1916–1919, 3/722/15-28, 31 Jan., 26 Feb., 2 Mar. 1917; 3/722/14-65, 18 June 1917; 3/722/20-49, 22 Dec. 1917.
[137] Press Censorship Records 1916–1919, 3/722/15-28, 17 Aug. 1916.
[138] Press Censorship Records 1916–1919, 3/722/15-128, 1 Feb. 1917.
[139] Press Censorship Records 1916–1919, 3/722/14-65, 19 July 1917.

Decies advised editors 'that the publication of any matter which is either directly or indirectly an incitement to armed rebellion or of any matter which is likely to inflame public opinion against the military could not be published'.[140]

Many provincial newspapers also operated an associated printing business and it was made clear that such papers also needed to be aware of the potential for infringement of the regulations. Immediately prior to the general election of December 1918, Irish newspapers were informed that the production of 'pamphlet, leaflets, election addresses, or other literature which contain matter offending against the Defence of the Realm Regulations' similarly risked censure.[141] The publication of letters from men arrested in Ireland and being held in England was also a cause of unease for Decies. In November 1916, he wrote to the Chief Secretary of his concern that newspaper reports regarding the treatment of prisoners at Frongoch were generating 'a bitter feeling towards the British government'.[142] In March of the following year, he advised newspapers that any letters from arrested prisoners that they wished to publish should first be submitted to his office.[143] It is clear also that the growing sympathy for the executed leaders of the Easter Rising was a cause of anxiety to the British authorities. Only five months after the rebellion, Decies advised the press that any mention of the 'late rebellion' made at a recent political meeting at Limerick needed to be 'submitted to the Press censor before publication'.[144] Just prior to the first anniversary of Easter 1916, Decies advised that the publication of 'memorial, anniversary, or other notices in your advertisement columns, which refer to the rebellion of last Easter' were to be submitted to his office before insertion.[145] While all of these directives created difficulties for Irish newspapers it was undoubtedly the instructions relating to the publication of political speeches that was the most problematic.

The ever-increasing popularity of Sinn Féin necessitated greater coverage of the party's activities within the print media. This created a predicament for most newspapers as the majority of speeches made at Sinn Féin meetings tended to be vehemently anti-British in nature. Hence, any reports of such speeches risked breaching censorship

---

[140] Press Censorship Records 1916–1919, 3/722/21-71, 30 Nov. 1918.
[141] Press Censorship Records 1916–1919, 3/722/18-1, 5 Dec. 1918.
[142] Press Censorship Records 1916–1919, 3/722/13-33, 18 Nov. 1916.
[143] Press Censorship Records 1916–1919, 3/722/15-128, 22 Mar. 1917.
[144] Press Censorship Records 1916–1919, 3/722/15-128, 28 Sept. 1916.
[145] Press Censorship Records 1916–1919, 3/722/15-128, 23 Mar. 1917.

regulations even if such views did not reflect the editorial policy of the paper. Early in his tenure, Decies endeavoured to clarify the matter by explaining that it was not his intention 'to interfere with reasonable criticism of political or military matters, as long as the language used was not calculated to incite the people'. He further added that 'any matter of a doubtful nature' should be referred to his office before publication.[146] Many newspapers availed themselves of this facility rather than risk possible suppression. Nevertheless, there is evidence to suggest that as Sinn Féin grew stronger censorship was utilised as a barrier to its aspirations.

In March 1918, Decies described many of the speeches at Sinn Féin meetings around the country as constituting 'the most violent anti-English propaganda' and stressed the need for censorship to be 'maintained over the reproduction of oratory of this description, which would greatly diminish its effect'.[147] By August 1918, Decies obviously felt that this policy was proving effective as he noted that 'the restrictions of censorship are proving an increasing embarrassment to the seditious activities of Sinn Féin'.[148] Two months later, the Chief Press Censor virtually conceded, albeit indirectly, that censorship was being deployed as a barrier to Irish republican aims when he reported that it had acted like 'a fire extinguisher on the dangerous element in Ireland' and that it could 'stand as the most immediate and visible obstacle to Sinn Féin aspirations'.[149] Following that party's success in the general election of December 1918, Decies still maintained that censorship had been an overall success. In an interview with the *New York Times*, he argued that this success was due to the 'loyal support of Irish newspaper men'. Sinn Féin's electoral success, he argued, was down to the British Government trying to justify their preoccupation with the war as an excuse for failing to deal comprehensively with the Irish situation.[150] Privately, though, Decies was questioning the necessity of ongoing censorship. In his monthly report for December 1918, he accepted totally its justification as a wartime measure but doubted its efficacy in peacetime. Praising the support he had received 'from all sections of the Irish press', he contended

---

[146] *Kerryman*, 17 June 1916. Decies made his comments at a meeting with local newspaper proprietors and editors in Tralee.

[147] Press Censorship Report, Mar. 1918, CO904/166/2.

[148] Press Censorship Report, Aug. 1918, CO904/167/1.

[149] Press Censorship Report, Oct. 1918, CO904/167/1.

[150] *Irish Independent*, 16 Jan. 1919. Extracts from Lord Decies's interview with the *New York Times* were quoted in the *Irish Independent*.

that such support constituted 'a strong argument for the discontinuance of censorship while yet it retains a measure of good-will'.[151]

Press censorship reports for the period confirm that it was, indeed, accounts of speeches made at Sinn Féin meetings, and to a lesser extent at meetings of local councils, that were censored to the greatest extent. Quite often the tone of such speeches was highly provocative (if not inflammatory) so it was hardly a surprise that permission to publish was refused. This trend is illustrated by a few brief examples. In July 1918, the *Wexford People* was not allowed to publish the text of a speech by Father Michael O'Flanagan in which he stated that any attempts to impose conscription would be countered by 'guerrilla warfare' carried out by 'bands of men up and down the country with little communi-cation between one another'.[152] O'Flanagan sometimes appeared to act like a magnet to the censor's attention; three months later, the *Meath Chronicle* was denied permission to publish the majority of a speech he made at Trim. This was not too difficult to understand given that during the course of his lengthy oration he referred to England as 'a hypocrite' that was 'professing to fight for freedom' when 'she was merely throwing dust in the eyes of the world'.[153] Indeed, in May 1918, Decies wrote to editors specifically to advise them that a speech made by O'Flanagan at Ballyjamesduff, Co. Cavan was 'not for publication'.[154] In Munster, the *Clare Champion* was prevented from publishing comments made by a local priest at a pre-election meeting in support of Eamon de Valera; references to 'English tyranny', 'armed hosts of militarism', 'strutting petty Czars in charge of the police', and 'England's tools of oppression' were hardly going to be passed by the censor.[155]

Sinn Féin's subsequent electoral success in December 1918 led to more militant public utterances that continued to keep the office of the censor busy. The following month, the *Wexford People* was refused permission to publish a report of a Sinn Féin meeting at which it was stated that Ireland need not fear 'British guns or British bayonets' and that resolutions passed at such meetings were of no consequence 'unless backed up by the resolution passed from the rifle'.[156] At a meeting of Mountmellick District

---

[151] Press Censorship Report, Dec. 1918, CO904/167/1.
[152] Press Censorship Report, July 1918, CO904/167/1. At the time, O'Flanagan held the position of joint vice-president of Sinn Féin.
[153] Press Censorship Report, Oct. 1918, CO904/167/1.
[154] Press Censorship Records 1916–1919, 3/722/21-71, 27 May 1918.
[155] Press Censorship Report, Dec. 1918, CO904/167/1.
[156] Press Censorship Report, Jan. 1919, CO904/167/2.

Council it was claimed that 'tyrants' with 'inhuman hearts' would treat domestic animals better than Irish political prisoners were currently being treated – the *Nationalist and Leinster Times* was not allowed report the comments.[157] The *Drogheda Independent* was similarly denied permission to publish comments made at a demonstration for returned prisoners at which it was stated that England used the tools of 'the prison and convict ship' to argue her case and that 'brute force' would be responded to by similar methods if required.[158]

There were some instances of editorial comment being censored but this did not occur with any great frequency. In several other cases the censorship ranged from the bizarre to what would simply be considered amusing almost a century later. On the bizarre front, the *Galway Express* was prohibited from publishing sections of a letter that suggested the spread of venereal disease in Ireland was increasing due to the number of soldiers returning from the front.[159] In a similar vein was the suggestion at a meeting of the Tipperary Board of Guardians in February 1919 that the killing of two members of the Royal Irish Constabulary (RIC) men at Soloheadbeg the previous month was engineered by the British Government in order to blacken Ireland's name 'before the nations of the world'. Unsurprisingly, the *Tipperary Star* had to edit these comments out of its report.[160] What would now most likely be regarded as light relief was provided by two cases from September 1918 and February 1919. In the earlier case, the *Irish Independent* was not allowed to report that mottoes such as 'Up the Rebels' and 'Join de Valera's IRA' had been painted on walls and public buildings around the town of Letterkenny.[161] Six months later, the strange combination of political prisoners and dog licences proved the unlikely reason why the *Irish Times* could not report on a Sinn Féin meeting at Mullingar. The meeting had passed a resolution calling on the party's supporters throughout Ireland 'to refuse to pay dog licences pending the release of Irish political prisoners in English and Irish jails'.[162]

---

[157] Press Censorship Report, Feb. 1919, CO904/167/2.

[158] Press Censorship Report, Mar. 1919, CO904/167/2.

[159] Press Censorship Report, July 1918, CO904/167/1. Letter was from a body called The Committee of Protection of Ireland from Venereal Disease.

[160] Press Censorship Report, Feb. 1919, CO904/167/2. The incident referred to at Soloheadbeg is generally regarded by historians as marking the start of the War of Independence.

[161] Press Censorship Report, Sept. 1918, CO904/167/1.

[162] Press Censorship Report, Mar. 1919, CO904/167/2.

The strange and even slightly comedic (by twenty-first-century standards) nature of a small section of censored newspaper items notwithstanding, the regulation of the press remained a problematic issue for both the British authorities and Irish newspapers. In August 1919, the post of Press Censor was abruptly abolished though it is not entirely clear why the British Government made the decision at this stage.[163] The move was not welcomed by Irish newspapers. As Kenneally points out, editors resented the fact that 'the censor may have gone but the restrictive regulations remained in place'.[164] One provincial newspaper commented that the closure of the censor's office would 'not leave the Irish press one whit more free hitherto'.[165] As will be seen in forthcoming chapters, it was a view shared by many other titles.

The problem was that while the office of the Press Censor was in operation newspapers could at least obtain some form of guidance as to what was permissible to publish. To a certain degree the Press Censor provided some form of protection but that protection ceased to exist after August 1919. For the next two years, as Ó Drisceoil notes, the censorship gave way to 'coercion and the blatant suppression of dissident media'.[166] The closure of the censor's office coincided roughly with the escalation of the situation in Ireland to a military conflict. As those in Sinn Féin who favoured pursuance of their goals by military rather than political means gained the upper hand the conflict with Britain grew decidedly more violent. In this hostile environment, provincial newspapers were frequently caught in the crossfire. Their experiences are documented and analysed in the following chapters.

---

[163] *Irish Times, Freeman's Journal*, 29 Aug. 1919.
[164] Kenneally, 'Truce to Treaty', p. 214.
[165] *Meath Chronicle*, 6 Sept. 1919.
[166] Ó Drisceoil, 'Keeping disloyalty within bounds?', p. 68.

2

The Pale and Beyond: Leinster

Introduction

In pure geographical terms, Leinster is the third largest of the four Irish provinces, with a land area of 19,800 square kilometres. According to the 1911 census, it had a population of 1,162,044, though Dublin city and county accounted for 477,196 of this figure.[1] Consequently, the population of the remaining eight counties was 684,848, with County Wexford the most populous (102,273) while County Carlow had the lowest population (36,252) of these counties. The urban centres with the largest populations were Kilkenny city, Wexford town, and Drogheda and Dundalk in County Louth. In total, thirty-five local newspapers served Leinster between 1914 and 1921. The four titles examined in this chapter, the *Meath Chronicle*, *Enniscorthy Echo*, *Kilkenny People*, and *Midland Tribune* were published in areas that displayed a variety of demographical characteristics.

The *Meath Chronicle* was published in Navan, which had a relatively small population of just fewer than 4,000. Nevertheless, the *Chronicle* was the only nationalist paper based in County Meath which had a population of just over 65,000, of which 93 per cent was Catholic. The situation was slightly different regarding the *Enniscorthy Echo*. It faced competition from a rival nationalist paper, the *Enniscorthy Guardian*, in the town of Enniscorthy, which had a population of 5,495. Furthermore,

---

[1] W.E. Vaughan and A.J. Fitzpatrick, *Irish historical statistics: population, 1821–1971* (Dublin, 1978), pp 3–68. All the demographical statistics and information provided in this section are based on the 1911 census and are cited from Vaughan and Fitzpatrick's work.

there were three other nationalist papers serving County Wexford: the *New Ross Standard*, *Wexford Free Press*, and *Wexford People*. The volume of competition, however, was somewhat offset by the fact that County Wexford, as noted, had the largest population of the Leinster counties (outside Dublin), with Catholics accounting for 93 per cent of the populace.

With a population of 10,514, Kilkenny city was one of the largest population centres in the province and was also where the *Kilkenny People* was published. The overall population of the county was just under 75,000, of which almost 95 per cent was Catholic. The *Kilkenny People*'s main rival in the area was the nationalist *Kilkenny Journal*, though the city and county was also served by the unionist *Kilkenny Moderator*. The *Midland Tribune*, published in Birr, County Offaly, did not have to contend with a nationalist rival in the same town. The county's only other nationalist paper was the *King's County Independent*, published in Tullamore. Birr, however, was also home to the unionist *King's County Chronicle*. The town's population at the time was just over 4,000 while County Offaly boasted a population of just over 57,000 of which 90 per cent was Catholic.

Leinster newspapers: an overview

In October 1915, the Lord Lieutenant of Ireland, Baron Wimborne, hosted a function at the Viceregal Lodge in the Phoenix Park in Dublin for editors of the Irish press. This gathering of representatives of the print media was held 'in order to consult with them as to the lines on which their co-operation could most effectively be given to the recruiting campaign' that had recently been inaugurated in Ireland.[2] According to news reports at the time, the Lord Lieutenant 'was glad to welcome the

---

[2] *Freeman's Journal*, 29 Oct. 1915; *Irish Times*, 29 Oct. 1915; 29 Jan. 1916; Mark O'Brien, 'With the Irish in France: the national press and recruitment in Ireland, 1914–1916' in *Media History*, 22, no. 2 (2016), p. 7. While the editors or representatives of many newspapers attended this event, many others sent letters of apology for non-attendance and others appear to have paid no attention to it at all. The eagerness on the part of the British authorities to enlist the assistance of newspaper editors to bolster recruitment is further evidenced by the fact that a number of them, including John Healy of the *Irish Times*, William J. Flynn of the *Freeman's Journal*, and Thomas J.W. Kenny of the *Connacht Tribune* were taken on a tour of the western front in Jan. 1916.

80 gentlemen who were present' despite the short notice, and he also 'paid a very cordial tribute to the assistance which the Press had already given in connection with the prosecution of the war'.[3]

Given the fractious relationship between the Irish print media and the British authorities in Ireland that was later to manifest itself, the Phoenix Park gathering was quite remarkable to the point of almost appearing anachronistic. Yet this ostensibly amiable meeting took place only six months prior to the 1916 Rising. Among the '80 gentlemen' present were editors of national newspapers plus other publications based in the three main cities (Belfast, Cork, and Dublin), but the vast majority of attendees were drawn from the Irish provincial press. Both unionist and nationalist titles were represented as were several longer-established titles in addition to numerous (principally nationalist) organs that had been established from around 1880 onwards. This diverse mixture obviously included representatives of the thirty-five provincial newspapers spread across eleven Leinster counties.

At the start of 1914, these Leinster newspapers (except for those published in Dublin city and county) comprised a mixture of nationalist, unionist, and independent titles. Similar to Connacht and Munster, the nationalist titles were in the majority, with most of these supporting the Irish Parliamentary Party. In a manner that was somewhat dissimilar to the other two provinces, several of these organs committed wholeheartedly to the Sinn Féin cause in the years that followed. Consequently, this chapter closely examines four such titles: the *Meath Chronicle*, *Enniscorthy Echo*, *Kilkenny People*, and the *Midland Tribune* (based in Birr, County Offaly). Certain other Leinster publications, most notably the *Westmeath Independent*, and to a lesser extent the *Dundalk Examiner*, also came to be regarded as Sinn Féin papers and their experiences are briefly considered. However, prior to investigating the aforementioned four titles it is necessary to assess the composition of the broader print media in Leinster during these years.

Outside Dublin, very few newspapers had been launched in the province prior to 1800 and an even smaller number had displayed any degree of longevity. The latter group included the *Drogheda Journal* (1772–1843) and the *Wexford Herald* (1787–1865), but the *Kilkenny Journal* was the only paper dating back to the eighteenth century that remained in existence by the early twentieth century. It had been established in 1766 as *Finn's Leinster Journal* but two changes of ownership resulted in it being renamed the *Leinster Journal* in 1802 and then the *Kilkenny*

---

[3] *Freeman's Journal, Irish Times*, 29 Oct. 1915.

Journal in 1830. The latter title remained in publication until 1965.[4] While the *Kilkenny Journal* was a nationalist organ, the political sympathies of most of the older provincial newspapers tended to be unionist while some others adopted an independent stance. By 1914, this was very much the case in Leinster where the majority of titles that had been launched in the first half of the nineteenth century were classified as either unionist or independent. This was exemplified by newspapers such as the *Kilkenny Moderator* (established in 1814), *Leinster Express* (1831), *Carlow Sentinel* (1831), *Drogheda Advertiser* (1837), *Longford Journal* (1839), *King's County Chronicle* (1845), and *Meath Herald* (1845). Possibly the most noteworthy of these titles were the *Kilkenny Moderator, King's County Chronicle*, and *Leinster Express*.

The *Kilkenny Moderator* was founded by Abraham Denroche in the early nineteenth century and was once edited by author and historian Standish James O'Grady. Despite its Protestant–unionist ethos, the paper was an enthusiastic supporter of the Gaelic League and at one stage even featured a weekly Irish language lesson. At the outbreak of World War I, Isabella Browne Lalor, one of the very few women involved at this level of the newspaper business, took over as editor–proprietor following the death of her husband, Michael Wilton Lalor.[5] In common with so many other unionist titles in the south of Ireland, the *Kilkenny Moderator* went out of existence shortly after the foundation of the Irish Free State, ceasing publication in 1925.

The *King's County Chronicle*, located in Birr, County Offaly, was acquired by Armagh-born John Wright in 1873. Wright was a staunch unionist and was reputed to have established Birr Orange Lodge in the early 1880s.[6] Despite its conflicting political outlook, the paper appears to have enjoyed a mostly amicable relationship with its nationalist counterpart in Birr, the *Midland Tribune*. When the *Chronicle*'s printing works were destroyed by fire in 1903, the *Tribune*'s plant was placed at its disposal and the favour was frequently reciprocated when the *Tribune* experienced difficulties with its own printing operation.[7] Indeed, when John Wright died in 1915, his obituary in the *Midland Tribune* described him as 'courteous and obliging, and ever ready if it was in his

[4] Michael O'Dwyer, 'A history of Kilkenny newspapers, 1767–2009' in John Bradley (ed.), *Kilkenny through the centuries: chapters in the history of an Irish city* (Kilkenny, 2009), pp 382–6.
[5] Ibid., pp 382–6.
[6] *Midland Tribune: 1881–1981 – 100 years of a family newspaper* (7 Nov. 1981).
[7] Ibid.; *Midland Tribune*, 7 Feb. 1914; 29 Jan. 1916.

power, to help fellow journalists in any difficulty'.[8] The *King's County Chronicle* somewhat bucked the trend for unionist newspapers in the south of Ireland to cease publication within the first decade or two of the formation of the Free State. In recognition of the new political situation it was renamed the *Offaly Chronicle* in 1922 and survived until 1948 when it was sold to the *Midland Tribune*. It remained as a separate title until it was finally discontinued in 1963.[9]

The *King's County Chronicle* had been established in 1845 by Henry W. Talbot who fourteen years earlier had launched the *Leinster Express* in Maryborough (now Portlaoise). Unlike the Birr-based paper it was an independent organ that has survived well into the second decade of the twenty-first century. It was owned and edited by Michael Charles Carey who succeeded his father as proprietor in 1903. Carey remained at the helm of the paper for forty years until his death in 1943.[10] Such prolonged editorial/proprietorial terms were very much a feature of the Irish provincial press. The independent status of the *Leinster Express* meant that it had no connections to the Irish Parliamentary Party, but this was certainly not the case at several other newspapers in Leinster.

Perhaps the most prominent example of such a link was the *Westmeath Examiner* based in Mullingar. The editor–proprietor of the paper was J.P. Hayden, who was elected as an MP for the South Roscommon constituency in 1897. A lifelong friend of Irish Parliamentary Party leader John Redmond, he held his seat until the 1918 general election, which effectively sounded the death knell for the party he represented. Hayden had established the *Westmeath Examiner* in 1882 and remained as editor–proprietor for a remarkable seventy-two years until his death in 1954.[11]

Such journalistic longevity was not in evidence at the *Longford Leader* though it similarly shared a strong connection with the Irish Parliamentary Party. The paper was established by J.P. Farrell in 1897 who had been elected an MP for West Cavan the previous year. Farrell subsequently served as MP for North Longford from 1900 until 1918.[12] In addition to his parliamentary activities he was also the first president of the GAA in the county and was later appointed president of Longford

8   *Midland Tribune*, 13 Nov. 1915.
9   *Midland Tribune: 1881–1981 – 100 years of a family newspaper* (7 Nov. 1981).
10   *Leinster Express*, 7 Aug. 1943.
11   *Westmeath Examiner*, 2 Oct. 1982; Jeremiah Sheehan, *Worthies of Westmeath: a biographical dictionary with brief lives of famous Westmeath people* (Moate, 1987), pp 54–5.
12   *75 years of Longford: The Longford Leader, 1897–1972* (29 Sept. 1972).

Wanderers, the first soccer club in the county.[13] In 1909, he became president of the newly established Ancient Order of Hibernians in Longford town.[14] In a report to Lord Decies shortly after the Easter Rising, J.P. Farrell was described as 'a slippery gentleman' who was 'at the bottom of all anti-British feeling' in the Longford area.[15] Despite such alleged credentials both he and his paper had, by the following year, incurred the wrath of local Sinn Féin members. They believed that the *Longford Leader*'s coverage of a Sinn Féin rally led to the arrest of Thomas Ashe (who later died as a result of attempted force-feeding while on hunger strike).[16] He was decisively defeated by Joe McGuinness of Sinn Féin in the 1918 general election. During the course of the campaign he had suffered a stroke; he died three years later at the relatively early age of fifty-six.[17]

The *Leinster Leader*, based in Naas, County Kildare, was another provincial newspaper with strong links to the Irish Parliamentary Party, though any direct connection had diminished somewhat by the 1914–21 period. It had been established as a limited liability company in August 1880 with many of its initial shareholders being drawn from the Catholic clergy in counties Kildare and Carlow. It went through a number of changes of editor in the first six years of its existence before ownership was transferred to James Laurence (J.L.) Carew and James Leahy, the parliamentary representatives for Kildare.[18] Leahy's involvement was believed to be only nominal and while Carew had little practical involvement in the running of the paper, it was to serve as a mouthpiece for his political views until his death in 1903.[19]

---

13 Tom Hunt, 'County Longford: sport and society, 1850–1905' in Martin Morris, James Kelly, and Fergus O'Ferrall (eds), *Longford: history and society: interdisciplinary essays on the history of an Irish county* (Dublin, 2010), pp 527–8; Mike Cronin, Paul Rouse, and Mark Duncan, *The GAA: county by county* (Cork, 2011), p. 255.

14 Gerard Morgan, 'The Ancient Order of Hibernians in County Longford' in Morris, Kelly, and O'Ferrall, *Longford*, p. 593.

15 Press Censorship Records 1916–1919, 3/722/14-83, 17 June 1916.

16 Marie Coleman, *County Longford and the Irish Revolution, 1910–1923* (Dublin, 2003), pp 71–4. Coleman states that 'Sinn Féiners in Longford blamed Ashe's arrest on J.P. Farrell, whose newspaper the *Longford Leader* was considered to have brought Ashe to the attention of the police by publishing the text of his speech at Ballinalee'.

17 Ibid., pp 86–7.

18 *Leinster Leader: Centenary Supplement* (15 Nov. 1980).

19 Ibid.

Although other newspapers in Leinster may not have featured elected MPs in the editor–proprietor role there was still a very close association between several titles and the Irish Parliamentary Party. This was the case at the *Drogheda Independent* whose origins can be traced to an Augustinian priest, Father James Anderson, who founded the Drogheda Independent Club in 1881 to promote nationalist ideals in the town. This led to the formation of the paper three years later, which became an enthusiastic advocate of Home Rule.[20] In 1889, Michael A. Casey was appointed editor at the request of William O'Brien MP. A devout Catholic, Casey played a key role in the development of the paper and remained in the editorial chair for almost fifty years.[21] Despite the close ties that had been forged with the Irish Parliamentary Party, shortly after its foundation the paper had, by 1919, moved to a position that was markedly more sympathetic to Sinn Féin.[22]

This contrasted with the other main newspaper in County Louth, the *Dundalk Democrat*. Unusually for a nationalist paper, it had been launched in the immediate aftermath of the Great Famine. The paper was established in 1849 by James Cartan, who was a strong supporter of land reform and the repeal of the Act of Union.[23] By the early years of the twentieth century, its ownership had passed to the Roe family and it was edited by Thomas F. McGahon, who held the position from 1902 until his death in 1941. In common with many of his peers within the journalistic trade, McGahon held a strong Catholic faith.[24] He was also an unwavering supporter of the Irish Parliamentary Party, but unlike many of his contemporaries he did not shift his allegiance towards Sinn Féin at any stage. Indeed, he was once quoted as saying that 'my heart died with John Redmond as far as politics are concerned'.[25] Despite McGahon's distaste for militant nationalism, the paper's reporting staff included Frank Necy (who later edited the paper for twenty years), a member of the Irish Volunteers who was imprisoned in Wales following the Easter Rising.[26]

The *Wexford People* was another paper that had significant links with the Irish Parliamentary Party (as noted in the previous chapter) through

[20] *Drogheda Independent: Centenary Supplement* (11 May 1984).
[21] *Drogheda Independent*, 25 Mar. 1938.
[22] Ted Greene, *Drogheda, its place in Ireland's history* (Julianstown, 2006), p. 365.
[23] *Dundalk Democrat*, 22 Oct. 1949; 16 Oct. 1999.
[24] *Dundalk Democrat*, 22 Oct. 1949.
[25] *Dundalk Democrat*, 2 Feb. 1941.
[26] *Dundalk Democrat*, 7 Mar. 1970.

the relationship between Edward Walsh, probably the *People*'s most celebrated editor, and Parnell. Following Walsh's death, the editorship passed to Edward O'Cullen, who occupied the position for a thirty-year period from around 1894. O'Cullen, who was a virtual invalid from an early age, was an enthusiastic supporter of the nascent GAA and also founded the *Ireland's Own* magazine in 1902.[27] While the *Wexford People* was not noted for any significant show of support for Sinn Féin, the same could not really be said for the *Nationalist and Leinster Times* in neighbouring County Carlow.

The paper was launched in 1883 by brothers Patrick and John Conlan, 'with the full support of the Irish Parliamentary at Westminster'.[28] By the early twentieth century, the management of the paper had passed to James Reddy. Similar to Edward O'Cullen of the *Wexford People*, Reddy was a loyal supporter of the GAA and also of the Gaelic League.[29] Clear indications that the paper had moved to a pro-Sinn Féin position came during the summer of 1919 when it published a series of articles penned by Kevin O'Higgins who had been elected as a Sinn Féin MP for Queen's County (Laois) the previous December. Despite the decidedly militant tone of these articles, none was censored.[30] Indeed, the *Nationalist and Leinster Times* avoided any threat of suppression although it was instructed by the Press Censor's Office to delete material on a regular basis between 1918 and 1919.[31]

Several other newspapers in the province were not so fortunate in avoiding official censure. One such case, albeit on a relatively mild scale, was the *Dundalk Examiner*, a publication that had initially been launched as the *Newry Examiner* in 1830. By 1919, it was regarded as a

---

[27] *Wexford People*, 16 Sept. 1933; 24 Dec. 2003.

[28] *Nationalist and Leinster Times: Centenary Issue 1883–1983* (23 Sept. 1983).

[29] *Nationalist and Leinster Times*, 8 Apr. 1944.

[30] *Nationalist and Leinster Times*, 31 May, 7, 14, 21, 28 June, 5, 12 July, 2 Aug. 1919. In this series of articles, O'Higgins repeatedly referred to England's 'army of occupation' in addition to using language such as 'the Prussianism of English rule', 'British rapacity', 'the force and fraud of England', as well as claiming how England's 'atrocities in Ireland made the worse deeds of the Prussian in Belgium look like peccadilloes'. This represents only a small sample of his comments but sufficiently indicates the overall tone of his contributions.

[31] Press Censorship Reports, Aug. 1918–Feb. 1919, CO904/167/1, CO904/167/2. The Press Censorship Reports that are available for this period indicate that the *Nationalist and Leinster Times* was required to delete content approximately ten times between August 1918 and February 1919. This was a significantly higher number of instances than most other provincial newspapers.

Sinn Féin organ and in September of that year it published a full-page advertisement for the Dáil Éireann loan. Consequently, the police visited its offices and seized all copies, and even 'newsboys selling the paper on the streets were requested to hand over all copies'.[32] However, the *Dundalk Examiner* suffered fairly minor disruption in comparison with some of the other newspapers in the province. The case of the *Westmeath Independent* provides an ample illustration of this point.

The *Westmeath Independent* was launched in 1846 by James Martin as a 'conservative journal' with a distinctly Protestant ethos.[33] Its political outlook underwent a dramatic shift under Thomas Chapman, who became proprietor in 1883. A Church of Ireland member, Chapman actively supported both the Land League and the Irish Parliamentary Party.[34] Both he and his paper firmly backed John Redmond and the recruitment campaign in the early stages of World War I and indeed two of Chapman's sons served in the British Army.[35] The *Westmeath Independent* was edited by Michael McDermott-Hayes, who was one of the founders of the Midland Volunteer Force in September 1913, a nationalist militia that joined with the Irish Volunteers a few months later.[36] In the wake of Easter 1916, however, the *Westmeath Independent* severed its ties with the Irish Parliamentary Party. By August 1917, Chapman had become president of the local Sinn Féin club while McDermott-Hayes was on its committee.[37] This new-found political allegiance soon incurred the wrath of the Press Censor.

In early 1918, the tone of the paper was deemed 'violent and of a nature to cause disaffection' and as 'having seriously transgressed the Defence of the Realm regulations'.[38] This resulted in the seizure of the *Independent*'s printing works in April 1918 and its suppression for one week.[39] Just prior to the suppression, McDermott-Hayes had complained bitterly to Decies at being instructed to remove segments of a report of an Irish

---

[32] *Irish Times*, 27 Sept. 1919.

[33] *Westmeath Independent: 150th Anniversary Special Supplement* (July 1996).

[34] *Offaly Independent*, 22 Apr. 1922.

[35] Michael Wheatley, *Nationalism and the Irish Party: provincial Ireland, 1910–1916* (Oxford, 2005), pp 240–1.

[36] John Burke, 'Evolving nationalism: Michael McDermott-Hayes and the *Westmeath Independent*, 1900–20' in Ian Kenneally and James T. O'Donnell (eds), *The Irish regional press, 1892–2018: revival, revolution and republic* (Dublin, 2018), pp 32–3.

[37] Wheatley, *Nationalism and the Irish Party*, p. 241.

[38] Press Censorship Report, Jan. 1918, CO904/166/1, Mar. 1918, CO904/166/2.

[39] *Irish Independent*, 6 Apr. 1918.

Volunteers' rally in Mullingar on St Patrick's Day.[40] In the aftermath of the suppression, his criticism grew more vociferous. Subsequent letters to Decies claimed that the censorship was backed by 'brute force' and had 'degenerated into tyranny and oppression'.[41] Just over two years later, a decidedly more serious fate befell the paper.

In October 1920, its printing works were attacked by Crown forces and partially wrecked. Despite the setback, the paper that only four months earlier had stated that 'English rule is broken in Ireland' was still published the following Saturday.[42] Only a fortnight later, a military force returned, and this time completely destroyed the printing works. One historian attributes the attack on the paper to Crown forces seeking a 'soft target for retribution' following increased republican activity in the area.[43] It is believed that Chapman, who was in a delicate state of health at the time anyway, never really recovered from the trauma. Even though he managed to start the paper up again in February 1922, Thomas Chapman passed away only two months later at the age of fifty-eight.[44]

The following sections closely scrutinise four newspapers in the province that came into conflict with the authorities to a similar or lesser degree to the *Westmeath Independent*. Each of these publications solidly committed to the Sinn Féin cause prior to the 1918 general election, which set them apart from most of their fellow-nationalist organs, not just in Leinster but also in the other three provinces. However, this shift of allegiance to Sinn Féin was clearly evident amongst a significant minority of nationalist titles in Leinster, a development that was not really replicated to any significant extent in the other provinces. Consequently, it renders this analysis of these four titles all the more relevant and is central to providing a comprehensive portrayal of the Irish provincial press during these years.

Meath Chronicle

Similar to the other three Leinster newspapers closely examined in this chapter, the *Meath Chronicle* was amongst that considerable number of nationalist newspapers established after 1880. The paper was founded

40 Press Censorship Records 1916–1919, 3/722/29-17, 28 Mar. 1917.
41 Press Censorship Records 1916–1919, 3/722/20-67, 7 and 13 May 1917.
42 Oram, *The newspaper book*, pp 143–4.
43 Burke, 'Evolving nationalism', p. 39.
44 *Westmeath Independent: 150th Anniversary Special Supplement* (July 1996).

in May 1897 by Tom Daly with the assistance of his brother Michael. Tom Daly began his career with the *Drogheda Independent* and went on to work for the *Wexford Free Press* before joining J.L. Carew's *Leinster Leader*. Carew then appointed Daly editor of what appears to have been the short-lived *Wicklow & Wexford Leader*. Daly subsequently assumed editorial control of the *Carlow Vindicator*, a Parnellite organ with which he remained until the foundation of the *Chronicle*. Tom Daly followed in the mould of so many provincial newspaper owners and editors of the time in that he was devoutly Catholic and a staunch supporter of the GAA. His considerable journalistic experience is said to have resulted in his friendship with several leading political figures, most notably Arthur Griffith. Tom Daly died in January 1917 at the relatively young age of forty-eight. His brother Michael, who had assisted in the foundation of the paper, died only a few months later while still serving as editor.[45] In its early years, the paper was printed in Kells, but this changed in 1907 when it was first produced in Navan by James Davis on a contract basis. Davis had moved there some years earlier from his native Fermoy and purchased the plant and goodwill of the defunct *Irish Peasant* newspaper. James Davis acquired the *Meath Chronicle* following the death of the Daly brothers in 1917. It was the beginning of a family association with the newspaper that has lasted well into the twenty-first century.[46]

The *Meath Chronicle* is an example of stability and longevity within the Irish provincial newspaper business. In the first century of its existence, it had only seven editors, and four of these had already served their editorship by 1919. Apart from the two Daly brothers, the paper was also edited for a short period by Michael Judge. Judge's membership of the provisional committee of the Irish Volunteers meant that he had a significant involvement in the Howth gun-running during which he received a bayonet wound to the stomach.[47] Unfortunately, little more is known of Judge, but considerably more is known of the fourth of these editors, Hugh G. Smith.

---

[45] *One hundred years of life and times in North Leinster: A Meath Chronicle centenary publication* (30 Aug. 1997); *Meath Chronicle*, 13 Jan., 28 July 1917.

[46] *One hundred years of life and times in North Leinster: A Meath Chronicle centenary publication* (30 Aug. 1997); *Meath Chronicle*, 2 May 1931. Similar to many printing operations around the country, Davis's business extended beyond newspaper publication and also included book-binding, paper bag-making, and wallpaper-making.

[47] *One hundred years of life and times in North Leinster: A Meath Chronicle centenary publication* (30 Aug. 1997); Maume, *The long gestation*, p. 186.

Smith was a nephew of Tom and Michael Daly, who established the paper in 1897. Born in 1895, in Kells, he took part in the Easter Rising as an IRA dispatch rider prior to joining the *Chronicle*.[48] Local historian Oliver Coogan credits Smith with the reorganisation of the Irish Volunteers in Meath in the aftermath of Easter 1916.[49] Coogan further describes Smith as 'the vitriolic anti-British columnist'; it is difficult to verify the accuracy of this description but there is little ambiguity as to Smith's allegiance to the IRA and Sinn Féin.[50] The paper's centenary issue describes him as a 'fearless freedom fighter', who on one occasion during the Anglo-Irish War 'carried a rifle and ammunition on his motorcycle' from Dublin to the Drumbaragh IRA Company in Kells.[51] While editor, Smith also worked for Sinn Féin on the campaign of Liam Mellows for the North Meath constituency in the 1918 general election.[52]

Smith was succeeded as editor in 1919 by Patrick Quilty, a Limerick man, who had worked on the *Ballina Herald* prior to joining the *Chronicle*. Although possibly not as active as Smith in militant circles, Quilty's political sympathies differed little from those of his predecessor. Already a Sinn Féin member before his move to Navan, he was said to have done 'splendid intelligence work' in the town while his home was 'a sanctuary for men 'on the run'. Unlike Smith who went on to other journalistic pursuits, Quilty remained with the paper for a prolonged period, serving as editor until his death in 1960.[53]

The *Meath Chronicle* also employed other like-minded journalists such as Seán Hayes, who was imprisoned at both the Curragh and Arbour Hill for his IRA activities during the War of Independence.[54] This accommodation of journalists so sympathetic to republican philosophy

---

[48] *One hundred years of life and times in North Leinster: A Meath Chronicle centenary publication* (30 Aug. 1997); *Irish Times*, 10 May 1975. Smith's obituary indicates he joined the *Meath Chronicle* after Easter 1916 though there seems to be a little uncertainty in this regard.

[49] Oliver Coogan, *Politics and war in Meath, 1913–23* (Dunshaughlin, 1983), p. 24.

[50] Ibid., p. 90.

[51] *One hundred years of life and times in North Leinster: A Meath Chronicle centenary publication* (30 Aug. 1997).

[52] *Meath Chronicle*, 4 Dec. 1918.

[53] *Irish Press*, 28 Nov. 1960; *Meath Chronicle*, 3 Dec. 1960; *Irish Times*, 10 May 1975. Hugh G. Smith moved to the *Irish Independent* and in 1924 joined the Censorship Department of the newly formed National Army. He was one of the original journalists in the *Irish Press* in 1931. He also served as resident Irish correspondent for the *New York Times* and as Dublin correspondent for the *Belfast Telegraph*.

[54] *Meath Chronicle*, 4 Apr. 1921; 24 Dec. 1921.

would probably not have taken place, however, without a proprietor of a similar political outlook. In this respect, the likes of Smith, Quilty, and Hayes had the ideal figure at the helm of their newspaper in the person of James Davis. On his death in 1931, his obituary stated that on assuming control of the paper in 1917 Davis 'determined that its proud national record should not suffer at his hands' and that 'he saw to it that it continued to support the policy of Sinn Féin'. Notably, it also declared that Davis preferred to leave 'the different departments to carry on with a reasonably free hand'.[55] With such an owner in place the output of the *Meath Chronicle* was bound to make for interesting consideration.

Editorial comment, 1914–1921

At the beginning of 1914, and indeed throughout the early years of World War I, the *Meath Chronicle* declared under its masthead that it was 'published in the principal towns and villages of Meath and adjacent counties'. By 1921, this had been replaced by the appended titles of *Cavan and Westmeath Herald*. The *Chronicle* usually constituted eight pages divided into seven columns, though the page count frequently dropped to four during the course of the war. The front page was generally a mixture of advertisements and news items, but this changed around 1919 when it became almost completely devoid of advertising. Those advertisements that appeared were principally comprised of the staples of Irish provincial papers such as local grocery and drapery shops, various items of clothing, bicycles, medications, and a broad range of farm machinery and supplies. Amongst the most regular brands to appear in the advertising sections were Ford Motor Cars, Bendigo Tobacco, and Findlater's Tea, while the *Meath Chronicle*'s own printing business also featured prominently.

As a nationalist organ, the *Meath Chronicle* was initially quite supportive of the Home Rule movement, but by 1918 its allegiance had unambiguously shifted to the Sinn Féin party. There were indications as early as 1915 that the paper was quite sympathetic to Irish republicanism, but support for Sinn Féin became more open as the fortunes of that party rose dramatically after Easter 1916. This support came at a cost as in December 1918 a force of police and military dismantled and removed the paper's printing machinery. Contemporary reports indicate that the reason for the raid was because the paper's plant had been used in the production of Sinn Féin election leaflets.[56] Press censorship reports

[55] *Meath Chronicle*, 2 May 1931.
[56] *Freeman's Journal*, 4 Dec. 1918.

for that time do not indicate any transgression by the paper so it seems reasonable to surmise that this was simply an effort to disrupt Sinn Féin's election campaign in County Meath. The printing machinery was returned about a week later but in no way did the occurrence restrain the *Meath Chronicle* from expressing its views about what it considered as efforts by the authorities to control the output of Irish newspapers.[57]

Three months earlier, a regulation had been introduced forbidding the reporting of meetings for which police permits had not been issued. The requirement prompted the paper to editorialise that censorship, ostensibly introduced in time of war, 'had slowly and deliberately filched away every little liberty a section of the Irish press enjoyed'. It further added that censorship was now being 'directed towards the extinction of the Sinn Féin movement'.[58] At the time of the raid on its printing works in December 1918 the paper claimed that no reason had been given for the action.[59] On the resignation of Lord Decies five months later the *Meath Chronicle* acknowledged that he had performed his duties 'with the utmost courtesy and urbanity' but protested at the continued 'curtailment of the liberty of the Irish press'.[60] Even when censorship was abolished in September 1919 it was not viewed as a conciliatory measure. The editorial at the time claimed that even though it had been intimated several months earlier that censorship was voluntary many publications had submitted content that might be deemed seditious 'for their own protection', but this protection, 'such as it was', had now been removed.[61] In the latter stages of the War of Independence, the paper railed against how 'the Irish press has to canvas the possibility of interference in publishing what it bona fide believes to be true'. 'The provincial press', it further commented, 'almost fears to call its soul its own'.[62]

The antagonism with which, by 1921, the *Meath Chronicle* regarded British rule in Ireland was somewhat distant from its editorial policy in the months leading up to the outbreak of World War I. As a nationalist newspaper, it was generally critical of the procrastination of the British Government in finding a resolution to the Home Rule issue. Its attitude to the war was accepting rather than supportive. As hostilities commenced, it prophetically editorialised that 'war with all its horrors threatens to

[57]   *Freeman's Journal*, 9 Dec. 1918.
[58]   *Meath Chronicle*, 31 Aug. 1918.
[59]   *Meath Chronicle*, 7 Dec. 1918.
[60]   *Meath Chronicle*, 3 May 1919.
[61]   *Meath Chronicle*, 6 Sept. 1919.
[62]   *Meath Chronicle*, 26 Feb. 1921.

devastate the old world'.[63] Prior to Easter 1916, most editorials dealt with the progress of the war and are probably only notable for how the delay in the relay of information regarding military operations was occasionally remarked upon.[64] However, an indication of the stance that the paper would later assume is provided by a column entitled 'Searchlights' that first appeared around October 1914.

This contribution was usually placed in a position of prominence close to the editorial and was generally signed by a columnist named 'Tara'. Oliver Coogan claims that 'Tara's' real identity was probably future editor Hugh G. Smith.[65] However, there is some doubt in this regard, as other reports indicate Smith only joined the *Chronicle* after the 1916 Rising. Regardless of the columnist's actual identity, 'Searchlights' was quite revelatory in signifying the underlying sympathies of the *Meath Chronicle*. As early as October 1914, 'Tara' was pouring scorn on those who encouraged recruitment to the British Army and reminding readers that 'every loyal son of Ireland should remember that his first duty should be to his own country'.[66] In general, this column was quite scathing in its attitude to John Redmond and the Irish Parliamentary Party. Redmond's assumption of control of the Volunteer movement was described as the fulfilment of his objective to 'crush every independent body that he cannot readily control'.[67] Redmond 'and his poltroons always disliked the Volunteers', and were 'bent on their destruction from the beginning', according to 'Tara'.[68] Indeed, the 'Searchlights' column made the point of distinguishing between the National Volunteers (under Redmond's control) and the Irish Volunteers, and stated categorically that its sympathies were entirely with the latter body.[69] The 'Searchlights' column ceased to appear in the wake

---

[63] *Meath Chronicle*, 8 Aug. 1914.

[64] *Meath Chronicle*, 13 Mar. 1915; 12 Feb. 1916. In March 1915, the paper noted how 'long weeks after a lengthy list of killed, wounded and missing lifts some of the supposed trifling incidents to quite a different level'. Almost a year later it was observed how 'war news remains meagre', which led to conjecture being 'more in evidence than plain fact at this stage of the war'.

[65] Coogan, *Politics and war in Meath*, p. 24.

[66] *Meath Chronicle*, 3 Oct. 1914; 24 Apr. 1915. Despite the opposition of this column to recruitment into the British Army, it was recognised that for some it was not really a matter of choice, such as 'the poor labourer whom perhaps necessity drives into donning the khaki'.

[67] *Meath Chronicle*, 24 July 1915.

[68] *Meath Chronicle*, 16 Oct. 1915.

[69] *Meath Chronicle*, 26 June 1915. 'Tara' acknowledged a letter from Bulmer Hobson

of the 1916 Rising, which seems to have marked a turning point in the outlook of the *Meath Chronicle*.

The first editorial after Easter 1916 noted that 'a sad page has been added to the gloomy record of insurrectionary outbreaks in our country' and regretted 'the folly of the men who disregarded the wise counsel of Eoin MacNeill'. Nevertheless, it unambiguously declared that the 'calamitous outbreak would never have occurred' had the British Government dealt firmly with the situation 'created in Ulster by Sir Edward Carson' by the use of 'violence and intimidation'.[70] While a subsequent editorial protested at 'the undue severity' in dealing with the leaders of the rebellion, considerable foresight was evident in its observation that the Irish Parliamentary Party, 'the only nationalist organisation capable of dealing with the situation', had not faced such a momentous challenge 'in all its history'.[71] Prior to Easter 1916, *Meath Chronicle* editorials dealt principally with the war in Europe; thereafter the focus increasingly shifted to developments in Ireland. The readiness to acknowledge that the Irish Parliamentary Party had an important role to play, articulated in the aftermath of the Easter Rising, soon dissipated. Outright antagonism towards British policy in Ireland and unwavering support for Sinn Féin soon became the order of the day.

The vehemence of the opposition to the British Government's actions with regard to Ireland was further fuelled by the introduction of conscription in April 1918. Opposition to such a measure had been articulated through the 'Searchlights' column as early as December 1915.[72] When conscription was finally enacted in Ireland, the paper was unqualified in its condemnation of the move. Over a number of editorials, the paper declared that 'England is committing a blunder at once the gravest and most criminal of those which have characterised her government since the outbreak of the war' and more bluntly that 'the English Government have declared war on the Irish people'.[73] In the months that followed, little opportunity was lost to label conscription as

that made a clear distinction between the 'National' Volunteers and the 'Irish' Volunteers.

70   *Meath Chronicle*, 6 May 1916.
71   *Meath Chronicle*, 13 May 1916; 20 May 1916.
72   *Meath Chronicle*, 11 Dec. 1915; 18 Mar. 1916. In December 1915, the column suggested that conscription could be prevented 'by joining the Irish Volunteers', while in March 1916 it was claimed that 'fear of the Irish Volunteers and nothing else' had saved the country 'from being included in the Compulsory Service Bill'.
73   *Meath Chronicle*, 13, 20 Apr. 1918.

the 'blood tax' that constituted 'the first act of the English Government in its declared war on the Irish nation'.[74]

By this time, Hugh G. Smith was editor of the *Meath Chronicle* and its support for Sinn Féin was as unstinting as its criticism of the British Government. Sinn Féin by-election victories in Roscommon and Longford in the first half of 1917 had certainly drawn editorial comment but outright support for the party had not been voiced (possibly because Smith had not yet become editor or James Davis had not yet become proprietor). The tone had changed markedly by the time of the Clare by-election in July 1917. Eamon de Valera's victory was hailed as a repudiation of 'the weak and foolish spirit that had been let creep into Irish national politics for close on a generation' and Clare voters had now pronounced 'the true voice of nationalist Ireland'.[75] It was around this time also that notices for Sinn Féin clubs began to appear for the first time. This possibly signified the *Meath Chronicle*'s wholehearted conversion to the Sinn Féin cause.

William T. Cosgrave's victory in Kilkenny in August 1917 was interpreted as merely a natural progression. The paper editorialised that in any nationalist constituency 'the defeat of a Sinn Féin candidate has become all but unthinkable'.[76] However, the defeat of the Sinn Féin candidate in South Armagh the following February was attributed to collusion between the Irish Parliamentary Party and Unionists when the 'virulent sectarian animosity that divided Hibernianism and Orangeism like a wedge, all suddenly evaporated before the menace of Sinn Féin'.[77] Damning criticism of the Irish Parliamentary Party had become a regular feature of editorials and it was labelled the 'West British Provincial Party' following its victory in Waterford in March 1918.[78] Such castigation of the rapidly weakening force in Irish politics had grown even more robust by the time of the East Cavan by-election three months later. J.F. O'Hanlon (managing-director of the *Anglo-Celt* in Cavan), who was standing in opposition to Sinn Féin's Arthur Griffith, was described as a 'pro-Britisher' and 'England's candidate'.[79] Griffith's resounding triumph was hailed as 'the greatest victory for Irish independence won for a generation'.[80]

---

[74] *Meath Chronicle*, 4, 19, 26 May 1918; 15 June 1918.
[75] *Meath Chronicle*, 14 July 1917.
[76] *Meath Chronicle*, 18 Aug. 1917.
[77] *Meath Chronicle*, 9 Feb. 1918.
[78] *Meath Chronicle*, 30 Mar. 1918.
[79] *Meath Chronicle*, 15 June 1918.
[80] *Meath Chronicle*, 29 June 1918.

As early as September 1918, the paper was anticipating a general election. 'The coming election', it stated, 'will be one of supreme importance to Ireland' and 'the only party that stands by the historical claim of the Irish nation to complete independence is the Sinn Féin party'.[81] The weeks leading up to the election saw a continuance of the now familiar pattern of stinging criticism of the Irish Parliamentary Party accompanied by near exultation of Sinn Féin ideals. As the election approached, the paper published the Sinn Féin manifesto (as passed by the Censor) and also included comprehensive portrayals of Liam Mellowes and Eamonn Duggan, the party's candidates in Meath.[82] Such endorsement was hardly surprising given that the editor was heavily involved in the party's campaign in the county.[83] The election itself was preceded by the aforementioned suppression of the paper plus an editorial reminder that the poll represented a choice between 'freedom or slavery'.[84] Sinn Féin's subsequent triumph was regarded as a victory for 'a force which even the strength of a mighty Empire cannot overcome'.[85]

Unsurprisingly, the first meeting of Dáil Éireann in January 1919 was viewed with great positivity. The fledgling assembly 'represented to the fullest the only democratic body that can be recognised as having the essentials upon which moral government rests, namely, the unfettered allegiance and consent of the people'.[86] Much of the *Chronicle*'s enthusiasm for republican strategy was based on the expectation of a favourable outcome for Ireland at the Peace Conference that had convened in Paris following the end of World War I. Such hopes were, to a great extent, based on the assumption of American support for the Irish cause. US President Woodrow Wilson's declarations about the rights of small nations seemed to give the paper particular cause for encouragement. When it became clear that Irish delegates would not even get a hearing at the Conference, the paper questioned whether Wilson's 'lofty principles' were 'mere diplomatic vapourings

---

[81] *Meath Chronicle*, 7 Sept. 1918.

[82] *Meath Chronicle*, 23, 30 Nov. 1918; 14 Dec. 1918.

[83] *Irish Independent*, 4 Dec. 1918, *Meath Chronicle*, 14 Dec. 1918. The *Irish Independent* reported Hugh G. Smith as one of the speakers for Liam Mellowes at the time of the paper's suppression while the *Meath Chronicle* itself reported Smith as in attendance at a rally in Kells at the close of the campaign.

[84] *Meath Chronicle*, 14 Dec. 1918.

[85] *Meath Chronicle*, 28 Dec. 1918.

[86] *Meath Chronicle*, 25 Jan. 1919.

as unmeaning and hypocritical as England's mouthings about freedom and justice'.[87]

As the situation in Ireland grew increasingly violent during the War of Independence the paper consistently maintained that Irish nationalists should pursue their goal by strictly peaceful means. Even though the two successive editors, Smith and Quilty, are credited with having IRA sympathies, the editorial message conveyed was one of restraint. 'Violence or crime will but play the game of the enemies of the nation', the paper declared in September 1919.[88] It could, of course, be argued that indicating support even for some of the aims of the IRA could risk suppression or even worse. Nonetheless, very little comment was passed regarding IRA activities though the killing of an RIC constable at Ballivor in November 1919 and an attack on the Protestant church in Navan in May 1920 were roundly denounced.[89] As hostilities intensified in 1920, vilification of Crown forces in Ireland became a regular feature. The country was 'being studded with the full panoply of warfare' while Irish people were 'setting about the necessary work of peacefully and constitutionally manning the public bodies'.[90] As the violence was reaching its zenith in 1921 the paper defiantly claimed that 'England has tried the methods of the terrorist and those methods have failed'.[91]

As hostilities ended with the calling of a ceasefire in July 1921, the *Meath Chronicle* counselled extreme caution. This was hardly surprising for a title that only recently had labelled David Lloyd George 'a pigmy in the breeches of a giant'.[92] Nonetheless, firm confidence in the Irish plenipotentiaries was expressed as final negotiations with the British Government approached. The paper regarded the conclusion of the talks and the formulation of Articles of Agreement as a vindication of this confidence. 'Ireland owes a deep debt of gratitude to Arthur Griffith and his colleagues for the magnificent handling of the situation', stated the first editorial following the culmination of the negotiations in London. In an almost celebratory manner, the same editorial, headed 'Saorstát na h-Éireann', voiced the belief that the Anglo-Irish agreement gave

[87] *Meath Chronicle*, 3 May 1919.
[88] *Meath Chronicle*, 20 Sept. 1919.
[89] *Meath Chronicle*, 8 Nov. 1919; 8 May 1920. While it decried the killing of RIC Constable Agar in November 1919, the same editorial also made the point that Sinn Féin had no connection with recent outrages.
[90] *Meath Chronicle*, 22 May 1920.
[91] *Meath Chronicle*, 24 Mar. 1921.
[92] *Meath Chronicle*, 16 Oct. 1920; 2 July 1921.

'substance to that freedom for which Ireland endured its Cavalry for the past four or five years, not to speak of what our forefathers had suffered'. The failure to achieve Irish unity was regretted but the hope was expressed that an 'All-Ireland Parliament with full powers to work for the advancement of the Irish Free State could soon come about'.[93] This was a significant change in tone for a paper that had consistently articulated its total opposition to any form of partition.[94]

As members of Dáil Éireann commenced debating the terms of the agreement, and tensions became apparent, the paper assumed a decidedly pro-Treaty stance. It counselled that it would be unwise to cast aside the Treaty to 'renew the struggle in the more virile fashion which would entail further blood sacrifice'.[95] This was a far cry from only a few months previously when the desire for peace was expressed, but the paper asserted that Ireland was 'prepared for the reverse should circumstances demand a continuation of sacrifice'.[96] Indeed, the evidence indicates a sense of *realpolitik* taking hold in the paper by December 1921. Addressing those it termed 'doctrinaire republicans', the penultimate editorial of 1921 argued that the achievement of an Irish Republic, 'standing in rigid isolation, was not practical politics'.[97] The final editorial of that year was most notable for criticism of Eamon de Valera for probably the first time within the pages of the *Meath Chronicle*. His failure to provide an alternative to 'bald rejection' of the Treaty prompted the paper to reason that there was 'only one constructive policy before the country', and that was 'acceptance of the peace treaty'.[98]

Conclusion

The *Meath Chronicle* was an unequivocally nationalist organ from its establishment in 1897. It was particularly supportive of organisations such as the GAA and the Gaelic League. A people 'who suffer their language to decay', it declared in a 1917 editorial, 'cannot claim to be a nation'.[99]

93 *Meath Chronicle*, 10 Dec. 1921.
94 *Meath Chronicle*, 20 Aug. 1921. Only three months earlier, the *Meath Chronicle* had declared that 'we will not have partition in any guise or form, Ireland is one and indivisible, geographically, politically, and historically'.
95 *Meath Chronicle*, 17 Dec. 1921.
96 *Meath Chronicle*, 16 July 1921.
97 *Meath Chronicle*, 24 Dec. 1921.
98 *Meath Chronicle*, 31 Dec. 1921.
99 *Meath Chronicle*, 6 Oct. 1917.

Unlike many other provincial titles, however, it never had any major links to the Irish Parliamentary Party. Indeed, by the middle of 1917, its nationalism had unambiguously translated into support for Sinn Féin. From this time forward it availed itself of every possible opportunity to rail against the continued British presence in Ireland. Despite this affinity for Irish republican ideals there were no direct calls for an independent Irish republic. Possibly this subtle differentiation allowed the *Chronicle* to adopt a somewhat more pragmatic approach at the time of the Anglo-Irish Treaty. Although it had repeatedly voiced vehement opposition to a settlement that included either partition or any British role in Irish affairs, it welcomed the Treaty with no little enthusiasm. Perhaps this could be explained by a sense of war weariness or a realisation that the attainment of goals that were simply articulated was far from simple in reality. The reasons for such a reaction notwithstanding, the *Meath Chronicle* ended up assuming a stance on the Treaty that broadly coincided with the majority of the members of Dáil Éireann and an even greater majority of the Irish people.

Enniscorthy Echo

On the occasion of its golden jubilee in 1952, the editorial of the *Enniscorthy Echo* suggested that when the history of the Irish provincial press came to be written, it would not be possible to ignore the part played by the paper and its staff in the movement for Irish independence.[100] This was an entirely reasonable claim as the significance of what the paper articulated during the 1914–21 period is almost outweighed by the personalities who plied their trade at the paper during these years. As the same editorial proudly pointed out, the paper did not appear for almost nine months following the Easter Rising. This was mainly due to the suppression of the paper, but also because most of its staff had been imprisoned in the aftermath of the Easter Rising. At the time, the *Echo* had been in publication for just under fourteen years, which made it the youngest of the five titles serving County Wexford.

The founding father of the *Enniscorthy Echo* in 1902 was undoubtedly William Sears. Originally from Ballinrobe, County Mayo, his journalistic career began with the *Western People* in Ballina.[101] His connection to County Wexford originally stemmed from time he spent early in his

---

[100] *Enniscorthy Echo*, 17 May 1952.
[101] *Western People*, 30 Mar. 1929.

career on the staff of both the *Wexford People* and the *Wexford Free Press*. He subsequently became the youngest member of Wexford District Council and married local woman Greta Morris when he was about thirty years of age.[102] One of the many newspaper obituaries written of Sears when he died in 1929 noted that 'he severed his connection with the old Irish Nationalist Party' around 1905 and became 'an ardent follower of the doctrines' of Arthur Griffith.[103] No reason is supplied for this sudden change of allegiance but there is one possible explanation.

In July 1905, Sears wrote to the Irish Parliamentary Party leader, John Redmond, seeking the latter's support for his candidacy for the South Mayo constituency. Sears pointed out to Redmond how he and his paper had done sterling work on the national question in County Wexford and he also informed Redmond that his uncle, Edward Jennings, had been honorary secretary of the Land League branch that led the protest against Captain Boycott in Mayo in 1879.[104] Redmond replied wishing Sears well in his quest for election to parliament but advised that selection of candidates for specific constituencies was a local party matter in which he could not interfere.[105] Sears then wrote back to the party leader asking that Redmond write him a letter of approval as a parliamentary candidate without any reference to a constituency.[106] There is little record of any further correspondence on the matter but Sears never stood for election on behalf of the Irish Parliamentary Party. Consequently, it seems that Sears' transfer of loyalty to Sinn Féin around this time could be more than mere coincidence. His ambition was ultimately fulfilled in 1918 when he was returned unopposed as Sinn Féin MP for South Mayo.[107] Nonetheless, his transfer of allegiance could hardly be described as one of political convenience. As his obituary noted in the paper he founded, his militant stance and support for Sinn Féin resulted in him serving prison terms totalling more than two years, spent in Frongoch and Ballykinlar internment camps and in Mountjoy Gaol.[108]

---

[102] *Enniscorthy Echo*, 30 Mar. 1929; *Irish Independent*, 25 Mar. 1929.

[103] *Mayo News*, 30 Mar. 1929.

[104] Sears to Redmond, 28 July 1905, MS 15,245/8.

[105] Redmond to Sears, 1 Aug. 1905, MS 15,245/8.

[106] Sears to Redmond, 23 Aug. 1905, MS 15,245/8.

[107] *Mayo News*, 30 Mar. 1929. Sears was also elected to Dáil Éireann in 1921 and 1922 but lost his seat in 1927 when he stood as a Cumann na nGaedheal candidate.

[108] *Enniscorthy Echo*, 30 Mar. 1929.

The ostensibly close relationship between the *Enniscorthy Echo* and the Irish Parliamentary Party in the early years of the paper is reasonably understandable given that one of its co-founders and financial backers was Sir Thomas Esmonde. In 1900, Esmonde was elected as the party's MP for the North Wexford constituency. By 1907, Esmonde appeared to be following the lead given by Sears as he withdrew from Westminster and joined Sinn Féin. However, Patrick Maume, in his portrayal of Esmonde, gives the impression that Esmonde's defection may have had more to do with internal party squabbling than with any major commitment to Arthur Griffith's party. This is borne out by the fact that he later returned to the Irish Parliamentary Party fold and loosened his links with the *Enniscorthy Echo*.[109]

Within a few years of Esmonde distancing himself from the *Echo*, the paper was attracting the attention of the police authorities. In January 1915, on the suspicion that what they termed 'seditious publications and leaflets' were being printed at the offices of the paper, the police identified Sears, Cornelius J. Irwin, Martin Donohoe, James Donohoe, John Bennett, and Patrick Kehoe as directors of the paper. The conclusion that the paper was a Sinn Féin organ is evident from the fact that the same report identified Patrick Byrne as a director who had signalled his intention to resign 'if the Sinn Féin policy was not dropped'.[110] With such a pro-Sinn Féin directorship in place it is hardly surprising that the *Echo* attracted journalists with an undisputed commitment to the republican cause.

One of the most prominent of these journalists was Laurence (Larry) de Lacy who was also named in the same police report that listed the paper's directors. He was identified as sub-editor and believed 'to be responsible for the printing of any seditious publications printed in the office'.[111] What was termed 'seditious publications' was most likely the *Irish Volunteer*, the newspaper of the Irish Volunteer movement. The police had earlier noted the *Irish Volunteer* as an 'extreme paper' and subsequently discovered that it was printed at the *Echo* offices with de Lacy, an Irish Republican Brotherhood (IRB) member, its editor.[112] Around February

---

[109] Maume, *The long gestation*. Esmonde remained as MP for North Wexford until 1918 when he lost his seat to Roger Sweetman of Sinn Féin.

[110] Seditious literature, censorship, publication of offensive articles, CO904/160/4.

[111] Ibid.

[112] Inspector General's and County Inspectors' monthly confidential reports, CO904/94-414, CO904/96-214; William Murphy, 'Enniscorthy's Revolution' in Colm Tóibín (ed.), *Enniscorthy: a history* (Wexford, 2010), p. 400.

1915, de Lacy fled to the USA after a quantity of explosives was found in the bedroom of his house.[113] A colourful character to say the very least, de Lacy spent quite an eventful number of years in the USA before returning to Ireland.[114] In a long journalistic career he served time as editor of the *Clare Champion* and the *Drogheda Argus* and was also a sub-editor at the *Irish Times* and *Irish Independent*. In his later years, he retired to his farm near Enniscorthy but also wrote a botany column for the *Irish Independent* under the nom de plume 'Fieldman'.[115] While de Lacy's absence from Ireland during the 1916–21 period meant he could not play a significant role in the upheavals of these years this was not the case with other journalists working at the *Enniscorthy Echo*.

Robert Brennan joined the staff of the *Echo* in 1909. In addition to his journalistic work he was also an organiser of the Gaelic League, Sinn Féin, the IRB, and the Irish Volunteers in his native County Wexford. He was sentenced to death for his part in the Easter Rising and while this was later commuted, he served several prison terms before hostilities finally ceased in July 1921. Brennan also worked for Sinn Féin's propaganda department (as mentioned in the previous chapter) and was involved in the production of the *Irish Bulletin*, the Dáil Éireann newssheet, between February 1921 and January 1922. He joined the Irish delegation in London in the early stages of the Treaty negotiations but ultimately assumed an anti-Treaty stance. Brennan was also involved in the establishment of the *Irish Press* and was the first general manager of the paper.[116]

Seán Etchingham, who worked for the *Echo* from its establishment in 1902 until 1915, similarly had a death sentence imposed after the Easter Rising that was later commuted. Like Brennan also, Etchingham opposed the Anglo-Irish Treaty of 1921. In common with the paper's editor, William Sears, he was also an elected representative. He was returned for the East Wicklow constituency in the 1918 general election and was subsequently elected in West Wicklow and then in North

---

[113] Personalities (Laurence de Lacy), CO904/198/99-7.

[114] Personalities (Laurence de Lacy), CO904/198/99-3; *Irish Journalist*, vol. 1, no. 13 (Nov. 1915); *Irish Independent*, 12 Jan. 1953; 19 Nov. 1973. While in America de Lacy found time to get married, work for Hearst Newspapers, and receive an eighteen-month prison sentence for conspiring to liberate a former German Consul-General. He also remained active in Irish republican circles and was closely associated with Éamon de Valera's tours of the USA.

[115] *Irish Independent*, 19 Nov. 1973; *Irish Times*, 20 Nov. 1973.

[116] Michael Kennedy, 'Brennan, Robert' in McGuire and Quinn, *Dictionary of Irish biography*; *Irish Independent*, *Irish Times*, 13 Nov. 1964.

Wexford. A devout Catholic, Etchingham was highly active in both the Gaelic League and the GAA in County Wexford.[117] Indeed, Etchingham may have been the reason the *Enniscorthy Echo* first came to the attention of the authorities. As early as September 1914, an RIC report singled him out as preaching 'veiled sedition' and encouraging 'anti-English feeling' through the pages of the newspaper.[118] Etchingham served several prison terms in the years after Easter 1916 that may have contributed to his death, due to ill health, at the relatively early age of fifty-six.

Although Sears, de Lacy, Brennan, and Etchingham are significant journalistic figures whose paths crossed at the *Enniscorthy Echo* it would be an injustice to the paper not to mention some of the other writers who also served on the staff of the paper during this critical period of Irish history. Thomas McCarthy was one such writer who, in addition to being involved in the labour movement, was also an IRB member and one of the early organisers of the Volunteer movement in the Enniscorthy area.[119] Aodh de Blacam (Hugh Blackham) was London-born of Ulster parents; he converted to Catholicism in 1913 and joined the *Echo* staff two years later. Described as 'intensely nationalistic', he was involved in the Gaelic League in Enniscorthy and even organised Irish classes for the paper's typographical staff.[120] James Bolger, brother-in-law of Robert Brennan, worked on the reporting staff of the *Echo* until 1916 and later served with both the Wexford and Dublin brigades of the IRA during the War of Independence.[121] David Sears, son of William, joined the staff of the paper in 1918 and was also a battalion commander in the IRA. He attended Patrick Pearse's St. Enda's school in Rathfarnham and as a sixteen-year-old student he participated in the Easter Rising, seeing action in the South Dublin Union.[122]

---

[117] *Enniscorthy Echo*, 28 Apr. 1923; *Irish Independent*, *Irish Times*, 25 Apr. 1923.

[118] Seditious literature, censorship, publication of offensive articles, CO904/160/4.

[119] Murphy, 'Enniscorthy's Revolution', p. 400.

[120] *Enniscorthy Echo*, 20 Jan. 1951; *Irish Independent*, *Irish Press*, *Irish Times*, 15 Jan. 1951. De Blacam later wrote for the *Irish Independent* and the *Irish Times* but most prominently he contributed a column to the *Irish Press* for almost seventeen years under the name 'Roddy the Rover'.

[121] *Enniscorthy Echo*, 27 Apr. 1963; *Irish Independent*, *Irish Press*, 22 Apr. 1963. Bolger later joined the *Irish Independent* and was the paper's GAA correspondent from 1924 until 1944.

[122] *Enniscorthy Echo*, 8 Sept. 1951; *Irish Independent*, 7 Sept. 1951. David Sears became chairman of the *Enniscorthy Echo* in 1929 following the death of his father. He was drama critic for the *Irish Independent* for many years and also authored several of his own plays.

The *Enniscorthy Echo* was one of the first provincial newspapers to attract the attention of the British authorities. In addition to the aforementioned identification of Etchingham in September 1914, the *Echo* was also noted in an RIC report from October 1914 as one of the 'few extreme papers' amongst the provincial press, though this was hardly borne out in its editorials.[123] The monitoring by the RIC continued and on the basis that 'seditious leaflets' were being printed at the paper's offices the authorities decided in January 1915 to detain, where it was deemed necessary, postal packages addressed to William Sears (editor), Cornelius J. Irwin (manager), and Laurence de Lacy (sub-editor).[124] Indeed, a personal file was maintained on de Lacy and his movements continued to be monitored after he fled to the USA around February 1915.[125]

With this level of surveillance, it is hardly surprising that the *Echo* was suppressed in the aftermath of the Easter Rising. The paper was published on 22 April 1916 but did not reappear until 3 February 1917. Robert Brennan recalled being told by William Sears (while both were detained) that it was not just the journalistic staff that had been arrested but also the printers and even the messengers. He further recollected how it seemed 'a bad joke that the military had also served on the proprietors a notice suspending publication of the paper indefinitely'.[126] On its return, the paper's editorial referred to the 'large number of the staff who had been interned without trial'.[127] The most notable of those arrested and detained was, of course, William Sears, proprietor and editor. It was not to be the last term of imprisonment Sears would endure and it was not the last brush his publication would have with the authorities. Significantly, though, no such clash again resulted in the non-appearance of the paper.

The *Echo* was still occupying police time in September 1919 when its offices were searched for 'seditious literature'. In its report of the incident, the only document that the *Irish Times* saw fit to report as having been seized was the programme of a concert hosted by the local GAA club the previous week.[128] Three months later, possibly in a sense

---

123   Police reports, CO904/94-414.

124   Seditious literature, censorship, publication of offensive articles, CO904/160/4.

125   Personalities (Laurence de Lacy), CO904/198/99-32. De Lacy was described as appearing 'to be living comfortably in New York in a god flat and to be a great deal at home'.

126   Robert Brennan, *Allegiance* (Dublin, 1950), p. 80.

127   *Enniscorthy Echo*, 3 Feb. 1917.

128   *Irish Times*, 25 Feb. 1919.

of solidarity from its own experiences, an *Echo* editorial was highly critical of Chief Secretary, Ian McPherson, and the Dublin Castle authorities for suppressing 'the very moderate, very respectable, staid old *Freeman's Journal*'.[129] While the suppression of the *Freeman's Journal* was deemed worthy of editorial comment, the IRA raid on the offices of the *Irish Independent* about a week later did not merit similar editorial attention.[130]

The increasing level of violence in Ireland saw Wexford declared a Martial Law area in 1921 which had a consequent effect on newspapers in the county. From early March until mid-August almost all editorials in the *Echo* were preceded by the proviso that all news and advertisements in the paper were 'censored by the Military Authorities, to whom the paper has to be submitted before being printed and published'. The restrictions did not discourage it from accusing the British Government of implementing a 'vindictive policy of reprisals in Ireland'.[131] Notably, though, no editorial comment was afforded to the incidents that gave rise to the reprisals. The censorship was only withdrawn in the middle of August, almost a month after the truce had been called in the War of Independence.[132]

According to the *Echo*: editorial comment, 1914–1921

Most unusually for an Irish provincial publication, the *Enniscorthy Echo* normally consisted of fourteen to sixteen pages prior to World War I, though this dropped to eight pages during the course of the war. Each page was printed in seven columns, which was the general standard for most provincial papers at the time. The appended title of *South Leinster Advertiser* appeared above a front page that was predominantly made up of lists of recent auctions and property sales. The diverse range of services advertised included ironmongery, dental surgery, tailoring, installation

---

[129] *Enniscorthy Echo*, 20 Dec. 1919; Ian Kenneally, *The paper wall: newspapers and propaganda in Ireland 1919–1921* (Cork, 2008), p. 9. The *Freeman's Journal* was suppressed for its persistent criticism of the authorities in Dublin Castle and 'for publishing offensive articles about the military, RIC and the proposed recruitment of a new auxiliary force'.

[130] As detailed in the previous chapter, the IRA took exception to the coverage in the *Irish Independent* of their attempt to assassinate the Lord Lieutenant, Lord French.

[131] *Enniscorthy Echo*, 4 June 1921.

[132] *Enniscorthy Echo*, 13 Aug. 1921.

of electric lights, insurance coverage in addition to a cargo steamship service (Coast Line) operating between Wexford and Liverpool. Various brands of bicycles were also advertised, as were motor cars, both for sale and hire. In common with many other provincial newspapers of the time, agricultural machinery and supplies also featured strongly in addition to frequent farming announcements and notices.

With the number of advanced-nationalist journalists on its staff, not to mention the proprietor and directors, it is scarcely surprising that a decidedly pro-Sinn Féin editorial policy was adopted, particularly in the years after 1916. To a certain extent, the paper's editorial comment did not differ greatly from that of the *Meath Chronicle*. Similar to its counterpart in County Meath, the paper enthusiastically embraced the Irish Ireland movement and frequently professed its support for the Irish language. 'We must not set aside the old tongue of our fathers', it warned in May 1915.[133] Also, any notion of partition was unequivocally opposed from the very start. The paper accused the British Tories of 'making a pawn of Ulster' and claimed that 'the entire country was disgusted' at the thought of any of the Ulster counties being excluded from Home Rule.[134] However, the attitude of the *Echo* was slightly different from that of the Navan-based title in one respect.

The *Enniscorthy Echo* did not join in the outright castigation of the Irish Parliamentary Party that became such a prominent feature of the *Meath Chronicle*. Indeed, the paper was occasionally willing to acknowledge the work of the party where and when it saw fit. With the impending ratification of the Home Rule bill in 1914, the *Echo* editorialised that it was a 'proud and happy' occasion for Mr Redmond who had 'led his party with faultless tact', and in whose hands 'Ireland's case was always safe'.[135] Over a year later, John Dillon was warmly praised for his opposition to conscription in the House of Commons and for 'making it perfectly clear to the Government' that 'Ireland had made up her mind that she would not have conscription'.[136] Even when the political atmosphere in the country had irrevocably changed by the time of John Redmond's death in 1918 the paper still had no qualms in accepting the sincerity of his efforts. In a genuinely heartfelt tribute it was acknowledged that 'no man did more than Mr. Redmond to bring about a kindly feeling between England and Ireland' but his 'profound faith

---

[133] *Enniscorthy Echo*, 29 May 1915.
[134] *Enniscorthy Echo*, 24 Jan., 21 Mar. 1914.
[135] *Enniscorthy Echo*, 30 May 1914.
[136] *Enniscorthy Echo*, 25 Sept. 1915.

in British democracy' was sadly misplaced.[137] Nonetheless, the political allegiance of the *Enniscorthy Echo* had by this time unquestionably shifted to the Sinn Féin party.

Following the initial Sinn Féin by-election victories in North Roscommon and South Longford the Echo stated unequivocally that 'complete self-government' could not be won by 'parliamentarianism' and that the country had now taken up 'the more up-to-date weapon of Sinn Féin'.[138] By the time Éamon de Valera won the East Clare by-election in July 1917, the paper was unambiguously asserting that nationalist Ireland had 'abandoned the policy of begging at Westminster and has nailed the Sinn Féin colours to the mast'.[139] The endorsement of the newly emerging political force became increasingly effusive as it claimed that 'The people in towns and villages are meeting in their thousands, and under the banner of Sinn Féin are pledging themselves to Ireland's service. In almost every case the local clergy lead the way'.[140]

One the eve of the general election the following year it editorialised that only one of the parties going to the polls stood for 'the absolute independence of Ireland' and 'that party is known the world over to be the Sinn Féin party'. The same editorial labelled the Irish Parliamentary Party an organisation that 'stands for an English settlement of the Irish question; for a decision by our enemies of what our destiny is to be'.[141] Much of the hope for Irish independence was based on the proclamations of President Wilson. However, the paper avoided criticism of the US President when it became apparent that the Peace Conference would not consider the aspirations of Irish nationalists. Instead, the *Echo* regarded Wilson as unfortunate in having 'to deal with two wily tricksters, Lloyd George and Clemenceau', who 'buttered up his Fourteen Points very thickly and then got the poor man to swallow the lot'.[142]

As the War of Independence grew more protracted during 1920, editorials became more damning in their condemnation of British rule in Ireland. Little restraint was evident as the paper bluntly stated that 'The

---

[137] *Enniscorthy Echo*, 9 Mar. 1918. The editorial published on the death of Mr Redmond also contended that 'if there was one spark of justice in the British nature it would have responded to his noble appeals', but his ambitions were scuppered by 'Carson's opposition, the Curragh mutiny, and Asquith's betrayal'.

[138] *Enniscorthy Echo*, 12 May 1917.

[139] *Enniscorthy Echo*, 14 July 1917.

[140] *Enniscorthy Echo*, 11 Aug. 1917.

[141] *Enniscorthy Echo*, 14 Dec. 1918.

[142] *Enniscorthy Echo*, 22 Nov. 1919.

British people are still the master hypocrites of Europe, of the world, of this age, and of all time. They still continue to speak of freedom and praise freedom and at the same time to keep shackles on Ireland, Egypt, and India'.[143]

Following reprisals carried out by Crown forces in Trim, Mallow, and Balbriggan, the paper compared them to the burning of Louvain in Belgium by the Germans in World War I. Accusing Britain of hypocrisy, the paper claimed that 'a crime when committed by the Germans, becomes excusable when committed by the British'. The same editorial alleged that the Black and Tans were specifically assembled 'to crush the movement supported by four-fifths of the people'.[144] Shortly afterwards, the paper asserted that the 'terrible pass in Ireland today' was solely due to 'the deliberately planned and ruthlessly executed campaign of the British cabinet'.[145] However, like the *Meath Chronicle*, the activities of the IRA merited little or no attention in the editorial columns of the *Enniscorthy Echo*.

The ceasefire of July 1921 was broadly welcomed and interpreted as 'the best indication of the genuine desire for an honourable peace uppermost in the hearts of the Irish people'.[146] If the reaction to the ending of hostilities was one of guarded optimism, the news of the conclusion of Articles of Agreement for the Anglo-Irish Treaty was greeted with a great degree of relief and extreme positivity. 'The realisation of the dream of the great patriots of the past was within sight', according to the editorial that also happily proclaimed that 'never again was England to have the appointing of judges, magistrates or police'. There appeared to be a realisation that the gap between what was desirable and what was achievable was not so easily bridged. This was most evident in the acknowledgement that 'Mr Griffith and his colleagues could never hope for a settlement if they were not prepared to give and take'.[147] As differences began to emerge, the paper solidly maintained its support for the agreement. This was most likely attributable to William Sears, who unambiguously supported the Treaty.[148] It accentuated the positive aspects of the Treaty such as the complete withdrawal of Britain's 'claim to domination in Irish affairs' and that Ireland would now be regarded as an equal rather than a subject.

---

143 *Enniscorthy Echo*, 13 Mar. 1920.
144 *Enniscorthy Echo*, 2 Oct. 1920.
145 *Enniscorthy Echo*, 16 Oct. 1920.
146 *Enniscorthy Echo*, 16 July 1921.
147 *Enniscorthy Echo*, 10 Dec. 1921.
148 *Enniscorthy Echo*, 30 Mar. 1929. William Sears was described as standing for the acceptance of the Treaty and being 'an unswerving supporter of Arthur Griffith'.

It was particularly critical of the comments in Dáil Éireann of Erskine Childers, who opposed the Treaty.[149] Unfortunately, this turned out to be a sad portent of events to come.

Conclusion

In common with many other provincial newspapers, the *Enniscorthy Echo* strongly supported the Irish Parliamentary Party in the paper's early years. This allegiance shifted rather swiftly, however, and was buoyed by the republican sympathies of both its directors and staff. Few other provincial, or indeed national, titles witnessed the involvement of so many of its own journalists in the movement for Irish independence. This involvement resulted in many of them serving terms of imprisonment, or, in the cases of Brennan and Etchingham, receiving death sentences. The *Enniscorthy Echo* is justifiably regarded by a number of historians as one of the earliest papers to support Sinn Féin. Nevertheless, from an editorial perspective this did not really manifest itself until after Easter 1916. Once this happened, however, that support was open and unequivocal. Support for the Anglo-Irish Treaty was enthusiastic and steadfast, quite possibly influenced by the respect William Sears had for Arthur Griffith. Nonetheless, in a microcosm of what happened in Dáil Éireann, former journalists with the paper (such as Brennan and Etchingham) took a rather different view than their erstwhile colleagues.

Kilkenny People

The history of the Irish provincial press in the late nineteenth century and the opening decades of the twentieth century are distinguished by a variety of editors who were inextricably and singularly linked to individual publications. This was a feature of all four provinces and was not confined to titles of any one political persuasion. Prime examples of such a characteristic in Leinster were Michael A. Casey at the *Drogheda Independent* and J.P. Hayden at the *Westmeath Examiner*. However, few

---

[149] *Enniscorthy Echo*, 31 Dec. 1921. The paper described the style of criticism adopted by Childers as 'very irritating' and was particularly irked by what it claimed was his acceptance that the Treaty would grant Ireland the same level of autonomy as Canada which was 'practically sovereign independence' but that the Treaty should still be rejected as 'Irishmen could not make the same use of their chance that the Canadians did'.

other newspapermen epitomised this aspect of provincial journalism to the same extent as Edward Thomas (E.T.) Keane of the *Kilkenny People*. Keane was co-founder of the paper in 1893 along with Patrick J. (P.J.) O'Keefe and was also the paper's first editor. He remained in this position until his death over fifty years later.[150]

Born in Listowel, County Kerry, he made his way to Kilkenny via the *Munster News* in Limerick and the *Clonmel Nationalist* before working at the *Kilkenny Moderator* prior to the establishment of the *Kilkenny People*. The *Kilkenny People* was founded as a Parnellite organ, as the *Kilkenny Journal* had become highly critical of Parnell in the late 1880s. Keane's co-founder at the paper, P.J. O'Keefe, was an IRB member and also served on the executive committee of the Kilkenny GAA. He later became mayor and borough treasurer of Kilkenny. O'Keefe tended to the commercial side of the paper's business while Keane directed editorial policy.[151]

Edward Thomas Keane

It is really not possible to discuss the fortunes of the *Kilkenny People* during these years without first considering its co-founder, proprietor, and editor, E.T. Keane. He was described by a former colleague (probably Frank J. Geary, who went on to edit the *Irish Independent* for over a quarter of a century) as being 'forthright in his speech and in his writings' and also someone who 'could hit hard' and 'did hit hard, many a time'.[152] In July 1917, the Press Censor, Lord Decies, labelled him 'a decidedly dangerous class of man'.[153] This attention from the office of the Press Censor arose out of Keane's involvement with the Sinn Féin party to whose cause Keane was converted after Easter 1916.

So swift was Keane's conversion to the republican ideology that he is regarded as a central factor in the election of William T. Cosgrave as Sinn Féin MP for Kilkenny city in August 1917.[154] One source even

---

[150] *Kilkenny People*, 19 May 1945.
[151] *Kilkenny People*; O'Dwyer, 'A history of Kilkenny newspapers, 1767–2009', pp 391–2.
[152] *Kilkenny People*, 19 May 1945; *Irish Independent*, 22 Dec. 1961. A section of Keane's obituary in the *Kilkenny People* in May 1945 was signed 'F.J.G.' – most likely Frank J. Geary, who worked for the paper from around 1916 until 1921.
[153] Seditious literature, censorship, publication of offensive articles, CO904/160/6-523.
[154] J.J. Comerford, *My Kilkenny IRA days: 1916–22* (Kilkenny, 1978), pp 188–9; Oram, *The newspaper book*, p. 131.

suggests that Keane wished to stand for election as Sinn Féin candidate: local Irish Parliamentary Party activist John Loftus, in a letter to leader John Redmond, claimed that Keane 'had no love for Cosgrave as he had hoped to be the Sinn Féin candidate himself'.[155] Regardless of his electoral ambitions, Keane was by this stage chairman of the local Sinn Féin club and through both his newspaper editorials and speeches at Sinn Féin rallies was converting increasing numbers of people to the republican cause.[156] He was arrested in August 1917 and October 1919, which roughly coincided with both suppressions of his newspaper and this only further solidified his status as a bastion of the independence movement in the Kilkenny area.

The 1917 arrest resulted from a seditious speech he had made at Ballingarry, County Tipperary, on 12 August. A large crowd gathered at the railway station in Kilkenny to cheer him off as he was being removed to Military Headquarters in Cork.[157] He was released about ten days later.[158] Keane's second arrest took place shortly after the second suppression of the *Kilkenny People*, though the two events were not connected.[159] This time he received a twenty-eight-day prison sentence for the possession of firearms. The conviction seems to have been fairly spurious as the small number of firearms found in his home were almost obsolete, with one being little 'more than a toy', according to Keane.[160] He was released about a week before the completion of his sentence due to ill health. Keane was said to be in a weak condition and had lost considerable weight during his incarceration.[161] While expressions of concern regarding the state of his health were genuine, Keane remained editor of the paper for another quarter century and he had an almost equally robust relationship with the authorities of the Irish Free State as he had had with their predecessors.[162]

---

155 Loftus to Redmond, 20 July 1917, MS 15,263/3. Loftus was seeking the nomination for his brother Pierce whom he claimed was 'a great friend of Keane'.
156 Comerford, *My Kilkenny IRA days*, pp 188–9.
157 *Irish Independent*, *Irish Times*, 28 Aug. 1917.
158 *Irish Times*, 8 Sept. 1917.
159 *Freeman's Journal*, 1 Oct. 1919; *Kilkenny People*, 4 Oct. 1919.
160 *Kilkenny People*, 18 Oct. 1919.
161 *Kilkenny People*, 1 Nov. 1919.
162 Marie Coleman, 'Keane, Edward Thomas ("E.T.")' in McGuire and Quinn, *Dictionary of Irish biography*.

Censorship and suppression

In a manner not totally dissimilar to the *Enniscorthy Echo*, the significance of the editorial comment of the *Kilkenny People* is somewhat diminished by the tribulations of its editor and the fact that the paper was twice suppressed during the 1916–21 period. Admittedly, the latter experience stemmed from what appeared in its editorial columns, but it is the mere fact that the paper was subjected to two fairly lengthy suppressions that has left a more indelible mark on Irish journalistic history. However, unlike its counterpart in neighbouring County Wexford, the *Kilkenny People* did not come under the police radar prior to 1916. The first instance of the paper attracting the attention of the authorities was in May 1916.

This attention was provoked by the editorial of 20 May 1916. In summary, this article was bitterly critical of police action in Kilkenny following the 1916 Rising. In a lengthy and rather long-winded editorial the question was posed as to why in Kilkenny, where 'there has never been the slightest suggestion of trouble', were so many citizens 'dragged from their homes, many of them humble wage-earners'. Possibly the authorities were most angered by the reference to General Sir John Maxwell as a 'military dictator'.[163] Subsequently, Maxwell wrote to Keane stating that he considered the aforementioned editorial was 'written with the intention of inciting the people against the military authorities'. Maxwell's letter additionally indicated that, until further notice, proofs of the paper were to be submitted 'to the County Inspector of the Royal Irish Constabulary at Kilkenny, before publication'. The letter was quoted in its entirety in the *Kilkenny People* of 3 June 1916, but Keane was not granted permission to publish his response to Maxwell. Accordingly, most of the editorial was left blank but preceded by a declaration that if the paper 'cannot speak free and untrammelled, it will not speak in the accents of slavery'.[164] The abrasive attitude of Keane to any form of censorship set the tone for Keane's relationship with the office of the Press Censor and resulted in the close monitoring of his paper for the next few years. In August 1916, Decies wrote to Keane expressing his concern at the tone of the paper's recent editorials. He advised Keane that there was 'no objection to any fair criticism' but comments 'tending to promote disaffection are not permitted'. He concluded by advising Keane that he hoped he would see his way to 'moderate the tone of your paper'.[165] At this stage Decies decided

163   *Kilkenny People*, 20 May 1916.
164   *Kilkenny People*, 3 June 1916.
165   Press Censorship Records 1916–1919, 3/722/13-20, 8 Aug. 1916.

against any immediate action being taken but the official monitoring of the *Kilkenny People* continued.[166]

As part of this ongoing monitoring, Decies contacted the Attorney-General in Dublin to discuss his continuing disquiet at the undesirable nature of Keane's editorials.[167] Correspondence between Decies and the Chief Secretary's Office the following January referred to 'the spirit of disloyalty fostered by this paper' while Keane was described as 'a difficult man to deal with' though 'he is better than he used to be but this is not saying a great deal'.[168] Nevertheless, the *Kilkenny People* still managed to avoid official censure but this was to change in late June 1917. At this stage, the Press Censor Decies wrote to Keane to remind him again 'that the publication of articles or other matter which infringe the Defence of the Realm regulations cannot be permitted'.[169] As no satisfactory response was received the decision to suppress the paper was taken in July 1917. Decies believed the suppression would have a 'salutary effect' and would 'serve as a warning to the Irish press as a whole'.[170] Decies may have had a point in this regard as the Press Censorship Report for the following month noted a 'greatly increased number of proofs submitted to this office by country papers'.[171] However, if the suppression of the *Kilkenny People* prompted a greater degree of caution on the part of other provincial titles it also strengthened the broader perception that the authorities were interfering with the freedom of the press.

The move even resulted in a question in the House of Commons as to the reason for the action to which the Chancellor, Andrew Bonar Law, bluntly replied that the paper was suppressed for contravening Defence of the Realm regulations. The question was then asked if similar action would be taken against the *Morning Post*, but no response was given.[172] At a more local level the suppression was condemned by both the

---

[166] Seditious literature, censorship, publication of offensive articles, CO904/160/6-580.

[167] Press Censorship Records 1916–1919, 3/722/13-20, 5 Sept. 1916.

[168] Press Censorship Records 1916–1919, 3/722/15-34, 22–3 Jan. 1917.

[169] Seditious literature, censorship, publication of offensive articles, CO904/160/6-526.

[170] Seditious literature, censorship, publication of offensive articles, CO904/160/6-519.

[171] Press Censorship Report, Aug. 1917, CO904/166/1.

[172] *Freeman's Journal*, 24 July 1917; *Irish Independent*, 24 July 1917; 22 Feb. 1918. The *Morning Post* of London was prosecuted for what was considered a similar contravention of Defence of the Realm regulations and subsequently fined £100 plus costs. According to the *Irish Independent* this was 'a mere bagatelle to a wealthy newspaper like the *Morning Post* and less than many shopkeepers have been fined for profiteering'.

Castlecomer Board of Guardians and Kilkenny Corporation.[173] Another provincial newspaper, the *Connacht Tribune*, weighed in with its support for Keane and his newspaper. While conceding that the *Kilkenny People* had recently 'taken a line with which we do not altogether agree', it described Keane as 'an able and fearless journalist' and protested strongly against the gagging of 'a newspaper owner by the Prussian policy of dismantling his machinery and doing incalculable injury to his business'.[174] The *Irish Independent* joined in the criticism, complaining that the *Kilkenny People* 'was suppressed for some unnamed offence' and accusing the authorities of selectively using 'all the formidable penalties which the Defence of the Realm Act' makes available to them.[175]

Ultimately, the paper did not appear from mid-July until mid-October 1917. The suppression was only lifted when Keane was compelled to agree that his paper would be subject to official censorship and that nothing would be published in the future 'to which official censorship could take exception'.[176] The solidarity of fellow newspapermen was expressed by the Irish Newspaper Owners' Association which congratulated Keane 'upon the restoration of his printing plant and machinery' and expressed the hope 'that he would have suffered nothing from the suspension of his newspaper'.[177] On its return the editorial announced that its 'long vacation' had terminated but acknowledged that the paper was 'only permitted to appear under official censorship'.[178] Nevertheless, in July 1918, the paper appeared to go on the offensive.

Through his solicitor, Keane complained to Lord Decies that a report of speeches made at a political meeting in Kilkenny, which had been deleted by the Censor's office from the proofs of the *Kilkenny People*, had been reported in both the *Kilkenny Journal* and the *Kilkenny Moderator*.[179] Lord Decies accepted the validity of Keane's complaint and effectively conceded that this was an oversight on the part of the Censor's office. Decies went on to state that the *Kilkenny People* editor 'may congratulate himself that by his actions he avoids any breach of the Defence of the Realm regulations' whereas the other two Kilkenny newspapers would

---

[173] *Freeman's Journal, Irish Independent*, 27 July 1917.
[174] *Connacht Tribune*, 15 Sept. 1917.
[175] *Irish Independent*, 6 Oct. 1917.
[176] Seditious literature, censorship, publication of offensive articles, CO904/160/6-518; *Irish Independent*, 4 Oct. 1917.
[177] *Freeman's Journal*, 18 Oct. 1917.
[178] *Kilkenny People*, 13 Oct. 1917.
[179] Seditious literature, censorship, publication of offensive articles, CO904/160/6-464.

'have to answer for their actions' as they saw fit to violate these regulations 'without any reference to this office'.[180] It is not altogether certain but Keane may have harboured a lingering sense of injustice at this incident and there is evidence to indicate that it was a similar occurrence that led to the second suppression of the paper in August 1919.

In summary, this second suppression resulted from the publication of certain items in the issue of 2 August 1919 that had already been deleted by the Censor's office from the proofs of the paper. The items again referred to speeches made at a recent political meeting in County Kilkenny and in reality were fairly innocuous by the standards of the time. Indeed, Major Bryan Cooper (who had now replaced Lord Decies as Press Censor) conceded that 'the actual offence was not a very serious one'.[181] Nonetheless, it was considered 'a deliberate and calculated defiance' of censorship regulations that swiftly led to the suppression of the paper.[182] Keane argued that the report of the speeches in question had already appeared in the *Kilkenny Journal* which had been published two days before his own paper. Accordingly, he contended 'that the prohibition of matter in one newspaper, which is allowed in another competing newspaper published in the same town, is a very grave injustice'.[183] Keane's case may not have been helped by the fact that he had questioned whether Cooper could perform his role in a totally objective manner given his unionist background.[184] This was a most unfair accusation to make against Cooper and indeed Keane acknowledged 'that it was a wrong suggestion for me to make' in a letter to Cooper some weeks later in which Keane effectively admitted that his contravention of the censorship regulations was due to a fit of temper.[185] In the first editorial after the ending of the suppression Cooper was referred to as 'an honourable man who would not consciously do what was unfair or unjust'.[186]

The paper reappeared on 13 September following considerable written correspondence with the authorities and a meeting between Keane and

---

[180] Seditious literature, censorship, publication of offensive articles, CO904/160/6-466.

[181] Press Censorship Records 1916–1919, 3/722/29-47, 25 Aug. 1919.

[182] Seditious literature, censorship, publication of offensive articles, CO904/160/6-485.

[183] Press Censorship Records 1916–1919, 3/722/23-136, 19 Aug. 1919.

[184] *Kilkenny People*, 2 Aug. 1919.

[185] Seditious literature, censorship, publication of offensive articles, CO904/160/6-480. Keane admitted that it was not always possible 'to bring to bear on my judgement and actions that calm judicial temperament, which would save me from the serious consequences that occasionally follow hasty decisions'.

[186] *Kilkenny People*, 13 Sept. 1919.

Major Cooper. By this time government censorship had officially ended. Nonetheless, this second suppression provides a pertinent example of the difficulties faced by newspapers during these years and of the dilemmas faced by editors. They had to decide whether to print content without reference to the Press Censor and risk the consequences or alternatively submit proofs for approval and face the possibility of being refused permission to publish. However, from September 1919 onwards, the latter option ceased to exist with the ending of official censorship.

'The voice of the *People*': editorial comment, 1914–1921

Prior to the outbreak of World War I, the *Kilkenny People* normally consisted of twelve pages (divided into seven columns), though this fell by four pages as the war progressed. The front page normally comprised classified ads – primarily details of public auctions – and conventional advertisements. The paper appeared to feature more advertisements than most, as a wide range of businesses were promoted in the advertising columns, as were a multitude of goods and services. In addition to the many local grocery, hardware, and clothing shops that appeared, the services of estate agents, dentists, and optometrists also featured significantly, as did the paper's own printing works. Farming-related advertisements and announcements were also a hallmark of the *Kilkenny People*, though this was scarcely surprising for a paper that included a regular column entitled 'All the news of interest to farmers'. There was also a highly notable concentration on Irish manufactures in the advertising sections, perhaps best exemplified by the Smithwick Brewery, which emphasised in its advertisement that it was the 'largest buyer of local barley'.[187]

There is little doubt that before Easter 1916 E.T. Keane and his newspaper were enthusiastic supporters of John Redmond and the Irish Parliamentary Party. Prior to Redmond's visit to Kilkenny in October 1914, when the implementation of Home Rule appeared imminent, an editorial recognised him as 'the leader of the movement which has won for us this measure of self-government' and 'the man who in the near future will be Prime Minister of Ireland'.[188] Indeed, Keane was quite supportive

---

[187] In November 1921, the paper claimed that some British manufacturers were attempting to pass off their products as Irish and accordingly started to publish lists of items (categorised into household, foodstuffs, and general) that the paper claimed were definitely home-produced.

[188] *Kilkenny People*, 17 Oct. 1914. All editorials appeared under the heading 'The Voice of the *People*'.

of Redmond's stance regarding the war and the paper frequently carried recruiting advertisements, particularly in the early months of 1915. The sinking of the *Lusitania* in May 1915 provided a stark illustration of the paper's outrage at Germany's prosecution of the war. The incident was labelled 'the crowning infamy of Germany's long series of barbarities since the war broke out' and the same editorial unambiguously declared that Germany 'should be wiped off the map'.[189] The scathing nature of such editorial comment can, in hindsight, be seen as an indicator of what was to appear in the lead columns of the *Kilkenny People* in the succeeding years. The crucial difference was that Keane's ire was to be focused in a completely different direction.

In the immediate aftermath of Easter 1916, the responsibility for the state of affairs that led to the Rising was laid firmly at the door of the British Government. Its capitulation to 'Carson and his criminal confederates' was angrily cited as the primary reason for this 'most appalling calamity' that 'has drenched the streets and the public places of the capital in human blood'.[190] This description of Dublin contrasted sharply with the depiction of Kilkenny, which, an editorial a few weeks later stated, almost with satisfaction, had remained 'as peaceful as a Sabbath evening in midsummer' amid all the disturbances in the capital city.[191] Despite this apparent pride in the complete absence of any violent unrest in Kilkenny, the editorial comment of the *Kilkenny People* grew decidedly more robust and the paper itself became increasingly associated with what the British authorities considered the militant strand of Irish nationalism.

By late 1917, the Irish Parliamentary Party was being referred to as an 'egregious collection of humbugs and charlatans', while Sinn Féin had 'already captured the country' and would 'go on from success to success'.[192] Barely ten months later the party previously led by John Redmond had become the 'West British Parliamentary Party' that was 'doomed to political extinction'.[193] In his memoir of his time in the IRA in Kilkenny, J.J. Comerford spoke of how E.T. Keane's 'writings and speeches made sense to all' and how his father used to cut certain editorials out of the paper and read them 'aloud to groups of people at Coolraheen crossroads

[189] *Kilkenny People*, 15 May 1915.

[190] *Kilkenny People*, 29 Apr. 1916. Carson's Ulster Volunteers were also described as 'the most violent, the most fanatical, and the most illiterate mob in all Europe'.

[191] *Kilkenny People*, 13 May 1916.

[192] *Kilkenny People*, 20 Oct. 1917; 3 Nov. 1917.

[193] *Kilkenny People*, 10 Aug. 1918.

and at the Salmonpool public house'.[194] While such a recollection may be slightly given to hyperbole, the editorial reaction to the introduction of conscription possibly renders such comments understandable. The contrast was made as to how it took the House of Commons twenty-five years 'to pass a Home Rule Act for Ireland', whereas the Conscription Act was 'put into force within a few weeks of its being placed on the Statute Book'. The same fiery editorial proclaimed that after the horrors of famine, emigration, and landlordism, conscription was now aimed 'at the annihilation of the Irish nation'.[195]

Broadly speaking, the editorial policy of the *Kilkenny People* did not differ greatly from that of the *Meath Chronicle* or *Enniscorthy Echo*. What was distinctive, however, was the highly belligerent tone of many of its editorials. As the situation in the country grew ever more violent, in 1920, the paper categorically stated that the 'supreme outrage' was 'the presence of an alien government detested by the people and maintained by brute force'.[196] The character of David Lloyd George was described as 'bitter, vindictive, and treacherous'.[197] Nonetheless, an editorial from early October provides the best example of the almost confrontational tone of some of the paper's editorials. The primary target was the Chief Secretary, Sir Hamar Greenwood, who had presided over a much criticised series of reprisals carried out by Crown forces. In an unusually short lead article Greenwood was variously referred to as the 'Canadian Pussyfoot', 'a beautiful liar', an 'accomplished liar', and then simply as 'Liar Greenwood'.[198] For a publication that had already experienced two suppressions, the tone and language of such an editorial was quite remarkable to say the least. Yet, despite the extremely abrasive nature of such editorials, the paper greeted the cessation of hostilities in July 1921 with considerable enthusiasm.

The fact that overtures for a ceasefire had originated on the British side was viewed by the *Kilkenny People* as an indication of 'a degree of sincerity' that had not existed previously.[199] Prior to the Treaty negotiations solid confidence was expressed in Arthur Griffith and Michael Collins who may not have been 'trained diplomatists' but were 'plain blunt men who are not going to let down their country'.[200] The agreement reached

---

[194]　J.J. Comerford, *My Kilkenny IRA days*, p. 189.
[195]　*Kilkenny People*, 20 Apr. 1918.
[196]　*Kilkenny People*, 22 May 1920.
[197]　*Kilkenny People*, 16 Oct. 1920.
[198]　*Kilkenny People*, 2 Oct. 1920.
[199]　*Kilkenny People*, 16 July 1921.
[200]　*Kilkenny People*, 8 Oct. 1921.

in December 1921 was greeted almost joyously. 'One of the greatest and most heroic fights for freedom ever put up in ancient or modern history by any small nation' had ended in victory the paper declared with almost unbridled enthusiasm. Griffith, Collins, and the remaining members of the negotiating team had 'won an unparalleled personal triumph'.[201]

As the Dáil debates on the Treaty commenced and opposition began to surface the *Kilkenny People* held firm in its support for both the agreement and the Irish signatories. Indeed, it was even acknowledged that neither Griffith nor Collins asked, or wanted, to be part of the negotiating team. They were not sent to London, the paper further argued, 'to demand an Irish Republic' and 'no one has asserted that they did'. According to the paper, rejection of the Treaty would mean choosing a policy of 'self-extermination' when self-determination had already been achieved. Resumption of military conflict would result in a 'bloody and ruthless war', not for an 'Irish Republic' but 'for a "shadow", for a "phrase", for one form of treaty as against another'.[202] The great difficulty of reconciling nationalist ideology with political reality seemed to be well appreciated in the editorial columns of the *Kilkenny People*. Similar to its counterparts in Meath and Wexford there was an acceptance that some degree of compromise was simply unavoidable.

Conclusion

Unlike the *Meath Chronicle* and *Enniscorthy Echo*, the *Kilkenny People* did not articulate any real support for Sinn Féin prior to Easter 1916. However, once E.T. Keane transferred his allegiance to the republican cause his paper quickly became a vociferous critic of British policy in Ireland. The nature of this criticism landed the paper in trouble with the authorities on several occasions. Much of the friction between the Censor's Office and the paper may well have been attributable to the abrasive and impulsive personality of E.T. Keane who went on to have an almost equally contentious relationship with the authorities of the Irish Free State. His imposing persona looms large over the experiences of the *Kilkenny People* in the years from 1916 to 1921. This only serves to emphasise the binding relationship between the editor and his publication that was a distinctive characteristic of Irish provincial journalism in the early twentieth century.

[201] *Kilkenny People*, 10 Dec. 1921.
[202] *Kilkenny People*, 24 Dec. 1921.

Midland Tribune

The Birr-based *Midland Tribune* did not find itself embroiled with the authorities to anywhere near the same extent as the *Enniscorthy Echo* or *Kilkenny People*. Nor is there any record of its proprietor or editor being imprisoned between 1916 and 1921, as was the case with William Sears and E.T. Keane. Nonetheless, this renders an examination of the paper's fortunes between these years and indeed the broader background of newspapers in County Offaly no less interesting. The *Midland Tribune* was ultimately regarded as a pro-Sinn Féin organ but as with so many other titles this is only part of the story.

At the start of the 1880s, the unionist *King's County Chronicle* was the only provincial title serving this part of County Offaly. This may have been one of the reasons that prompted three Catholic priests to establish the *Midland Tribune* in 1881, the primary aim of which was to provide a nationalist organ to an area that had previously been devoid of such an influence. The three priests, Robert Little, Denis Sheehan, and Patrick Brennan, occasionally wrote for the paper in its early years but the most significant figure in the opening decades of its existence was John Powell, who assumed control in 1888. Powell is credited with putting the paper on a firm footing and significantly improving its fortunes as the first ten years of the *Tribune*'s existence had proved quite difficult. By the time of Powell's death in 1901, the paper's circulation had reached around 5,000 and it had also been equipped with new machinery.[203]

Originally from Ennis, Powell had worked at the *Kilrush Herald* and the *Clare Examiner* and spent some time in America before returning to Ireland. He had been involved in the establishment of the *Tribune* and had already served four years as editor prior to taking ownership of the paper in 1888. Powell's tenure as editor was also marked by several brushes with the law. He appeared before the courts on no fewer than eight occasions and served three separate prison terms arising out of those appearances. The periods of imprisonment resulted mainly from his advocacy of tenant rights and are believed to have broken his health and impaired his eyesight. These setbacks may have been a contributory factor to his death in 1901 at the relatively young age of forty-five.[204]

His wife Margaret had assumed legal ownership in 1892 while a number of the ten young children he left behind later worked for

---

[203]   *Midland Tribune: 1881–1981 – 100 years of a family newspaper* (7 Nov. 1981).
[204]   Ibid.

the paper. John Powell was succeeded as editor by his brother Daniel. Within a year of taking editorial control Daniel Powell received a four-month prison term after being convicted of intimidating a local solicitor who had refused to re-let a house to a tenant he had previously evicted. Margaret Powell was also charged with the same offence, but her brother-in-law took full responsibility for articles published in the *Midland Tribune* that were intended to bring pressure to bear on the solicitor.[205] On his release he received a 'royal welcome' at Roscrea but his incarceration had a detrimental effect on his previously robust health. He died in 1907 at a relatively young age similar to his brother.[206]

Margaret Powell was proprietor of the *Midland Tribune* from 1892 until her death in 1931. The paper had been conveyed to her so that her husband could speak freely without the fear of the sheriff's seizure as a result. In addition to the somewhat premature loss of her husband, two of her children also died while quite young. Leo Powell died in 1907 and Bluebell Powell died in 1917.[207] Two of her sons joined the British Army while one of her daughters, Clare, joined the army medical service at the outbreak of World War I but was invalided out of service in 1917.[208] Another son, John B. Powell, emigrated to the USA around 1913 and became a successful journalist in Boston.[209]

While Margaret Powell took legal ownership of the *Midland Tribune* in 1892, she did not take an active part in the running of the paper. Accordingly, a period of difficulty and uncertainty followed the death of Daniel Powell in 1907. In the five years after his death several of the children of John and Margaret Powell assisted in the production of the paper, most notably the aforementioned John B. Powell.[210] However, a sustained period of stability followed the appointment of James Pike as editor in 1912. Pike was another newspaperman who bolstered the sense of longevity that was characteristic of Irish provincial journalism, remaining in the editorial chair of the *Midland Tribune* until his death in 1948. Hailing from Tullamore, Pike was initially a teacher before turning his hand to journalism. His first journalistic posting was on the staff of Thomas Chapman's *Westmeath Independent* and was later assistant

---

[205] Ibid.

[206] *Irish Independent*, 30 May 1907.

[207] *Midland Tribune: 1881–1981 – 100 years of a family newspaper* (7 Nov. 1981).

[208] Ibid.; *Irish Independent*, 1 June 1917.

[209] *Midland Tribune: 1881–1981 – 100 years of a family newspaper* (7 Nov. 1981).

[210] Ibid.

editor to W.P. Ryan at the *Irish Peasant* in Navan and subsequently at the renamed *Peasant and Irish Nation* in Dublin.[211]

Described by Hugh Oram as 'dour' and 'walrus-moustached', James Pike was also a member of the IRB and the Irish Volunteers.[212] Originally supportive of the Irish Parliamentary Party, Pike and his paper switched allegiance in the months after Easter 1916.[213] In the following months and years Pike was swift to embrace Irish republican ideology and canvassed for Sinn Féin during the 1918 general election campaign. Birr was then a town with a significant unionist community whose antipathy Pike's political activity appears to have aroused. When loyalists in the town lit a bonfire in Emmet Square (then Cumberland Square) to mark the end of World War I, they added Pike's effigy to that of the Kaiser.[214] Around the same time, Pike was accosted on the street by a woman who thrust a Union flag in his face, yelling, 'Make the rebel eat it', and 'Where now is Sinn Féin and German gold?'[215]

The antagonism directed at Pike by members of Birr's unionist community had little effect on his journalistic career and the *Tribune*'s support for Sinn Féin remained solid. In later years Pike joined the Fianna Fáil ranks and his obituary described him as being 'a staunch member of the Birr Comhairle Ceanntair and Birr Cumann'.[216] As Pike was a dominant personality at the newspaper there is little record of any other journalists who worked for the *Midland Tribune* during these years. This may simply be due to the fact (as will be outlined in the next section) that the *Tribune* was a significantly smaller operation than titles such as the *Enniscorthy Echo* and the *Kilkenny People*. However, one of those who did work for the paper was Cornelius O'Mahony, who joined the reporting staff around 1920. O'Mahony had edited the *Kerry Weekly News* for over ten years until the destruction of the paper's printing machinery by Crown forces. O'Mahony was credited as a supporter of Sinn Féin and an active member of the party from a very early stage.[217] Another journalist to work at the *Midland Tribune* during this period, albeit for a short time, was the aforementioned Frank J. Geary. As previously noted,

211   *Midland Tribune*, 7 Feb. 1948.
212   Ibid.; Oram, *The newspaper book*, pp 139–40.
213   *Irish Independent*, 9 Oct. 1916. The *Irish Independent* of this date described the *Midland Tribune* as 'a strong party and partition organ till a few weeks ago'.
214   Oram, *The newspaper book*, pp 139–40.
215   *Irish Independent*, 13 Nov. 1918.
216   *Midland Tribune*, 7 Feb. 1948.
217   *Irish Press*, 30 May 1939; *Midland Tribune*, 3 June 1939.

Geary had cut his journalistic teeth under E.T. Keane at the *Kilkenny People* but spent some time with the Birr title before his long association with the *Irish Independent* commenced in 1922.[218]

Editorial comment, 1914–1921

During the 1914–21 period, County Offaly was served by four different titles that curiously were evenly split between nationalist and unionist. However, this statistic may be a little misleading as it is not really possible to determine the influence exerted by individual titles as there are no figures available for either sales or circulation. The two unionist titles were the *King's County Chronicle* and the *Leinster Reporter*, the latter being the Tullamore edition of the former publication. The other nationalist organ apart from the *Midland Tribune* was the Tullamore-based *King's County Independent* (later the *Offaly Independent*), which was the owned by the same company (Athlone Printing Works) that published the *Westmeath Independent*.[219]

The masthead of the *Midland Tribune* also displayed the appended title of the *Tipperary Sentinel and King's County Vindicator*. At six pages in volume it was somewhat smaller than several other provincial newspapers. It also differed from other titles in that it was divided into eight columns. Its front page contained both advertisements and news items though frequently only the latter appeared. Local businesses accounted for much of the advertising space though overall there was a slightly lesser proportion of advertisements than many other papers. Apart from the promotion of local businesses, the advertising columns featured advertisements for several different medications, a variety of foodstuffs, and numerous agriculture-related items. One further noticeable aspect of the *Tribune* was regular advertisements for cinemas in Birr, Roscrea, and Nenagh, which was an evolving feature of many local papers at that time.

Editorials in the *Midland Tribune* often tended to be quite brief (sometimes only five or six sentences) and frequently dealt with matters specific to County Offaly. This may well have been due to the simple fact that the paper was a smaller journalistic and publishing entity than many other provincial titles of the time. Many issues comprised only four pages, which differed considerably from the *Meath Chronicle*, *Enniscorthy Echo*, and *Kilkenny People*, which almost always consisted of eight pages. This tendency towards a smaller paper and brief editorials lessened

---

[218] *Irish Independent, Irish Times*, 22 Dec. 1961.
[219] *Newspaper press directory and advertisers' guide 1922*, p. 216.

noticeably after Easter 1916. Nevertheless, it remained quite a distinctive feature throughout the years from 1914 to 1921. Despite the frequently brief nature of the leading articles the paper's editorial comment is still deserving of serious consideration.

In general terms, the *Midland Tribune* was clearly supportive of the Irish Parliamentary Party up to Easter 1916. Indeed, in 1914, James Pike took the time to write to the national newspapers to dispel any uncertainty as to his paper's support for the party led by John Redmond. The situation arose due to a minor controversy that had attracted some outside attention concerning the selection of candidates for the upcoming election. Pike's letter, published in both the *Freeman's Journal* and the *Irish Independent*, declared that 'far from being hostile to the Irish Party' his paper had 'consistently supported what we conceived to be its best interests'.[220] The publication of a full-page recruiting advertisement the following year seemed to indicate that the *Tribune* was quite supportive of John Redmond's stance on the war.[221] Nonetheless, there had already been indications that the paper was not entirely in agreement with those calling for support for the British war effort. A few weeks after the shootings that followed the Howth gun-running, an editorial bluntly stated that 'nationalists who are now spouting as to the defence of the Empire should not forget the happenings on the streets of Dublin a few Sundays ago, when unarmed Dublin citizens were shot down by Scottish soldiers'.[222]

In the aftermath of Easter 1916, the paper regretted the absence of a Parnell-like figure that 'could have controlled the situation as it existed'. In a similar vein to several other provincial newspapers it also cited what it considered the British Government's capitulation to Sir Edward Carson 'and the hanging up of Home Rule' as the immediate cause of the rebellion.[223] Nonetheless, the paper still considered the violence in Dublin 'a very mad and foolish undertaking'.[224] By October, the *Tribune* was clearly distancing itself from the parliamentary party, accusing John Redmond of 'toadying to English opinion' and of being 'largely responsible for the rebellion' due to his part in splitting the Volunteer movement.[225]

---

220 *Freeman's Journal, Irish Independent*, 15 Dec. 1914.
221 *Midland Tribune*, 6 Nov. 1915.
222 *Midland Tribune*, 15 Aug. 1914.
223 *Midland Tribune*, 6 May 1916.
224 *Midland Tribune*, 13 May 1916.
225 *Midland Tribune*, 14 Oct. 1916. 'Had there been no Volunteer split', the paper's editorial claimed, 'the "extremists" in the movement would have worked in harmony with, or would have been controlled by the more moderate section'.

The following year witnessed the *Midland Tribune*'s total conversion to the Sinn Féin cause. The party's victory in South Longford was seen as 'a nail in the coffin of the present Irish Party' while de Valera's victory in East Clare 'sounded the death-knell of parliamentarianism'.[226] The Sinn Féin defeat in South Armagh early the following year saw the sentiments of the *Meath Chronicle* being echoed with 'Redmondites and Ulster Orange Partitionists' now marching 'shoulder to shoulder'.[227] The advent of the conscription crisis in April 1918 unsurprisingly elicited the paper's opposition but the *Tribune* was eager that its readers did not lose sight of the fact that it coincided with the first unopposed return of a Sinn Féin candidate. Following Dr Pat MacCartan's by-election victory, the paper proudly stated that 'North Offaly can now claim in all truth to be Ireland's premier constituency'.[228] Sinn Féin's resounding victory at the general election several months later was considered 'the final stroke towards the demolition of England's effort to disguise the thorough dissatisfaction of the Irish people with the system of rule by force which now reigns supreme in Ireland'.[229]

As a Sinn Féin paper the *Midland Tribune* did not find itself attracting the attention of the Press Censor to anywhere near the same degree as other provincial titles of similar allegiance. It was, however, sternly warned in August 1917 that its recent reproduction of 'speeches of a seditious nature' was 'in clear violation of the Defence of the Realm Regulations'.[230] Press Censorship Records indicate the paper being instructed to delete content on only three occasions. Nevertheless, the *Midland Tribune* certainly expressed strong opinions on the broader issue of censorship. In August 1918, it complained that the phrase 'as passed by censor' had become increasingly familiar in relation to the depiction of events in Ireland.[231] Nevertheless, its most vociferous criticism of what it regarded as the muzzling of the press came with the announcement in April 1919 that press censorship was to continue.[232] Similar to many other provincial publications the *Tribune* was quite complimentary of Lord Decies and his staff whom it described as 'both efficient and courteous'.

---

[226] *Midland Tribune*, 12 May, 14 July 1917.
[227] *Midland Tribune*, 9 Feb. 1918.
[228] *Midland Tribune*, 27 Apr. 1918.
[229] *Midland Tribune*, 28 Dec. 1918.
[230] Press Censorship Records 1916–1919, 3/722/21-81, 2 Aug. 1917.
[231] *Midland Tribune*, 10 Aug. 1918.
[232] This announcement coincided with the resignation of Lord Decies as Chief Press Censor and the appointment of Major Bryan Cooper as his successor.

Regrettably, they were 'tools in the hands of higher powers', whose functions were 'on an exact par with the German censorship'. The same editorial railed against the notion of voluntary censorship and claimed that it was really 'based on arbitrary force'. Yet censorship was no longer in force when the paper was suppressed less than six months later.

The suppression followed the publication in its issue of 20 September 1919 of a full-page advertisement for the Irish National Loan that had been instigated by Dáil Éireann. Copies of the paper were also seized at Roscrea and Cloghan.[233] The suppression did not last long, and the paper only missed one issue. On its return the editorial voiced its strong opinion on what it regarded as attempts to control the output of the print media in Ireland. The recent closure of the office of the Press Censor had made matters more difficult for Irish newspapers, the paper argued, to the extent that 'it is now almost impossible to know what will or will not leave a paper open to drastic measures'.[234] The *Midland Tribune* attracted little further police attention though the lodgings of James Pike and the offices of the paper were searched in May 1921 after exception was taken to comments made with regard to the funeral of an RIC constable.[235]

A notable feature of editorials during 1920 and 1921 was that there was less focus on the violent incidents that were taking place around the country than was the case in papers such as the *Enniscorthy Echo* and *Kilkenny People*. This should not imply that the *Tribune* remained oblivious to such occurrences. Nevertheless, when describing violent outbreaks in November 1920 in Nenagh, Tullamore, and Templemore as 'tragic experiences' that would have 'shocked the public opinion of the civilised world', its tone was a little more guarded than some of its counterparts.[236] It was, however, happy to articulate its antipathy for Lloyd George, stating that where 'other coercionists' such as Cromwell and Pitt had failed he was 'not likely to succeed'.[237] It was in its reaction to the Anglo-Irish Treaty of 1921 though that the *Midland Tribune*'s stance was markedly different from the other three pro-Sinn Féin organs discussed in this chapter.

Its most immediate response to the London agreement was to comment that it 'falls short of the ideal Republic' but equally warned of the dangers of divisions 'in the Irish ranks here at home'. Precious little recognition was afforded the Irish negotiators other than an acknowledgement 'that

[233] *Irish Independent, Freeman's Journal*, 22 Sept. 1919; *Irish Times*, 27 Sept. 1919.
[234] *Midland Tribune*, 4 Oct. 1919.
[235] *Irish Independent*, 24 May 1921.
[236] *Midland Tribune*, 13 Nov. 1920.
[237] *Midland Tribune*, 7 Aug. 1920.

the plenipotentiaries in London during the last fateful day were confronted with a very difficult situation'. To the paper's credit it argued that the Treaty 'perpetuates partition' whereas other papers glossed over the Ulster situation or simply ignored it. Its recognition that 'the country is in favour of the acceptance of the Treaty' appeared to be dispelled by its comment that Home Rule would have been accepted in 1914 but 'many things have happened since 1914'.[238] The *Tribune*'s final editorial of 1921 offered the cryptic comment that those people now vigorously calling for ratification of the Treaty refused their services to Dáil Éireann when called on and that 'Griffith and Collins are now applauded by these people'.[239] Crucially, though, it did not elaborate as to who 'these people' were. In summary, the *Midland Tribune* appeared to oppose the Anglo-Irish Treaty but stopped short of making an outright declaration of opposition. Perhaps the paper may not have wished to encourage divisions but the more cynical might suggest that it saved it from the tricky task of proposing an alternative to rejection of the Treaty.

Conclusion

The *Midland Tribune* displayed many similar traits to the other three newspapers examined in detail in this chapter. This included support for the Gaelic League, which it described as kindling 'the spark from which the present national fire is burning'.[240] It also included a swift transfer of allegiance to Sinn Féin after Easter 1916 (though its previous support for the Irish Parliamentary Party could hardly be labelled as staunch) and subsequent suppression albeit for a minimal period. It differed from the other three titles from an editorial perspective in that it did not focus on national issues to the same extent. This is not to suggest that its commitment to the movement for Irish independence was not as strong as other papers. It merely indicates that the *Tribune* obviously considered local issues as also being of great importance to its readers. However, by far the most notable manner in which the *Midland Tribune* distinguished itself from the other three titles under scrutiny in this chapter was its stance on the Anglo-Irish Treaty of 1921. The paper's centenary issue describes it as being 'neither for or against', but a more accurate description would be that it was non-committal and rather evasive.[241]

---

[238] *Midland Tribune*, 24 Dec. 1921.

[239] *Midland Tribune*, 31 Dec. 1921.

[240] *Midland Tribune*, 5 Apr. 1919.

[241] *Midland Tribune: 1881–1981 – 100 years of a family newspaper* (7 Nov. 1981).

Summary: Leinster newspapers

Quite apart from the political allegiances of individual newspapers there were several discernible features of the provincial press in Leinster between 1914 and 1921. These included prolonged editorial reigns, lengthy periods of family ownership, a highly dominant personality directing the fortunes of the paper, and a distinctly Catholic dimension that manifested itself either at the paper's foundation or in the strong Catholic faith of the editor or proprietor. Also, the province featured a significant number of unionist titles though almost all of them ceased publication within the first few decades of the establishment of the Irish Free State.

The most remarkable example of such lengthy editorial tenures was unquestionably at the *Westmeath Examiner*, where J.P. Hayden fulfilled the role for an incredible seventy-two years (1882–1954). Nevertheless, this trend was also exemplified at other newspapers, where editors such as Michael A. Casey (*Drogheda Independent*), E.T. Keane (*Kilkenny People*), and Thomas F. McGahon (*Dundalk Democrat*) served for close on half a century. Other journalists such as Michael Charles Carey (*Leinster Express*) and Patrick Quilty (*Meath Chronicle*) occupied the editorial chair for forty years or more. Such remarkably long periods at the helm of an individual newspaper meant that dominant personalities such as Keane and Casey were inextricably linked to specific titles, though such a characteristic could also apply to J.P. Farrell (*Longford Leader*), Thomas Chapman (*Westmeath Independent*), and James Pike (*Midland Tribune*).

Pike served at a paper that more than adequately illustrates the sense of family involvement at individual publications over a prolonged period of time. When John Powell assumed control of the *Midland Tribune* in 1888 it marked the commencement of almost one hundred years of family ownership. In a similar vein, the acquisition of the *Meath Chronicle* by James Davis in 1917 was the beginning of a family association with the paper that has lasted for nearly a century. The highly significant family element to the provincial print media is also evident at the *Nationalist and Leinster Times*, where Liam D. Bergin, a grandson of one of the co-founders, occupied the editorial chair when the paper celebrated its centenary in 1983.[242] The conspicuously Catholic dimension to many Leinster titles was clearly illustrated not only by the establishment of provincial organs such as the *Leinster Leader*, *Drogheda Independent*, and *Midland Tribune* but also in the devoutly Catholic faith of newspapermen

---

[242] *Nationalist and Leinster Times: Centenary Issue 1883–1983.*

such as Tom Daly (*Meath Chronicle*), Thomas F. McGahon (*Dundalk Democrat*), and Michael A. Casey (*Drogheda Independent*).

This strong sense of Catholicism was understandably not a feature of the significant amount of unionist titles within Leinster. By the outbreak of war in 1914 most of these organs had been in existence for well over half a century, with the *Kilkenny Moderator* actually celebrating its centenary that year. However, all bar one of these titles ceased publication less than two decades after the foundation of the Irish Free State. The exception was the *King's County Chronicle* in County Offaly, which survived until 1948 when it was sold to the *Midland Tribune* but was discontinued as a separate title in 1963. These unionist titles had once occupied a position of prominence within the print media in Leinster but by the second decade of the twentieth century it was recently established nationalist organs such as the *Meath Chronicle*, *Kilkenny People*, *Enniscorthy Echo*, and *Midland Tribune* that had assumed such a role.

These four Leinster newspapers shared a number of common characteristics. All had declared their support for Sinn Féin quite soon after the Easter Rising and well before the general election of 1918. Although none of the four titles expressed any degree of solidarity with the 1916 rebels there appeared to be a consensus that much of the fault lay with the British Government. It was more or less agreed that the apparent refusal of the British Government to deal with the threat of violence posed by Sir Edward Carson and the Ulster Volunteers created a mood of frustration amongst nationalists that led some to resort to extreme measures. Once this shift in allegiance took place these titles were not shy about pouring scorn on the Irish Parliamentary Party. Strangely, this was far less the case with the *Enniscorthy Echo*, whose personnel, from its establishment, largely comprised either Sinn Féin members or sympathisers. Additionally, all four titles were quite supportive of movements such as the Gaelic League and the GAA, though the *Kilkenny People* was slightly less vocal in this regard. With the exception of the *Midland Tribune* these papers enthusiastically embraced the Anglo-Irish Treaty of 1921. Finally, at the gathering of the Irish print media hosted by the Lord Lieutenant mentioned at the outset of this chapter, only the *Meath Chronicle* amongst these four titles sent a representative. The *Midland Tribune* sent an apology for non-attendance, but the *Enniscorthy Echo* and *Kilkenny People* appear to have paid no heed to the meeting.[243] It may be just mere coincidence but it seems curious that these two non-attendees were the Leinster newspapers that subsequently came into

[243] *Freeman's Journal*, *Irish Times*, 29 Oct. 1915.

more conflict than most with the authorities. Nonetheless, these four publications were, of course, not the only papers in Leinster.

Other titles such as the *Nationalist and Leinster Times* of Carlow and the *Westmeath Independent* displayed similar pro-Sinn Féin sympathies, but it was only the latter that attracted the unwanted attention of the authorities. However, it should not be concluded that the province of Leinster was awash with republican organs between 1916 and 1921. Titles such as the *Westmeath Examiner*, *Longford Leader*, *Dundalk Democrat*, and *Drogheda Independent* had long-established associations with the Irish Parliamentary Party and were not as quick to change their loyalties. What might well be considered like-minded publications in other provinces are the subject of detailed scrutiny in succeeding chapters. The *Meath Chronicle*, *Enniscorthy Echo*, *Kilkenny People*, and *Midland Tribune* assumed a very definite political stance and suffered the consequences to varying degrees and accordingly merit such attention in this period of Irish journalistic history. Titles that took a different or completely opposing position are also deserving of such scrutiny and this is a matter that is addressed in the upcoming chapters.

3

West of the Shannon: Connacht

Introduction

Connacht's land area of 17,788 square kilometres makes it the smallest of the Irish provinces and it has traditionally been the least populous. This was certainly the case at the start of the second decade of the twentieth century when its total population was 610,984.[1] The largest population centres were Galway city (13,255) and Sligo town (11,163). The next largest centres of population were Ballina and Ballinasloe, with populations of just over and under 5,000 respectively. In total, the province was served by twenty-two local newspapers during the 1914–21 period. The four Connacht titles examined in this chapter, the *Tuam Herald*, *Roscommon Herald*, *Mayo News*, and *Leitrim Observer*, were based in areas exhibiting a variety of demographical features.

The *Tuam Herald* was published in a town with a relatively small population of just under 3,000 though it was the only paper based in Tuam. Despite such a relatively small population the paper could compete for readers amongst County Galway's considerable population of 182,224 of which 98 per cent was Catholic. Boyle in County Roscommon, where the *Roscommon Herald* was published, accounted for a population 2,691 out of County Roscommon's total population of 93,956. Similar to County Galway, 98 per cent of the populace was Catholic. The *Western Nationalist* was also published in Boyle while the county was similarly served by two titles based in Roscommon town,

---

[1] Vaughan and Fitzpatrick, *Irish historical statistics*, pp 3–68. All the demographical statistics and information provided in this section are based on the 1911 census and are cited from Vaughan and Fitzpatrick's work.

the *Roscommon Journal* and the *Roscommon Messenger*, and also by the *Strokestown Democrat*.

The *Mayo News* was the only title published in Westport, which had a population of 3,674. At the time, Mayo was the most populous county in Connacht, with a population of just over 192,000, and, similar to Galway, 98 per cent of the population was Catholic. The *Mayo News* competed for readers amongst the populace, with two titles based in Ballina: the *Ballina Herald* and the *Western People*, and one in Castlebar, the *Connaught Telegraph*, though this was later joined by the short-lived *Mayoman*. County Leitrim, which was home to the *Leitrim Observer*, had a population of 63, 582, making it the least populous county in the province. Catholics accounted for just over 91 per cent of the county's populace, which was a lower ratio than most of the other Connacht counties. The only other paper published in the county was the *Leitrim Advertiser*, published in Mohill.

Connacht newspapers: an overview

The structure of the provincial press in Connacht shared certain characteristics with that of Leinster but in certain other respects it was distinctly different. The emergence of markedly nationalist titles during the late nineteenth and early twentieth centuries was undoubtedly a similar feature in the western province. However, none of the existing papers at the start of World War I dated back to the 1700s or even the early 1800s. Additionally, only a small number of unionist titles were published in Connacht. Furthermore, only two nationalist organs, the *Mayo News* and *Leitrim Observer* (both of which are examined in detail in this chapter), converted unreservedly to the Sinn Féin cause prior to the 1918 general election. However, two other Connacht publications, the *Galway Express* and the *Sligo Nationalist*, were purchased by local Sinn Féin interests. Such developments may have set the provincial press in Connacht slightly apart from other provinces but suppressions, imprisonment of proprietors and editors, plus attacks on certain newspaper offices were just as much a part of the print media landscape in Connacht during the 1914–21 period as they were elsewhere; all of these characteristics are investigated in this chapter.

Amongst the limited number of titles that were launched in Connacht during the 1700s, there were only two, the *Sligo Journal* (1752–1866) and the *Connaught Journal* (1754–1840), that displayed any degree of longevity. This differed from Leinster where several titles that had been established in the late eighteenth and early nineteenth centuries were still being published in the second decade of the twentieth century. Additionally, the province only featured two unionist titles, neither of which could lay claim to being amongst the oldest in Connacht. The *Ballina Herald* had actually started out as a unionist organ upon its launch in 1870 but appears to have drifted towards nationalism in the late nineteenth century.[2] By the 1914–21 period, it was owned by the Duncan family and was regarded as politically neutral.[3] Such neutrality failed to prevent the brief suppression of the paper in December 1918 for printing a Sinn Féin election leaflet.[4] The two remaining unionist papers in the province had somewhat contrasting experiences during these years.

The first of these was the *Sligo Independent*, which was founded in 1855 by brothers Alexander and William Gillmor.[5] In 1921, the paper was acquired by William David Peebles, who had commenced his career as a journalist at the *Mid-Ulster Mail* in his home town of Cookstown, County Tyrone. He had worked as a reporter at the *Sligo Independent* since 1914 and ultimately spent close on fifty years at the paper.[6] Under his proprietorship it effectively ceased to argue the unionist cause and accepted the inevitability of Irish self-government.[7] This may have contributed to the fact that the paper differed from many unionist publications in the south of Ireland in lasting well beyond the establishment of the Free State. The *Sligo Independent* only ceased publication in 1962. A rather different fate befell the other unionist title that was published in Connacht at the start of World War I.

The paper in question was the *Galway Express*, which had been established in 1853 by a Scotsman, J.C. McDougall. By 1914, the paper was edited by Harry D. Fisher, a Church of Ireland member from Waterford, two of whose sons died while serving in the British Army.[8] In September 1917, the *Galway Express* was sold to Sinn Féin interests in

[2] *Western People, 125th Anniversary 1883–2008* (18 Nov. 2008).

[3] Ibid.; *Newspaper press directory and advertisers' guide 1917*, p. 207.

[4] *Connaught Telegraph, Irish Times*, 28 Dec. 1918. The incident led the *Connaught Telegraph* to remark sardonically that 'the only unionist paper in the county has been suppressed'.

[5] *Sligo Champion – Sesquicentenary Issue 1836–1986* (5 Dec. 1986).

[6] *Irish Times*, 6 Jan. 1962; *Sligo Champion*, 14 Dec. 1984; Padraig Deignan, *The Protestant community in Sligo, 1914–49* (Dublin, 2010), p. 176.

[7] Deignan, *The Protestant community*, p. 176.

[8] *Irish Times*, 2 May 1939; *Irish Independent* 3 May 1939.

the city for £535.[9] The principal instigator of the acquisition was Thomas Walshe, a pathology lecturer in University College Galway who was also highly involved in both the Gaelic League and the Irish Volunteers.[10] The tone of the paper predictably changed under the new ownership, which led to the receipt of a warning from the Press Censor in January 1918 as to its future conduct.[11] In September 1920, however, the *Galway Express* was dealt a far more serious blow. During what was described by the *Connacht Tribune* as the 'city's night of horror', the paper's offices were destroyed by Crown forces. This followed an incident at the railway station in the city that resulted in the death of an English policeman and a local man.[12] Later the same year, the owners submitted a claim for £10,000 for damage to premises and loss of business but the *Galway Express* ceased publication around the same time.[13]

The other Connacht title to be purchased by Sinn Féin interests was the *Sligo Nationalist*. This publication had only been founded in 1910 by Bernard McTernan, who had previously served as editor of the *Sligo Champion*. In April 1920, it was acquired by a group of Sinn Féin supporters and renamed the *Connachtman* (or *Connachtach*).[14] Under the new title it was edited by Robert George Bradshaw, who was active in the Sligo branch of the IRA.[15] When it was still operating as the *Sligo Nationalist* the paper had been closed down for advertising the Dáil Éireann loan while under its new title it was fined £250 for contravening the Restoration of Order in Ireland Act.[16] The *Connachtman* opposed the Anglo-Irish Treaty and was later suppressed by Free State forces before finally ceasing publication in 1925.[17]

Two other relatively short-lived newspapers with broadly republican sympathies, the *Western Nationalist* (1902–20) and the *Mayoman* (1919–21), were also published in Connacht. Despite its brief lifespan, the latter title, which was published in Castlebar, was still a noteworthy publication. It

---

[9]   *Freeman's Journal*, 21 Sept. 1917; *Irish Independent*, 22 Sept. 1917.

[10] *Connacht Tribune*, 23 July 1960.

[11] Press Censorship Report, Jan. 1918, CO904/166/1.

[12] *Connacht Tribune*, 11 Sept. 1920.

[13] *Connacht Tribune*, 30 Oct. 1920.

[14] Michael Farry, *The Irish revolution, 1912–1923: Sligo* (Dublin, 2012), pp 7–8.

[15] Michael Farry, *The aftermath of revolution: Sligo, 1921–23* (Dublin, 2000), p. 23.

[16] Farry, *The Irish revolution, 1912–1923*, p. 41; *Sligo Champion*, 4 Oct. 1919; *Sligo Nationalist*, 30 Sept. 1919; *Irish Times*, 26 Jan. 1921.

[17] Farry, *The Irish revolution, 1912–1923*, pp 7–8; *Sligo Champion – Sesquicentenary Issue 1836–1986* (5 Dec. 1986).

was established by John J. (J.J.) Collins and grew to become quite an influential paper during the War of Independence. Collins was a cousin of Archbishop Gilmartin of Tuam, whose pronouncements were frequently published in the *Mayoman*.[18] Collins, a noted supporter of Irish Ireland movements, also served as an official on the Connacht Council of the GAA and later worked for both the *Mayo News* and *Connacht Tribune*.[19] However, the most notable feature of the print media in the province was the predominance of titles that supported constitutional nationalism. This was undoubtedly exemplified by provincial organs such as the *East Galway Democrat* (1910–49) and the *Galway Observer* (1881–1966), but it was the nationalist papers that have lasted into the twenty-first century that provide the clearest illustration of this particular characteristic. These include titles such as the *Connacht Tribune*, *Tuam Herald*, *Connaught Telegraph*, *Western People*, and *Sligo Champion*. The origins of some of these newspapers can be traced back to the first half of the nineteenth century while others emerged in the late 1800s and early 1900s.

The *Tuam Herald*, which is profiled in the next section, dates back to 1837, whereas the *Connacht Tribune* is of a slightly more recent vintage, being established in 1909. It was founded by Corkman Thomas J.W. Kenny, who remained as editor until his death in 1940 and who was also a founding director of the Catholic journal, the *Standard*.[20] Initially, the *Connacht Tribune* was a solid supporter of the Irish Parliamentary Party, as evidenced by John Dillon writing in one of its early issues of the importance of 'a vigorous and able provincial press'.[21] Although the paper certainly did not evolve into a republican organ it still provoked the ire of Lord Decies during 1917, who reprimanded it for reporting speeches made at Sinn Féin meetings without reference to the office of the Press Censor.[22]

The launch of the *Western People* in Ballina, County Mayo, pre-dated that of the *Connacht Tribune* by over a quarter of a century. Informal links between the Catholic Church and provincial newspapers were again to

---

18 Dominic Price, *The flame and the candle: war in Mayo, 1919–1924* (Cork, 2012), pp 43–7.

19 *Connacht Tribune*, *Mayo News*, 15 May 1948.

20 *Connacht Tribune – 100th anniversary: souvenir centenary supplement* (22 May 2009); *Connacht Tribune*, 11 May 1940; *Irish Times*, 18 May 1940; O'Brien, 'With the Irish in France', p. 7. Kenny was the only editor of a specifically provincial paper to be brought on the tour of the western front referred to in Chapter 2.

21 *Connacht Tribune*, 22 May 1909.

22 Press Censorship Report, Jan. 1918, CO904/166/1.

the fore at the *Western People*, which was established in 1883 following a meeting at St Muredach's Cathedral in the town that was organised by Fr Anthony Finnerty. The meeting had been arranged with the intention of starting up a newspaper that would reflect the town's Catholic ethos.[23] Terence Devere, one of the main personalities involved in the foundation of the *Western People*, served with the paper for almost sixty years. He became sole proprietor in 1923 and remained in that position until his death in 1941.[24] The paper also provided an example of the close affiliation between the provincial press and the GAA. The first editor of the *Western People* was Patrick Smyth, who had strong links to the fledgling association, while Devere was a founder member of the Ballina Stephenites club.[25]

The Castlebar-based *Connaught Telegraph* was one of the few newspapers in the province that dated back to the first half of the nineteenth century. It started out as the *Telegraph or Connaught Ranger* in 1828 having been established by a titled English Protestant, Lord Frederick Cavendish. Despite his background, Cavendish strongly endorsed nationalist causes such as Daniel O'Connell's repeal movement of the 1840s, and he was also an early advocate of tenant rights.[26] The title ceased publication in 1870 (fourteen years after the death of Cavendish) but was acquired by James Daly in 1876 and renamed the *Connaught Telegraph*.[27] Daly, a native of County Mayo, was a devout Catholic and was also significantly involved in the formation of the Land League in the county.[28] In 1892, Daly sold his interest in the paper to one of his employees, Richard C. Gillespie, which marked the commencement of a family connection with the *Connaught Telegraph* that was still going strong over a century later.[29] In 1899, Gillespie's son, Thomas H. Gillespie, assumed control of the paper and remained as editor–proprietor until his death in 1939.[30]

---

23   *Western People, 125th Anniversary 1883–2008* (18 Nov. 2008).
24   Ibid.; *Western People*, 12 Apr. 1941; Rosa Meehan, *The story of Mayo* (Castlebar, 2003), pp 206–9.
25   *Western People, 125th Anniversary 1883–2008* (18 Nov. 2008); *Western People*, 12 Apr. 1941.
26   *Connaught Telegraph – Commemorative Issue* (Apr. 1996).
27   Donald E. Jordan Jr, *Land and popular politics in Ireland: County Mayo from the plantation to the land war* (New York, 1994), p. 267.
28   Gerard Moran, 'James Daly and the rise and fall of the Land League in the West of Ireland, 1879–82' in *Irish Historical Studies*, 29, no. 114 (Nov. 1994), pp 201–2.
29   *Connaught Telegraph – Commemorative Issue* (Apr. 1996).
30   *Connaught Telegraph*, 5 Apr. 1939.

The other relatively long-established nationalist paper in the province was the *Sligo Champion*. It was launched in 1836 as an organ of the Liberal Party by Edward Howard Verdon. Prior to this, Dublin-born Verdon had moved to the west of Ireland to become editor of the *Ballina Impartial*.[31] However, the figure that is undoubtedly most associated with the *Sligo Champion* is P.A. McHugh, who acquired the paper in 1885. Similar to several other fellow-newspapermen McHugh was also elected to parliament. He served as an MP of the Irish Parliamentary Party for North Leitrim from 1895 to 1906 and for North Sligo from 1906 to 1909. He died in 1909 at the relatively early age of fifty-one. However, the esteem in which McHugh was held in the region is illustrated by the fact that a memorial to him was unveiled outside Sligo town hall in October 1916 at a ceremony attended by John Redmond.[32]

At the outbreak of World War I, the *Sligo Champion* was considered to be 'still firmly loyal to the Irish Party and mouthpiece of Sligo's bourgeois, Catholic establishment'.[33] Nonetheless, this allegiance to the Irish Parliamentary Party had declined considerably by 1918 when the paper was even warned by the Press Censor that its tone was 'distinctly bad'.[34] This quite possibly resulted from its vehement opposition to conscription, which, the *Champion* warned, would have to be enforced 'at the point of a bayonet'.[35] The truce of July 1921 was warmly welcomed and the *Sligo Champion* also firmly supported the Anglo-Irish Treaty of December 1921.[36]

The four newspapers that are profiled in the upcoming sections of this chapter also displayed support for constitutional nationalism at certain stages. However, this began to change as the political climate within the country began to shift irrevocably towards a more separatist form of nationalism. In the case of papers such as the *Mayo News* and *Leitrim Observer* this support pre-dated any electoral manifestation of this shift. The nature of the *Roscommon Herald*'s eventual move to support for Sinn Féin was somewhat less simple. On the other hand, the *Tuam Herald* only began to voice any tolerance of the republican cause following Sinn Féin's landslide victory at the 1918 general election.

---

[31] *Sligo Champion – Sesquicentenary Issue 1836–1986* (5 Dec. 1986).

[32] Owen McGee, 'McHugh, Patrick Aloysius' in McGuire and Quinn, *Dictionary of Irish biography*.

[33] Wheatley, *Nationalism and the Irish Party*, p. 177.

[34] Farry, *The Irish revolution*, p. 7; Press Censorship Report, Mar. 1918, CO904/166/2.

[35] Farry, *The aftermath of revolution*, p. 40; *Sligo Champion*, 6 Apr. 1918.

[36] Farry, *The aftermath of revolution*, p. 203.

Consequently, these four provincial organs provide a representative cross-section of nationalist sentiment in Ireland between 1914 and 1921 that renders both their experiences and their editorial output during this period all the more relevant.

Tuam Herald

The *Tuam Herald* did not emerge amongst the substantial number of nationalist newspapers launched in the late nineteenth and early twentieth centuries. In fact, the origins of the *Tuam Herald* pre-date the Great Famine by almost ten years. The story of the paper begins in 1837 when Richard Kelly bought the type, press, and goodwill of the *Connaught Advertiser* from Mary Bradley. The first issue of the paper subsequently appeared on 13 May 1837. Born in Loughrea, in 1810, Richard Kelly came from quite an affluent background. His grandfather, having attained the requisite social standing, had married into a landowning family, the Ousleys of Prospect, Dunmore.[37]

Prior to the establishment of the *Tuam Herald*, the young Richard Kelly had enthusiastically supported Catholic emancipation. His Catholicism also inspired his opposition to the payment of tithes to the established Church of Ireland. This was just one of the issues robustly tackled in the early years of the *Herald*. Kelly was also a strong supporter of Daniel O'Connell and the repeal movement of the 1840s. As with so many other editor–proprietors Kelly's active interests extended considerably beyond the print media. While the *Herald* premises also served as a stationery and book shop as well as a general printing office, Kelly additionally fulfilled numerous of other roles. During his lifetime, Kelly also acted as a Justice of the Peace, Peace Commissioner, Town Commissioner, and Poor Law Guardian. Towards the end of the 1850s he transferred the editorship of the paper to his son, Jasper. Jasper Kelly died at a relatively young age in 1873 and the ownership of the paper was ultimately inherited by his son Richard John (R.J.) Kelly. The paper's founder, Richard Kelly, retained an interest in the running of the paper, despite having moved to Dublin, where he died in 1884. R.J. Kelly subsequently assumed full control and remained at the helm of the *Tuam Herald* until 1930 when the paper passed from the ownership of the Kelly family after almost a century.[38]

---

[37] *Tuam Herald: 150th anniversary supplement* (21 May 1988).
[38] Ibid.; *Tuam Herald*, 16 May 1987; 10 May 1988.

R.J. Kelly died in 1931, approximately one year after he had resigned his active interest in the *Herald*. On his departure, Kelly had served over fifty years as editor and proprietor, yet again illustrating the tradition of continuity that existed within the ranks of the Irish provincial press. In much the same way as his grandfather before him, R.J. Kelly's interests extended well beyond the journalistic field, except to an even greater extent. He was a senior barrister and wrote legal texts on subjects such as newspaper libel, registration of tithe, plus a large volume on the Land Acts from 1860 to 1896. Additionally, he authored many pamphlets on topics such as peasant proprietary, land reclamation, and Irish industries and railways. His keen Catholicism is evident from his authorship of pamphlets on the lives of Pope Pius X and Benedict XV plus the fact that he was one of the founders of the Catholic Truth Society. R.J. Kelly is also credited with several published volumes of Irish patriotic verse, a history of the Aran Islands, plus works on the lives of Charles Kickham and Saint Jarlath.[39]

Kelly was an unwavering supporter of constitutional nationalism. As a very young man he reported on the first meeting of the Land League at Irishtown, County Mayo, in 1879. He was a loyal supporter of Parnell, who was described as a 'trusted friend' in Kelly's obituary. Subsequently, Kelly became an equally loyal supporter of John Redmond, which was reflected significantly in the editorials of the *Tuam Herald*. The 150th anniversary issue of the paper states that 'one thing R.J. Kelly was not was a Sinn Féiner' and this is entirely accurate.[40] The same could certainly not be said of John Burke, Kelly's long-time manager at the *Herald*, and ultimately his successor as editor–proprietor.

It is one of the curious characteristics of the Irish provincial press of this era that the two competing strands of Irish nationalism often encountered each other in the editorial ranks of local newspapers. In complete contrast to R.J. Kelly, John Burke was not only a committed republican but was elected for Sinn Féin as a Town Commissioner in

---

[39] *Tuam Herald: 150th anniversary supplement* (21 May 1988); *Tuam Herald*, 5 Sept. 1931; *Irish Times*, 12 Sept. 1931. R.J. Kelly's obituary also credits him with a variety of other roles. From 1903 to 1911, he acted as an assistant legal land commissioner and for a time he was a Crown Prosecutor for County Sligo and a magistrate for County Galway. He was a fellow of the Royal Society of Antiquaries. Additionally, Kelly was known in commercial circles as a director of the National Bank. He also acted as a consular representative of Romania and Estonia and was additionally the Free State consul for the Republic of Bolivia.

[40] *Tuam Herald: 150th anniversary supplement* (21 May 1988).

1907. His journalistic career began at the *Tuam News* and he also worked for the *Mayo News* before spending some time in the USA where he worked at the *Irish World* in New York. He joined the *Tuam Herald* in 1901 and became manager a few years later. Unfortunately, little is known of the potentially fascinating relationship between Burke and Kelly though it is known that the latter principally resided in Dublin and sent his editorials by train for publication. However, Burke is credited with penning an appreciation of Kelly upon the death of the latter in 1931 in which he described him as 'always a true and staunch friend'.[41]

Burke displayed characteristics similar to so many members of the provincial press of that era in that he was a devout Catholic and a keen supporter of both the Gaelic League and the GAA. His Sinn Féin activities led to his house being raided on several occasions during the War of Independence. Burke opposed the Anglo-Irish Treaty of 1921 and his support for Eamon de Valera led to his involvement in the organisation of the fledgling Fianna Fáil party. Subsequently, he served as chairman of the local Fianna Fáil Cumann for several years, and he continued in his role as a Town Commissioner (as a Fianna Fáil representative in later years) until his retirement from public life due to ill health in 1943.[42]

Thirteen years earlier, Burke had become editor–proprietor of the *Tuam Herald*. In 1930, R.J. Kelly, whose main interest by this time was his legal career in Dublin, indicated his desire to sell the paper. It was initially sold to a Dunmore man, Gabriel Diskin, who attempted to run the paper as a going concern but gave up the idea within a matter of weeks. It was quickly sold on to Burke who had borrowed a few hundred pounds from relatives to pursue the venture.[43] The *Herald* has remained in the ownership of the Burke family well into the second decade of the twenty-first century meaning that despite being one of the oldest of the Irish provincial titles it has remarkably remained in the ownership of only two families during its entire existence.

[41] Ibid.; *Tuam Herald*, 12 Sept. 1931. The same appreciation also noted the many people 'who got their start in life through the kindness of the late Mr Kelly' and where 'possible to do a good turn he [Kelly] never failed to do his utmost'.

[42] *Tuam Herald*, 13 Feb. 1954.

[43] *Tuam Herald*, 16 May 1987; 10 May 2012.

Editorial comment, 1914–1921

In somewhat of a contrast to most of its provincial counterparts the *Tuam Herald* comprised only four pages, usually divided into six columns, and this remained constant for almost the entirety of the 1914–21 period. It bore the appended title of *Great Western Advertiser* and its front page was normally devoted to advertisements. Similar to the *Midland Tribune*, cinema listings were a developing feature of the paper. The heavy concentration on agriculture was clearly visible in the *Tuam Herald* and was typified by advertisements for Goulding's Manures, Dickson's Seeds, and the intriguing Oaks' Pig Powder. Advertisements for alcoholic drinks such as Power's Apple Cider, O'Connell's Ale, and D'Arcy's Stout also appeared regularly. Apart from this, the *Herald* contained a roughly similar proportion of advertisements for local retailers and services as other provincial papers, while advertisements for shipping companies (Cunard, American Line, Anchor Line) was something it had in common with other newspapers.

The only indication of the *Tuam Herald* having any contact with the Office of the Press Censor dates from November 1917. Following the publication of an article entitled 'The Convention Crisis', the paper was warned that any reporting of the proceedings of the Irish Convention 'are most undesirable and infringe the Defence of the Realm Regulations'.[44] Apart from this there is no further record of the paper incurring the displeasure of the Press Censor or provoking the anger of the British authorities. This is hardly surprising given the political sympathies of its editor–proprietor, R.J. Kelly, who remained steadfast in his support for the Irish Parliamentary Party to the very end. However, this absence of any conflict with the British authorities renders the paper's editorial commentary no less worthy of examination and certainly no less interesting. Indeed, it is not unreasonable to suggest that the lead articles in the *Tuam Herald* between 1914 and 1921 represent an example of a nationalist viewpoint that much of the historiography of the period has overlooked. Nonetheless, at the start of this period, the *Herald*'s editorials indicated little that distinguished its nationalism as substantially different from that of the four Leinster titles considered in the previous chapter.

Such a trait was particularly evident in the *Tuam Herald*'s attitude towards the Ulster Unionists. The paper expressed its utter disdain at how 'the Covenanters are allowed to organise, drill, and march, to possess arms, to act as if they were part of the armed forces of the Crown' and

[44] Press Censorship Records 1916–1919, 3/722/23-152, 29 Nov. 1917.

how 'their leaders preach the doctrines of revolt' and 'can with impunity resort to any extreme of lawlessness'.[45] The Larne gun-running in April 1914 was described as 'the most audacious series of illegal acts ever perpetrated in a country which was not in a state of war'.[46] For the greater part of 1914, the *Tuam Herald* differed little from the *Kilkenny People* or the *Enniscorthy Echo* in that it was unambiguous in expressing its confidence in John Redmond as the leader of nationalist Ireland. Redmond was considered the 'trusted leader of the Irish people' and his 'statesmanlike instinct' was lauded when he pledged Irish support for the British war effort.[47] It was the *Herald*'s attitude to World War I, and the attendant issues it provoked, however, that began to cast the paper in a different light from other nationalist titles.

Without any equivocation the *Herald* considered Ireland a part of the Empire and accordingly had a contribution to make in fighting 'German barbarism'.[48] Consequently, the paper wholeheartedly promoted enlistment in the British Army and in January 1915 it proudly declared that Ireland was 'contributing more men to the fighting line than is England in proportion to its teeming population of capable adults'.[49] Recruitment advertisements appeared regularly during the first half of 1915 and the appeal of the Lord Lieutenant in November 1915 for 50,000 new recruits was regarded as a 'reasonable demand'.[50] This 'reasonable demand' also included the publication, in December 1915, of a letter from the Lord Lieutenant appealing for recruits. The editorial of the same date expressed the hope that the 'appeal of the Lord Lieutenant to the manhood of Ireland would not fall upon deaf and unreceptive ears but, as far as possible, meet with a response which the merits of the case and the necessities of the situation require'.[51] Almost a year later, the paper cited the Easter Rising as the reason 'Ireland has failed in its duty' to supply recruits and was thus 'deliberately guilty of a dishonourable and discreditable breach of agreement'.[52]

---

45   *Tuam Herald*, 24 Jan. 1914.
46   *Tuam Herald*, 2 May 1914.
47   *Tuam Herald*, 11 Apr., 10 Oct. 1914.
48   *Tuam Herald*, 12 Sept., 3 Oct. 1914.
49   *Tuam Herald*, 16 Jan. 1915.
50   *Tuam Herald*, 6 Nov. 1915. This appeal formed part of the campaign that included the gathering of newspaper editors at the Viceregal Lodge referred to at the start of the last chapter.
51   *Tuam Herald*, 4 Dec. 1915.
52   *Tuam Herald*, 7 Oct. 1916.

Even though the *Herald* was an unstinting advocate of recruitment it vehemently opposed any suggestion of conscription. As early as January 1916, it sternly warned that 'coercion, in any shape or for any purpose never did succeed in Ireland' and that nothing was more likely to hinder recruitment in Ireland than a 'foolish attempt to push it or rush it and to force it unwillingly upon the Irish people'.[53] The introduction of conscription over two years later drew an uncharacteristically harsh reaction from this relatively staid organ that possibly indicates the depth of resentment to the move amongst a variety of political persuasions. The *Herald* unambiguously censured the decision that the government sought to enforce 'against the wishes of the representatives of the Irish people' while 'a solemn undertaking, four years ago, entered into to give this country self-government, is still in suspense'.[54] It was a decision, the paper feared, that would rouse 'young hot blood' and lead to 'loss of life and general disorder'.[55]

By this stage the ultimately irreversible shift to the Sinn Féin party was well established. Nonetheless, the party had come under the radar of the *Tuam Herald* well before this shift had commenced. The enmity that R.J. Kelly held for the party was quite apparent in several editorials leading up to Easter 1916. During April 1916, Sinn Féin and their advocates were variously referred to as 'degenerates amongst us who affect to be democrats', 'young men of misguided views and imperfect knowledge', 'every form of crank and discontent', while those supporting the party from abroad were 'under the banner of the German War Lord'.[56] In the aftermath of the rebellion, the *Herald*, in line with much of the broader print media, had little hesitation in labelling it the '"Sinn Féin" rebellion' ('the lunacy of the Sinn Féiners') but even went a little further as this editorial from May 1916 illustrates:

> The Germans it is clear, organised this insurrection. They cleverly financed it in town and country, their agents in America, aided by some deluded Irishmen there, were active in bringing it to a head. Their complicity in it is undeniable and will we trust be fully and quickly exposed. Their ships with munitions, money and officers were on the high seas on Easter Monday, prepared to come to Ireland's aid, and forty-eight hours before the actual rising at home it was suspiciously announced in New York as about to take place.

[53]   *Tuam Herald*, 15 Jan. 1916.
[54]   *Tuam Herald*, 13 Apr. 1918.
[55]   *Tuam Herald*, 20 Apr. 1918.
[56]   *Tuam Herald*, 1 Apr., 15 Apr. 1916.

The same editorial claimed that it did not wish to 'disparage the dead' but categorically stated that 'the ring leaders have properly been executed'.[57] The paper continued the theme of alleged German collaboration in a later editorial when it was asserted that the 'Irish revolt formed part of Germany's 'low game of treachery, trickery and intrigue' and that 'Ireland was to be its playground now as were Turkey, Bulgaria, South Africa, and the United States'.[58] With the benefit of hindsight, it is quite easy to dismiss such statements as absurdities and even an insult to the subsequently lionised men of 1916. Yet such editorial commentary can serve a valuable historical purpose in that it may well convey the dismay and anger at the rebellion felt among certain sections of the population and also the extent to which Germany was believed to be the manifestation of supreme evil.

The distrust of Sinn Féin and its policies notwithstanding, the *Herald* clearly realised that a new force in nationalist politics was emerging. The initial Sinn Féin by-election victories in early 1917 in North Roscommon and South Longford did not merit editorial comment but the Irish Parliamentary Party was defended as not being 'a perfect organisation' but could 'boast of achievement and it can claim success' while 'other roads leads certainly to dissension and disaster'.[59] The East Clare by-election of July 1917, however, did not escape editorial attention. Victory for Sinn Féin, it was claimed, would mean 'a wrench' for constitutional politics 'which may be disastrous'.[60] Yet Eamon de Valera's victory was attributed to a county that was never 'very constitutionally inclined' plus 'the lawless spirit that is abroad' combined with 'the unsettledness of the public mind'.[61]

The inexorable rise of Sinn Féin provoked a response from the *Tuam Herald* that was somewhat tinged with desperation. Its defence of the Irish Parliamentary Party appeared to be constantly qualified by an acceptance that the party had erred in the past but was still the political organisation best equipped to deliver on nationalist aspirations. Also, throughout 1917, considerable editorial attention was devoted to the ill-fated Irish Convention. Yet its editorial comment prior to the East Cavan by-election of June 1918 (won by Arthur Griffith) was perhaps the best indication of how out of touch the paper was with the broader electorate. The lead

---

[57]   *Tuam Herald*, 13 May 1916.

[58]   *Tuam Herald*, 20 May 1916.

[59]   *Tuam Herald*, 10 Mar. 1917. Sinn Féin were not actually mentioned in this editorial so the reference seems to have been implied.

[60]   *Tuam Herald*, 7 July 1917.

[61]   *Tuam Herald*, 14 July 1917.

article referred to Griffith's pamphlet, 'The Resurrection of Hungary' (already out of print as the paper acknowledged) and cited events from Austria and Hungary over half a century previously.[62] Its argument may well have been historically sound but in the world of practical politics a lesson in European history was hardly likely to have much effect on voters in East Cavan. Griffith's victory and the onward march of Sinn Féin did not deter the *Tuam Herald* in the prelude to the general election of December 1918. Sinn Féin's abstentionist policy was described as 'politically suicidal and patriotically disastrous' resulting in the country 'rushing madly along a certain road to political ruin'.[63]

Sinn Féin's resounding victory brought about a considerable alteration in the *Herald*'s opinion of that party. The first post-election editorial described it as 'a compact, homogeneous body of active and intelligent young men, sincerely honest and unpurchasably patriotic, who may yet become the means and be the medium of bringing to this country the fullest measure of self-government'.[64] This apparent volte-face was certainly not the signal for the *Tuam Herald* to become a pro-Sinn Féin organ but editorial criticism of the party all but disappeared from this time onwards.[65] The principal editorial concern ultimately became the increasingly violent situation prevailing in the country. The paper was particularly concerned with the plight of the RIC which it described as 'the finest police force in the world' and whose members were 'true Irishmen in every sense of the word'.[66] Attacks on RIC barracks were labelled 'ruffian raids' and 'an onslaught on the ordinary machinery of law and order' that were 'a hindrance to the realisation of the aspirations of the true nationalist'.[67] Significantly, though, such attacks were not ascribed to any specific movement and the haste with which the events of Easter 1916 were attributed to Sinn Féin was markedly absent. Indeed, as hostilities intensified during 1920, the *Herald* was careful not to criticise

[62] *Tuam Herald*, 11 May 1918.

[63] *Tuam Herald*, 12 Oct. 1918; 7 Dec. 1918.

[64] *Tuam Herald*, 4 Jan. 1919.

[65] *Tuam Herald*, 7 June 1919. The only editorial that could possibly be interpreted as criticism of Sinn Féin appeared in June 1919 in reference to the Peace Conference when the folly of what would be regarded 'as a hostile attack on England' by the other three Allied Powers – France, Italy, and the USA – was highlighted, However, the tone of the editorial was certainly not condemnatory and Sinn Féin were not specifically mentioned.

[66] *Tuam Herald*, 20 Sept. 1919.

[67] *Tuam Herald*, 17 Jan. 1920.

either warring party. Even the police reprisals in Tuam itself in July 1920 met with quite a restrained editorial response. It was simply stated that some of the police had 'committed great havoc' but only after being 'goaded by the dastardly murder of their comrades on the way home to Dunmore'.[68]

From around this time until the end of the War of Independence, the predominant tone in the editorials of the *Tuam Herald* was one of despair and dismay. Following the events in Tuam an almost equal sense of repulsion was expressed at similar occurrences in Templemore, Galway, Balbriggan, and Clifden.[69] Condemnation of such violence was rarely punctuated by criticism of either side in the conflict. The only notable exception came in April 1921 when the British Government was severely criticised for its 'perverse persistency in the wrong course they are taking'.[70] Yet the *Herald* was rather unique amongst local newspapers upon the calling of a truce in July 1921 when it applauded the British Prime Minister's act of 'characteristic boldness' and 'real statesmanship'.[71] Similar praise for David Lloyd George was one of the most notable features of its reaction to the Anglo-Irish Treaty. In the first editorial following the conclusion of the talks in London the paper stressed the need to acknowledge Lloyd George's contribution, without whom 'there would never have been an Irish settlement'.[72]

Reaction to the Treaty was almost as enthusiastic as the response to the ending of the military conflict five months earlier.[73] The work of the Irish negotiators was warmly praised but special mention was reserved for the role of Arthur Griffith.[74] No person stood 'higher in the public

---

[68] *Tuam Herald*, 24 July 1920; *Daily News*, 21 July 1920. These reprisals received significant coverage in the British broadsheet press as did many of the actions of the Crown forces during 1920. The highly restrained nature of the *Herald*'s editorial response is perhaps best illustrated by contrasting it with the report in the *Daily News* of London that described Tuam as resembling 'some of the ruined Belgian and French town' following the police actions.

[69] *Tuam Herald*, 21 Aug., 25 Sept. 1920; 26 Mar. 1921.

[70] *Tuam Herald*, 2 Apr. 1921.

[71] *Tuam Herald*, 2 July 1921.

[72] *Tuam Herald*, 10 Dec. 1921.

[73] *Tuam Herald*, 23 July, 10 Dec. 1921. In addition to being described as 'eminently creditable to all parties concerned', the ending of hostilities in July 1921 was considered 'beyond all praise' and 'simply marvellous'. The news of agreement being reached in London in early December constituted 'glad tidings of a great joy' at which the nation 'first exalted itself and gave thanks to God'.

[74] *Tuam Herald*, 22 Oct., 10 Dec. 1921. Even before the talks in London had

esteem' than the Sinn Féin founder who 'defended its policy in the dark days' and 'who never swerved from devotion to the cause'.[75] This was a far cry from only three years earlier when such a cause was labelled 'fatuous folly' and a 'suicidal course'.[76] The wholehearted approval of the Treaty was matched by an equal lack of tolerance for the emerging opposition. The agreement 'must be accepted in its entirety', the final editorial of 1921 claimed, and those who took a different view 'must be prepared to take the consequences of our rejection'.[77]

Conclusion

In common with newspapers such as the *Dundalk Democrat* and *Enniscorthy Echo* the curious situation existed at the *Tuam Herald* that the two conflicting strands of Irish nationalism were represented within its senior ranks. Editor–proprietor R.J. Kelly was a staunch supporter of the Irish Parliamentary Party while manager John Burke was an elected Sinn Féin representative from a very early stage. Ultimately, it was, of course, Kelly who decided editorial policy, which, until the general election of 1918, was notable for the vehemence of its opposition to Sinn Féin. This opposition subsided almost completely thereafter, and indeed by late 1921 the paper was highly positive in its regard for the party. This belated endorsement of the Sinn Féin movement could possibly be regarded as a cynical move that was simply following public opinion in an attempt to avoid being left out in the cold amongst nationalist titles. Alternatively, it could be interpreted as an honest acknowledgement of an overly hasty judgement of a political movement still in its infancy. The actual reason for such a change was most likely a combination of both. Regardless of what prompted the shift, by the time of the Anglo-Irish Treaty the *Tuam Herald*, like so many other nationalist titles, was quite supportive of Sinn Féin. Its journey to such a point simply started considerably later and was not disrupted by unwanted attention from either side in the conflict.

ended, confidence was expressed in the Sinn Féin representatives who, it was asserted, had handled the country's affairs 'in many respects with extraordinary skill and success'. Upon the conclusion of negotiations the Irish plenipotentiaries were lauded for how 'they acquitted themselves like true statesmen and born diplomatists' and 'how ably and skilfully they did their work'.

[75] *Tuam Herald*, 24 Dec. 1921.
[76] *Tuam Herald*, 5 Oct. 1918.
[77] *Tuam Herald*, 31 Dec. 1921.

Roscommon Herald

In the previous chapter the almost inextricable nature of the link between some editors and their specific newspaper was highlighted. Possibly no one epitomised this aspect of the Irish provincial press more than Jasper Tully of the *Roscommon Herald*. Tully's personality simply towered over the Boyle-based publication to such an extent that the paper's origins and even its editorial commentary appear as almost of secondary importance. This is perhaps understandable for a man who controlled the paper from 1881 until 1938, was imprisoned in Kilmainham Gaol at the same time as Charles Stewart Parnell, served as MP for South Leitrim from 1892 to 1906, stood for election (unsuccessfully) against Count Plunkett of Sinn Féin in the North Roscommon by-election of 1917, suffered an attempt on his life in 1927, and was, for a considerable period, according to Michael Wheatley, 'an influential figure in the region's politics' but also 'obsessive, quarrelsome, and litigious'.[78]

Jasper Tully

Jasper Tully was born in 1858, a year prior to the birth of the *Roscommon Herald*. It was launched as a 'Liberal weekly newspaper' by his father George, who was also the paper's first editor. George Tully died at quite a young age, leaving his wife Honoria to run the paper until her two sons, Jasper and George (junior), came of age. Having spent a few years in America, Jasper returned to join the staff of the *Herald* and took over as managing-director upon the death of his mother, while his brother George served as a director until his death in 1921.[79] Jasper Tully married Mary Ellen Monson, whose family owned the Royal Hotel in Boyle, but the union was far from a happy one. Both were of such a single-minded and strong-willed temperament that they had a very acrimonious relationship and consequently lived apart for years.[80] The aggravated nature of Tully's marital relationship was mirrored during his journalistic and political career.

---

[78]   Oram, *The newspaper book*, p. 164; Wheatley, *Nationalism and the Irish Party*, p. 99.
[79]   *Roscommon Herald: Centenary Supplement* (5 Dec. 1959).
[80]   Ibid.; Oram, *The newspaper book*, pp 165–6. The centenary issue of the *Roscommon Herald* stated that the couple lived their separate lives for years 'until frayed tempers cooled, and a reconciliation took place which lasted until her death'. Oram notes more bluntly that 'after his wife's death, Tully used to readdress letters to her with the legend "not known at this address – try Hell"'.

Despite his membership of the Irish Parliamentary Party and election as an MP Tully's relationship with the party was fraught to say the least. He was unreservedly anti-Parnellite but continued to be at the centre of much internal dissension even after the party reunited under John Redmond in 1900.[81] Tully's combative personality and penchant for controversy were hardly conducive to a unified and disciplined party. Even Tully's obituary acknowledged that he was the '*enfant terrible*' of the Irish Parliamentary Party and that his retirement from the party in 1904 was greeted with much relief.[82] Thereafter, Tully became 'an unremitting enemy of the Irish Party' and this was certainly evident in his editorials during the period covered by this study.[83] His abrasive nature resulted in his inheritance of 'the family dislike of the Haydens', a prominent nationalist family in the region that included J.P. Hayden of the *Westmeath Examiner* and his brothers Luke and Joseph. All three brothers in turn were proprietors of the *Roscommon Messenger*. The origins of this family feud are not entirely clear though Wheatley describes it as 'bitter and protracted' and it lasted from the early 1880s until Tully's death in 1938.[84]

The difficult and obstinate nature of Tully's character is clearly decipherable from the recollection of those who worked with him. Cahir Healy, later a director of the *Irish News* and a nationalist member of the Northern Ireland parliament, worked as a reporter at the *Roscommon Herald* around the turn of the twentieth century. Healy admitted that 'we had not a few rows in the office arising out of his impetuosity and his inability to bear even the wise gladly'. According to Healy, 'Jasper liked or disliked people – there was no middle way with him'. Martin F. Coffey, who worked at the paper from the early 1920s until 1936, described the

---

[81] Callanan, *The Parnell split*, p. 162; Wheatley, *Nationalism and the Irish Party*, pp 99–104. Callanan describes the denigration of 'Parnell's physical aspect and demeanour' in 'Jasper Tully's fiercely anti- Parnellite *Roscommon Herald*'. Wheatley outlines Tully's numerous clashes and controversies including a court case to overturn local election results, allegations that he provided information 'on the grazier connections' of senior officials of the United Irish League (UIL) to Dublin Castle, prosecution 'on charges of publishing incitements to boycott', and attacks on the profligacy of Roscommon County Council.

[82] *Roscommon Herald: Centenary Supplement* (5 Dec. 1959). A year previously Tully had been the cause of much embarrassment when he moved the writ for a by-election in Cork against the wishes of the party.

[83] Wheatley, *Nationalism and the Irish Party*, p. 15.

[84] Ibid., pp. 15, 99. The feud may have been further fuelled by both families taking different sides during the Parnell split.

'absolute ruthlessness' of Tully's 'attitude towards those he deemed his enemies'. Coffey also noted the 'extraordinary Jekyll and Hyde-like traits in his character' with little evidence of a sense of humour.[85]

Coffey's first encounter with Tully was as an election worker with Sinn Féin during the North Roscommon by-election campaign in early 1917 and says much about Tully's impulsive nature. Coffey was a junior member of a Sinn Féin delegation that visited Tully seeking the paper's support for the candidacy of Count Plunkett. According to Coffey the delegation was received 'most cordially' and Tully 'promised the co-operation of the *Herald*' only then casually to announce 'that, of course, he would be a candidate himself'.[86] Tully may well have found the temptation to run against the other two candidates, whom he personally disliked, simply too much to resist. He had dismissed Plunkett as 'an amiable old Whig' while the Irish Parliamentary candidate was 'his old Boyle enemy T.J. Devine', who had previously been a target of Tully's litigiousness.[87] Whatever his motivation for standing for election it was a hasty and ill-advised decision. There were only eleven days remaining prior to polling day and he appeared to have no proper campaign in place. He did not undertake any real canvas of the constituency, rarely appeared on election platforms, and seemed to be relying solely on his reputation.[88] All these factors ultimately told on him as he finished a poor third and Count Plunkett won Sinn Féin's first parliamentary seat.[89]

This marked Tully's final attempt for election to public office.[90] A few years before his death he appointed Thomas J. McDermott to succeed him as editor. McDermott had been with the *Roscommon Herald* since 1913 having previously worked at the *Western Nationalist*.[91] Despite Tully's rather unique personality there were a number of aspects to his career that

85 *Roscommon Herald: Centenary Supplement* (5 Dec. 1959).

86 Ibid.

87 Wheatley, *Nationalism and the Irish Party*, p. 113; *Roscommon Herald*, 27 Jan. 1917. Tully had indicated that he 'would always stand down in favour of a real Sinn Féiner such as Eoin MacNeill'. In 1905, Devine had been prevented from standing for the County Council following a court action taken by Tully.

88 Shane Reynolds, 'Fr Michael O'Flanagan and the North Roscommon by-election of 1917: sowing the seeds of republican constitutionalism' (MA thesis, St Patricks College, 2010), pp 41–2.

89 Cyril Mattimoe, *North Roscommon: its people and past* (Boyle, 1992), pp 190–1.

90 Wheatley, *Nationalism and the Irish Party*, p. 99. In 1905, Tully became a county councillor after bringing a court challenge to the result of an election he had narrowly lost. However, he failed to be re-elected three years later.

91 *Roscommon Herald*, 23 Dec. 1939.

closely resembled those of other editor–proprietors of his day. In common with James Daly of the *Connaught Telegraph* his early journalistic career was noted for his involvement in land agitation and he endured a prison sentence for his involvement as had William Hastings of the *Western News*.[92] He also served as a nationalist MP at Westminster as did P.A. McHugh of the *Sligo Champion*, J.P. Farrell of the *Longford Leader*, J.L. Carew of the *Leinster Leader*, and J.P. Hayden of the *Westmeath Examiner*. Notably, Tully was also an enthusiastic supporter of the GAA. In addition to lending the paper's support to the nascent body he also served as chairman of Roscommon County Board.[93] Nonetheless, with the possible exception of E.T. Keane of the *Kilkenny People* (coincidentally, a close friend of Tully), there were few editors of such an individualistic nature as Jasper Tully.[94] With such a character penning the leading articles the editorials of the *Roscommon Herald* could hardly fail to prove compelling reading.

Editorial comment, 1914–1921

Unlike many of its provincial peers the *Roscommon Herald* mostly remained at a constant eight pages between 1914 and 1921. Unusually, it was normally divided into ten columns per page which was quite a deviation from the normal standard in addition to being a strain on the eyesight of its readers. Nonetheless, the number of columns was reduced at certain times during these years. The appended title of *Leitrim, Longford, Sligo, and Mayo News* may well have assisted the paper in securing advertising not only from businesses in its base of Boyle but also in towns such as Sligo, Carrick-on-Shannon, and Longford. The *Roscommon Herald* differed from most other provincial papers at the time in displaying a minimal number of advertisements for alcohol- and tobacco-related products. Agriculture, however, featured even more prominently in its advertising sections. This was illustrated by a high frequency of advertisements for items such as seeds, fertilisers, harrows, tractors, drills, harvesting machinery, animal medications and vaccinations, and even shotgun cartridges. Amongst the other items to appear regularly in the same sections were Raleigh Bicycles,

---

[92] Mattimoe, *North Roscommon*, p. 177. Mattimoe notes that when Tully was imprisoned in Kilmainham in 1881 with Parnell he 'was given a great send-off from Boyle' where 'a large crowd assembled at the station'. He was also given 'a tumultuous reception' on his release.

[93] M. O'Callaghan, 'The GAA in County Roscommon' in Martin F. Coffey (ed.), *Roscommon, past and present* (Dublin, 1961), p. 87.

[94] *Roscommon Herald: Centenary Supplement* (5 Dec. 1959).

Paisley Flour, Dixon's Soap, Laurence's Hair Dye, Rathborne's Irish-made Altar Candles, and Veno's Lightning Cough Cure.

With a personality as combative as Tully at the helm, the *Roscommon Herald* would have seemed destined for clashes with the authorities. Yet this was only the case to quite a limited extent during the 1914–21 period. In October 1914, an RIC report noted that 'the tone of the provincial press is satisfactory' except for the *Roscommon Herald*, amongst others.[95] Apart from this rather innocuous observation, there is little evidence of the paper attracting further attention from the authorities. It does seem, however, that the paper was contacted by the Press Censor in November 1917 with regard to the publication of a report of a local Sinn Féin meeting. In response, Tully appeared to try to shift responsibility elsewhere, explaining that the item was taken from the *Anglo-Celt*, and adding that he 'did not imagine' that the printers of the *Anglo-Celt*, 'who are Cahill & Co. of Dublin', would risk breaching the censorship regulations.[96] Despite the minimal evidence of any serious clash with the authorities both Hugh Oram and the paper's centenary issue claim that Tully was visited by Crown forces at some stage during the War of Independence and warned to 'tone down his comments about the Black and Tan atrocities'. According to Oram, the soldiers 'received such a tongue lashing from Tully that they fled'. The paper's centenary edition claimed that Tully 'informed them of his firm intention to write to their superiors in Dublin'.[97] The alleged incident seems somewhat far-fetched or perhaps the stuff of urban legend considering that neither press censorship reports nor police reports from the time indicate any matters of contention with the *Roscommon Herald*. Indeed, police reports for County Roscommon during the War of Independence single out the *Irish Independent* and the *Freeman's Journal* as being 'the chief sources of sedition and disaffection' in the county and make no mention whatever of the *Roscommon Herald*.[98]

[95] Inspector General's and County Inspectors' monthly confidential reports, Oct. 1914, CO904/94/414.

[96] Press Censorship Records 1916–1919, 3/722/23-147, 22 Nov. 1917.

[97] Oram, *The newspaper book*, p. 165; *Roscommon Herald: Centenary Supplement* (5 Dec. 1959). The centenary supplement also claimed that Tully told Crown forces that he would write 'to Lloyd George, then British Prime Minister, and a personal friend of Mr Tully's', which seems unlikely to say the least given the paper's comments regarding the British Prime Minister during the War of Independence.

[98] Inspector General's and County Inspectors' monthly confidential reports, July 1920, CO904/112-284; June 1921, CO904/115-719.

Regardless of the question marks over Tully's encounters with the Crown forces there is still an abundance of material within the pages of his paper to justify detailed historical scrutiny. The *Roscommon Herald* was rather unique within the Irish provincial press in that it featured photographs, cartoons (frequently caricatures), sketches, maps, and diagrams to a much greater extent than most other local newspapers. Quite often the cartoons ridiculed those who had incurred Tully's wrath while sketches and maps regularly featured in the paper's coverage of World War I. Unlike the *Tuam Herald*, it was non-committal about Ireland's contribution to the British war effort but carried recruitment advertisements throughout 1915.[99] Once the war had started, the editorials of the *Roscommon Herald* dealt predominantly with its progress and tended to be quite lengthy. The concentration on military developments most likely stemmed from Tully's interest in Napoleon. Cahir Healy recalled the numerous books about Napoleon owned by Tully and described him as 'a lover of the little Corsican'.[100] The editorial emphasis on the prosecution of the war did not waver until the armistice in 1918. However, the obvious fascination with the war seemed to bring out one of the more distasteful elements in Tully's character.

Jasper Tully was never one to have any reluctance in denigrating individuals, but the contemptuous dismissal of entire countries or religions was quite a different matter. This most unappealing attribute was clearly evident upon the outbreak of war in 1914 when the *Roscommon Herald* editorial declared that 'Servia [Serbia] is one of the most contemptible nations on God's earth' and that 'Austria is right in taking vengeance on this cowardly clan'.[101] Six months later, those in the Jewish community were the target of the *Herald*'s leading article. In commenting on Romania's entry into the war as an ally of Britain it was stated that their soldiers had a 'good fighting reputation' though 'the country itself is the most Jew-ridden place in the world'.[102] Anti-Semitic traits were again evident in the months following the end of World War I. It was alleged that it was 'the Jews who are the Bolsheviks in Russia' who 'have plundered and crucified that unfortunate country'.

[99] *Roscommon Herald*, 3, 13, 20 Mar., 3, 10 Apr., 19 June, 4 Sept., 6, 13 Nov. 1915. The paper actually published more recruitment advertisements than the *Tuam Herald* during 1915, which was the year that witnessed the biggest push for recruits.

[100] *Roscommon Herald: Centenary Supplement* (5 Dec. 1959).

[101] *Roscommon Herald*, 1 Aug. 1914.

[102] *Roscommon Herald*, 30 Jan. 1915.

The same editorial stated that 'the international Jew put all his money in German investments before the war' and was now 'moving heaven and earth to save the Kaiser and to save the Germans from having to pay up'.[103] Later editorials variously asserted that 'theatrical outbreaks in Berlin and other German towns are the handiwork of German Jews'; 'international Jews' would 'free the Germans from the burden of a war indemnity'; 'the international Jew is working against old Catholic Poland'; the hands of the 'Jew Bolsheviks' were 'dripping with the blood of the Czar'; 'international finance, which is mainly Jewish, has been very kind to the Germans'; and that 'a gang of international Jews' had seized power in Russia and 'plundered all that French money'.[104]

The editorial fascination with matters beyond Ireland's shores continued after the war had ended. Leading articles throughout 1919 dealt overwhelmingly with the Peace Conference and its aftermath while similarly in 1920 and the first half of 1921 foreign affairs or British domestic politics predominated. Accordingly, Irish affairs did not garner the same editorial attention as was the case in many other provincial titles, but it does not render the *Herald*'s commentary on this period of Irish history any less fascinating. Initially, the paper mirrored the views of many other nationalist publications in expressing its dismay at the notion of partition, anger at the unhindered operation of the Larne gun-running, and its enthusiastic endorsement of the Irish Volunteers.[105] The Easter Rising provoked an editorial response that resembled that of the *Tuam Herald* in that it articulated some decidedly far-fetched notions:

> It was an act of lunatics spurred on by clever intriguers paid by Germany. Very few people have seen gold during the last twelve months, yet in a village in Galway wrecked by shell fire, £600 in sovereigns was found by the police in a modest house, and in the pockets of Sinn Féiners sums such as £100 and £30 were found in gold. In other parts of the country there have been instances of newly rich people, whose new-found wealth could not be easily accounted for. It paid Germany to make this expenditure to produce this disaster for Ireland at this moment, and little the Kaiser and his agents reck the red ruin they have brought on Dublin and on thousands of their dupes.

[103]　*Roscommon Herald*, 4 Jan. 1919.
[104]　*Roscommon Herald*, 18 Jan., 25 Jan., 1 Feb., 6 Sept., 15 Nov. 1919.
[105]　*Roscommon Herald*, 14 Mar., 2 May, 6 June 1914.

Nonetheless, like several other provincial organs, the paper identified the seeds of the rebellion being sown when 'the Asquith Cabinet allowed the Carson armed volunteers to be formed in Ulster'. However, the overall attitude to the Easter Rising was condemnatory, the leaders being 'men blinded by the lust of conquest' who wished to pursue 'the alliance with Germany'.[106]

Although the rebellion and its leaders were roundly vilified it may well have sparked a realisation that the days of the Irish Parliamentary Party were numbered. Some months later the paper castigated the Irish representatives who 'sold themselves to the Government and did the Government's fetch and carry work for ten years'.[107] It cannot be categorically stated that this sense of the Irish Parliamentary Party's impending demise was a factor that motivated Tully to stand in the North Roscommon by-election. His motivations notwithstanding, the editorial columns of the *Roscommon Herald* were not employed to promote his election campaign and the aforementioned dismissal of Count Plunkett appeared elsewhere in the paper. The subsequent Sinn Féin victory was interpreted as the first death-blow to the Irish Parliamentary Party resulting from its 'failure to win anything for Ireland in the midst of golden opportunities'.[108]

Michael Wheatley comments that following the North Roscommon by-election the *Roscommon Herald* became 'the leading campaigning paper for Sinn Féin in Counties Roscommon, Leitrim, and Longford', but this is not entirely the case from an editorial perspective.[109] The paper was certainly supportive of Sinn Féin in the next by-election in South Longford but its editorial policy was more anti-Irish Parliamentary Party than pro-Sinn Féin.[110] The ensuing Sinn Féin victory prompted the response that 'the present Irish Party no longer represents Ireland' and that 'the next general election will see the end of them'.[111] With increasing frequency during the remainder of 1917, the Irish Parliamentary Party leaders were ridiculed in front-page cartoons while John Dillon was

---

[106] *Roscommon Herald*, 6, 13 May 1916.

[107] *Roscommon Herald*, 21 Oct. 1916.

[108] *Roscommon Herald*, 10 Feb. 1917. The same editorial stated that the Irish Parliamentary Party 'must be promptly consigned to the scrap heap'.

[109] Wheatley, *Nationalism and the Irish Party*, p. 113.

[110] *Roscommon Herald*, 25 Apr. 1917. Prior to the South Longford by-election the paper carried a photograph of the Sinn Féin candidate, Joe McGuinness, under the heading 'The man for South Longford'.

[111] *Roscommon Herald*, 12 May 1917.

similarly derided on an almost weekly basis in the months leading up to the general election in December 1918. Even before the results of the poll were declared the *Herald* confidently predicted that it would 'mark the passing of a rotten and corrupt phase in Irish politics'.[112]

With the mortal blows administered to the Irish Parliamentary Party, the *Herald* then shifted its ire in the direction of Lloyd George and his government. Possibly due to concerns over official censure, criticism of the British Government was not marked by the same ferocity to which the Irish Parliamentary Party had been treated. Nonetheless, this did not prevent the paper from publishing a cartoon in September 1920 with a caption referring to the 'regime of military frightfulness instituted by Lloyd George's cabinet'.[113] Later editorials accused the British Prime Minister of having an attitude of 'brazen hypocrisy' towards Ireland and of being the 'inspirer and instigator' of the reprisals campaign.[114] In complete contrast to the *Tuam Herald*, the truce of July 1921 was greeted with extreme scepticism. According to the *Roscommon Herald*, 'no one trusts his [Lloyd George's] promises' and his 'peace trap' was 'designed to put de Valera in the wrong before the other peoples of the world'.[115]

The most remarkable aspect of the paper's coverage of the Anglo-Irish Treaty was that it reported de Valera's opposition a week before almost all other provincial papers. Following the conclusion of the negotiations in London, the first issue of the majority of such publications was on Saturday, 10 December 1921. On this date, most provincial papers published details of the agreement and their reaction to it, but the *Roscommon Herald* appeared to have had a 'scoop' in reporting de Valera's rejection. It was acknowledged that only limited information was available at that stage, but it was also conceded that 'theoretically de Valera is right'. However, the paper commented that 'Sir Thomas Moore built his famous Republic of Utopia on theory' but 'Utopia has not yet arrived on earth'.[116] This injection of political realism was an indicator of the *Herald*'s subsequent pro-Treaty stance. It was a case of

---

[112] *Roscommon Herald*, 14 Dec. 1918. Under the heading 'Imbecile leadership' the paper based its prediction on the concession of twenty-five uncontested seats to Sinn Féin and labelled John Dillon 'an utterly incompetent, worthless leader, even from the standpoint of his own narrow interests'.

[113] *Roscommon Herald*, 4 Sept. 1920.

[114] *Roscommon Herald*, 11 Sept., 2 Oct. 1920.

[115] *Roscommon Herald*, 2 July 1921.

[116] *Roscommon Herald*, 10 Dec. 1921.

'fire and sword' being 'loosed on our people' if the Treaty was rejected 'or whether peace with all it denotes will fall on our parched soil like the gentle rain from heaven'.[117] The paper also accentuated the positives of the Treaty such as the departure of Crown forces, the establishment of an Irish Army, and the operation of a Free State Parliament in Dublin.[118] Ultimately, and perhaps even with a little foresight, the *Herald* predicted that, once ratified, the country was tied to the Treaty only as 'long as it serves Ireland's material interests'.[119]

Conclusion

By December 1921, the *Roscommon Herald* did not differ from most Irish provincial newspapers in expressing its solid support for the Anglo-Irish Treaty. Yet most of the other characteristics of this paper set it apart from its counterparts within the broader print media. Its use of cartoons, caricatures, sketches, and maps was a most unique feature, as was the volume of editorial focus on the prosecution of the war, and international politics thereafter. This level of attention to affairs outside the country meant that substantially less editorial space was devoted to matters in Ireland than in many other provincial titles (though such matters were certainly not ignored in the remainder of the paper). Yet even this reduced amount of editorial coverage of Irish affairs still proved intriguing and was particularly notable initially for its stinging criticism of the Irish Parliamentary Party, and latterly for its damning indictment of Lloyd George and his government. These distinguishing traits of the *Roscommon Herald* were almost undoubtedly attributable to the personality of editor–proprietor, Jasper Tully. Frequently prone to personal animosities and given to highly prejudicial views, Tully was unarguably one of the most colourful characters in the ranks of the Irish provincial press in the late nineteenth and early twentieth centuries.

[117] *Roscommon Herald*, 17 Dec. 1921.
[118] *Roscommon Herald*, 24 Dec. 1921.
[119] *Roscommon Herald*, 31 Dec. 1921.

Mayo News

The two brothers

The history of the Irish provincial press in this period is distinguished by individual figures who were synonymous with specific publications, Jasper Tully (*Roscommon Herald*), J.P. Farrell (*Longford Leader*), and J.P. Hayden (*Westmeath Examiner*) being some of the prime examples. In the case of the *Mayo News* such a distinction falls to two people, brothers William and Patrick Joseph (P.J.) Doris. The two brothers established the paper in 1892 as an indisputably nationalist organ reflecting the ideals of its co-founders. Both had been centrally involved in the activities of the nascent Land League and were closely associated with Michael Davitt. In its early years, the paper continued to push for land reform in addition to becoming a persistent critic of British Government policies in Ireland. William Doris subsequently embarked on a political career that resulted in the brothers taking opposite sides in the emerging split within Irish nationalism in the first two decades of the twentieth century. This was the cause of an estrangement between the two brothers that was not resolved within their lifetimes.[120]

William Doris, the older of the brothers, had already gained considerable experience of print media prior to the establishment of the *Mayo News*. He began his journalistic career at the age of eighteen with James Daly's *Connaught Telegraph*. Around this time, he commenced his Land League activities that ultimately resulted in six months' imprisonment in Dundalk Gaol.[121] On his release, he moved to Dublin, joining the parliamentary staff of the *Freeman's Journal*. Subsequently, he worked on the staff of the *Leinster Leader* (Naas) and the *Nationalist and Leinster Times* (Carlow). William Doris's political career began in 1898 when he was elected to the inaugural Mayo County Council. In the same year, he was a founding member of the United Irish League (UIL), an organisation established by William O'Brien MP, to address the depressed state of agriculture and which was principally concerned with the redistribution of large estates.[122] In 1910, he stood as the Irish Parliamentary Party

---

[120]   *Mayo News: Centenary Supplement* (2 Mar. 1994).

[121]   *Connaught Telegraph*, 18 Sept. 1926. William Doris had taken part in the 'no rent manifesto' and had spent a few months 'on the run' after the warrant for his arrest had been issued.

[122]   *Connaught Telegraph*, 18 Sept. 1926; D.J. Hickey and J.E. Doherty, *A new dictionary of Irish history from 1800* (Dublin, 2005), p. 494.

candidate in West Mayo and was elected as an MP, defeating O'Brien who had held the seat as an independent nationalist. He was re-elected in 1915, but lost his seat to Joseph MacBride of Sinn Féin in the general election of 1918.[123]

Like so many other provincial editors and proprietors, P.J. Doris held a deep Catholic faith. He also shared his brother's zeal for land reform. His obituary described him as having 'devoted his life to the cause of land reform'. However, on the national question, he became a convert to the more separatist ideals of Sinn Féin. As his obituary also noted, P.J. Doris 'was a personal friend and keen follower of Arthur Griffith' and propagated Sinn Féin principles in the pages of the *Mayo News*.[124] The conflicting nationalist principles formed the basis of a lifelong rift between the two brothers. The paper's centenary issue pinpoints the split becoming permanent upon William's election as an MP and his subsequent move to London to sit in Westminster.[125] Thereafter, P.J. Doris effectively assumed sole control of the paper resulting in it ultimately being considered a pro-Sinn Féin organ. Accordingly, in the 1918 general election campaign, the *Mayo News* lent its support to Joseph MacBride of Sinn Féin in his contest against its own co-founder. However, prior to polling day, William's name was rarely mentioned, most of the criticism being reserved for the increasingly emasculated Irish Parliamentary Party.[126] William Doris died eight years later, in 1926, while P.J. passed away in 1937. The depth of the rift between them is perhaps illustrated by the fact that P.J. did not attend his older brother's funeral.[127] The estrangement was not detrimental to the survival of the *Mayo News*, however, even though P.J. Doris, like his brother before him, was imprisoned for several months in the aftermath of the Easter Rising, whilst the paper was additionally suppressed for five weeks during 1918.

---

[123] Hickey and Doherty, *A new dictionary of Irish history from 1800*; *Mayo News: Centenary Supplement* (2 Mar. 1994).

[124] *Mayo News*, 6 Mar. 1937.

[125] *Mayo News: Centenary Supplement* (2 Mar. 1994).

[126] Ibid.

[127] *Connaught Telegraph, Mayo News, Irish Times*, 18 Sept. 1926; *Irish Independent*, 22 May 1951. The death of William Doris received little attention in the *Mayo News* and simply quoted comments from the Dublin papers. P.J. Doris was not listed among the mourners, though their younger brother, John P. (J.P.), did attend. J.P. Doris was also a journalist, having begun his career with the *Mayo News*. He also worked at the *Wexford People, Nationalist and Leinster Times, Westmeath Independent*, and *Irish Independent*.

Incarceration and suppression

P.J. Doris was arrested at his home in Westport on 12 May 1916. The official report of his arrest acknowledged that he had not played any part in the rebellion but that his 'writings in the *Mayo News*' had 'encouraged preparations for the rebellion'.[128] Unlike the *Enniscorthy Echo*, however, the *Mayo News* was not forced to suspend publication as P.J. Doris was the only member of staff to be arrested. About a month after his arrest an editorial appeared in the paper that was severely critical of 'the continued imprisonment of Mr P.J. Doris, editor and proprietor of this paper, for now five weeks without any charge being made against him'. Nevertheless, the most fascinating aspect of the editorial was the description of an incident that allegedly preceded the arrest of P.J. Doris:

> The editor of this paper was arrested on Friday morning 12th May. Now it so happened that four days previously he was taking his customary morning's walk on the Mall, when the Redmondite MP for West Mayo came down the Mall by the Ulster Bank. The MP stood at the corner of the middle bridge, and the editor of this paper heard him shouting some remarks down the Mall towards him, at the same time pointing him out with his hand. There were crowds on the streets at the time, amongst them the District Inspector of Police. The MP then proceeded to the opposite side of the river in front of the chapel, and walking up and down by the river wall he continued to shout vigorously, and went on with this performance for some time. The editor of this paper discovered immediately afterwards what the substance of his remarks had been, and was astonished to learn that he had been called a Sinn Féiner who had carried on a Sinn Féin campaign.[129]

The most remarkable aspect of this report is not even the suggestion that an Irish Parliamentary Party MP was complicit in the arrest of P.J. Doris but that the 'Redmondite MP for West Mayo' was, of course, William Doris, his older brother. The same editorial claimed that P.J. Doris 'had never been a Sinn Féiner, and was not a member of any organisation of any sort or kind in the country, but had always maintained an independent point of view'.[130] Regardless of P.J. Doris's affiliation or

---

[128] Personalities (P.J. Doris), CO904/200/14-9. The same report stated that he had fallen out with his brother three years earlier and adopted a Sinn Féin policy.

[129] *Mayo News*, 17 June 1916.

[130] Ibid.

otherwise to any particular organisation he was arrested and eventually transferred to Reading Gaol. Five months later, a *Mayo News* editorial reported that, in response to a parliamentary question, Mr Flavin of the Irish Parliamentary Party had been informed that P.J. Doris was arrested for being 'reasonably suspected of aiding and abetting the recent rebellion'. In addition to utilising the opportunity to castigate the Irish Parliamentary Party for what the paper perceived as its belated concern for those arrested in the aftermath of Easter 1916, the paper also dubbed the House of Commons the 'place in which the highest citizen in the Empire can lie with impunity'.[131]

By this stage, P.J. Doris's case had been raised with the Chief Secretary's office by John Chartres, a British patent lawyer.[132] English-born Chartres had spent his early years in Ireland due to his father's position as a staff surgeon in the British Army. His involvement in Irish politics dates from 1917 when he first met Arthur Griffith and he eventually served as second secretary to the Irish treaty delegation.[133] It is not clear why Chartres took up Doris's case as he acknowledged in his correspondence with the Chief Secretary's office that he had never met nor was he acquainted with P.J. Doris, but had heard about his case on a recent visit to the West of Ireland. Chartres pointed out that Doris 'took no part in the volunteer movement and was opposed to the policy of physical force'. It was accepted that the *Mayo News* had refused to publish recruiting advertisements but that this provided no basis for his imprisonment.[134]

Following some initial correspondence, it was proposed that P.J. Doris could be released upon the provision of an undertaking to keep the peace and a bond 'in the sum of £100'.[135] It was an offer that was not appreciated by Chartres and certainly cut no ice with P.J. Doris. Chartres described it as an 'attempt to make it appear that an innocent man is in the wrong

---

[131]   *Mayo News*, 4 Nov. 1916.
[132]   Francis Costello, *The Irish revolution and its aftermath, 1916–1923: years of revolt* (Dublin, 2003), p. 247. Costello describes Chartres as 'a little-known British patent lawyer, but nonetheless someone who had proved an invaluable intelligence source to [Michael] Collins in Britain'.
[133]   Pauric J. Dempsey and Richard Hawkins, 'Chartres, John Smith' in McGuire and Quinn, *Dictionary of Irish biography*.
[134]   Personalities (P.J. Doris), CO904/200/14-22. In his correspondence, Chartres asserted that 'large numbers of persons in the West of Ireland are convinced that the imprisonment of Mr Doris is a tyrannical act for which no justification of any kind exists'.
[135]   Personalities (P.J. Doris), CO904/200/14-24.

and so to inflict further undeserved ignominy upon him'.[136] P.J. Doris, meanwhile, responding to the proposal via a letter to the Governor of Reading Gaol, stated uncompromisingly that it added 'insult to the irreparable injury which has been done me'. He was particularly irked that the requested undertaking for 'future good behaviour' implied that he had not previously been of 'good behaviour'. Doris concluded his letter by demanding that he either be charged or released.[137] P.J. Doris was eventually released in December 1916 at the same time as many others who had been interned following the Easter Rising. In the final *Mayo News* editorial of 1916, P.J. Doris thanked readers, advertisers, and contributors for their 'wholehearted support' during his 'eight months of brutal imprisonment'. The same editorial contended that 'the incidents of 1916' had, 'in great part, cleared the air' and that 'the struggle for the uplifting of Ireland will be continued until her rights to nationhood be restored to her'.[138] From around this time onwards the paper began to assume an unambiguously pro-Sinn Féin stance and within less than eight months had attracted the unwanted attention of the authorities once more.[139]

In July 1917, Lord Decies wrote to the *Mayo News* to express his concern at 'the tone of your paper lately' and warned against 'the publication of seditious matter or matter tending to promote disaffection'. P.J. Doris replied, declaring his surprise, and requested specific details of the offending items. Decies promptly responded, citing six separate articles from the previous few weeks (mainly concerned with local Sinn Féin activity) and also referred to 'the general tone' of the paper's editorials.[140] The following month Decies contacted the paper to request an explanation as to why it had published items that had not appeared in the proofs submitted to his office.[141] He again contacted the *Mayo News* in December 1917 to warn that several of its recent reports of Sinn Féin and republican gatherings contained 'matter which is in violation of the Defence of the Realm Regulations'.[142] These various warnings may well have been a contributory factor leading to the paper's suppression the following year.

---

[136] Personalities (P.J. Doris), CO904/200/14-15.
[137] Personalities (P.J. Doris), CO904/200/14-24. P.J. Doris also accused the authorities of attempting to ruin 'my paper without suppressing it directly'.
[138] *Mayo News*, 30 Dec. 1916.
[139] McGee, 'Doris, William' in McGuire and Quinn, *Dictionary of Irish biography*.
[140] Press Censorship Records 1916–1919, 3/722/14-83, 18, 19, and 23 July 1917.
[141] Press Censorship Records 1916–1919, 3/722/21-82, 18 Aug. 1917.
[142] Press Censorship Records 1916–1919, 3/722/21-82, 3 Dec. 1917.

On 1 April 1918, in execution of the appropriate warrant, police entered the premises of the *Mayo News* and seized the paper's plant and machinery and suppressed the paper. The police action resulted from the publication of a number of items in the edition of 23 March to which the Press Censor and the Dublin Castle administration took offence.[143] The offending items included an editorial that referred, among other things, to Ireland's 'opportunity to rid her of the cursed influence which has ground her down for 700 years'. Notably, the same editorial declared that this end could be achieved 'without any recourse to physical force'. One of the other articles reported, in fairly glowing terms, on a St Patrick's Day Sinn Féin parade in Westport and asserted that 'Ireland will soon have crushed its last binding reptile'. The remaining articles were severely critical of the recent behaviour of the police in Westport, accusing them of carrying out unprovoked baton charges and labelling them 'an infuriated imported police mob'.[144] In his letter to the Chief Secretary, the Press Censor, Lord Decies, described the items as 'likely to cause disaffection' and stated that 'the tone of the *Mayo News* has been bad for a long time, and has a large circulation'.[145]

Two days after the police had entered his premises, P.J. Doris travelled to Dublin in an attempt to have the suppression lifted. While waiting in Dublin Castle in the hope of securing an interview with the Under-Secretary, Doris composed a letter to him protesting at the enforced closure of his business and claiming that he was 'quite unconscious of any reason why I should be suppressed'.[146] Doris's visit to Dublin proved fruitless and he was merely advised that the action taken 'was caused by the publication in the *Mayo News* of reports and statements which were grave infringements of the Defence of the Realm regulations'.[147] However, he was not informed of which specific 'reports and statements' had infringed the regulations. Doris continued to protest at what he perceived as the injustice of his case but received little sympathy.[148] Nonetheless, he was

---

[143]   Seditious literature, censorship, publication of offensive articles, CO904/160/5.

[144]   *Mayo News*, 23 Mar. 1918.

[145]   Seditious literature, censorship, publication of offensive articles, CO904/160/5.

[146]   Seditious literature, censorship, publication of offensive articles, CO904/160/5. In the same letter Doris claimed that 'since the censorship was established the Censor has constantly sent me circulars of instruction and on all such instructions I have always acted to the letter, and he never complained that I did not do so', though it seems clear that this was not entirely correct.

[147]   Seditious literature, censorship, publication of offensive articles, CO904/160/5.

[148]   Seditious literature, censorship, publication of offensive articles, CO904/160/5.

politely advised by Decies that he should refer to the numerous circulars issued by the Office of the Press Censor for guidance as to what was permissible to publish. Decies further confirmed that he was happy to provide clarification 'if there are any specific points on which you desire information'.[149]

The *Mayo News* eventually resumed publication on 11 May 1918 though it is not entirely clear why the suppression was lifted at this particular stage. The editorial of that date stated that 'we have not been informed why we were suppressed' and that 'we resume publication with our views on Irish affairs absolutely unaltered'.[150] Although the paper was not suppressed again during this period its tribulations were not at an end. In February 1921, the Black and Tans raided the offices of the paper and occupied the house of P.J. Doris for a brief period. As a consequence, he spent some time on the run like his older brother had done some forty years before.[151] However, this did not lead to the non-publication of the *Mayo News* which continued to provide compelling editorial comment, as it had done since early 1914.

Editorial comment, 1914–1921

In the months leading up to the start of World War I, the *Mayo News* generally consisted of eight pages, divided into seven columns, though the number of pages dropped to four over the course of the succeeding years. Underneath the masthead a list of between fifty and sixty towns and villages in County Mayo appeared in which the paper claimed circulation. By 1918 this had been revised to the far more concise claim that the paper circulated 'in every town and village in Mayo'. Similar to many other titles the front page was fully taken up with advertisements though the overall proportion of advertising was noticeably less than papers such as the *Kilkenny People* and *Enniscorthy Echo*. Nonetheless, the promotion of

Doris again wrote to the Under-Secretary on 17 April 1918 claiming that he had still not been given any clear reason for the suppression of his paper.

[149] Press Censorship Records 1916–1919, 3/722/21-82, 10 May 1918.

[150] *Mayo News*, 11 May 1918. The same editorial articulated that censorship was reasonable in time of war 'to prevent the publication of matter which might be of use to "the enemy"' but that 'we are not conscious of having at any time published matter which could have been by any stretch of the imagination of use to the enemy'.

[151] *Mayo News*, 6 Mar. 1937; McGee, 'Doris, William' in McGuire and Quinn, *Dictionary of Irish biography*.

local businesses, various types of foodstuffs, and medications was just as much an attribute of the *Mayo News* as of most other provincial titles. Agricultural items such as fertilisers, seeds, sacks, and tarpaulins also appeared regularly in the paper's advertising columns. Other items to make similarly frequent appearances were a variety of flours (Summit, Spillers, Millocrat, Portia), Rudge-Whitworth Bicycles, and Golden-Spangled Cigarettes. By 1918, an increasing amount of Sinn Féin announcements plus notices of Gaelic Football matches were appearing in these columns.

One of the most striking features of the editorial comment of the *Mayo News* from the very start of this period was its clear indication that it regarded Home Rule as only a stepping stone towards full independence. As early as the first week of January 1914, it unambiguously articulated that it believed the Home Rule bill to be 'the best that can be hoped for at present' and only 'a first step – much impeded – on the road to complete and practical self-government'.[152] The paper shared the same disdain for the demands of the Ulster Unionists as most other nationalist titles in the provinces and recoiled at any notion of partition, which it considered 'an outrage to our nationhood'.[153] However, if the paper did not voice open support for Sinn Féin until after Easter 1916 (as noted in the previous section), criticism of the Irish Parliamentary Party was discernible from a much earlier stage.

Even two months prior to the outbreak of World War I and John Redmond's call to Irishmen to enlist in the British Army, the *Mayo News* dubbed the Home Rule movement 'a pawn to be used in the dirty game of British politics'.[154] If this was the regard in which the Irish Parliamentary Party was held before the outbreak of war it is scarcely surprising that the criticism intensified as the war dragged on. By the autumn of 1915, the paper was accusing the party of having 'gone on lowering the flag bit by bit until a policy of downright sycophancy has been reached'.[155] Unlike the *Tuam Herald* and *Roscommon Herald* in neighbouring Galway and Roscommon, the *Mayo News* did not carry any recruitment advertisements. P.J. Doris's obituary claimed that he

---

[152] *Mayo News*, 3 Jan. 1914.

[153] *Mayo News*, 11, 25 Apr. 1914. The paper did, however, indicate some understanding of the unionist mindset when stating that 'the belief that a parliament consisting mainly of Catholics would endeavour to injure and oppress them is very strong and deep-rooted in the mind of the average Ulster Unionist, and is not to be readily displaced'.

[154] *Mayo News*, 20 June 1914.

[155] *Mayo News*, 11 Sept. 1915.

'vigorously opposed recruitment in Ireland' as 'he doubted the sincerity of England's solicitude in the interests of "small nations", while she herself continued to oppress one of the oldest and smallest of them'.[156] An understandable consequence of such sentiments was the vilification of such a senior member of the Irish Parliamentary Party as John Dillon for calling on Irishmen to enlist in the British Army: 'Has Mr Dillon sent his son, or sons, into the firing line? If he has not done so, is it not a piece of audacious impudence on his part to call on our people to do so.'[157]

From late 1916 onwards, stinging criticism of the Irish Parliamentary Party was accompanied by the espousal of the Sinn Féin agenda. The editorial response to the Rising itself was actually rather muted, quite possibly due to the enforced absence of P.J. Doris. Nonetheless, the *Mayo News* echoed the response of many other provincial titles when it stated that 'the root and foundation of all the trouble was permitting armed forces to be formed in the north of Ireland for the open and avowed purpose of resisting Ireland's constitutional demands'.[158] Seven months later, with P.J. Doris back in the editorial chair following his imprisonment, a far more assertive view of the Rising was articulated. 'The tragedy of Easter Week', its first lead article of 1917 claimed, and 'the horrors which accompanied its suppression, the shootings, the lootings, the indiscriminate arrest and ill-treatment of innocent men' had ultimately provided 'a much needed stimulant which made the blackest incidents of 1916 blessings in disguise for our oppressed country'.[159] This reappraisal of Easter 1916 preceded a period in which support for Sinn Féin was expressed more openly and castigation of the Irish Parliamentary continued apace.

The electorate of North Roscommon, where Sinn Féin won its first by-election victory, was lauded for the 'noble blow you have struck for Irish freedom'. The same editorial presciently observed that the result 'spells the end of Redmond's misrepresentation of Irish feeling' while it also believed that it was an expression 'of the disgust which prevails in every part of Ireland with the inept and craven policy by which her so-called represent-atives have disgraced our country in the last decade'.[160] The second Sinn Féin by-election victory in South Longford in May 1917 was similarly greeted as 'a glorious victory for Ireland's freedom' and a 'magnificent triumph of pure and unselfish patriotism over the worst elements of

---

156   *Mayo News*, 6 Mar. 1937.
157   *Mayo News*, 8 Jan. 1916.
158   *Mayo News*, 13 May 1916.
159   *Mayo News*, 6 Jan. 1917.
160   *Mayo News*, 10 Feb. 1917.

political corruption and chicanery'.[161] The growing appeal of Sinn Féin to the Irish electorate was outlined in fairly concise terms in June 1917:

> Hitherto Sinn Féin was regarded as the ideal band of dreamers, and by some as a physical force movement, but gradually the efficiency of Sinn Féin as a policy is impressing itself on the popular mind and the youth of Ireland have begun to recognise in it the most powerful weapon yet devised for the attainment of Ireland's national aspirations.[162]

Editorial reaction to subsequent Sinn Féin by-election victories in East Clare, Kilkenny City, and East Cavan followed a similar pattern. However, it was Sinn Féin's only defeat in a by-election outside Ulster prior to the 1918 general election that gave rise to the most interesting editorial response. This occurred in March 1918 when Captain William Redmond won the seat for the Irish Parliamentary Party in Waterford City. The *Mayo News* promptly dubbed it a 'British victory' and suggested that any 'Irish city capable of such a choice is not worthy of the franchise which it prostitutes in such a fashion'.[163] This indictment of the Waterford electorate for exercising its democratic choice echoed the reaction of the *Meath Chronicle* which had lambasted the result as 'just what one would expect from a city whose escutcheon for seven hundred years has never been stained by any disloyalty to England'.[164]

The Waterford by-election immediately preceded the five-week suppression of the *Mayo News*. On its return from suppression in May 1918 the paper unequivocally restated its advocacy of the policy of Sinn Féin.[165] One of the defining features of such pro-Sinn Féin provincial organs was the promotion of the Irish language and in this respect the *Mayo News* was no exception. The Irish language, the paper declared, 'is a mirror and reflex of the Irish mind' that 'enshrines and preserves the religion and piety of our people' and 'is the guardian and bulwark of Ireland's nationality'.[166] Nonetheless, the paper's view of the language was not entirely romanticised as it warned that if 'we lose our language we cease to be a nation' and questioned the sincerity of those claiming to be patriots but 'make no effort to revive the language of Patrick and

[161]   *Mayo News*, 12 May 1917.
[162]   *Mayo News*, 30 June 1917.
[163]   *Mayo News*, 30 Mar. 1918.
[164]   *Meath Chronicle*, 30 Mar. 1918.
[165]   *Mayo News*, 11 May 1918.
[166]   *Mayo News*, 18 Mar. 1916.

Brigid'.[167] The rapidly changing situation that began to evolve, however, from early 1919 onwards meant that ongoing events took precedence over any discussion of the Irish language.

With the Irish Parliamentary Party no longer a threat following the general election of 1918 the *Mayo News* shifted its attention to the attainment of Sinn Féin objectives. From an early stage, however, it was suspected that US assistance could not be relied upon. President Wilson may 'be another political hypocrite of the Lloyd George type' the paper editorialised and it feared that Irish representatives would be excluded from the Paris Peace Conference.[168] When the paper's fears were realised only two months later it accused the US President of being 'struck dumb' in the face of 'the abandonment of all that was best in his historic fourteen points'.[169] Once it became clear that a hearing at the Peace Conference was most unlikely the focus of attention was shifted to the increasingly hostile situation within the country. The *Mayo News* was rather unique in that it was one of the few provincial papers outside County Tipperary to pass editorial comment on the killing of two RIC men at Soloheadbeg in January 1919. The paper compared the incident to 'the class of crime which became quite the rule in Ireland in the early eighties when Parnell and over 2,000 of the Land League leaders were locked up in Irish jails'. Responsibility for such crimes, it added, rested with 'the Executive which provokes them and which aims at destroying the influences which are a check on the extremist elements in our midst'.[170]

The depiction of the incident at Soloheadbeg as a 'crime' was indicative of the attitude of the *Mayo News* towards the use of physical force in achieving nationalist objectives. The shooting dead of Resident Magistrate J.C. Milling (while putting his clock forward to British Summer Time) at Westport in March 1919 was a further case in point.[171] The first editorial to appear following the killing had no hesitation in deeming it a 'foul crime' and a 'vile outrage' that should arouse 'the indignation of the community'.[172] Even the IRA attack at Fermoy, County Cork in September 1919, that preceded what is regarded as

---

167   *Mayo News*, 22 Apr. 1916.
168   *Mayo News*, 4 Jan. 1919.
169   *Mayo News*, 1 Mar. 1919.
170   *Mayo News*, 1 Feb. 1919.
171   Hopkinson, *The Irish War of Independence*, p. 133. Hopkinson suggests that the shooting 'was probably carried out by the "Young Turks" in the IRB and meant to pressurise senior Volunteer officers to initiate action in West Mayo'.
172   *Mayo News*, 5 Apr. 1919.

the first reprisal of the War of Independence, was strongly censured. The *Mayo News* editorialised that the success of the attack on a group of fourteen soldiers attending the Wesleyan church in the town relied 'largely on the helplessness of the military party who were arched out in full war kit without ammunition'.[173] Nevertheless, by the following year criticism of IRA activities was wholly replaced by outright castigation of the British authorities, brought about by the campaign of 'reprisals' first witnessed in the aftermath of the IRA attack at Fermoy.

The Irish Administration in Dublin Castle was initially accused of 'brutal coercion methods' but the British Government itself soon became the target of the paper's editorial outrage.[174] In September 1920, it concluded that the British Government had 'at last adopted a settled policy' in Ireland. 'That policy', it continued, 'was one of reprisal' inspired by 'Sir Hamar Greenwood's Cromwellianism'.[175] This set the editorial tone as the violence continued, with Lloyd George in particular incurring the wrath of the *Mayo News*. 'Not since 1798', it was declared, had a 'British Cabinet been so successful in sowing the seeds of hate in Ireland' until 'this vile campaign' initiated by Mr Lloyd George.[176] Given such contempt for Lloyd George and his government it was only to be expected that the initiation of peace negotiations in July 1921 was regarded with outright cynicism.

Lloyd George's offer of peace negotiations was dubiously considered as part of the 'olive branch and sword tactics' of an 'arch-political trickster' who could have no cause for complaint if the invitation was 'received with suspicion and contempt'.[177] The prospect of Sir Hamar Greenwood's inclusion on the British negotiating team provoked similar feelings of mistrust. Greenwood's 'infamies in Ireland rank him with Cromwell for brutality without any of Cromwell's redeeming characteristics', the paper bluntly stated, mirroring the sentiments of the *Kilkenny People*.[178] Yet the *Mayo News* warmly welcomed the Treaty agreement of December 1921. Its reaction may not have been as effusive as other recognised pro-Sinn Féin titles such as the *Meath Chronicle* and *Enniscorthy Echo* but it still regarded the agreement as 'the crowning victory of the Sinn Féin movement'.[179]

---

[173] *Mayo News*, 20 Sept. 1919; Hopkinson, *The Irish War of Independence*, p. 108.
[174] *Mayo News*, 3 Apr. 1920.
[175] *Mayo News*, 11 Sept. 1920.
[176] *Mayo News*, 13 Nov. 1920.
[177] *Mayo News*, 2 July 1921.
[178] *Mayo News*, 8 Oct. 1921.
[179] *Mayo News*, 10 Dec. 1921.

As possible difficulties with Dáil ratification began to surface the paper somewhat echoed its views on the Home Rule bill eight years previously in describing the Treaty as 'a very substantial step' that could 'materially advance the interests of the country' even if it was 'not free from defects'. The opposition of Mr de Valera and others was accepted as genuine and an illustration of 'the depth of the sincerity of their desire to secure for their people the fullest possible measure of liberty'.[180]

The *Mayo News* was one of the few provincial newspapers to acknowledge the partition of the country as one of the Treaty's main defects. Nonetheless, it simultaneously demonstrated a distinct lack of foresight in deeming partition 'an evil for which the Irish people can easily find a remedy'. In the short term, however, the paper voiced a similar opinion to many other provincial newspapers, whether with Sinn Féin affiliations or otherwise. It predicted that 'the people of Ireland would accept the Treaty by an overwhelming majority' and vehemently asserted that precious little was to be gained by rejection other than 'a return to the dreadful conditions which prevailed in Ireland twelve months ago'.[181] The notion that most of the populace was in favour of the Treaty and the fear that rejection could bring about a return to war-like conditions were sentiments that had appeared to take hold amongst large sections of the provincial print media.

Conclusion

Although the *Mayo News* provided fascinating editorial commentary between 1914 and 1921, the rift between William Doris and P.J. Doris, the two brothers who co-founded the paper, is undoubtedly the most abiding (and unfortunate) feature of the paper's history. The diverging paths of Irish nationalism that they separately followed ultimately led to their estrangement. Yet they shared much in common: their involvement in agitation for land reform, their pursuance of the goal of Irish self-government (albeit by different routes), and indeed the fact that both endured terms of imprisonment in pursuit of these aspirations. The election of William Doris, the older of the two brothers, to Westminster in 1910 most likely marked the point at which the rift between them became more or less irreversible. Thereafter P.J. Doris assumed almost total control of the *Mayo News*.

The paper did not come to be regarded as a pro-Sinn Féin organ until

---

180   *Mayo News*, 17 Dec. 1921.
181   *Mayo News*, 24 Dec. 1921.

after Easter 1916 but there were signs well beforehand that it favoured a more advanced form of nationalism. This was particularly evident in its attitude to the Home Rule bill of 1914 and in its criticism of the Irish Parliamentary Party even before the outbreak of World War I. Such an editorial tone may possibly have contributed to the prolonged detention of P.J. Doris after the 1916 Rising. Regardless of what prompted his arrest and detention, his release almost seven months later saw his paper adopting a stance that was openly supportive of Sinn Féin. The editorial reaction to that party's by-election victories during 1917 and 1918 provides clear evidence of such support. The harsh criticism of the British Government, and Lloyd George and Sir Hamar Greenwood in particular, suggest that the paper's five-week suppression in 1918 did little to restrain the tone of the *Mayo News*. By the end of 1921, however, the paper did not differ greatly from even some of the more conservative provincial titles in regarding the Anglo-Irish Treaty as a hugely beneficial step forward and a considerable achievement for those who negotiated it.

Leitrim Observer

The *Leitrim Observer* was founded by the Mulvey family from Ballinaglera, County Leitrim, in 1890. However, like so many other Irish provincial newspapers it came to be associated with one dominant personality. In the case of the *Leitrim Observer* that personality was Patrick Dunne, who took ownership of the paper in the first decade of the twentieth century. There is a slight degree of uncertainty as to Dunne's acquisition of the *Leitrim Observer*. Hugh Oram states that he bought it for £5 in 1910 but the centenary issue of the *Observer* credits Dunne with purchasing the paper in 1904 for a sum thought to be around £150.[182] Regardless of the specific date of Dunne's assumption of ownership and the amount he paid, he remained at the helm of the paper for almost sixty years, his tenure as editor–proprietor only ceasing upon his death in 1968.

Patrick Dunne was born in Carrick-on-Shannon in 1879. Upon leaving school he became an apprentice printer at the *Leitrim Observer* that was then owned by Frank Mulvey, a member of the family that originally established the paper. In order to gain further experience of the printing trade Dunne left the *Observer* to work at both the *Longford Leader* and *Roscommon Herald* where he served under J.P. Farrell and

---

[182]   *Leitrim Observer: 1890–1990 – One hundred years of history in the making* (28 Nov. 1990); Oram, *The newspaper book*, pp 146–7.

Jasper Tully respectively. He later returned to the *Leitrim Observer* and purchased the paper upon the retirement of Frank Mulvey.[183] Oram describes Dunne as 'an extraordinary character' and 'the Jasper Tully of County Leitrim'.[184] There is little available evidence to discern what would merit such a label, but a description of Dunne as a 'colourful' character and someone whose 'adversaries, or those perceived as such played no part in Pat's life or newspaper', makes the comparison somewhat more comprehensible.[185]

Dunne differed from Tully though in that he was never elected to public office. Nonetheless, it was certainly not the case that he had any less interest in the national question. In fact, Dunne's nationalism was of a significantly more militant nature than the editor–proprietor of the *Roscommon Herald*. He joined the Irish Volunteers at an early stage and was subsequently a member of the South Leitrim Brigade of the IRA. He facilitated clandestine meetings of like-minded nationalists by making his premises available for such a purpose.[186] It is not certain whether such activities, or the sentiments expressed in his paper, attracted the attention of the military authorities but in November 1920 Crown forces paid the offices of the paper an unwelcome visit.

On 10 November 1920, Crown forces raided the premises of the *Leitrim Observer* and caused damage that was to keep the paper out of print for over two years. At the time the *Irish Times* reported that Patrick Dunne and his sister Eliza were held at gunpoint and within a few hours 'the machinery and plant were a mass of wreckage' while 'the type and type frames were scattered about'. It was also stated that the printing office was 'set on fire in two places' and as a consequence a large staff was 'thrown out of employment'.[187] The Dáil Éireann newssheet, the *Irish Bulletin*, reported that the offices and works of the *Leitrim Observer* and the residence of the proprietor had been 'wrecked and fired by constabulary' while shop windows in Carrick-on-Shannon had also been smashed.[188] Within days Patrick Dunne lodged a claim for £12,000 for the destruction of his plant and machinery but three weeks later he was arrested.[189]

183   *Leitrim Observer*, 30 Nov. 1968.
184   Oram, *The newspaper book*, pp 146–7.
185   *Leitrim Observer: 1890–1990 – One hundred years of history in the making* (28 Nov. 1990).
186   *Leitrim Observer*, 30 Nov. 1968; *Irish Times*, 26 Nov. 1968.
187   *Irish Times*, 11 Nov. 1920.
188   *Irish Bulletin*, 2 Dec. 1920.
189   *Freeman's Journal*, 13 Nov. 1920; *Irish Independent*, 7 Dec. 1920.

He was interned at Ballykinlar camp in County Down where numbered among his fellow-prisoners were Seán Lemass and Peadar Kearney, composer of the Irish national anthem.[190]

It is not clear why the *Observer* was targeted nor why Patrick Dunne was arrested. The office of the Press Censor was no longer in existence at that stage but even prior to its enforced closure there was little to indicate that the *Leitrim* Observer had attracted the attention of the authorities. Dunne's obituary claimed that his paper was such a powerful 'medium to imbue the national spirit into the people of Leitrim that the Black and Tans, on arrival in the county went first to the office, destroyed the plant and burned the premises'.[191] While such obituaries can be prone to overstatement it is possible that the tone of the paper at the time may have incurred the disapproval of the authorities. Nonetheless, although the paper was highly critical of British Government policy in Ireland, its editorial tone (as outlined in the next section) was scarcely more excessive than many other nationalist titles. Whatever the reasons for targeting the *Leitrim Observer*, it remained out of print until January 1923. On its return, it stated that 'in the past we endeavoured to sustain the faith and courage of the people during the blackest days of the war, and accordingly we were singled out for ruthless treatment and the attempted extermination of our paper and our livelihood'.[192] Although this provides no further clue as to why the paper was specifically targeted it does provoke a certain curiosity as to the editorial message being articulated in the paper.

'Pars. and points': editorial comment, 1914–1921

The *Leitrim Observer* bore the appended title of *Roscommon, Longford, Cavan, and Sligo News* and usually comprised eight pages, divided into seven columns, with the front page containing only advertisements. The number of pages dropped as low as four at certain times between 1918 and 1920. The paper contained a variety of weekly articles whose theme was self-evident from the title. Such articles included 'Garden Gossip', 'Home Hints', 'Dress of the Day', 'Field and Farm', and 'Woman's Corner'. An almost equally regular feature was the advertisement for the *Observer*'s own printing works, which could supply posters, handbills, billheads, memos, circulars, and programmes. In a similar vein to most

---

[190] *Leitrim Observer: 1890–1990 – One hundred years of history in the making* (28 Nov. 1990).

[191] *Leitrim Observer*, 30 Nov. 1968.

[192] *Leitrim Observer*, 6 Jan. 1923.

other provincial titles the considerable rural readership was evidenced by the amount of farming-related advertisements. Eckford's High Grade Manures, Richardson & Fletcher's Fertilisers, Fordson Tractors, and Drummond's Seeds were just a few of the agricultural items to appear in the advertising sections. A broad array of other items was also advertised such as Neave's baby food, Austin Motor Cars, Savar's Instant Toothache Remedy, and the ubiquitous Raleigh Bicycles.

By far the most striking feature of the editorial columns of the *Leitrim Observer* between 1914 and 1921 is that quite frequently there were simply no opinion pieces.[193] Instead they regularly only consisted of brief local announcements, sometimes no more than two or three sentences. This makes it even more surprising as to why the paper ultimately attracted the undesired attention of the Crown forces. Nonetheless, this rather unique characteristic of its editorial columns was as much in evidence in 1914 as it was at the height of the War of Independence in 1919 and 1920. Such an editorial trait contrasted hugely with organs such as the *Tuam Herald*, *Enniscorthy Echo*, and *Kilkenny People*, whose leading articles were almost without exception quite lengthy and dealt with both national and international affairs. In this respect the *Observer* most resembled the *Midland Tribune*, which often featured only brief local announcements in its editorial columns though not with the same frequency. Yet when its lead articles did turn their attention to national issues it did not fail to provide compelling reading.

This was most evident in the opening months of World War I. In response to the German destruction of the Belgian city of Louvain the paper asked, 'How many Louvains were destroyed in Ireland?' In an unequivocal manner, it additionally claimed that 'the same England that is hypocritically wringing its hands in horror at German atrocities today' was responsible for 'destroying our priceless treasure' and had also 'destroyed our language and laid waste this beautiful island'.[194] It was further asserted that Britain's involvement in the war was a totally self-serving exercise. 'The great mills and factories of England' were, the paper editorialised, 'taking on men daily in order to cope with the rush of trade they expect to capture from Germany'.[195] Even allowing for the vehemence of such sentiments the *Observer*'s response to Lord Kitchener's call for more Irish recruits was still quite remarkable:

[193] Editorial columns in the *Leitrim Observer* were headed 'Pars. and Points'.
[194] *Leitrim Observer*, 12 Sept. 1914.
[195] *Leitrim Observer*, 26 Sept. 1914.

Why does he not make an appeal to all the 'swanky' tennis players, golfers, and cricketers in "appy Hengland' [*sic*] to join his new army? Those English 'Joonies' who sing Rule Britannia in time of peace, and who read novels and play cricket in war time when Irishmen are fighting their battles, they should be compelled to enlist. Certainly, the average Englishman is only a coward. He is good for nothing only eating beef, drinking beer and sleeping.[196]

Quite remarkably, such open antagonism to enlistment in the British Army did not attract the attention of the authorities. However, perhaps even more remarkable was the fact that the editorials in the *Leitrim Observer* did not turn their attention to either national or international matters for about another eighteen months. Also, the paper did not carry any recruitment advertisements except on two occasions following the gathering of newspaper editors at the Viceregal Lodge in the Phoenix Park in October 1915, though the *Observer* did not send any represent-atives to the meeting.[197] Even the Easter Rising provoked only a minimal response from the paper. Events in Dublin were reported but the only editorial comment appeared well over a month after the rebellion when it was simply referred to as 'a sad and regrettable affair'.[198] The introduction of conscription in April 1918 similarly drew no editorial response. Such silence was highly strange considering the extreme nature of the anti-enlistment messages articulated in the opening months of the war. Nevertheless, a distinctly pro-Sinn Féin outlook was detectable, if not clearly obvious, from 1917 onwards.

The first Sinn Féin by-election success in North Roscommon in February 1917 was not greeted with the same enthusiasm expressed by the *Mayo News*, *Enniscorthy Echo*, or *Meath Chronicle*. Instead, Count Plunkett's victory was simply described as 'a timely warning to the Irish Party that they must awaken to their duty'.[199] By June 1918, however, the *Observer* hailed Arthur Griffith's by-election victory in East Cavan as 'historic and a great setback to all opposed to the cause of Sinn Féin'. Significantly, the paper was keen to point out that the widespread celebrations of Griffith's victory held in County Leitrim 'passed off quietly and without a single untoward incident occurring'.[200] Support for

---

196   *Leitrim Observer*, 19 Sept. 1914.
197   *Irish Times*, 29 Oct. 1915.
198   *Leitrim Observer*, 10 June 1916.
199   *Leitrim Observer*, 10 Feb. 1917.
200   *Leitrim Observer*, 29 June 1918.

Sinn Féin, if somewhat understated, was not all that surprising as notices for meetings of Sinn Féin clubs had begun to appear in the *Observer* from around September 1917. Any tentativeness in displaying pro-Sinn Féin sentiment had all but disappeared by the time of the campaign for the general election of December 1918. Prior to the poll the paper published a photograph of the Sinn Féin candidate for Leitrim, James N. Dolan (then interned) under the sub-heading, 'a well-known and popular Manorhamilton Gael', and described him as 'an ardent Gaelic Leaguer, highly educated and a powerful and leading orator'.[201] Sinn Féin's subsequent victory, not only in Leitrim but across the country, was described in the first editorial of 1919 as one that 'speaks in the highest for the good men in charge of Sinn Féin, which is the respected and universal policy of the great masses of the people of Ireland'.[202]

In its own unique fashion, the *Leitrim Observer* editorial columns then reverted to the more familiar terrain of local issues and announcements. This remained the case for quite some time and it was only around May 1920, when hostilities in Ireland were intensifying, that the editorial focus reverted to national issues with any degree of regularity. The paper accused the British Cabinet of attempting to choke 'republicanism out of us' and despite 'the most intense period of repression in modern times' Ireland was 'still under the sentence of death'.[203] The condemnation of the British Government during the summer of 1920 was probably as strong, if not as frequent, as many other nationalist organs. British Prime Minister, David Lloyd George, was accused of implementing a strategy of 'shooting on sight, the sacking of towns, midnight incendiarism, and the bombing of houses occupied by women and children'. The paper caustically suggested that the only tactic not yet employed was a 'house to house slaughter'.[204] Editorial indictment of the actions of Crown forces in Ireland, however, only reached its zenith in August 1920:

---

[201] *Leitrim Observer*, 12 Oct. 1918. The paper also promoted Dolan's candidacy by reminding readers that his brother, Charles, had been the first ever Sinn Féin parliamentary candidate in 1908. Charles Dolan had originally been elected in 1906 as an Irish Parliamentary Party MP for North Leitrim but resigned his seat after transferring his allegiance to Sinn Féin. He contested the subsequent by-election on behalf of Sinn Féin but was defeated by UIL candidate, Francis Meehan.

[202] *Leitrim Observer*, 4 Jan. 1919.

[203] *Leitrim Observer*, 1 May 1920.

[204] *Leitrim Observer*, 31 July 1920.

The officers of the Army of Occupation are to have the power of life and death over Irish civilians. They may arrest and imprison without trial any persons whom they suspect of hostility to them in thought, word, or deed. They may impose savage sentences for offences such as the doing of acts calculated to promote the objects of the Gaelic League, an 'unlawful association'. They may use the starvation blockade against every or any district in Ireland. They can shoot down Irish civilians without provocation and then hold a court of inquiry themselves and pronounce themselves justified. No such terrible weapons have been used to break a people's will since the Tsar of Russia was forced to abdicate.[205]

It is not possible to determine whether such unrestrained criticism was a factor that led Crown forces to the offices of the *Leitrim Observer* less than three months later. The difficulty in identifying a reason for the actions of the military is compounded by the fact that in the two months prior to the raid on the *Observer* editorial comment had been largely confined to more mundane local matters. Regardless of what prompted the unwelcome visit, it unfortunately leaves it as a matter of speculation as to how Patrick Dunne and his newspaper would have reacted to the truce of July 1921 and the Anglo-Irish Treaty six months later.

Conclusion

The case of the *Leitrim Observer* is rather unique among the ranks of the provincial print media between 1914 and 1921. Although unquestionably pro-Sinn Féin in sympathy from around 1917 onwards, its editorials dealt predominantly with local matters both before and after this time. Even when leading articles turned their attention to national issues its tone was rather understated. This was perhaps best illustrated by the fact that the *Observer* did not engage in the damning criticism of the Irish Parliamentary Party that was a hallmark of papers such as the *Kilkenny People* and *Roscommon Herald*. Nonetheless, there were exceptions to the rather reserved editorial tone. This was most evident in its anti-enlistment proclamations in the early months of World War I and even more so in its castigation of Lloyd George and his government during the summer of 1920. In the latter instance, the paper certainly did not hold back in its vilification of the actions of Crown forces in Ireland but its commentary was hardly more severe than many other nationalist titles. Yet the *Leitrim*

---

[205] *Leitrim Observer*, 28 Aug. 1920.

Observer suffered a fate far worse than most other provincial papers in having its plant and machinery destroyed and being forced out of print for over two years. While the reason that the *Observer* was targeted by Crown forces is somewhat perplexing it is perhaps best to regard it as a salient example of the extremely difficult circumstances under which newspapers had to operate during these years.

Summary: Connacht newspapers

The history of provincial titles in Connacht during these years displays many of the characteristics that were common to newspapers in other provinces. Nonetheless, it similarly displays certain factors that were rather unique to the province. The common characteristics include the undoubted sense of continuity and longevity within many publications, the sense of affiliation and allegiance to institutions such as the Catholic Church and the GAA, and not least the suppressions and enforced closures of several newspapers accompanied by the imprisonment of their editor–proprietors. Aspects of the history of the provincial press that were not replicated to any great extent elsewhere include the singularly individual personality of Jasper Tully of the *Roscommon Herald*, the irrevocable fraternal split between William and P.J. Doris of the *Mayo News*, and the takeover of certain newspapers by Sinn Féin interests.

The sense of continuity and longevity was evident in a variety of publications in the province. The ownership of the *Tuam Herald* has been shared between two families over its entire lifespan since its launch in 1837. Richard C. Gillespie's takeover of the *Connaught Telegraph* in 1892 marked the start of over a century of ownership by the same family. The sense of longevity in the provincial press is exemplified by figures such as Thomas J.W. Kenny, editor–proprietor of the *Connacht Tribune* for over thirty years, and by Terence Devere, who was centrally involved in the foundation of the *Western People* in Ballina in 1883 and remained with the paper until his death in 1941. This longevity is even further exemplified by William David Peebles, who spent almost half a century at the *Sligo Independent*, much of that time as editor–proprietor, and to and even greater extent by Jasper Tully and Patrick Dunne, editor–proprietors of the *Roscommon Herald* and *Leitrim Observer* respectively for close on sixty years.

Tully also provided an example of the strong support for the GAA within the senior ranks of the provincial print media. The aforementioned Terence Devere equally displayed this trait as evidenced by his involvement in the foundation of the Ballina Stephenites club. J.J. Collins of the *Mayoman* further re-enforced this strong connection as demonstrated by his service on the Connacht Council of the GAA. The *Mayoman* also provided an example of the considerable links between provincial newspapers and the Catholic Church with its publication of the edicts of Archbishop of Tuam. This close relationship is further illustrated by the staunch Catholicism of James Daly of the *Connaught Telegraph* and the strong clerical involvement in the establishment of the *Western People*.

Connacht newspapers also sustained their share of suppression and enforced closures not to mention imprisonment of editor–proprietors. The unfortunate experience of the *Leitrim Observer* mirrored that of the *Westmeath Independent*, while its owner, Patrick Dunne, was imprisoned in common with William Sears of the *Enniscorthy Echo* and P.J. Doris of the *Mayo News*. At least the *Mayo News* did not suffer the destruction of its plant and machinery as was the case with the *Leitrim Observer* and *Galway Express*, but it was subjected to a relatively lengthy suppression that mirrored somewhat the experience of the *Kilkenny People*. The case of the *Ballina Herald*, suppressed in 1918 despite historically being considered a unionist paper, showed that suppression could befall even the most unlikely of candidates. Nevertheless, while many Connacht newspapers shared both the traits and experiences of those in other provinces there were other discernible features that were not replicated to any great extent elsewhere.

Although it was not solely restricted to the province, one of the most notable features was the takeover of two titles in the interests of Sinn Féin. The acquisition of the *Sligo Nationalist* and its subsequent relaunch as the *Connachtman* plus the purchase of the *Galway Express* clearly demonstrated the desire of the Sinn Féin party to possess its own organs within the provincial print media. Nevertheless, an arguably more unique feature of the print media in Connacht during this time was the personalities associated with several papers and their attendant stories. The political and journalistic career of Jasper Tully of the *Roscommon Herald* could provide sufficient material for a historical study in its own right. The experiences and ultimate estrangement of brothers William and P.J. Doris, co-founders of the *Mayo News*, is not only an intriguing narrative but illustrates in microcosm the split that occurred in Irish nationalism in the early twentieth century. With such a backdrop the editorial comment of these two papers was always likely to prove interesting, but this was just as much the case with the other two titles considered in this chapter, the *Tuam Herald* and *Leitrim Observer*.

Indeed, from an editorial perspective, all four titles proved quite distinctive in their own right. The *Tuam Herald* was unambiguously supportive of the British war effort, a wholehearted advocate of Irish enlistment in the British Army, and a persistent critic of Sinn Féin prior to the 1918 general election. This criticism dissipated almost completely after that election and the *Tuam Herald* not only strongly supported the Anglo-Irish Treaty of 1921 but was fulsome in its praise of Sinn Féin for securing such a settlement. The *Roscommon Herald* was not entirely supportive of Sinn Féin but was almost virulent in its castigation of the Irish Parliamentary Party, though this was perhaps more because of Jasper Tully's chequered relationship with that party than with ideological differences. Its editorial concentration, possibly even fascination, with the progress of the war and subsequently with British and international affairs set it clearly apart from the other three newspapers. Editorially, the *Mayo News* was initially most notable for its view of Home Rule as only a stepping stone to greater independence. Such a stance allied with its stinging criticism of the Irish Parliamentary Party from a very early stage meant that its more open support for Sinn Féin after Easter 1916 came as no great surprise. The *Leitrim Observer* was the least editorially vocal of these four titles yet ended up having its plant and machinery destroyed by Crown forces. Unfortunately, this prevented the paper from passing opinion on the Treaty of December 1921.

The other three publications all backed the settlement though some, in particular the *Tuam Herald*, more enthusiastically than others. As these were all nationalist titles a certain degree of uniformity of opinion was to be expected at some stages between 1914 and 1921. However, in order to provide a broad portrayal of the Irish provincial press during this period it is necessary to scrutinise closely titles other than those with clear nationalist sympathies. Accordingly, a considered study and analysis of provincial organs regarded as independent and indeed unionist is required; such a requirement is fulfilled in the next two chapters.

4

Southern Exposure: Munster

Introduction

With a land area of 24,675 square kilometres Munster is the largest of the four Irish provinces. At the time of the 1911 census, it had the third-largest population at just over 1.03 million. Cork city accounted for 76,673 of that total while Limerick city (38,518), and Waterford city (27,464) were the other main population centres. County Waterford was, however, the least populous (83,966) of the six Munster counties. Even with the population of Cork city excluded, County Cork had a population of just over 315,000, which was by far the largest in the province.[1]

A total of thirty-two provincial titles operated in Munster during the 1914–21 period and five of them are examined in this chapter. Three were based in Cork, the most populous county. One of these, the *Cork Constitution*, was based in the city, while the other two, the *Skibbereen Eagle* and the *Southern Star*, were based in Skibbereen. The unionist *Cork Constitution* most likely drew a significant amount of its readers from the 11 per cent of Cork city's populace that were of the Protestant denomination though it is equally likely that it also attracted readers from across the province. Outside Cork city Skibbereen was the only town in the county in which any newspapers were published. Curiously, though, it was not the most populous town as its population of just over 3,000 was exceeded by Fermoy (6,863), Youghal (5,648), and by Mallow and Kinsale, which both had populations of just over 4,000.

---

[1] Vaughan and Fitzpatrick, *Irish historical statistics*, pp 3–68. All the demographical statistics and information provided in this section are based on the 1911 census and are cited from Vaughan and Fitzpatrick's work.

County Cork's considerable population outside the city was just over 91 per cent Catholic.

The two other titles examined in this chapter, the *Kerryman* and the *Clonmel Chronicle*, were published in some of the largest centres of population outside the cities of Cork, Limerick, and Waterford. Tralee, where the *Kerryman* was published, boasted a population of 10,300, making it the most highly populated urban centre outside the province's three cities. Between 1914 and 1921, the *Kerryman* competed with as many as eight other newspapers published in Tralee, all of which were nationalist except for the unionist *Kerry Evening Post*. Such a relatively large number of titles endeavoured to attract readers from County Kerry's population of just fewer than 160,000, of which 97 per cent was Catholic. Clonmel also had a population of just over 10,000 – slightly less than that of Tralee. In the town, the *Clonmel Chronicle* faced competition from the *Clonmel Nationalist*, while its main rivals within the county were based in Nenagh (*Nenagh Guardian* and *Nenagh News*) and Thurles (*Tipperary Star*). At the time, County Tipperary's population amounted to just over 152,000 of which almost 95 per cent was Catholic.

Munster newspapers: an overview

There were several characteristics that the provincial press in Munster shared with other Irish provinces but there were also some other features that were noticeably different. Newspapers were published in various parts of the province as far back as the eighteenth century and indeed some of them were still in operation upon the outbreak of World War I. Additionally, a significant number of unionist and independent titles were published in the southern province. Nonetheless, the print media within Munster also comprised several nationalist titles that were established from the 1880s onwards in a manner that was similar to Leinster and Connacht and, to a lesser extent, Ulster. Finally, several provincial newspapers in Munster similarly experienced censorship and suppression while this period also witnessed the arrest and detention of editors and proprietors plus attacks on newspaper offices. However, in the southern province it was not only one side in the Anglo-Irish conflict that targeted newspapers. In addition to the *Cork Examiner*, papers such as the *Cork Constitution* and *Skibbereen Eagle* incurred the wrath of the IRA and suffered consequently as detailed in this chapter.

It was in Munster that Ireland's first known newspaper was printed when the armies of Oliver Cromwell published the *Irish Monthly Mercury* on two occasions between 1649 and 1650.[2] Nevertheless, this distinction is perhaps of limited relevance to the history of the Irish provincial press as it was published in the city of Cork, one of the largest urban centres in the country. However, what is far more noteworthy in this respect is the fact that newspapers were published in each of the province's six counties as far back as the eighteenth century. In Cork, such publications were confined to the city itself but papers exhibiting highly respectable degrees of longevity also operated in the other five counties of Munster. Some of the most pertinent examples were titles such as the *Waterford Chronicle* (1765–1849), *Ennis Chronicle* (1784–1831), and *Andrew Welsh the Limerick Journal* (1739–77). This trait was best exemplified, however, by newspapers that were launched in the 1700s and were still being published in the second decade of the twentieth century.

The *Clare Journal*, which was established in 1778, was one such newspaper. Its most celebrated editor was John St George Joyce, a staunch nationalist who was also highly active in the Land League.[3] Following a suspension of publication in May 1917 due to a scarcity of paper, the *Clare Journal* joined forces with the Ennis-based *Saturday Record* to become the *Saturday Record and Clare Journal*.[4] The owner of both publications was John B. Knox and Sons and the amalgamated title remained in print until 1935.[5] While the *Clare Journal* displayed nationalist sympathies, the other Munster publications that traced their origins back to the eighteenth century were solidly unionist organs.

One of these was the *Kerry Evening Post*, which was launched in 1774 as the county's first newspaper. It ceased publication in 1917, at which stage its editor was George Raymond whose family had been proprietors for the entirety of its existence.[6] Amongst the other unionist titles in the province was the *Limerick Chronicle*, which was one of the oldest provincial newspapers in the country. It was launched in 1766 by a Limerick poet named John Ferrar.[7] In 1908, John Augustus (J.A.) Baldwin was appointed editor, a position in which he served until shortly before his death in 1935.[8]

---

[2] Oram, *The newspaper book*, p. 21.
[3] *Freeman's Journal*, 8 July 1922; *Connacht Tribune*, 15 July 1922; *Tuam Herald*, 22 July 1922.
[4] *Irish Times*, 5 May 1917.
[5] *Newspaper press directory and advertisers' guide 1917*.
[6] *Freeman's Journal*, 4 Oct. 1917; *Connaught Telegraph*, 6 Oct. 1917; *Irish Times*, 6 Sept. 1933.
[7] Oram, *The newspaper book*, p. 35.
[8] *Limerick Leader*, 9 Oct. 1935.

The *Limerick Chronicle* remained in print until 1953 when it was taken over by the *Limerick Leader*.[9] Several other notable unionist titles operated in Munster though they did not all date back to the eighteenth century.

The *Waterford Standard*, a unionist organ based in Waterford city, was owned by Robert Whalley who had been one of the paper's founders in 1863.[10] However, the curious situation existed at the *Waterford Standard* that David Cuthbert (D.C.) Boyd, a journalist with strong republican links, was appointed editor in 1916. Originally from Dundonald, County Down, and despite his Protestant–unionist background, Boyd became a member of the IRB and was involved in the Howth gun-running of July 1914. He even spent a period 'on the run' following the Easter Rising before obtaining a position as a reporter with the *Waterford Standard*, which, according to one commentator, afforded him 'a level of cover from the eyes of the British authorities'.[11] In 1921, Boyd became editor–proprietor of the paper which remained in print until 1953.[12]

The *Nenagh Guardian* was another of the unionist organs operating in Munster at the start of World War I. However, a change of ownership took place in 1916 that resulted in a reversal of its political outlook. The paper was established in 1838 by John Kempston as a solidly conservative organ that was decidedly antagonistic towards many nationalist aspirations. Following the death of Kempston in 1857, it was acquired by George Prior and remained in the ownership of the Prior family until 1916.[13] In the latter part of that year the paper was sold to a concern that supported Home Rule.[14] One of the principal figures involved in the acquisition of the *Nenagh Guardian* was Jeremiah Ryan who subsequently became editor, a position in which he served until his death in 1928.[15]

The significant unionist element to the provincial press in Munster was further swelled by the *Cork Constitution*, which is examined in detail

9   Oram, *The newspaper book*, p. 260.
10   *Newspaper press directory and advertisers' guide 1917*; *Irish Times*, 7 May 1921; *Freeman's Journal, Irish Independent*, 9 May 1921.
11   Anthony Keating, 'Criminal libel, censorship and contempt of court: D.C. Boyd's editorship the *Waterford Standard*' in Kevin Rafter and Mark O'Brien (eds), *The state in transition: essays in honour of John Horgan* (Dublin, 2015), p. 217.
12   *Irish Independent*, 13 July 1953; *Irish Press, Irish Times, Munster Express*, 29 Oct. 1965.
13   Joseph C. Hayes, *Guide to Tipperary newspapers, 1770–1989* (Tipperary, 1989), p. 8.
14   *Nenagh Guardian*, 16 Dec. 1916.
15   *Nenagh Guardian*, 24 Nov. 1928.

in this chapter. Nevertheless, the print media landscape in the province during this period was effectively dominated by nationalist titles, most of which were launched after 1880 though some dated from before this time. Two titles from the former category, the *Southern Star* and the *Kerryman*, are profiled in this chapter but it is still necessary briefly to consider some of the other nationalist organs in the province. Highly significant titles in this respect include the *Munster News*, *Tipperary Star*, *Waterford News*, and *Waterford Star*, but possibly the most noteworthy were papers such as the *Munster Express*, *Limerick Leader*, *Clonmel Nationalist*, and *Clare Champion*.

The *Munster Express*, based in the city of Waterford, was launched in 1860 and accordingly pre-dated the advent of so many nationalist titles later in the century. It was established by Joseph Fisher but was acquired by Edward Walsh in 1908, which marked the commencement of over one hundred years of family ownership. The paper was a supporter of the Irish Parliamentary Party and indeed Walsh was elected as a party councillor.[16] Upon its establishment in 1889, the *Limerick Leader* was similarly supportive of constitutional nationalism. In the early 1900s, Jeremiah Buckley, who is considered the paper's founding father, assumed control. Originally from County Cork, Buckley also qualified as both a barrister and a chartered accountant.[17] In later years, Buckley became a strong supporter and close friend of Eamon de Valera. Buckley assisted de Valera in the foundation of the *Irish Press* and it was from the offices of his accountancy practice in Dublin that the new paper was launched in 1931.[18] The editor of the *Limerick Leader* for most of Buckley's proprietorship and beyond was Cornelius (Con) Cregan. A devout Catholic, Cregan joined the paper in 1908 and served as editor from 1910 until his retirement almost fifty years later.[19]

In County Tipperary, the *Clonmel Nationalist* was probably the most notable nationalist paper to emerge in the decades leading up to the establishment of the Irish Free State. It was first published in June 1890 after a group of local businessmen pooled their resources to purchase the plant and machinery of the defunct *Tipperary Nationalist*. Amongst this group was Thomas J. Condon, who served as MP for Tipperary East from 1885 until 1918.[20] James J. Long, who had assisted in the paper's launch,

---

[16] *Munster Express: Waterford through the ages, 1860–2010* (8 Oct. 2010); *Munster Express*, 12 July 1946.

[17] *Limerick Leader*, 30 Sept. 1989.

[18] *Limerick Leader*, 18 Sept. 1937, 30 Sept. 1989.

[19] *Limerick Leader*, 2 July 1966.

[20] *The Nationalist – Centenary Supplement 1890–1990* (29 Dec. 1990).

became its first editor and remained in the position until his death in 1909.[21] His son, Brandon J. Long, succeeded him as editor, and similar to his father before him he was an enthusiastic advocate of the Gaelic League and an ardent supporter of the GAA.[22] Several other notable personalities also worked at the *Clonmel Nationalist* such as Richard Stapleton and William Myles. Stapleton worked as a journalist at the paper for many years but was also involved in numerous other activities. In addition to playing Gaelic football for Tipperary he became a trade union activist at an early age, served two terms as Mayor of Clonmel, and was elected a Labour Party TD in 1943.[23] William Myles first entered journalism as cub reporter with the *Clonmel Nationalist* at the age of fourteen and later joined the South Tipperary brigade of the IRA under the command of Seán Treacy and Seamus Robinson.[24] In 1919, Myles became vice-commandant of the brigade while two years previously he had been appointed secretary of the first Sinn Féin club in Clonmel.[25] Following the Treaty of 1921 Myles attained the rank of captain in the army of the Free State. However, he resumed his journalistic career in 1925 as editor of the *Tipperary Star* and remained in the position until his retirement in 1975.[26]

The *Clare Champion* was another highly significant nationalist publication that was launched in Munster in the decades preceding independence. In many respects the paper encapsulated a lot of the distinctive characteristics of Irish provincial newspapers during this period and beyond. These included prolonged family ownership, lengthy editorial reigns, and a decidedly Catholic outlook. The *Clare Champion* emerged from the ashes of the *Clareman*, a paper established by Tom Galvin in 1896 but which was forced to close seven years later as the result of a libel action. Galvin subsequently launched the *Clare Champion* in March 1903 and the paper was still owned by the Galvin family a century later. Tom Galvin died only six months after its foundation, at which stage his sister Josephine and her editor husband Sarsfield Maguire assumed control.[27]

[21] Martin O'Dwyer, *A bibliographical dictionary of Tipperary* (Cashel, 1999), p. 221.
[22] Seán O'Donnell, *Clonmel 1900–1932: a history* (Clonmel, 2010), p. 243; *Clonmel Nationalist*, 20 Apr. 1938.
[23] O'Dwyer, *A bibliographical dictionary of Tipperary*, p. 402; *Clonmel Nationalist*, 6 Aug. 1949.
[24] Witness Statement (Bureau of Military History, William Myles, WS795).
[25] O'Donnell, *Clonmel 1900–1932*, pp 314–15.
[26] *Tipperary Star*, 25 Sept. 1976.
[27] *Clare Champion*, 28 Mar. 2003.

Sarsfield Maguire remained as editor of the *Clare Champion* for almost forty years, matching the editorial longevity of many of his fellow provincial editors.[28] His wife, Josephine Maguire, also had a significant input into the paper. Following her death in 1937 her obituary noted her determination that the title founded by her brother should be 'a most staunchly Catholic journal' and that it should convey 'a virile Catholic tone in every article that appeared in its weekly issue'.[29] Politically, the *Clare Champion* was initially supportive of the Irish Parliamentary Party but this changed in the aftermath of the Easter Rising when Sarsfield Maguire transferred his allegiance to Sinn Féin.[30]

This change was clearly noticed by the Chief Press Censor, Lord Decies, who took particular offence at an editorial that appeared in November 1917. The specific editorial, a prolonged endorsement of Clare's enthusiasm for militant nationalism, contained phrases such as the 'full weight of England's machinery of oppression', 'the calculated brutality of England', and 'English hypocrisy'. Decies wrote to the paper to warn that such commentary was in breach of the Defence of the Realm Regulations.[31] Sarsfield Maguire replied in a somewhat oblique manner, stating that the 'complaint and the penalties that follow' could be published in the paper.[32] The tone of the *Clare Champion* continued to draw the ire of Decies, who advised the Chief Secretary that he had written to the paper three times during the previous month and that he believed it would 'have a good effect if it was closed for a certain time'.[33]

This probably influenced the decision to move against the paper in April 1918, when its printing machinery was seized by police. The *Clare Champion* was subsequently suppressed for almost six months.[34] Similar action had been taken against a number of other papers around the country at the same time though none suffered such a lengthy suppression. The most notable of these other titles were the *Westmeath Independent* and the *Mayo News*, though two Munster titles, the *Southern Star* and the *Weekly Observer*, were also suppressed. The latter paper, based in Newcastle West, County Limerick, had just been established in late 1914

28   *Irish Times*, 26 July 1945.
29   *Clare Champion*, 20 Feb. 1937.
30   *Irish Times*, 6 Apr. 1918; 26 July 1945.
31   Press Censorship Records 1916–1919, 3/722/29-47, 17 Nov. 1917.
32   Seditious literature, censorship, publication of offensive articles, CO904/122/2-1183.
33   Seditious literature, censorship, publication of offensive articles, CO904/122/2-1182.
34   *Irish Independent*, 30 Sept. 1918.

and only remained in publication until 1927.[35] Just over a year later, the *Waterford News* was deemed to have published 'statements likely to cause disaffection' and was suppressed for three months as a consequence.[36] Its suppression appears to have stemmed from an article published in February 1919 that Decies believed was 'written with the intention of running down the Irish Constabulary'. The article in question referred to the 'naked Prussianism, merciless and unabashed', of the police force in Ireland and appeared to label individual officers as 'public tyrants'.[37] The *Waterford News* was owned by Edward Downey who became a strong supporter of Sinn Féin from 1916 onwards and served as honorary treasurer of the party during the War of Independence.[38] Later in 1919 Limerick city's three nationalist papers, the *Limerick Leader*, *Limerick Echo*, and *Munster News*, were all briefly suppressed for publishing the prospectus for the Dáil Éireann loan.[39] There were, however, a number of other newspapers in Munster that suffered to a significantly greater extent during this period.

The *Southern Star* in Skibbereen, County Cork, cumulatively endured the longest period of suppression of any provincial newspaper. The *Kerryman*, based in Tralee, was briefly suppressed but was later forced to close for a prolonged period because of an attack on its premises. Accordingly, the experiences of both these titles are examined in detail in this chapter. Nonetheless, it was not only nationalist papers in Munster that were caught up in the Anglo-Irish conflict. The unionist *Cork Constitution* was subjected to threats and intimidation by the IRA. The *Skibbereen Eagle*, which has sometimes been referred to (perhaps mistakenly) as a unionist organ, also endured similar treatment. Consequently, both these titles are also subjected to detailed scrutiny in this chapter. In order to provide as broad a portrayal as possible of the provincial press during these years the final newspaper that is considered is the *Clonmel Chronicle*, an independent organ in County Tipperary. It managed to avoid any undesired attention from either and hence provides somewhat of a contrast with the other four papers that are profiled.

---

[35] Bureau of Military History, Seán Brouder, WS1236.

[36] *Freeman's Journal*, 14 May 1919; *Ulster Herald*, 17 May 1919; *Waterford News & Star: 150th Anniversary Supplement* (6 Nov. 1998).

[37] Press Censorship Records 1916–1919, 3/722/29-47, 18 Feb. 1919.

[38] *Irish Independent*, *Irish Times*, 12 Feb. 1937.

[39] *Freeman's Journal*, *Irish Bulletin* 24 Sept. 1919.

Cork Constitution

The *Cork Constitution* first appeared in June 1822 as a bi-weekly publication and became a daily in 1867. For many years the paper was owned by the Savage family but in 1882 it was purchased by Henry Lawrence (H.L.) Tivy for the sum of £5,310.[40] In 1897, he was joined at the paper by one of his sons, Henry Francis (H.F.), and in 1915 they both purchased the Dublin *Evening Mail*.[41] Another of H.L. Tivy's sons, George L.W. Tivy, became a director of the *Cork Constitution* and also served with the Royal Artillery during World War I.[42] The paper's editor for approximately forty years from around the time of the Land War was William J. Ludgate, but records indicate that he may have retired due to ill health at some stage before 1920, at which point H.L. Tivy assumed editorial control.[43]

The *Cork Constitution* was rather unique among newspapers in the south of Ireland not simply because of its staunchly unionist sympathies but also because it unashamedly claimed to possess a decidedly more well-heeled readership than almost all other papers. It was described as circulating 'most extensively among all the nobility, gentry, landed proprietors, and mercantile classes in the city and county of Cork and generally through the counties of Kerry, Limerick, Waterford, and Tipperary'.[44] Such a description easily explains why the *Constitution's* leading articles were frequently preceded by the claim that it was 'read daily and exclusively by people representing a greater purchasing power than the readers of all the other papers published in Munster'.[45] Evidence of this apparently affluent readership could possibly be discerned from a cursory perusal of the paper during this period. Normally eight pages

---

[40] *Southern Star 1889–1989: Centenary Supplement* (11 Nov. 1989); *Irish Independent*, 30 June 1929; Tim Cadogan and Jeremiah Falvey, *A biographical dictionary of Cork* (Dublin, 2001), p. 326.

[41] *Irish Times*, 13 Oct. 1960. The *Evening Mail* was acquired by the *Irish Times* in 1960.

[42] *Irish Times*, 7 Feb. 1961; George L.W. Tivy also served as a director of the *Evening Mail*.

[43] *Cork Examiner, Irish Independent*, 26 Nov. 1935; Kenneally, *The paper wall*, p. 67. Ludgate's obituary stated he served as editor of the *Cork Constitution* for forty years but did not indicate the precise dates though the 1911 census records him as still being a working journalist. Kenneally refers to H.L. Tivy fulfilling the editorial role around 1920.

[44] *Newspaper press directory and advertisers' guide 1917*, p. 210.

[45] This wording appeared at the top of most editorial columns but appears to have been discontinued from around 1919 onwards.

in length, three were usually devoted to advertisements that regularly featured travel on cruise liners, motor cars, women's clothes shops, and concerts at the Cork Opera House. Allied to the regular listing of prices on the London Stock Exchange, this seemed to add strong substance to the claim to circulation amongst a somewhat wealthier cohort of people.

With its circulation drawn from a wealthier section of the local population and its strongly unionist tradition it might reasonably be concluded that the *Constitution* was unlikely to have any great influence over the majority of nationalists. This clearly seemed to be the conclusion arrived at by the IRA in 1921. While categorising the paper as 'openly hostile' it was also acknowledged that it was doing neither harm nor good to the organisation as it circulated only 'to confirmed unionists'.[46] Despite the recognition that the *Constitution* was no real hindrance to the republican movement the paper was still targeted. During the War of Independence, the presses of the *Constitution* were wrecked by the IRA while H.L. Tivy was ordered out of the country. Clearly a newspaperman of some integrity, Tivy refused and the paper managed to continue publication throughout the Anglo-Irish conflict.[47]

Although it survived the hostilities between 1919 and 1921, the paper's centenary year of 1922 marked the beginning of the end for the *Constitution*. In July of that year it suspended publication in the face of attempts by anti-Treaty forces to enforce military censorship on the entire Cork Press. The following month, with the Civil War becoming more protracted, its plant and machinery were destroyed by republican forces in the city. The paper's unionist tradition most likely did not prompt this action, however, as the *Cork Examiner* suffered a similar fate.[48] Nevertheless, it proved a fatal blow to the *Constitution* and although it remained in publication for another two years (by which time it had been reduced to a single sheet) the demise of the century-old newspaper finally arrived in 1924.[49]

---

[46] Schedule No. 1 – Newspapers, MS 31,208; the exact same conclusion was drawn in respect of the *Irish Times*.

[47] John Borgonovo, *Spies, informers and the 'Anti-Sinn Féin Society': the intelligence war in Cork city, 1919–1921* (Dublin, 2007), p. 93; Kenneally, *The paper wall*, p. 67.

[48] *Irish Independent*, 24 July, 12 Aug. 1922; Cadogan and Falvey, *A biographical dictionary of Cork*, p. 326.

[49] Oram, *The newspaper book*, p. 152.

According to the *Constitution*: editorial comment, 1914–1921

The *Cork Constitution* can reasonably be considered one of the principal journalistic fatalities during this period. Other provincial papers endured the tribulations of suppression, imprisonment of staff, destruction of their premises, and enforced closure for long periods arising out of the events that took place between 1914 and 1921. However, most of them resumed publication sooner or later but the *Cork Constitution*, one of the longest established newspapers in the country at the start of the twentieth century, failed to emerge from this turbulent period. Accordingly, a detailed analysis of its lead articles during these years is all the more relevant in order to ascertain what may have offended republican sensibilities but more importantly to determine how such a solidly unionist organ dealt with such dramatic developments as they unfolded.

The *Cork Constitution* was a daily paper and consequently its editorial output was far greater than almost all other papers in Munster (aside from the *Cork Examiner*). For most of 1914 such editorial output was dominated by the Home Rule issue. The paper vehemently objected to the imposition of Home Rule upon Ulster which it considered to be the perpetration of a 'great crime'.[50] Unlike most of its nationalist counterparts the *Constitution* frequently referred to the possibility of Civil War in the northern province even before the Larne gun-running had taken place in April 1914. Home Rule, the paper claimed on more than one occasion, was the result of a 'corrupt bargain' between the Irish Parliamentary Party and Asquith's government.[51]

Following the landing of arms at Larne and other ports in Ulster a form of veiled approval was articulated when it was stated that the government may have been within its rights if they arrested Sir Edward Carson and other unionist leaders just as it may have been 'justified in using British troops to shoot down British people for insisting on remaining British'.[52] The militant opposition to Home Rule continued to be voiced throughout the summer of 1914: Home Rule, it stated, would provoke 'the armed resistance of the determined and efficient Ulster Volunteers'.[53] Despite its unambiguous support for the Ulster Volunteers, the *Constitution* did not really clarify if it was proposing that the entire island of Ireland should remain in the Union, quite an omission for the only unionist daily paper

---

50   *Cork Constitution*, 17 Jan. 1914.
51   *Cork Constitution*, 9 Feb., 16 July 1914.
52   *Cork Constitution*, 29 Apr. 1914.
53   *Cork Constitution*, 19 June 1914.

outside Ulster (apart from the *Irish Times*). From August 1914, however, Home Rule took a back seat to the paper's war coverage.

Unlike most nationalist titles, support for the British war effort was never likely to present a dilemma for the solidly unionist *Cork Constitution*. Recruitment advertisements regularly appeared in the paper from an early stage of the war and throughout 1915. At the same time, the nationalist community was criticised for what the *Constitution* claimed to be its failure to supply recruits in any substantial numbers. As early as September 1914, the Irish Volunteers were accused of showing 'no inclination to follow the example of their countrymen in Ulster, who unconditionally placed themselves at the service of their country'.[54] Even after John Redmond's call to Irishmen to enlist in the British Army, it claimed that 'nationalist Ireland' had yet to adopt his advice and abandon 'the disloyal counsels of the irreconcilables who seek to perpetuate ancient feuds'.[55] This theme of disloyalty was one that surfaced a number of times as the war progressed and was unsurprisingly a significant feature of the paper's reaction to the Easter Rising.

In a similar manner to the *Tuam Herald*, the Sinn Féin party attracted a significant amount of editorial attention even before Easter 1916. In a slightly derisive tone the *Constitution* claimed it had 'no quarrel whatever with the Sinn Féin party as a political organisation' as 'the more factions there are in the Nationalist Party the better we like it'.[56] Nevertheless, the attitude towards Sinn Féin changed significantly in a relatively short space of time. Barely a month prior to the rebellion the paper berated the Irish Executive for assuming a position of 'benevolent neutrality' in respect of a movement that 'openly and secretly obstruct[s] efforts being made to stimulate recruiting for the Army' and additionally plays 'the part of Germany's agents in Ireland'.[57] Accordingly, one of the earliest editorials in the aftermath of the events of Easter Week welcomed the resignation of the Chief Secretary, Augustine Birrell, 'who is mainly responsible for the shocking state of Ireland today'.[58] Although a unionist organ, the *Cork Constitution*'s editorial reaction to the Rising was quite similar to that of nationalist titles such as the *Tuam Herald* and *Roscommon Herald*. Labelling the events of Easter Week 'the Irish-German insurrection', the paper claimed that 'these Irish republicans' had 'laid their plans to

---

[54] *Cork Constitution*, 17 Sept. 1914.
[55] *Cork Constitution*, 14 Nov. 1914.
[56] *Cork Constitution*, 29 Feb. 1916.
[57] *Cork Constitution*, 22 Mar. 1916.
[58] *Cork Constitution*, 1 May 1916.

facilitate a Prussian invasion of Ireland, and that these preparations were of such a widespread and determined character that they went within measurable distance of succeeding'.[59]

The rise of the Sinn Féin party in the wake of Easter 1916 was met by the *Constitution* with grave warnings that another rebellion was imminent. Sinn Féin were accused of 'urging their followers to avail of every opportunity to perfect their military training' so 'that they may be ready to strike when the order reaches them to do so'.[60] Such a mindset combined with the aforementioned conviction of German involvement in the Easter Rising meant that the *Constitution* was quite willing fully to accept the veracity of the later discredited 'German plot' during 1918. The paper gladly accepted 'that the Government had the clearest evidence in their possession that the Sinn Féin organisation is, and has been, in alliance with Germany'.[61] The prospect of an election later the same year was greeted by the warning that it promised to excel in violence anything hitherto experienced, even in Irish parliamentary contests'.[62] Following Sinn Féin's subsequent landslide victory, the Irish electorate was censured for having 'deliberately disenfranchised themselves'.[63]

The first meeting of Dáil Éireann in January 1919 was described as 'theatrical protestations against British rule' while Sinn Féin was also accused of complicity in the 'cold-blooded murder' of the two policemen at Soloheadbeg, County Tipperary, on the same day.[64] This might give the understandable impression that the *Cork Constitution* was quite content to link Sinn Féin to all the violence that followed and condemn the party accordingly. Yet, quite remarkably, this was not the case. Gerard Murphy contends that for a staunch unionist newspaper the *Cork Constitution*'s coverage of events during the War of Independence was 'surprisingly even-handed' and there is quite a degree of accuracy in this assertion.[65] Indeed, there is much evidence to suggest that even before this time the *Constitution* demonstrated a particular understanding of Irish nationalist politics that was noticeably absent from a number of nationalist titles.

---

[59] *Cork Constitution*, 13 May 1916.
[60] *Cork Constitution*, 28 Nov. 1917. Editorials dated 2 Aug. 1917 and 18 Jan. 1918 also claimed that plans were in place for another rebellion.
[61] *Cork Constitution*, 20 May 1918.
[62] *Cork Constitution*, 19 Sept. 1918.
[63] *Cork Constitution*, 31 Dec. 1918.
[64] *Cork Constitution*, 23 Jan. 1919.
[65] Gerard Murphy, *The year of disappearances: political killings in Cork, 1920–1921* (Dublin, 2010), pp 251–2.

Even as early as May 1914 the *Constitution* recognised that 'by consenting to a temporary exclusion' of Ulster from Home Rule the Irish Parliamentary Party 'have already strained the loyalty of their followers to breaking point'.[66] Despite its outright condemnation of the Easter Rising the paper was still perceptive enough to observe that many nationalists believed 'that the rising has done more to arouse English statesmen to a sense of the need of a speedy settlement of the Home Rule question than twenty years of parliamentary action'.[67] The *Cork Constitution* was also quicker than several nationalist titles to foresee the irreversible shift in nationalist sentiment. Following Sinn Féin's first by-election victory in February 1917 the paper declared that the Irish Parliamentary Party 'now realise that the political ground is disappearing from beneath their feet' and shortly afterwards it predicted that Sinn Féin would win fifty-three seats if a general election was held at that time.[68]

While the *Constitution* initially had few qualms about linking Sinn Féin to instances of violence it later conceded that the party 'may in at least some instances be more sinned against than sinning', as extreme elements, the paper contended, had almost always managed to exert some degree of control over popular political movements in Ireland.[69] It was also acknowledged that republican courts had 'a disposition to deal out impartial justice' and possessed the ability to give effect to their decisions 'in many parts of the country' where 'the King's writ has ceased to run'.[70] There were even echoes of the criticism of the British Government so common in nationalist newspapers when, in January 1921, Sir Hamar Greenwood was accused of refusing 'to take the Irish Republican Party seriously' in the vain hope that a more moderate element of Irish nationalism would once again assert itself.[71]

Both the truce of July 1921 and the Anglo-Irish Treaty in December of the same year were warmly welcomed by the *Cork Constitution*.[72] However, the paper also displayed a considerable degree of perception when it identified the likelihood of Eamon de Valera's estrangement from his erstwhile colleagues a full three months before the signing of the

---

[66] *Cork Constitution*, 2 May 1914.
[67] *Cork Constitution*, 19 June 1916.
[68] *Cork Constitution*, 12 Feb., 18 Apr. 1917.
[69] *Cork Constitution*, 27 Apr. 1920.
[70] *Cork Constitution*, 2 July 1920.
[71] *Cork Constitution*, 8 Jan. 1921.
[72] *Cork Constitution*, 11 July, 7 Dec. 1921.

Treaty.[73] In voicing its approval of the Treaty the *Constitution* cited US newspaper magnate William Randolph Hearst (described as 'the pro-Sinn Féin and anti-British newspaper proprietor') who had supported 'de Valera's propaganda in [the] USA' but had declared firmly in favour of the London agreement.[74] By contrast, de Valera was decried for his 'irreconcilable attitude'.[75]

One issue that was noticeably absent from the *Cork Constitution*'s editorial discussion of the Treaty was that of partition. Indeed, the paper's stance on this particular issue was quite puzzling throughout the 1914–21 period. Despite its quite vocal support for the Ulster Unionists the notion of partition was often mentioned in decidedly unflattering terms in the editorial columns. At the height of the Home Rule crisis in 1914 it was referred to as having the potential to 'accentuate racial and religious differences' that were already at a heightened state.[76] Six years later, this attitude had not changed as the paper asserted that all Irishmen were 'in full agreement that a partition scheme is the most objectionable that could be devised'.[77] Such vehement opposition to partition combined with such enthusiastic endorsement of the Ulster Unionist cause makes the editorial policy of the *Cork Constitution* in this regard rather difficult to understand. Possibly the paper felt that the strength of Ulster opposition to Irish self-government could save all of Ireland from any severance of the union but unfortunately this can only be a matter of speculation. Nonetheless, as late as June 1921 the paper's distaste for partition even seemed to be tinged with bitterness. Referring to the Government of Ireland Act as the 'ill-advised partition act', the British Government was roundly criticised for 'having sundered the six counties from the rest of the country' while Ulster Unionists now appeared to be classified as 'northern secessionists'.[78] By late December 1921, the *Cork Constitution* hardly differed at all from its nationalist counterparts in making little or no mention of partition.

---

[73] *Cork Constitution*, 31 Aug. 1921. The paper suggested that de Valera had 'lost some of the confidence of his party' and that the Parnell split of 1891 seemed 'almost parochial'. Nonetheless, its prediction that the likely 'division of the country into moderate and extremist elements' that would result in 'decades of warfare' was rather overstated.

[74] *Cork Constitution*, 14, 16 Dec. 1921.

[75] *Cork Constitution*, 20 Dec. 1921.

[76] *Cork Constitution*, 2 May 1914.

[77] *Cork Constitution*, 1 Apr. 1920.

[78] *Cork Constitution*, 14 June 1921.

<u>Conclusion</u>

In order to provide a balanced portrayal of the Irish provincial press between 1914 and 1921 it would be quite remiss to overlook a publication such as the *Cork Constitution*. Not only was it one of the principal unionist organs outside Ulster but it was also one of the oldest titles across the other three provinces. In many ways, the *Constitution* displayed the characteristics that might be expected of a staunchly unionist newspaper. Unequivocal opposition to Home Rule was followed by unqualified support for the British war effort. Outright condemnation of the Easter Rising was succeeded by an apparent conviction that another rebellion was imminent. The rise of Sinn Féin was met with grave warnings as to that party's aims and how it hoped to achieve them. However, the *Cork Constitution* was catering for an affluent unionist readership that had virtually no influence on nationalist opinion.

Even though republican ideals were hardly ever likely to find favour amongst the readership of the *Constitution* the IRA still saw fit to issue threats against the newspaper. Such action further illustrates how both warring factions desired to influence and control the output of the print media and equally it also clearly demonstrates that both sides in the conflict had a rather ambivalent attitude towards the freedom of the press. As it happened, the *Cork Constitution*, despite its staunchly unionist background, displayed a comprehension of nationalist politics and sentiment that was not always replicated in newspapers with indisputably nationalist sympathies. Ultimately, however, the *Constitution* echoed the views of many nationalist titles in accentuating the practical benefits of the Anglo-Irish Treaty while remaining silent on the thorny question of partition.

Skibbereen Eagle

Despite only enjoying a relatively brief lifespan (1858–1922) the *Skibbereen Eagle* has attained an unlikely fame within the annals of Irish journalistic history. This derives from an editorial that appeared in the paper in November 1898 that famously declared that it was keeping its eye on the Tsar of Russia. At the time, the Tsar of Russia was one of the world's most powerful and most autocratic rulers, and the incident, as Matthew Potter points out, 'has resulted in the phrase entering the English language as an example either of absurd self-importance or plucky courage and plain speaking'.[79] It has proven a popular point of reference ever since. Potter further notes an allusion to the episode in James Joyce's *Ulysses*, while in 1946 it formed the basis of a cartoon in the satirical journal *Dublin Opinion* that lampooned a recent meeting between Eamon de Valera and Joseph Stalin.[80] Even as recently as July 2014, veteran RTÉ sports presenter, Bill O'Herlihy, referenced the incident in his farewell address to viewers prior to his retirement.[81]

The person responsible for the warning to the Russian monarch that he was being closely monitored from West Cork was the paper's editor–proprietor, Frederick Peel Eldon Potter, more commonly known as Fred Potter. The *Eagle* was established in 1858 by Fred Potter's father, John William Potter. Originally from Pembrokeshire in Wales, John William Potter's family already had significant connections to the newspaper trade before he moved to Ireland in the mid-1820s. The *Skibbereen and West Carbery Eagle*, as the paper was titled upon its launch, was initially only a single-sheet monthly publication containing a column of local advertisements and a minimal amount of local news. By the early 1870s, it had developed into quite a successful weekly organ, due in no small part to the efforts of Fred Potter who had followed his father into the business. In 1874, Fred Potter was left in complete control of the paper following the death of his father.[82]

By this stage the paper had been renamed the *West Cork Eagle*, which was one of a number of name changes it experienced during its lifetime. Indeed, it was never officially entitled the *Skibbereen Eagle* but over time it has come to be known by this name and is referred to accordingly in this work. In addition to such name changes, Fred Potter's tenure as editor–proprietor was marked by a number of other developments. A price reduction from twopence to one penny allied to considerably more attention being devoted to Irish and local news resulted, according to

---

[79] Matthew Potter, 'Keeping an eye on the Tsar: Frederick Potter and the *Skibbereen Eagle*' in Rafter, *Irish journalism before independence*, p. 49.

[80] Ibid. One of the characters in *Ulysses*, J.J. O'Molloy, refers to 'our watchful friend, the *Skibbereen Eagle*', while in the *Dublin Opinion* cartoon Joseph Stalin is depicted as explaining the Soviet Union's vetoing of Ireland's application for United Nations membership by saying to de Valera: 'Between ourselves, Dev, Russia has never quite forgotten that article in the *Skibbereen Eagle*'.

[81] 'Bill O'Herlihy bids farewell after 49 years on RTÉ'; RTÉ World Cup Final coverage, 13 July 2014, available at https://www.youtube.com/watch?v=WEYBSz79ZJM (accessed 1 Feb. 2019).

[82] *Southern Star 1889–1989: Centenary Supplement* (11 Nov. 1989).

Fred Potter, in the paper achieving a considerable increase in circulation. Possibly buoyed by such progress Potter launched a daily newspaper in 1871, the *Irish Daily Telegraph and Southern Reporter*, but the venture was not successful and barely lasted two years. Although a Protestant of British extraction, the developments in nationalist politics that took place from the 1870s onwards did not prove any great hindrance to Fred Potter who 'was a born newspaperman and entrepreneur'.[83] Fred Potter died in September 1906, by which time the paper was officially entitled the *Cork County Eagle*, the name it retained for the remaining sixteen years of its publication.

Following Fred Potter's death in 1906, the paper was inherited by his son Eldon. However, this effectively marked the end of the Potter family's involvement in the newspaper as Eldon Potter had already embarked on a legal career and did not share his father's passion for the newspaper business. From early 1908, the proprietors were listed as 'Eagle Ltd' and although Eldon Potter was the largest shareholder he did not hold a controlling interest. The two other principal shareholders were also engaged in the legal profession, R.W. Doherty from Bandon and Jasper Travers Wolfe from Skibbereen.[84] Although he was not really a newspaperman and was described as 'minimally qualified' for the newspaper trade it was Wolfe who was mostly associated with the proprietorship of the *Eagle* for the rest of its lifetime.[85]

A member of the Methodist Church, Wolfe was born in Skibbereen and qualified as a solicitor in 1893. He served as Crown Solicitor for Cork City from 1916 to 1923 and was elected to Dáil Éireann as TD for West Cork on three occasions between 1927 and 1933 but did not seek re-election to the eighth Dáil in 1933.[86] Other people, such as R.W. Greenfield, John Topping, and James O'Driscoll, were more closely involved in the daily administration of the paper but the most influential figure was Patrick Sheehy who was appointed editor in August 1915.[87] Sheehy, like Jasper Wolfe, was a qualified solicitor but was also a strong supporter of John Redmond and the Irish Parliamentary Party.[88] However, unlike many other provincial newspapermen Sheehy did not

83 Potter, 'Keeping an eye on the Tsar', p. 52.
84 *Southern Star 1889–1989: Centenary Supplement* (11 Nov. 1989).
85 Jasper Ungoed-Thomas, *Jasper Wolfe of Skibbereen* (Cork, 2008), p. 211.
86 *Southern Star*, 30 Aug. 1952; Cadogan and Falvey, *A biographical dictionary of Cork*, p. 344.
87 *Southern Star 1889–1989: Centenary Supplement* (11 Nov. 1989).
88 *Southern Star*, 21 Sept. 1940.

switch his allegiance to Sinn Féin and his criticism of republican strategy was to land both him and his newspaper in trouble.

In September 1917, there was a break-in at offices of the *Eagle* during which the printing machinery was vandalised.[89] Interestingly, the pro-Sinn Féin *Kerryman* newspaper published a rather restrained account of the incident, reporting merely that printing parts had been 'stolen' after being 'skilfully removed'. The *Kerryman* did acknowledge, nonetheless, that the raid was probably politically motivated as the *Eagle* had 'advocated a vigorous policy of anti-Sinn Féinism'.[90] After this the *Eagle* was not only boycotted but its editor, Patrick Sheehy, was also attacked. In May 1920, a group of about twelve armed men broke into his home and bound him with ropes following which he was kicked and tarred. Contemporary newspaper reports indicated that the attack resulted from Sheehy's consistent stance as 'a vigorous adverse critic of Sinn Féin in the columns of the *Eagle*'.[91] This series of incidents was to sound the death knell of the *Skibbereen Eagle* and it ceased publication in 1922, two years before the *Cork Constitution* was to suffer the same fate.[92]

The experience of the *Skibbereen Eagle* and more particularly the manner in which it met its end illustrates once again that Irish republicans were not reluctant to adopt heavy-handed tactics against newspapers that saw fit to criticise Sinn Féin or the IRA. Just as the British authorities demonstrated little hesitancy in suppressing publications that criticised its administration in Ireland, the IRA displayed a similar lack of tolerance towards those organs that expressed opposition to its policies or tactics. Ultimately, both sides had a rather selective attitude towards the maintenance of a free press. Yet in targeting the *Eagle* the IRA was directing its ire at a paper that was broadly nationalist in its sympathies. Hugh Oram describes it as a unionist organ but this is quite misleading.[93] Mathew Potter provides a more accurate indicator of the *Eagle*'s political disposition when he states that the paper was supportive of Home Rule

[89] *Anglo-Celt*, 29 Sept. 1917; *Southern Star 1889–1989: Centenary Supplement* (11 Nov. 1989).

[90] *Kerryman*, 29 Sept. 1917.

[91] *Irish Times*, 14 May 1920; *Freeman's Journal*, 17 May 1920.

[92] Potter, 'Keeping an eye on the Tsar', p. 58; Ungoed-Thomas, *Jasper Wolfe*, p. 211; *Southern Star 1889–1989: Centenary Supplement* (11 Nov. 1989). Although the paper ceased publication, the 'Eagle Ltd' remained in existence until 1929. At that stage Wolfe was apparently the only remaining shareholder and the sale of the company to the *Southern Star* was agreed on amicable terms.

[93] Oram, *The newspaper book*, p. 131.

from the movement's infancy in the 1870s.[94] Indeed, as Gerard Murphy notes, Jasper Wolfe and his brother Willie campaigned enthusiastically for Home Rule between 1910 and 1912 while Patrick Sheehy was an unwavering supporter of constitutional nationalism.[95] Nevertheless, to comprehend fully the political sympathies of the *Skibbereen Eagle* it is necessary to examine closely its editorial comment.

'The outlook from the *Eagle* Watchtower': editorial comment, 1914–1921

Unlike the city-based *Cork Constitution*, the *Skibbereen Eagle* was a weekly publication. It was normally eight pages in length containing seven columns each though the number of pages sometimes dropped during World War I, most likely due to paper shortages. The 'Eagle' of the title was positioned in the masthead and towered over the front page in a manner that distinguished it from most other provincial publications.[96] It carried a similar amount of advertising space to other provincial papers, nonetheless, promoting items such as medications, drapery stores (mostly directed at women), and some agricultural products. Other advertisements, however, appear to indicate a slightly more affluent readership such as those for auctioneer services, holidays, and travel on Cunard liners. While this may have intimated a similar cohort of readers to that of the *Cork Constitution* the editorial comment of the *Skibbereen Eagle* suggested otherwise.

From early 1914, the *Skibbereen Eagle* displayed an unequivocally nationalist outlook as the paper contemplated the passing of the Home Rule bill. The prospect of 'our country enjoying a satisfactory measure of self-government' was eagerly anticipated while unionist opposition was afforded little credibility. Ulster was described as 'menacingly disloyal' as the paper claimed that the real reason for unionist objections to Home Rule was 'the old spirit of ascendancy, and not any fear of ill-treatment or opposition at the hands of their Catholic fellow-countrymen'.[97] The *Eagle* echoed most other nationalist titles in expressing its utter disdain at any suggestion of Ulster's exclusion from Home Rule. The paper angrily declared that such a move 'would merely create another Orange Free

---

[94] Potter, 'Keeping an eye on the Tsar', pp 58–9.

[95] Murphy, *The year of disappearances*, p. 237; *Southern Star*, 21 Sept. 1940.

[96] 'The Outlook from the *Eagle* Watchtower' was the wording that appeared above all the *Eagle*'s editorials.

[97] *Skibbereen Eagle*, 3 Jan. 1914.

State, and would set up a new Act of Disunion in Ireland'.[98] Although solidly supportive of the Irish Parliamentary Party, its leader, John Redmond, was censured for his 'bungling and treachery' in agreeing to Ulster's temporary exclusion from Home Rule that had resulted in the country 'being rapidly turned into two hostile armed camps'.[99]

The outbreak of war in August 1914 gave rise to a new set of editorial priorities. In many respects the response of the *Skibbereen Eagle* to World War I was very similar to that of the *Tuam Herald*. Ireland was considered 'an integral part of the United Kingdom' and by consequence was 'one of the component parts of the Allies'.[100] The proposal, articulated in a few other provincial newspapers, that the Irish Volunteers should be reserved for home defence in case of invasion received short shrift in the 'Eagle Watchtower'. The suggestion was dismissed as 'sickly twaddle' and indeed it was quite reasonably explained that the Irish Volunteers comprised a body of men who were 'unskilled in the use of arms, untrained, and unacquainted with the profession of the soldier – defending their country'.[101] The criticism of John Redmond that had been voiced before the outbreak of war was replaced by fulsome praise for his call to Irishmen to enlist in the British Army. 'No man', the paper declared, 'will merit a more splendid panegyric – no figure will stand out in greater or more dignified relief than that of the distinguished Irishman'.[102]

Despite the *Eagle's* wholehearted support for the war effort its reaction to the Easter Rising was far from condemnatory and even quite considered. Although it labelled the events of Easter Week 'insane folly' it did not refer to the insurrection as the 'Sinn Féin rebellion' nor did it allege German involvement. The paper articulated similar sentiments to many nationalist titles in asserting that the seeds of rebellion were sown 'on the day when Sir Edward Carson called his northern "braves" into existence'.[103] The Rising, however, did not signal a shift in the paper's political allegiance. Sinn Féin's electoral successes the following year were greeted with a mixture of frustration and resignation. Unlike the *Cork*

---

[98] *Skibbereen Eagle*,14 Mar. 1914.

[99] *Skibbereen Eagle*, 27 June 1914.

[100] *Skibbereen Eagle*, 17 Oct. 1914.

[101] *Skibbereen Eagle*, 2 Jan. 1915.

[102] *Skibbereen Eagle*, 22 Jan. 1916.

[103] *Skibbereen Eagle*, 6 May 1916. Significantly, the *Eagle* differed from most other papers in proposing that the causes of the rebellion were 'by no means all political' but that 'the hideous social conditions of Dublin's under-world' was also a contributory factor.

Constitution, the *Eagle* initially failed to acknowledge the enormity of the shift in the electoral mood and passed off the Sinn Féin by-election victory in South Longford in May 1917 as 'purely the result of disinclination for warfare'.[104] Nonetheless, the Irish Parliamentary Party's defeat at the hands of Sinn Féin's William T. Cosgrave in the Kilkenny by-election in August 1917 appeared to bring about a far more realistic appraisal of political developments. In endeavouring to explain the decline in the fortunes of the Irish Parliamentary Party the paper recognised 'that when Mr John Redmond made his historic offer of Ireland's assistance to the Empire, he took, and probably knew he was taking a risk no Irish leader had yet undertaken'.[105]

A series of by-election results early in 1918 appeared to convince the *Eagle* that the rise of Sinn Féin was slowly coming to a halt. The Irish Parliamentary Party's success in South Armagh in February 1918 was viewed as a 'clear indication that the fever of revolution is abating'.[106] Captain William Redmond's victory in Waterford the following month was cited as further evidence of a reversal in the fortunes of Sinn Féin that denoted 'the close of an era' and the 'beginning of a new chapter in Irish history'.[107] As the general election approached later that year, however, the *Eagle* appeared to acknowledge its misreading of the situation. It reluctantly conceded 'that thousands of young Irishmen will light-heartedly vote Sinn Féin' but were somewhat deluded if they believed their vote would swiftly lead to an Irish Republic.[108]

Sinn Féin's resounding victory at the general election was accepted as marking 'the extinction, absolute and complete' of the Irish Parliamentary Party, though the first meeting of Dáil Éireann was described as a 'farce'.[109] Unlike the *Tuam Herald*, the attitude of the *Skibbereen Eagle* towards Sinn Féin did not soften following the general election. Yet the paper did not engage in any blanket denigration of the party and was even willing to accept that there were certain laudable aspects to its policies. Even though the *Eagle* reacted with dismay to the party's initial electoral successes in 1917, it recognised the part Sinn Féin had played in 'the awakening of intellectual Ireland' and additionally that it had provided 'an incentive to the study of our native language and the patronage of

104   *Skibbereen Eagle*, 19 May 1917.
105   *Skibbereen Eagle*, 18 Aug. 1917.
106   *Skibbereen Eagle*, 9 Feb. 1918.
107   *Skibbereen Eagle*, 30 Mar. 1918.
108   *Skibbereen Eagle*, 14 Sept. 1918.
109   *Skibbereen Eagle*, 4 Jan., 1 Feb. 1919.

our home industries'.[110] In complete contrast to the *Cork Constitution*, the *Eagle* did not avail itself of the revelation of the 'German plot' in May 1918 to deride republicans. Indeed, the paper was quite forthright in expressing its scepticism and categorically stated its refusal 'to believe, until convinced by overwhelming evidence', that Sinn Féin was guilty of soliciting assistance from Germany.[111]

Although the paper remained a persistent critic of Sinn Féin until the truce of 1921, it did not tend to allege that the party was involved in the increasingly frequent instances of violence. Instead the *Eagle* concentrated on what it believed to be the unrealistic pursuit of an Irish Republic. As early as 1917, the paper poured cold water on the notion of an Irish delegation receiving a hearing at any post-war peace conference.[112] In the weeks prior to the general election of December 1918, it argued that the pursuit of a policy of abstention from Westminster while simultaneously 'begging an Irish Republic off every power in the world from President Wilson to the Emperor of Japan' posed little realistic chance of success.[113] As several of the pro-Sinn Féin provincial organs celebrated the general election result as the vindication of the republican cause, the *Eagle*'s response was more grounded in reality. It warned that the creation of an Irish Republic was 'no child's play' and pointedly commented that Sinn Féin was 'not as clear or definite on the means of attaining their ideal as on its necessity'.[114] Allied to its ongoing criticism of Sinn Féin's abstentionist policy, the paper continued to argue that the blunt demand for an Irish Republic was both fanciful and dangerous:

> An Irish Republic, as the silliest Sinn Féiner must realise, means a 'fight for it'; and a fight with the British Empire for it; nothing less will do. Now the most frenzied 'Irish Republican' has common sense enough to know that, after such a fight there would be no Irish Republic; there would only be no Ireland; that is all.[115]

Nonetheless, the relentless questioning of Sinn Féin strategy should not mask the fact that the *Skibbereen Eagle* was just as critical of the British Government as many more recognisably nationalist papers. In the aftermath of the 1918 general election, the *Eagle* claimed that the

---

[110] *Skibbereen Eagle*, 19 May 1917.
[111] *Skibbereen Eagle*, 25 May 1918.
[112] *Skibbereen Eagle*, 3 Nov. 1917.
[113] *Skibbereen Eagle*, 23 Nov. 1918.
[114] *Skibbereen Eagle*, 4 Jan. 1919.
[115] *Skibbereen Eagle*, 29 Nov. 1919.

attainment of an Irish Republic was even further complicated by the fact that the new British government would be led by David Lloyd George whose 'record on the Irish question is beyond cavil, a revelation of the British statesman at his worst'.[116] At the height of the War of Independence, in 1920, the British Prime Minister was lambasted for 'his present method of ruling our country', which has 'no approval outside north-east Ulster' and 'has brought us to our present deplorable condition'. Accordingly, the *Eagle* angrily declared, he 'should either govern or clear out' while also accusing him of being a totally self-serving politician who 'thinks only of the dangers to his power or his ambition'.[117]

The truce of July 1921 was greeted with neither relief nor joy. Instead, the paper reflected on 'all that might have been spared our unfortunate country' had John Redmond been sufficiently supported eight years earlier in his efforts 'to arrange with Ulster'. However, the same editorial also remarked with some degree of perception that, in agreeing to negotiations with the British Government, 'Mr de Valera must realise he leaves outside the door, every possible hope of the Irish Republic'.[118] Even at this late stage, the *Eagle* continued to argue that Ireland would have been better served had it followed a constitutional and non-abstentionist path:

> Given a powerful disciplined Irish Party in Westminster for the past five years, there would never have been an Ulster Parliament. The passing of the Partition Act against their opposition would simply have been impossible.[119]

Nonetheless, the paper accepted the changed situation and gave 'unqualified support to the representatives of Southern Ireland' to achieve what it hoped would be 'a permanent and satisfactory Anglo-Irish agreement'.[120] The warm approval for the agreement reached in London, in December 1921, was accompanied by fulsome praise for the Irish negotiators for doing 'a brave and a wonderful thing when they put their names to the Treaty'. The practical benefits of the agreement were articulated enthusiastically but a lack of foresight was evident on some issues. The *Eagle* confidently stated that 'the Irish Question, as it has been known to generations of Irishmen and Englishmen' has 'passed from the stage'. The consequences of partition were similarly underestimated.

116   *Skibbereen Eagle*, 4 Jan. 1919.
117   *Skibbereen Eagle*, 14 Aug., 18 Sept. 1920.
118   *Skibbereen Eagle*, 2 July 1921.
119   *Skibbereen Eagle*, 23 July 1921.
120   *Skibbereen Eagle*, 6 Aug. 1921.

Ireland's 'one reluctant province', the paper reasoned, would soon yield 'to the pressure of economic laws' and throw in her lot with the Irish Free State.[121] In the face of the emerging opposition to the Treaty, the *Eagle*'s final two editorials of 1921 continued to cite how much the country stood to gain from the agreement. Central to its argument was its endorsement of the leadership of Michael Collins and Arthur Griffith who were described as stamped 'with the mark of statesmanship'.[122] The *Skibbereen Eagle*, however, like Collins and Griffith, did not survive to witness even the first year of the Irish Free State.

Conclusion

The *Skibbereen Eagle* is best remembered for its warning to the Tsar of Russia but its experiences and also its editorial output between 1914 and 1921 arguably justify an equally significant place in the broader history of Irish newspapers. The paper's wholehearted support for Home Rule in conjunction with its sense of allegiance to Britain (which manifested itself in its unequivocal support for the war effort) was a combination that was brushed aside following the ascension of Sinn Féin from 1917 onwards. Despite this, the editorial commentary of the *Skibbereen Eagle* held firm in its support for constitutional nationalism. In this respect the paper illustrated that not every area of the so-called 'Munster Republic' was a hotbed of militant nationalism. Nonetheless, the *Skibbereen Eagle* did not in any way deride this newly popular form of nationalism. Indeed, the paper's commentary on this period of Irish history was predominantly measured and fair. On occasion, like the *Cork Constitution*, it demonstrated a grasp of developments that eluded many more traditionally nationalist newspapers.

The sense of fairness was particularly evident in it is response to the Easter Rising. Unlike the *Tuam Herald* and the *Roscommon Herald*, the *Skibbereen Eagle* did not engage in any sensationalist allegations of German intrigue but concentrated on identifying the factors that led to the rebellion. Equally, the *Eagle*'s criticism of Sinn Féin did not descend into insinuations of treasonable activities based on supposed collaboration with Germany. Nor did it carelessly link Sinn Féin to instances of violence. Instead, it focused on what it believed was the unrealistic nature of Sinn Féin's primary demand of an Irish Republic. Its warning to

---

[121]   *Skibbereen Eagle*, 10 Dec. 1921. The paper believed that 'everybody instinctively feels this severance is but temporary'.
[122]   *Skibbereen Eagle*, 24 Dec. 1921.

Eamon de Valera in July 1921 that agreeing to negotiate with the British Government effectively nullified any prospect of an Irish Republic was to prove prophetic. Despite the considered and reasoned nature of the *Eagle*'s coverage it was still targeted by the IRA. Along with the *Cork Constitution*, *Cork Examiner*, and *Irish Independent*, the *Skibbereen Eagle* discovered that criticism of republican tactics or strategy would not be allowed to go unchecked. In the *Eagle*'s case, such attention marked the beginning of the end for the paper, and less than twenty-five years after it saw fit to issue a warning to the Tsar of Russia it disappeared from the Irish newspaper scene for good.

Southern Star

Origins

In his famed memoir of his experiences during the Irish War of Independence, the renowned IRA leader, Tom Barry, did not hold back in his disdain for the town of Skibbereen and its residents. According to Barry, 'its inhabitants were a race apart from the sturdy people of West Cork' who 'with a few exceptions were spineless, slouching through life meek and tame, prepared to accept ruling and domination from any clique or country'. In his prolonged condemnation of the town he also remarked that the town posed no threat to the IRA as the citizens of Skibbereen 'lacked the energy and gumption to be actively hostile to anything'.[123] Regardless of the supposed indolence and docility of the town's populace, Skibbereen had at least shown an energy and enthusiasm for the newspaper trade that was not evident anywhere else in the county outside of the city of Cork. At the start of the twentieth century, Skibbereen, quite remarkably, was the only town in County Cork to have sustained a local press of any significance.[124] Indeed, by this time the town was served by two successful newspapers, the aforementioned *Skibbereen Eagle* and the *Southern Star*, which was first published in 1890.

Mathew Potter notes that 'the perceived pro-British and Protestant tone of the *Eagle*' led to the establishment of 'the much more strongly nationalist *Southern Star*'.[125] The paper was founded by John O'Sullivan

---

123 Tom Barry, *Guerrilla days in Ireland* (Dublin, 1981), p. 89.
124 *Southern Star 1889–1989: Centenary Supplement* (11 Nov. 1989).
125 Potter, 'Keeping an eye on the Tsar', p. 53.

with the assistance of his brother Florence. Little is known of John O'Sullivan except that he was involved in the printing trade while Florence O'Sullivan was a qualified solicitor. However, the O'Sullivan brothers did not retain a controlling interest in the paper for very long. In 1892, the *Southern Star* was sold to a consortium led by Monsignor John O'Leary of Clonakilty. The consortium consisted of ten shareholders, including another two priests (Father Michael Cunningham and Father Daniel O'Brien), once again signifying the highly notable clerical involvement in Irish provincial newspapers during this period.[126] Nonetheless, unlike many other provincial titles the *Southern Star* was not dominated by an individual personality as was the case at newspapers such as the *Westmeath Examiner* (J.P. Hayden), *Kilkenny People* (E.T. Keane), and *Roscommon Herald* (Jasper Tully). Accordingly, the paper experienced a rather high turnover of editors in the first two decades of its existence.

During this period, the *Southern Star* appears to have had as many as six different editors. Florence O'Sullivan was succeeded by J.J. Comerford, while others who edited the paper included Michael J. Flynn, Patrick J. O'Driscoll, and Seumas O'Kelly. Flynn later moved to the *Freeman's Journal* but ended his career at the *Brisbane Courier* in Australia, having emigrated there after his health became impaired.[127] O'Driscoll's tenure as editor was quite brief, only lasting from 1901 until 1902. He then established the *West Cork People* in his home town of Clonakilty, one of the very few papers in the county to be established outside either Cork City or Skibbereen. The paper only lasted a few years, however, closing in 1907 due to an expensive libel action. O'Driscoll was a brother-in-law of Michael Collins, having married his sister Margaret. He later served on the editorial staff of the *Cork Free Press* as well as acting as Irish correspondent of the *Catholic Herald*.[128] O'Kelly became editor of the *Southern Star* around 1903 before moving on to the editorship of the *Leinster Leader* about three years later. He subsequently developed a close friendship with Arthur Griffith and even edited *Nationality* for a brief spell during 1918 while Griffith was imprisoned. Seumas O'Kelly died suddenly in November 1918 after being taken ill at the Sinn Féin offices at Harcourt Street in Dublin.[129] However, the most celebrated

---

[126] *Southern Star 1889–1989: Centenary Supplement* (11 Nov. 1989).

[127] *Irish Times*, 15 Oct. 1928.

[128] *Southern Star*, 7 Sept. 1940; *Southern Star 1889–1989: Centenary Supplement* (11 Nov. 1989).

[129] *Irish Independent*, 15 Nov. 1918; *Irish Times*, 6 Oct. 1969. Seumas O'Kelly is additionally remembered as a noted playwright and was also a brother of Michael

editor of the *Southern Star* in its first twenty years of publication was D.D. Sheehan. Originally from Kanturk, County Cork, Sheehan was a teacher prior to embarking on a journalistic career. He initially worked at the *Glasgow Observer* and the *Catholic News* of Preston while he also served on the staff of the *Cork Constitution*. His time in the editorial chair of the *Southern Star* was quite brief (1898–1901) as he resigned the post after being elected MP for Mid-Cork in 1900. He retained this seat until 1918, being returned unopposed on a number of occasions, but did not stand at the general election in December of that year.[130]

Suppression, takeover, suppression

Any disruption that the *Southern Star* may have experienced due to the high turnover of editors in its first twenty years pales into insignificance in comparison with the turbulent times it endured from around 1916 onwards. The first instance of such turbulence arrived on 13 November 1916 when police seized the paper's plant and machinery and duly suppressed the *Southern Star*. In correspondence with the Under-Secretary beforehand, Lord Decies commented that a recent issue of the paper contained 'many undesirable passages'.[131] Following the police action, the *Irish Independent* reported that the *Star*'s editor believed the suppression was due to the publication of an article entitled 'Masons and Mollies' that dealt with police agitation.[132] At the time, the editor was James Michael (J.M.) Burke, who had been appointed shortly before the Easter Rising and was to have a long association with the paper.[133] The matter of the paper's suppression was raised in the House of Commons by Joseph Devlin of the Irish Parliamentary Party. After questioning why such action was taken against the paper, Devlin was brusquely informed

O'Kelly, who succeeded him as editor of the *Leinster Leader* and was arrested after the Easter Rising.

[130] *Southern Star 1889–1989: Centenary Supplement* (11 Nov. 1989); *Irish Independent*, 29 Nov. 1948; *Southern Star,* 4 Dec. 1948. At the outbreak of World War I, Sheehan joined the Munster Fusiliers while three of his sons also enlisted in the British Army, two of whom were killed in action. Along with William O'Brien, he declared his support for Sinn Féin following the failure to implement Home Rule. He retired from active politics in 1918 and was engaged in journalism and business until his death in 1948.

[131] Press Censorship Records 1916–1919, 3/722/13-19, 6 Nov. 1916.

[132] *Irish Independent*, 14 Nov. 1916.

[133] *Southern Star 1889–1989: Centenary Supplement* (11 Nov. 1989).

by the Chief Secretary, Mr Duke, that the suppression was due to the publication of statements likely to cause disaffection.[134] The *Southern Star* was permitted to resume publication just under a month later though little indication was forthcoming as to why it was allowed recommence operations at that stage.[135] The curious aspect of the suppression was that at that time the paper had no real or perceived link to Sinn Féin, which was a factor common to the actions taken against other provincial newspapers in the months following the Easter Rising. The absence of such a republican link was to change dramatically just over a year later.

On 26 December 1917, the *Irish Independent* reported that the *Southern Star*, 'hitherto an advocate of the Irish Party, has been purchased by the Sinn Féin Party' for £570.[136] Prior to the Sinn Féin acquisition, the paper was still owned by the consortium assembled by Monsignor John O'Leary over twenty-five years earlier. One of the main facilitators of the takeover was Peadar O'Hourihane, who was to play a significant role under the new ownership. Among the large group that constituted the new proprietorship were three men who were later to become TDs: Seán Buckley, Seán Hales, and Seán Hayes. Michael Collins (along with his brother John M. Collins) was listed as one of the early shareholders though Peter Hart further credits Collins with assisting in putting together the group of investors that bought the paper.[137] Collins's enthusiasm for the project no doubt stemmed from what Tim Pat Coogan describes as his 'interest in newspapers which never left him' after he worked as a very young man at the *West Cork People*, the paper owned by his brother-in-law, the aforementioned Patrick J. O'Driscoll.[138] With such an overtly republican ownership in place it was highly unlikely that the paper would escape the attention of the British authorities for very long.

In total, the *Southern Star* was suppressed three times between 1918 and 1919. The first occasion was in April 1918 when it was deemed by Lord Decies to be one of a number of newspapers whose tone was 'distinctly bad, and likely to cause disaffection'. The suppression lasted four weeks though some of the other titles suppressed at the same time,

134 *Irish Times*, 18 Nov. 1916.
135 *Cork Examiner*, 11 Dec. 1916.
136 *Irish Independent*, 26 Dec. 1917.
137 *Southern Star 1889–1989: Centenary Supplement* (11 Nov. 1989); Peter Hart, *Mick: the real Michael Collins* (London, 2005), p. 121.
138 Tim Pat Coogan, *Michael Collins: a biography* (London, 1990), p. 15. At the *West Cork People* Collins 'learnt to type, acted as a copyboy, and wrote up sporting events'.

most notably the *Clare Champion*, were subjected to longer periods of enforced closure.[139] The second suppression began in late August 1918 and turned out to be the lengthiest. The reason given for the police action in dismantling and removing the printing machinery was the increasingly standard line that the paper had published content 'likely to cause disaffection'.[140] The previous month, Decies had written to the paper to advise that its publication of a letter from an Irish prisoner being held in England was in breach of censorship regulations.[141] Nonetheless, this may not have been the reason for its suppression. Local IRA commander Liam Deasy later claimed that it was because the *Southern Star* had been the first newspaper to publish an account of an attempt by Crown forces to capture Tom and William Hales, both brothers of Seán Hales. According to Deasy, the two brothers had been involved in 'hiding material that was intended for use in manufacturing shotgun bayonets'.[142] While this could have been a contributory factor, Michael Collins believed there may have been another reason. In a letter to a local Sinn Féin activist Collins indicated that the suppression may have been due to the alleged production of some handbills (possibly relating to the upcoming general election) at the *Southern Star* plant.[143]

Whatever the reason for the initial action against the paper, it appears that Decies did not favour such a lengthy ban on the *Southern Star*. In a memo to the Under-Secretary in September 1918 he advised that the paper would 'give any guarantee necessary if allowed to resume work' and that he believed 'the suppression of the paper has been a good lesson to them'.[144] Indeed, there is a level of confusion around this particular suppression. This is evident from a letter sent by the paper's business manager, Seamus O'Brien, to Ernest Blythe, then editor of the paper but imprisoned at Belfast following his arrest in March 1918. O'Brien stated that 'Lord Decies knew nothing of the suppression and did not seem to like the idea of the military authorities taking the full

---

[139] Press Censorship Report, Mar. 1918, CO904/166/2. The most notable of the other papers to be suppressed at the same time were the *Mayo News*, *Galway Express*, *Westmeath Independent*, and *Weekly Observer*.

[140] *Freeman's Journal*, *Irish Independent*, *Irish Times*, 26 Aug. 1918.

[141] Press Censorship Records 1916–1919, 3/722/20-66, 9 July 1918.

[142] Liam Deasy, *Towards Ireland free: the West Cork brigade in the War of Independence, 1917–1921* (Dublin, 1973), p. 22.

[143] Collins to Kelly, 18 Nov. 1918 (University College Dublin, Irish Volunteers papers, P16).

[144] Press Censorship Records 1916–1919, 3/722/29-47, 12 Sept. 1918.

power into their own hands'.[145] With the suppression well into its fifth month, O'Brien decided to write to the national newspapers to publicise the *Star*'s plight. In a letter to the *Irish Independent* he protested that no reason had been given for the banning of the paper, it had taken place without the knowledge of Lord Decies, and that requests to meet with the military authorities at Cork to try resolve the matter had not even merited a response.[146]

The *Southern Star* was eventually permitted to resume publication in April 1919 though no specific reason was provided for the lengthy suppression or why the ban was lifted at that particular time.[147] In its first editorial upon its return the paper claimed that the only response to its many requests for information on the matter was that the 'action was taken under the Defence of the Realm regulations'.[148] The suppression of almost thirty weeks was one of the longest endured by any Irish provincial newspaper. However, it was not long before the authorities focused its attention on the *Southern Star* once more. On 27 October 1919, a force of about a dozen policemen arrived at the paper's offices and duly dismantled and removed its printing machinery.[149] This third suppression resulted from the publication of the Dáil Éireann loan prospectus.[150] Although a number of newspaper reports in January 1920 indicated that the ban had been lifted, this third suppression lasted until March 1920.[151] In total, the paper was banned for almost fifty-six weeks during the two-year period from March 1918. Consequently, the challenge faced by the new owners of the *Southern Star* was all the more difficult.

The people behind the *Star*

Many of those who owned, managed, or edited the *Southern Star* from the time of the Sinn Féin takeover in late 1917 until the end of the War of Independence could well justify substantive scrutiny in their own right.

---

[145] O'Brien to Blythe, 15 Jan. 1919 (University College Dublin, Ernest Blythe papers, P24/1028).

[146] *Irish Independent*, 17 Jan. 1919.

[147] *Irish Independent*, 31 Mar. 1919; *Irish Times*, 5 Apr. 1919.

[148] *Southern Star*, 5 Apr. 1919.

[149] *Cork Examiner, Irish Independent*, 28 Oct. 1919; *Irish Times*, 1 Nov. 1919.

[150] Inspector General's and County Inspectors' monthly confidential reports, Oct. 1919, CO904/110-250.

[151] *Irish Independent*, 15 Jan. 1920; *Cork Examiner*, 15, 16 Jan., 19 Mar. 1920; *Freeman's Journal*, 15 Jan., 19 Mar. 1920; *Irish Times*, 27 Mar. 1920.

In the case of Michael Collins, a shareholder in the paper, such detailed scrutiny already exists in abundance. Nevertheless, it is both worthwhile and instructive to consider some of the other figures centrally involved in the paper during these years. Seán Hayes, a member of the group that acquired the *Southern Star* in 1917 and who also edited the paper for a time, fought in the GPO in Dublin during Easter Week 1916 and was subsequently imprisoned at Frongoch internment camp in Wales. He was elected MP for the West Cork constituency in December 1918, was re-elected in 1921 and took a pro-Treaty stance.[152]

From about 1916 onwards, Seán Buckley, another of those involved in the acquisition, was actively involved in Sinn Féin and the Irish Volunteers and was imprisoned at Belfast during 1918. He was a member of the West Cork brigade of the IRA from 1919 until the truce of July 1921. Buckley took the republican side following the Anglo-Irish Treaty and endured further terms of imprisonment at Cork, Mountjoy, Newbridge, and Kilmainham.[153] Seán Hales, also involved in the Sinn Féin takeover, had even stronger republican credentials. He joined the Irish Volunteers in 1915 and was imprisoned at Frongoch in Wales following the Easter Rising. He became a battalion commander in the West Cork brigade of the IRA and was involved in many operations during the Anglo-Irish conflict, most notably at Crossbarry in March 1921. Later that year he was elected to Dáil Éireann for the Cork mid, north, south, south-east, and west constituency and was the only IRA brigadier from Cork to support the Anglo-Irish Treaty. He was re-elected to Dáil Éireann in June 1922 but was shot dead by republican gunmen in Dublin in December of that year.[154]

Buckley and Hales had little involvement in the ongoing management of the *Southern Star* but the republican connections of those who played a more significant role were also quite considerable. The main instigator of the acquisition, Peadar O'Hourihane (or Peadar O'hAnnracháin, as he preferred to be known) was a renowned Gaelic League organiser, which resulted in his activities being monitored by the RIC as early as

---

[152] *Southern Star 1889–1989: Centenary Supplement* (11 Nov. 1989); *Irish Independent*, 25 Jan. 1928. Hayes was also a close friend of Michael Collins and is not be confused with Seán Hayes of the *Meath Chronicle* as detailed in Chapter 2.

[153] *Irish Press*, 2 Dec. 1963. Buckley later represented Fianna Fáil in Dáil Éireann for the West Cork constituency from 1938 until 1948 and for South Cork from 1948 to 1954.

[154] Maurice Cronin, 'Hales, Seán' in McGuire and Quinn, *Dictionary of Irish biography*.

June 1914.[155] An early Sinn Féin activist in his home town of Skibbereen he was imprisoned at Wakefield and Reading following the Easter Rising and later took an active part in the War of Independence.[156] The aforementioned Seamus O'Brien, business manager at the paper for a time during this period, was arrested and imprisoned during the War of Independence. He later married Nora Connolly, daughter of James Connolly.[157] Similarly, Dick Connolly, who succeeded O'Brien as the paper's business manager during 1919, was a prominent IRA member and described as a 'War of Independence courier for Michael Collins'.[158] Connolly briefly edited the paper during 1920 and was one of a number of people to occupy the editorial chair between 1916 and 1921.[159]

In all, there appears to have been seven different editors of the *Southern Star* between 1916 and 1921. By mid-1920, the aforementioned J.M. Burke, Peadar O'Hourihane, Seán Hayes, and Dick Connolly had each edited the paper for relatively short spells. They were succeeded by Arthur Nix in late 1920 and subsequently by Eoin Sharkey, both of whom had similarly brief terms in the editorial chair. Nix ultimately took a legal action against the paper for wrongful dismissal in which, by coincidence, he was represented by Jasper Wolfe of the *Skibbereen Eagle*.[160] The last of these seven editors also only enjoyed a brief tenure but was, nonetheless, the most famous figure to occupy the position. Ernest Blythe became editor of the *Southern Star* early in 1918, principally due to the influence of Peadar O'Hourihane.[161] Blythe's lengthy career is well documented. A member of the Gaelic League, the Irish Volunteers, the IRB, and Sinn Féin, he was elected as an MP for North Monaghan in December 1918

---

155 Police Reports, June 1914, CO904/120/4-98; May 1915, CO904/120/6-134; Nov. 1915, CO904/120/9-197; Dec. 1915, CO904/120/10-214; Inspector General's and County Inspectors' monthly confidential reports, Jan. 1917, CO904/102-13.

156 *Southern Star* 1889–1989: Centenary Supplement (11 Nov. 1989); *Irish Times*, 30 Mar. 1965. Peadar O'hAnnracháin also contributed to nationalist publications such as *An Claidheamh Soluis* and *Irish Freedom* and was a respected author in both Irish and English. His most noted work was *Fé bhrat an chonnartha*, a diary of his Gaelic League days.

157 *Southern Star 1889–1989: Centenary Supplement* (11 Nov. 1989).

158 Ibid.; Lawrence William White, 'O'Brien, Nora Connolly' in McGuire and Quinn, *Dictionary of Irish biography*.

159 *Cork Examiner*, 16 Jan. 1920. Connolly's term as editor seems to have been quite brief but he signed himself as editor in a letter to the *Cork Examiner* in January 1920 to refute reports that the suppression of the *Southern Star* had been lifted.

160 *Freeman's Journal*, 12 Apr. 1921.

161 *Southern Star 1889–1989: Centenary Supplement* (11 Nov. 1989).

and later held several different ministerial positions in the Free State Government. However, his time at the *Southern Star* was cut short when he was arrested in early March 1918 for contravening an undertaking to reside within a short distance of his father's house in County Antrim.[162]

The editorial instability only ended late in 1921 when J.M. Burke was reappointed editor. Burke's connection to the *Star* pre-dated the Sinn Féin acquisition, which he did not favour as he did not appear to hold republican sympathies. Indeed, even after his reappointment as editor in 1921 Burke had a frequently fractious relationship with the directors of the paper. Like many of his predecessors he was elected to political office, being returned as a Cumann na nGaedheal TD for West Cork in the 1933 general election. Unlike most of his predecessors, J.M. Burke remained as editor for a sustained period: his tenure lasted almost fourteen years and provided the paper with a period of stability that had proved highly elusive during the first three decades of its existence.[163]

Editorial comment, 1914–1921

Even a cursory perusal of the contents of the *Southern Star* during these years provides some indication that it was catering to a slightly different readership from the other two Cork newspapers already profiled in this chapter. Normally comprising eight pages, the paper was generally divided into eight columns. Two or three pages usually comprised of advertisements. Unlike the *Cork Constitution* and the *Skibbereen Eagle*, advertisements for motor cars and foreign travel were rare.[164] Amongst the most regular items being promoted were medications to deal with ailments such as backache, toothache, and sore throats. Also featuring prominently in the advertising sections were agricultural items such as farm implements, cart and rick covers, seeds, feedstuffs, and animal medications. Indeed, the paper featured a farming column as well as a lady's column that mostly contained household and cookery tips. The outward appearance of the paper did not change significantly following the Sinn Féin takeover apart from the masthead, which was altered to display the paper's title in Irish,

---

[162] *Freeman's Journal*, 5 Mar. 1918; Witness Statement (Bureau of Military History, Ernest Blythe, WS939).

[163] *Southern Star 1889–1989: Centenary Supplement* (11 Nov. 1989); *Southern Star*, 12 Sept. 1936.

[164] Even though such notices were quite infrequent the paper occasionally featured advertisements for sea travel with the Canadian Pacific Company accompanied by a note promising 'special arrangements for the celebration of holy mass'.

Réalt a'Deiscirt. Unsurprisingly, the content of the paper's editorial columns is somewhat more difficult to summarise.

The *Southern Star*'s editorial comment is quite fragmented during this period, particularly from late 1916 onwards. This is principally due to the various suppressions that collectively meant that the paper lost just over a year of publication. The change of ownership in addition to the unusually high turnover of those occupying the editorial chair did little to help mitigate this situation. Nevertheless, at certain stages the leading articles of the *Star* displayed some similarities with those of its provincial counterparts. Even allowing for the considerably reduced amount of editorial output and its unambiguous affiliation to one side in the Anglo-Irish conflict, the *Star*'s editorials still merits detailed scrutiny.

As 1914 dawned, the *Southern Star* did not differ from so many other nationalist newspapers in anticipating the passing of Home Rule in an almost celebratory manner. It not only expressed its gratitude to 'John Redmond and his faithful, pledge-bound, and disciplined party' but also dismissed unionist opposition in the belief that 'the most bellicose covenanter of last year' was 'to become the most harmless lamb of 1914'.[165] Although this attitude changed with the arming of the Ulster Volunteers, the paper still doubted the resilience of Ulster opposition when the Home Rule bill was placed on the statute book nine months later. It accepted that the convening of a new parliament in Dublin was not feasible in wartime but also confidently predicted that 'many of the most influential unionists in Ulster are disinclined to offer further opposition to Home Rule once the bill has received the Royal Assent'.[166]

The *Southern Star* differed from titles such as the *Tuam Herald* and *Skibbereen Eagle* by not articulating any specific allegiance to Britain or the Empire but there was little doubt that it supported the British war effort. One of its more notable editorials in the early months of the war not only declared that 'this is Ireland's war as well as England's' but also excoriated Sinn Féin for its attitude to the war even though the party scarcely occupied any position of prominence at the time. In a prolonged editorial assault, Sinn Féin was accused of wishing to 'substitute Prussian militarism for British Government' and furthermore was willing to 'substitute the German language for the Irish'. The sustained attack also asserted that 'the Sinn Féiner is a political humbug whose sense of patriotism is generally confined to the depths of his own pocket'.[167]

165 *Southern Star*, 3 Jan. 1914.
166 *Southern Star*, 19 Sept. 1914.
167 *Southern Star*, 12 Dec. 1914.

Despite the obvious contempt for Sinn Féin, the paper refrained from automatically linking the party to the Easter Rising as was the case with so many other newspapers.

Although it deplored 'this late, insane, and hopeless rising' the *Star*'s editorial response was by no means condemnatory. In calling for an end to the executions of 'the vanquished and misguided insurgents' a considerable degree of admiration and respect was clearly evident. Without qualification, the paper acknowledged the 'pluck, bravery, honesty of motive and high purposed endeavour' of the rebels and recognised the fact that many of them were willing to make 'the supreme sacrifice of laying down their lives for a cause which they believed to be a just one'. Any anger that the Rising had engendered was reserved for Sir Edward Carson. It was Carson, the paper declared, who had 'preached open treason', 'defied the Government', and 'lunched with the Kaiser' and consequently was 'primarily responsible for the tragic rising'.[168]

The shift in political sympathy that followed the Easter Rising at papers such as the *Kilkenny People* and *Mayo News* was not evident to any great extent at the *Southern Star*. The Sinn Féin by-election victories during 1917 were afforded scant editorial attention. Instead, the paper focused on the ill-fated Irish Convention, though there was obviously a realisation that Sinn Féin was an emerging force as the *Star* encouraged the party to participate.[169] Shortly before the change of ownership this realisation had developed into a grudging acceptance that most Sinn Féin members were 'patriotic Irishmen, sincerely interested in the advancement and betterment of their country'.[170] The suppression of the paper at various stages during 1918 and early 1919 meant that the *Star* was prevented from passing comment on landmark developments such as the 1918 general election results and the first meeting of Dáil Éireann. Nonetheless, it is not unreasonable to speculate that with a republican ownership in place the main thrust of its editorial output was unlikely to have differed substantially from other pro-Sinn Féin organs such as the

---

[168]   *Southern Star,* 6 May 1916. In the same issue the paper also published a tribute to 'The Late P.H. Pearse' signed by 'A Friend'. In a moving testimonial, the writer expressed disapproval for Pearse's actions but proceeded to describe him as being 'incapable of a mean act or an unworthy thought', 'a brilliant scholar, an attractive writer, a thorough gentleman' whose 'head may have gone wrong but his heart was right' and the motives that inspired him and his colleagues 'were genuine and pure'.

[169]   *Southern Star*, 23 June 1917.

[170]   *Southern Star*, 27 Oct. 1917.

Enniscorthy Echo, *Meath Chronicle*, or *Mayo News*. What is of significantly more value from a historical perspective is an examination of how a Sinn Féin organ such as the *Southern Star* responded to the Anglo-Irish Treaty of 1921.

In this respect, the *Southern Star* reflected the sentiments of the majority of other nationalist newspapers whether pro-Sinn Féin or otherwise. The Irish plenipotentiaries were praised as 'far-seeing statesmen that could not be bought or bullied, cajoled or coerced into a settlement'. The agreement they had secured 'may not be ideally perfect but this is a world of stern realities and disagreeable imperfections'.[171] The Ulster question was not overlooked as it was by many other papers but, in common with the few titles that saw fit to consider the issue, the *Star* fell into the trap of assuming that Unionists would eventually come to their senses and throw in their lot with the Irish Free State:

> The solution of the Ulster problem may not be wholly satisfactory, but the Orangemen are Mammon-worshippers and are sometimes wise in their generation. They have no more to expect from Westminster, in fortune and in name, by tradition and geographical necessity they are bound to the rest of Ireland and they may be as reluctant to leave an Irish Free State as they were slow to enter it.[172]

As it became clear that not all republicans were willing to accept the Treaty's imperfections the *Southern Star* angrily dismissed any associated criticism of Michael Collins. 'No sane person', the paper asserted, 'would for a moment entertain the thought that Mr M. Collins would be a party to any lowering of the nation's honour'.[173] Yet it was quite evident that it had no wish to encourage any division in republican ranks as it deemed de Valera 'a chivalrous, dauntless soldier'. Nevertheless, the suggestion of an alternative oath of allegiance was considered excessively pedantic and a simple matter of 'Tweedledum and Tweedledee'.[174] The paper's final editorial of 1921 expressed the same fear and articulated sentiments akin to those of many other provincial titles. 'What is the alternative proposal?', the *Star* asked before stating bluntly that 'the other alternative is hideous war, red ruin, destruction and desolation'.[175]

---

[171]   *Southern Star*, 10 Dec. 1921.
[172]   Ibid.
[173]   *Southern Star*, 17 Dec. 1921.
[174]   *Southern Star*, 24 Dec. 1921.
[175]   *Southern Star*, 31 Dec. 1921.

Conclusion

The editorial commentary of the *Southern Star* between 1914 and 1921 might almost seem of secondary importance when compared to the overall turbulence experienced by the paper in the first three decades or so of its existence. Between 1890 and 1921, the *Southern Star* had three different sets of owners, as many as thirteen different editors, and was suppressed on three separate occasions. Amongst the figures associated with the paper was one who was elected an MP (D.D. Sheehan), three who were elected both as MPs and TDs (Michael Collins, Ernest Blythe, and Seán Hayes), and three others who were also elected as TDs (Seán Buckley, Seán Hales, and J.M. Burke). The disruption caused by changes in ownership and editorship, plus the multitude of personalities that assumed roles in the paper, meant that it did not display some of the traits that were evident at so many other Irish provincial papers such as family ownership or a prolonged period under the guidance of a specific individual. Consequently, the sense of continuity that was a mark of several of its counterparts was absent from the *Southern Star*. Nevertheless, the overall editorial comment between 1914 and 1921 displayed many similarities to that of other provincial organs. This is best illustrated by its support for the Allied war effort, criticism of Sir Edward Carson and the Ulster Unionists following the Easter Rising, and perhaps most pertinently, its strong defence of the Anglo-Irish Treaty. Nonetheless, it is the *Southern Star*'s own particular history that is the most compelling and earns it such a prominent place in the broader history of the Irish provincial press.

Clonmel Chronicle

Joseph Napier Higgins was the main driving force behind the foundation of the *Clonmel Chronicle* in 1848. Higgins was a barrister and went on to amass a fortune in London as a recognised authority on joint-stock company law. The paper was printed by Edmond Woods who eventually assumed the role of sole proprietor and editor.[176] The *Chronicle* became an official organ of the Conservative Party but unlike many of its contemporaries it did not engage in personalised attacks and consequently steered clear of costly libel actions. Indeed, the paper soon gained a reputation for

---

[176] William P. Burke, *History of Clonmel* (Kilkenny, 1983), p. 356.

accurate and reliable reporting.[177] Edmond Woods died in 1893 following which the *Chronicle* was acquired by David Montgomery and two other journalists who had been involved in the management of the paper along with Montgomery.[178] The paper ceased publication for two months during 1910 and on its return declared itself an independent organ. A new board of directors was also in place following the resumption of publication. The new directors were Thomas Morrisey, Thomas Skehan, James Reidy, Denis Lowry, and John Mulcahy. All of them were prominent Clonmel businessmen and all were from a nationalist background.[179]

Despite the nationalist sympathies of those now controlling the *Clonmel Chronicle* the editor that was appointed under the new ownership was a northern Presbyterian with a solidly unionist background. Arthur Ross Burns was from Newry, County Armagh and a son of Joseph F. Burns who had founded the *Newry Reporter* in 1867. Following his father's death in 1900, Arthur Ross Burns sold the paper and moved on to edit the *Lisburn Standard*. He subsequently edited the tri-weekly *Derry Standard* but a difference of opinion with the proprietor, J.G. Glendenning, about Lloyd George's 'People's Budget' of 1909, resulted in Burns parting company with the paper. It was at this stage that he moved south to Clonmel to take over as editor and manager of the *Clonmel Chronicle*. He remained at the helm of the paper until his death in 1927.[180]

Information regarding other journalists who worked for the *Chronicle* is in short supply though the same could be said for most other Irish provincial newspapers. Nonetheless, it is known that John Griffin, who succeeded Brandon J. Long as editor of the *Clonmel Nationalist*, worked as a reporter at the *Clonmel Chronicle* for about three years before moving on to the town's rival newspaper around 1919.[181] Another journalist to follow a similar path was a more celebrated figure. Tommy O'Brien spent forty years as a broadcaster with RTÉ radio but as a young man in the early 1920s he was a cub reporter with the *Clonmel Chronicle* before moving to the *Clonmel Nationalist*, which he later edited. O'Brien joined Fianna Éireann at the age of fifteen and was later a dispatch rider for the South Tipperary Brigade of the IRA where he encountered both Dan Breen and Seamus Robinson.[182]

---

[177] Hayes, *Guide to Tipperary newspapers*, p. 6.
[178] O'Donnell, *Clonmel 1900–1932*, pp 215–16.
[179] Ibid., p. 216; Hayes, *Guide to Tipperary newspapers*, p. 6.
[180] *Clonmel Chronicle*, 12 Mar. 1927; *Newry Reporter*, 16 Nov. 1967.
[181] *Clonmel Nationalist*, 7 Feb. 1942.
[182] *Irish Times*, 23 May 1987; 1 Jan., 25 Feb. 1988; Gus Smith, *Tommy O'Brien,*

Editorial comment, 1914–1921

Rather unusually for a provincial newspaper the *Clonmel Chronicle* was published twice weekly. Appearing on Saturday and Wednesday, it normally consisted of eight pages though this dropped to four for a period during 1918. Similar to so many other papers, its front page was completely comprised of advertisements. Such advertisements and those on other pages embraced the standard fare of drapery stores and agricultural machinery though a significant amount of motor car advertisements suggests a slightly more affluent readership. The *Clonmel Chronicle* also operated its own printing business that also featured prominently amongst the paper's advertisements.

If the *Clonmel Chronicle*'s advertising sections differed little from other provincial newspapers the same could certainly not be said of its editorial comment. This was not due to the paper's leading articles containing any sensational declarations; rather, it was attributable to the simple fact that no editorial comment was passed on almost all the major events that took place between 1914 and 1921. The Home Rule crisis, the outbreak and progress of World War I, the 1916 Rising, the rise of Sinn Féin, and the many violent incidents during the War of Independence all received a certain amount of coverage in the *Chronicle*, but from an editorial perspective the paper maintained a silence on these matters. Indeed, for much of the 1914–21 period the editorial columns merely consisted of a few brief local announcements under the heading 'local and general pars.' (i.e. paragraphs). To a considerable extent, the editorial policy of the *Chronicle* reflected that of the *Leitrim Observer*, though the leading articles of the Carrick-on-Shannon-based newspaper were more regularly interspersed with strong views on contemporary developments.

The editorial trend of featuring only brief local announcements began to change during 1920 and 1921. However, it was by no means a radical change. Actual leading articles rather than brief announcements began to appear but invariably they dealt solely with local matters. Editorial headings such as 'Clonmel's waterway', 'Street dangers in Clonmel', 'Sanitation in Clonmel', 'Support local industries', 'Clonmel mental hospital milk supply', and 'Clonmel town clerkship' more than

good evening listeners (Dublin, 1987), pp 8–9. Although O'Brien's obituary in the *Irish Times* credits him with being an IRA dispatch rider while working as a cub reporter it seems more likely that his career in journalism started just after the Anglo-Irish Treaty of 1921.

adequately illustrate how the *Chronicle* obviously considered itself a local newspaper in every sense of the word.[183] Even the editorial response to the outbreak of war in 1914 confined itself to how it would affect local affairs such as the cancellation of a local cattle mart, the indefinite postponement of a local horse show, and the fact that 'it seems clear that Powerstown Park Races cannot now be held'.[184] The truce of July 1921 was warmly welcomed as was the Anglo-Irish Treaty several months later, though the paper was extremely careful not to tread on any political sensibilities.[185]

Conclusion

Editorially, the *Clonmel Chronicle* assumed the role of a disinterested bystander during the 1914–21 period. While the paper may have aspired to maintaining an appearance of absolute impartiality, this unstated policy was still rather strange. After all, County Tipperary was one of the most militant counties during this period and, as Michael Hopkinson has noted, South Tipperary in particular has been most strongly identified with the War of Independence.[186] Accordingly, the editorial silence of the *Chronicle*, one of South Tipperary's two newspapers at the time, with regard to ongoing developments, seems more like a disservice to its readers than a noble attempt to avoid any sense of bias. Possibly the paper's unionist editor, Arthur Ross Burns, disapproved of the militant nationalism that was asserting itself in his midst but felt that discretion was the better part of valour and that he could not vent such feelings in a catchment area that was predominantly nationalist. Unfortunately, this is only speculation, but what is known is that the *Chronicle* ultimately went the way of so many other Irish newspapers that had originally been established as solidly unionist organs. The *Clonmel Chronicle* ceased publication in 1935 when the company was purchased by the *Clonmel Nationalist*.[187]

[183] *Clonmel Chronicle*, 16 Oct., 3 Nov. 1920, 4 June, 27 July, 19 Oct., 10 Dec. 1921.

[184] *Clonmel Chronicle*, 5 Aug. 1914.

[185] *Clonmel Chronicle*, 30 July, 14, 17, 31 Dec. 1921.

[186] Hopkinson, *The Irish War of Independence*, p. 115.

[187] *Cork Examiner, Irish Independent, Irish Press*, 30 Mar. 1935.

Kerryman

Upon its establishment in 1904, the *Kerryman* joined a comparatively large group of newspapers serving County Kerry, all of which were published in Tralee. The new paper faced the very difficult task not only of remaining financially viable in a town that was already served by a comparatively large number of newspapers, but also of simply surviving in an extremely precarious newspaper environment. The clearly perilous nature of launching a newspaper in such conditions obviously did not discourage Maurice Griffin, and cousins Thomas and Daniel Nolan, the founding fathers of the *Kerryman*.[188] To compound such a hazardous venture Griffin was the only member of the triumvirate to have any previous experience in journalism, having worked as a legal correspondent at the *Kerry Weekly Reporter*. Originally from Dingle, Griffin spent eleven years working on the commercial staff of a building firm in Tralee, which was where he first came into contact with Thomas Nolan, the future co-founder of the paper.[189] The new publication demonstrated similar traits to many other provincial organs launched during this era such as strong support for 'Irish Ireland' movements, most notably the Gaelic League and the GAA, and a keen Catholicism.[190] This was particularly exemplified by Daniel Nolan who in 1896 became secretary of the first branch of the Gaelic League in the county and was also a founder member of the Tralee Catholic Literary Society.[191]

One distinguishing feature of the *Kerryman* when it was launched in 1904 was that it did not carry advertisements on its front page, which certainly set it apart from almost all other newspapers. Its early issues usually comprised ten pages, which was somewhat unusual for such a fledgling publication. By the outbreak of World War I, ten years later, the *Kerryman* normally consisted of ten to twelve pages, though this dropped to six during 1916 and rose to eight following the end of the war. The masthead contained the wording, 'All the News of Interest to Kerrymen' above a front page filled with news. Those advertisements that appeared within the paper were principally for clothing stores, household items, foodstuffs, agricultural machinery and supplies, while there were occasional advertisements for motor cars, motorcycles, and bicycles. There were also frequent notices relating to farming matters in

---

[188] *The Kerryman: 1904–2004* (5 Aug. 2004).

[189] *Kerryman*, 7 Apr. 1928.

[190] *The Kerryman: 1904–2004* (5 Aug. 2004); *Kerryman*, 8 Apr. 1939.

[191] *Kerryman*, 23 Apr. 1938.

addition to similar announcements promoting Irish language events and GAA activities. However, what really set the *Kerryman* apart from most other provincial organs was its advocacy of the Sinn Féin cause from a very early stage.[192]

Of the paper's three co-founders, Maurice Griffin personified this support for Sinn Féin to the greatest extent. Griffin, who was elected to Tralee Urban District Council in 1908, became a member of the party well before it started to gain any national popularity.[193] A deep-rooted antipathy developed between Griffin and Thomas O'Donnell, the Irish Parliamentary Party MP for West Kerry from 1900 to 1918. The hostility between the two men was not solely due to their divergent political loyalties. While contracted as an auditor to the Tralee and Dingle Railway, of which O'Donnell was Chief Executive, Griffin was highly critical of certain accounting practices at the company that led O'Donnell to dispense with his services.[194] The enmity between Griffin and O'Donnell was mirrored in exchanges between the *Kerryman* and the *Kerry Advocate*, the paper established by O'Donnell in conjunction with Maurice P. Ryle. Throughout the latter publication's brief existence, it excoriated Sinn Féin and its supporters while the *Kerryman* responded with similar severity in its criticism of O'Donnell and the Irish Parliamentary Party.[195]

As the British authorities detained large numbers of Sinn Féin activists following the Easter Rising, Griffin was amongst those arrested. His detention, however, was considerably shorter than that of William Sears (*Enniscorthy Echo*) and P.J. Doris (*Mayo News*) as he was released from Wakefield Prison after a few weeks.[196] Nevertheless, it was not long before the paper had another brush with the authorities. Lord Decies informed the *Kerryman* that a report in its evening issue, the *Liberator*, should have been submitted to his office before publication. The particular item related to a resolution passed by the Listowel Board of Guardians

---

[192] *Irish Times*, 21 Apr. 1938; *Kerryman*, 7 Apr. 1928, 8 Apr. 1939. Daniel Nolan's obituary noted that the *Kerryman* 'was an advocate of Sinn Féin almost from its foundation' while the obituaries of Maurice Griffin and Thomas Nolan similarly noted the paper's support for the party well before any significant electoral success had been secured.

[193] *Kerryman*, 8 Feb. 1908; 7 Apr. 1928. The *Kerryman* of 8 Feb. 1908 records Griffin addressing a Sinn Féin meeting in Killorglin.

[194] J. Anthony Gaughan, *A political odyssey: Thomas O'Donnell, M.P. for West Kerry, 1900–1918* (Dublin, 1983), pp 117–18.

[195] Ibid., p. 91.

[196] *Cork Examiner*, 30 Aug. 1916.

concerning the execution of Roger Casement. Maurice Griffin replied stating that he had not had sufficient time to forward a proof of the paper but undertook to do so in the future when necessary.[197] This clearly did not satisfy the authorities as the *Kerryman* was suppressed on 29 August and only recommenced publication in early October.[198]

In November 1920, the *Kerryman* suspended publication for two weeks due to the extreme level of violent incidents in the Tralee area.[199] In March 1921, it was subjected to threats by the Anti-Sinn Féin Society, a clandestine body that had first appeared in Cork in the summer of 1920. This organisation was most likely a cover for unofficial attacks by the British police force on civilians and IRA supporters.[200] However, this was only a prelude to even greater trauma. The following month, the IRA shot dead Major John Alastair McKinnon at the golf links outside Tralee. In the aftermath, Crown forces visited the offices of the *Kerryman* and demanded that the *Liberator* of that day be printed in black-ruled mourning columns as a mark of respect to their dead colleague. The publishers subsequently decided not to print at all. During a series of aggravated reprisals, the printing works and offices of the paper were completely destroyed.[201] The *Irish Independent* reported at the time that the *Kerryman* was not expected to resume publication for six months.[202] The paper actually remained out of print for over two years, only resuming publication in August 1923.

[197]   Press Censorship Records 1916–1919, 3/722/15-135, 22 and 23 Aug. 1916.
[198]   *Irish Independent*, 30 Aug. 1916; *The Kerryman: 1904–2004* (5 Aug. 2004). The *Kerryman*'s centenary issue in 2004 suggested that the suppression stemmed from the publication of a letter congratulating Maurice Griffin on his release from prison. The same letter was also highly critical of the continued detention of Austin Stack.
[199]   *Kerryman*, 20 Nov. 1920.
[200]   *Irish Independent*, 10, 11 Mar. 1921; *Freeman's Journal*, 11 Mar. 1921; Borgonovo, *Spies, informers and the 'Anti-Sinn Féin Society'*, p. 179. Borgonovo details the appearance of this society in Cork city stating that there 'is no conclusive evidence that a pro-British civilian intelligence group' was actually in operation but suggests that 'it is plausible that such a network existed in Cork'. The *Kerryman* received a letter from the Anti-Sinn Féin Society warning against the publication of statements made at the Tralee Assizes regarding allegations that a man named John Houlihan had been murdered by Crown forces.
[201]   *Irish Independent*, 21 Apr. 1938; *The Kerryman: 1904–2004* (5 Aug. 2004).
[202]   *Irish Independent*, 21 Apr. 1921.

'All the news of interest to Kerrymen': editorial comment, 1914–1921

As the passing of the Home Rule bill seemed imminent in early 1914, the *Kerryman* made the same mistake as several other Irish newspapers in grossly underestimating the desire and resolve of Ulster Unionists. The 'doleful prophecies of the Orange leaders are absolutely without foundation' the paper asserted, and added that 'when the Ulster trouble has disappeared' the pending legislation would 'make it a real state of independence'.[203] However, the paper differed from many other provincial titles by assuming a decidedly guarded stance in anticipation of the implementation of a measure of Irish self-government. Such wariness was also very much in evidence at the start of World War I as it questioned whether Ireland's 'loyalty' to England would reap any genuine benefit.[204] By October 1914, the *Kerryman* declared itself 'not in favour of sending Irishmen wholesale to be butchered on the continent – just at present'.[205]

The reluctance to enthusiastically embrace the Home Rule settlement and the unwillingness to wholly support the British war effort developed into unconcealed hostility towards the Irish Parliamentary Party by the following year. The party's failure to secure a satisfactory settlement for nationalists drew sarcastic praise for the 'marvellous patience' it had shown though it had 'valuable incentive to persevere in the "hopping-on" process by the receipt of a salary of £400 a year each'.[206] Even though John Redmond's party had expressed its opposition to any form of conscription it was still 'wobbling and weak-kneed' and most likely to do 'what their English superiors command'.[207] Unlike most other provincial organs, the *Kerryman* passed little editorial comment on the Easter Rising except to cite it as a by-product of the Irish Parliamentary Party's inaction in addressing nationalist grievances.[208] As early as July 1916, the paper called on John Redmond 'and his lieutenants' to resign as a consequence of throwing away 'countless chances for securing Irish legislative independence'.[209]

Castigation of John Redmond and his party continued apace into 1917 as the paper confidently predicted its demise following by-election

---

[203]   *Kerryman*, 3 Jan. 1914.
[204]   *Kerryman*, 8 Aug. 1914.
[205]   *Kerryman*, 10 Oct. 1914.
[206]   *Kerryman*, 26 June 1915.
[207]   *Kerryman*, 25 Sept. 1915.
[208]   *Kerryman*, 13 May 1916.
[209]   *Kerryman*, 29 July 1916.

defeats at the hands of Sinn Féin. The results of the by-elections in North Roscommon and South Longford were viewed respectively as deliverance from 'English Whiggery' and proof of the 'patriotic integrity of the people' in the face of 'bribery, misrepresentation and intimidation'.[210] Subsequent Sinn Féin victories in East Clare and Kilkenny provoked similar editorial comment as the paper now focused its ire on the Irish Convention. Seven months after its commencement and with no indication of any concrete result emerging, the *Kerryman* derisively remarked that the assembly was 'going great guns' and showing 'no sign of tiring yet'.[211]

Despite its well-established antagonism for the Irish Parliamentary Party the paper did not engage in any form of editorial triumphalism following Sinn Féin's sweeping general election victory in December 1918. Instead, it focused on the possibility of Ireland obtaining a favourable hearing at the Paris Peace Conference. The *Kerryman* was, however, far more circumspect than papers such as the *Meath Chronicle* and *Enniscorthy Echo* in this regard. It more reflected the cautious attitude of the *Mayo News* in merely speculating that the conference 'may, or may not, fail us'.[212] President Wilson's subsequent refusal to give any consideration to the Irish question resulted in him being dubbed 'the world's chief hypocrite' and 'just as supercilious as his friend and partner, Lloyd George'.[213]

As levels of violence in Ireland increased dramatically from 1919 onwards, the *Kerryman* reported events extensively but, curiously, passed little editorial comment on actions carried out either by Crown forces or by the IRA. Leading articles were notable for their harsh criticism of the British Government and what the paper regarded as its totally inadequate efforts to resolve the situation in Ireland. The Government of Ireland Act was dismissively labelled the 'Partition Bill' and described as 'the handiwork of Carson, who commanded Lloyd George to put it through the British Parliament'.[214] As hostilities intensified even further during 1920, the paper declared that 'the English are pious hypocrites' who were out 'to humiliate and despoil this unfortunate nation'.[215] However, in common with so many other nationalist titles, the *Kerryman* reserved particular contempt for British Premier, Lloyd George.

[210]   *Kerryman*, 10 Feb., 12 May 1917.
[211]   *Kerryman*, 12 Jan. 1918.
[212]   *Kerryman*, 18 Jan. 1919.
[213]   *Kerryman*, 22 Mar., 14 June 1919.
[214]   *Kerryman*, 13 Mar. 1920.
[215]   *Kerryman*, 29 May 1920.

'A notorious opportunist and trimmer' who 'hates this country with an abiding, wholehearted hate' was how the paper described him in August 1920.[216] The British Prime Minister's alleged loathing of all things Irish was a continuing theme in the editorial columns of the *Kerryman* as it further labelled him 'the most unblushing hypocrite and prevaricator of his time' who 'made no attempt to conceal the malignant hatred he entertains for this country'.[217] In one of its final editorials before its enforced closure in April 1921 the resentment felt towards the British Prime Minister surfaced yet again as the paper asserted that no English minister since 1798 had 'travelled so far along the path of coercion as he has done'.[218] Unfortunately, the attack on the *Kerryman*'s premises barely two weeks after this editorial leaves it a matter for speculation as to how such a pro-Sinn Féin organ would have reacted to the truce of July 1921 and the Anglo-Irish Treaty six months later.

Conclusion

Although the *Kerryman* was ultimately classified as a pro-Sinn Féin organ along with titles such as the *Enniscorthy Echo*, *Kilkenny People*, and *Midland Tribune*, it differed significantly from the three latter newspapers. Unlike its Leinster counterparts, the *Kerryman* never really articulated any degree of support or appreciation for the Irish Parliamentary Party. It is quite likely that this principally stemmed from Maurice Griffin's very early conversion to the Sinn Féin cause and the bitterness that developed between Griffin and the sitting MP for West Kerry, Thomas O'Donnell. Despite the link to Sinn Féin that pre-dated that of many other provincial titles the paper did not engage in any sense of *schadenfreude* at the demise of the Irish Parliamentary Party. Indeed, as the War of Independence became more protracted, the *Kerryman*'s editorial comment was certainly damning in its criticism of the British Government but hardly reached the same level of belligerence as that of the *Kilkenny People* or even the *Mayo News*. The admonition of Lloyd George was undoubtedly bitter in its tone but even the *Skibbereen Eagle*, which most definitely had no republican tendencies, saw fit similarly to rebuke the British Prime Minister.

The *Kerryman* reflected the experiences of several other nationalist newspapers in undergoing periods of suppression plus the detention of

---

[216] *Kerryman*, 21 Aug. 1920.
[217] *Kerryman*, 9 Oct. 1920.
[218] *Kerryman*, 2 Apr. 1921.

one of its proprietors. However, only the *Westmeath Independent* and *Leitrim Observer* suffered to the same extent as the *Kerryman* by being forced out of business for over two years due to an attack on its premises. Nonetheless, it differed from many other provincial organs in that no individual personality was at the helm of the paper for a prolonged period as was the case at the *Westmeath Examiner* (J.P. Hayden), *Roscommon Herald* (Jasper Tully), *Drogheda Independent* (Michael A. Casey), and *Limerick Leader* (Con Cregan). Maurice Griffin passed away in 1928 at the relatively young age of fifty-three, Daniel Nolan died in 1938, while Thomas Nolan died the following year. Even though two of the co-founders had overseen the paper's fortunes for over three decades it was not a remarkably long stewardship by the standards of the Irish provincial press. Yet the publication they established proceeded to display impressive durability, far outliving all its contemporaries in Kerry at the time of its foundation.

Summary: Munster newspapers

Many of the characteristics of provincial newspapers in Leinster and Connacht are similarly discernible across the provincial print media in Munster during these years. Dominant figureheads at the helm, prolonged editorial reigns, remarkably lengthy periods of family ownership, and enthusiastic support for the GAA and Gaelic League were a feature of many nationalist titles in Munster though perhaps to a slightly lesser extent than the other two provinces. Munster newspapers also fell foul, possibly to a greater degree, of the Press Censor and Crown forces with a number of nationalist titles suffering considerably as a result. However, other titles suffered at the hands of the IRA as it attempted to enforce its own form of censorship. Finally, and perhaps most importantly, the output of some of the unionist and independent organs located in the province provide a rather unique perspective on this turbulent period of Irish history.

The *Clare Champion* most embodied features that were common to many newspapers across the three southern provinces. Over a century of ownership by the Galvin family, Sarsfield Maguire's four decades in the editorial chair, and his wife Josephine's determination that the paper should reflect her devout Catholicism mark the *Clare Champion* as exemplifying many of the primary features of Irish provincial newspapers. The fact that the paper experienced quite a lengthy suppression lends further weight to this assertion. On the other hand, dominant personalities such as

E.T. Keane and Jasper Tully, plus prolonged occupancy of the editorial chair by a single individual, were probably not as much in evidence in Munster as elsewhere. Con Cregan's fifty years as editor of the *Limerick Leader*, however, provides at least one example of the latter. The promotion of the activities of organisations such as the GAA and the Gaelic League was also evident in Munster, particularly in publications such as the *Southern Star*, *Clonmel Nationalist*, *Tipperary Star*, and *Kerryman*.

Munster newspapers had to contend with the possibility of suppression and attacks on their premises possibly to a greater degree than in any of the other three provinces. A variety of titles in counties Clare, Limerick, Cork, Kerry, and Waterford were either suppressed or suffered malicious raids on their printing works and offices. The suppression of the *Southern Star* even before it became a Sinn Féin organ highlights the sense of uncertainty under which papers had to operate. Cumulatively, the *Southern Star* probably endured the longest period of suppression of any provincial newspaper in Ireland though the *Clare Champion* and *Waterford News* were also subjected to considerable periods of suppression. All four nationalist newspapers in Count Limerick were also suppressed, with the *Weekly Observer* in Newcastle West additionally enduring an attack on its offices. In Kerry, the *Killarney Echo* did not reappear following an attack on its premises by Crown forces. It was the *Kerryman*, however, that bore the worst excess of the British military as it was forced out of publication for over two years. Nonetheless, it was not only Crown forces that were making the operation of a newspaper such a hazardous business. In addition to targeting the *Cork Examiner*, the IRA issued threats and carried out attacks on both staff and premises of both the *Cork Constitution* and *Skibbereen Eagle* that ultimately led to the demise of both titles.

From an editorial standpoint, the five newspapers considered in this chapter differ significantly from those titles in Leinster and Connacht similarly analysed. The papers scrutinised in the previous two chapters were nationalist organs, if not all necessarily pro-Sinn Féin. In Munster, the situation is somewhat different. The *Kerryman* certainly held pro-Sinn Féin sympathies from a very early stage so its reluctance to fully embrace Home Rule was hardly surprising. Unfortunately, its reaction to Sinn Féin's achievements under the terms of the Anglo-Irish Treaty can only be speculated upon as the paper was not in publication at the time. The editorial comment of the *Southern Star* is somewhat fragmented due to the change of ownership, high turnover of editors, and lengthy periods of suppression. However, the paper unambiguously supported the Anglo-Irish Treaty. The *Clonmel Chronicle* also voiced support for the

Treaty though otherwise it remained editorially oblivious to almost all significant developments between 1914 and 1921.

This most certainly was not the case at the *Cork Constitution* and *Skibbereen Eagle*. The leading articles of both these titles provide quite a unique perspective on developments in Ireland between 1914 and 1921. As a staunchly unionist organ, the *Constitution* voiced strong support for the Ulster Unionists but curiously expressed utter disdain at the prospect of partition. It was also far quicker than many of its nationalist contemporaries in foreseeing probable developments within nationalism such as the electoral meltdown of the Irish Parliamentary Party and the estrangement of Eamon de Valera from his erstwhile Sinn Féin colleagues.

The editorial commentary of the *Skibbereen Eagle* refutes any suggestion that it was a unionist organ. The *Eagle* wholeheartedly welcomed the prospect of Home Rule and was quite antagonistic in its attitude to the Ulster Unionists or any notion of partition. Nevertheless, the paper had little time for Sinn Féin's brand of nationalism and, similar to the *Cork Constitution*, adopted a far more realistic attitude than many nationalist titles. This was most evident in its prediction that Sinn Féin's appeal to the Paris Peace Conference would fall on deaf ears and that an Irish republic was never likely to result from the negotiations that followed the truce of July 1921. Yet the *Eagle* did not join with other papers in blandly labelling the Easter Rising as the 'Sinn Féin rebellion'. It most honourably refused to accept that Sinn Féin had any involvement in the 'German plot' of 1918 and it expressed warm praise for the negotiating skills of Michael Collins and Arthur Griffith following the conclusion of the Anglo-Irish Treaty.

The *Clonmel Chronicle*, *Cork Constitution*, and *Skibbereen Eagle* operated in a region where the majority of their fellow-newspapers were solidly nationalist. Consequently, analysis of their response to the evolving situation in Ireland during these years lends a much-needed sense of balance to this examination of the Irish provincial press. This sense of balance can only be fully achieved by comprehensive scrutiny of provincial newspapers in an area where nationalist titles were not in the majority. Accordingly, this study can only be fittingly concluded by closely examining the wide variety of provincial papers across the nine counties of Ulster.

5

Northern Drumbeats: Ulster

Introduction

The nine counties of Ulster cover a geographical area of just under 22,000 square kilometres, making it the second-largest Irish province after Munster. However, during the 1914–21 period it was by some distance the most populous province. According to the 1911 census, the nine counties of Ulster boasted a population of 1.58 million.[1] Even with the considerable population of Belfast (387,000) excluded, the province of Ulster still possessed the largest population. At 204,000, County Down had the greatest population while County Fermanagh had the lowest at just under 62,000.

In addition to having the largest population, the province also boasted the largest number of provincial newspaper titles. A total of forty-six local papers were published in Ulster between 1914 and 1921. Four of them, the *Impartial Reporter*, *Londonderry Sentinel*, *Anglo-Celt*, and *Donegal Democrat* are scrutinised in this chapter. Apart from the *Londonderry Sentinel*, these titles were published in urban centres with relatively small populations. The unionist *Impartial Reporter* was based in Enniskillen which had a population of just under 5,000. Its main competition for unionist readership was the *Fermanagh Times*, also based in Enniskillen. The town was also home to the nationalist *Fermanagh Herald*. The aforementioned population of County Fermanagh was 56 per cent Catholic with most of the remainder unsurprisingly comprised of Protestant denominations.

---

[1] Vaughan and Fitzpatrick, *Irish historical statistics*, pp 3–68. All the demographical statistics and information provided in this section are based on the 1911 census and are cited from Vaughan and Fitzpatrick's work.

Amongst these the Church of Ireland was most dominant at 34 per cent, with 7 per cent Methodist and 2 per cent Presbyterian.

With a population of 41,000, the city of Derry was the largest urban centre of population outside Belfast. The county had a total population of just under 141,000 which was served by two Coleraine newspapers, *Coleraine Chronicle* and *Northern Constitution*, while the *Londonderry Sentinel*'s main rivals in the city were the unionist *Derry Standard* and the nationalist titles, the *Derry Journal* and the *Derry People*. The split of religious denominations was somewhat different in County Derry compared with County Fermanagh. In the city of Derry, the population comprised roughly 56 per cent Catholic, 18 per cent Church of Ireland, 21 per cent Presbyterian, and 3 per cent Methodist. In the county, the figures were 42 per cent Catholic, 20 per cent Church of Ireland, 34 per cent Presbyterian, and 1 per cent Methodist.

The *Anglo-Celt* was published in Cavan town which had a population of slightly fewer than 3,000. County Cavan's population of 91,173 was the third lowest of the Ulster counties. However, the *Anglo-Celt* had the advantage of being the county's only nationalist paper. Additionally, the county was home to the highest proportion of Catholics of all the Ulster counties (81 per cent). The *Donegal Democrat* was based in Ballyshannon which had a relatively small population of just over 2,000. However, the total population of County Donegal was 168,000, of which 79 per cent was Catholic. Only two other papers were published in the county, the *Donegal Vindicator*, also based in Ballyshannon, and the *Donegal Independent*, which served as the Letterkenny edition of the former paper.

Ulster newspapers: an overview

It can scarcely be regarded as any major historical revelation to state that the composition of the provincial press in Ulster differed significantly from that of any of the other three Irish provinces. While the distinctive traits of the print media in Leinster, Connacht, and Munster were not so clearly identifiable this was not the case in the northern province. In complete contrast to the other provinces, unionist organs accounted for the largest number of provincial papers in Ulster which was a clear reflection of the region in which support for the union with Great Britain was at its strongest. Nevertheless, there were still some aspects of the provincial print media in Ulster that were slightly less discernible though still highly noteworthy. The actual extent of the dominance of unionist newspapers was one such feature. Allied to this was the remarkably broad spread of towns in which these unionist titles were published. Additionally, and in contrast with the nationalist section of the provincial press, unionist titles did not emerge within a relatively brief and clearly identifiable timeframe. This contrasted sharply with the limited number of nationalist papers based in the province, most of which were only launched after 1900. However, there were some traits that the provincial print media in Ulster shared with the other provinces. These included the significant religious dimension (though not a Catholic one), the tendency for single individuals to remain as editor or owner for several decades, and finally the propensity of prolonged periods of family ownership of newspapers.

Across the nine counties of Ulster a total of forty-six titles were in publication between 1914 and 1921 of which only nine were nationalist. Although there was a significant number of neutral or independent publications, the unionist dominance was quite remarkable. This dominance was most pronounced within the six counties that ultimately came under the authority of the Stormont Parliament. All but two of the province's twenty-eight unionist titles were published within this area while only six nationalist papers existed within the same area. The extent of the predominance of unionist organs was best exemplified in Antrim, Armagh, and Down, where only one nationalist title (Newry's *Frontier Sentinel*) featured amongst the twenty-two provincial papers located across the three counties. Counties Antrim and Down provided the best illustration of how newspapers were published across a far greater spread of towns than was the case in any of the other three provinces. Despite the proximity to Belfast, and the more regional appeal of papers such as the *Belfast Newsletter*, *Belfast Telegraph*, *Northern Whig*, and *Irish News*, there were eighteen provincial titles operating in these counties published across eleven different towns. In County Antrim, these papers were based in Ballymena, Ballymoney, Carrickfergus, Larne, and Lisburn, while County Down's newspapers were published in the towns of Banbridge, Bangor, Downpatrick, Dromore, Newry, and Newtownards.

Ulster boasted a greater number of provincial newspapers than any of the other Irish provinces yet strangely only one of these dated back to the eighteenth century. Outside of Belfast the only existing paper that had been established prior to the 1800s was the nationalist *Derry Journal*. Unionist titles were launched throughout the nineteenth century rather than in one clearly identifiable period which was the case with the majority of nationalist titles. The oldest of these unionist titles was the *Newry Telegraph* which was established in 1812. This was followed by the *Impartial Reporter* (1825) and *Londonderry Sentinel* (1829), both of which are examined in detail in this chapter. Other unionist titles to be launched in the first half of the nineteenth century included the *Derry Standard*, *Down Recorder* (both established in 1836), *Coleraine Chronicle*, *Tyrone Constitution*, and *Ulster Gazette* (all three dating from 1844). The second half of the nineteenth century witnessed the foundation of several other unionist titles. These included the *Ballymena Observer* (1855), *Portadown News* (1859), *Ballymoney Free Press* (1863), *Northern Constitution* (1875), *Lisburn Standard* (1876), *Tyrone Constitution*, *Fermanagh Times* (both 1880), *Lurgan Mail* (1890), and *Lisburn Herald* (1891).

In Ulster, nationalist titles occupied the minority position that their unionist counterparts occupied in the other three Irish provinces. This position was most pronounced in the six counties that ultimately constituted the Northern Ireland state. Within this region only six nationalist newspapers were published, and, except for the *Derry Journal*, all were launched after 1900. The *Derry Journal* was established in 1772 as the *Londonderry Journal* by a Scottish Protestant, George Douglas. Originally a conservative organ with a firm allegiance to the British monarchy, its ethos began to change somewhat in the first half of the nineteenth century with its support for Catholic emancipation.[2] However, it was under the ownership of the McCarter family, which commenced in 1858, that a decidedly nationalist editorial policy began to evolve and in 1880 the title was shortened to the *Derry Journal*.[3] In 1908, a limited company was formed to take over the business of the *Derry Journal* and of the 198 initial shareholders fifty-six were members of the Catholic clergy.[4] This transition to a limited company resulted in the emergence of James Joseph (J.J.) McCarroll as the main driving force behind the paper. McCarroll was noted for his strong Catholic faith and as a loyal supporter of both the Gaelic League and the GAA.[5]

Some other nationalist titles in Ulster did not display the same degree of durability as the *Derry Journal*. The *Dungannon Democrat* only lasted ten years (1913–23) but the *Frontier Sentinel*, although it did not survive to the latter part of the twentieth century, remained in publication for almost seventy years (1904–72). The personality most associated with

---

[2] *Derry Journal*, 9 June 1972; *Derry Journal: 225th Anniversary Supplement* (6 June 1997).

[3] *Derry Journal: 225th Anniversary Supplement* (6 June 1997); Brian Lacy, *Siege city: the story of Derry and Londonderry* (Belfast, 1990), p. 204.

[4] *Derry Journal: 225th Anniversary Supplement* (6 June 1997).

[5] *Derry Journal*, 3 and 5 Mar. 1937; *Fermanagh Herald*, 5 Mar. 1937; *Londonderry Sentinel*, 4 Mar. 1937.

this paper was undoubtedly Joseph Connellan, who was appointed editor around 1908 and remained in the position for almost sixty years. Similar to J.J. McCarroll, he was an enthusiastic advocate of both the GAA and the Gaelic League.[6] Another noted supporter of the Gaelic League was Patrick Joseph (P.J.) Flanagan, who was the first editor of the nationalist *Derry People* launched in 1902.[7] Both the *Frontier Sentinel* and the *Derry People* were owned by the North West of Ireland Publishing Company who also owned the *Fermanagh Herald*. This was County Fermanagh's only nationalist paper and was edited for over thirty years, following its foundation in 1902, by Patrick A. (P.A.) MacManus, a fervent nationalist and devout Catholic.[8]

The remaining nationalist title within the six-county area was the *Ulster Herald*, which was launched in Omagh, County Tyrone, in 1901. It was also owned by the North West of Ireland Publishing Company whose managing-director for close on thirty years, until his death in 1935, was Michael Lynch. In common with so many of his nationalist counterparts Lynch was a devout Catholic and a keen GAA enthusiast.[9] Enduring family ties to provincial newspapers were again epitomised at the *Ulster Herald* where the Lynch family still held the reins of the paper over a century after its establishment.[10] As outlined in Chapter 1, Michael Lynch sought the endorsement of John Redmond prior to the establishment of the *Ulster Herald*.[11] Lynch, who had been involved in many Land League activities in County Tyrone, later transferred his political allegiance from the Irish Parliamentary Party to Sinn Féin following which he became closely acquainted with Arthur Griffith.[12] The most noted editor of the *Ulster Herald* was Anthony Mulvey, who was appointed in 1917 and remained in the position for thirty years. Originally from County Leitrim, Mulvey had a considerable journalistic pedigree, having started his career working under Patrick Dunne at

6 *Irish Times*, 12 Apr. 1967; *Frontier Sentinel*, 15 Apr. 1967.

7 *Derry Journal*, 21 Feb. 1961.

8 *Impartial Reporter*, 20 Dec. 1934; *Ulster Herald*, 22 Dec. 1934; *Fermanagh Herald*, 29 Dec. 1934.

9 *Ulster Herald*, 20 Apr. 1935.

10 *Ulster Herald*, 3 Jan. 2002.

11 Muldoon to Redmond, 27 Mar. 1901, MS 15,208.

12 *Ulster Herald*, 20 Apr. 1935; 3 Jan. 2002; Pádraig Ó Baoighill, 'The Irish language in Tyrone'; and Éamon Phoenix, 'Nationalism in Tyrone, 1880–1972' in Charles Dillon and Henry A. Jefferies (eds), *Tyrone: history and society* (Dublin, 2000), pp 676 and 781.

the *Leitrim Observer* before moving to the *Roscommon Herald* where he served under Jasper Tully. Prior to his appointment as editor of the *Ulster Herald*, Mulvey worked at the *Wexford People* and following his retirement from journalism in 1947 he served as an MP in the Stormont Parliament.[13]

Outside the six counties that went on to comprise the Northern Ireland state, a further three nationalist titles were published in the province. Two of these, the *Anglo-Celt* in Cavan, and the *Donegal Democrat*, are closely scrutinised in this chapter. Curiously, no nationalist title was published in County Monaghan though it was served by the *Monaghan Democrat* which was a localised edition of the moderately nationalist *Dundalk Democrat*.[14] The unionist *Northern Standard*, owned by Philip McMinn, was published in Monaghan town and principally catered for the Protestant population of north and west Monaghan.[15] Nonetheless, the paper occupies a rather unique place in the history of the Irish print media as it was virtually the only provincial title of a unionist persuasion located outside Northern Ireland to survive past the first few decades of the Irish Free State and indeed well beyond. Much of the credit for this achievement was attributable to John Joseph (J.J.) Turley, who was appointed editor in 1928. During his editorship, he succeeded in gradually making the paper that had previously been run 'along strictly Presbyterian lines' more acceptable to Catholics.[16]

The remaining nationalist title in the province was the Ballyshannon-based *Donegal Vindicator*. The paper was owned and edited by John McAdam from its foundation in 1889 until his death in 1925. McAdam was born in Glasgow to Irish parents and was noted for his wholehearted Catholicism, as was his daughter Marie, who succeeded her father as editor–proprietor.[17] County Donegal was also served by the *Donegal Independent*, which operated as the Letterkenny edition of the *Donegal Vindicator*.[18] The former title had initially operated as a

---

13 *Ulster Herald*, 19 Jan. 1957.
14 *Newspaper press directory and advertisers' guide 1917*, p. 214.
15 Peadar Livingstone, *The Monaghan story: a documented history of the County Monaghan from the earliest times to 1976* (Enniskillen, 1980), pp 661–2.
16 Ibid.; Oram, *The newspaper book*, p. 158; *Northern Standard*, 22 Dec. 1961. Turley had stood as the unsuccessful Irish Parliamentary Party candidate for the North Monaghan constituency in opposition to Ernest Blythe at the 1918 general election.
17 *Donegal Vindicator*, 13 June 1925; *Donegal Democrat*, 7 May 1938.
18 *Newspaper press directory and advertisers' guide 1917*, p. 213.

separate entity and appears to have emerged from the ashes of the defunct *Ballyshannon Herald*, which had been established in 1831.[19]

Amongst the province's many unionist titles there were several distinct characteristics. Some of these were shared with the nationalist print media across all four provinces. These included the regularity of remarkably lengthy editorial and proprietorial tenures and the numerous instances of prolonged family ownership. Similarly, there was an undoubted political and religious dimension to the unionist press in Ulster. However, where editors and proprietors of nationalist papers displayed allegiance to the GAA, Gaelic League, Irish Parliamentary Party, and latterly Sinn Féin, their peers within unionist publications exhibited an equivalent loyalty to the Ulster Volunteers, the Orange Order, the British war effort, and the unionist cause in general. Likewise, the devout Catholicism of so many senior nationalist journalists was frequently matched by steadfast Presbyterianism within the senior ranks of unionist newspapers.

The remarkable longevity of Irish provincial editors and proprietors was certainly in evidence at papers such as the *Lurgan Mail*, *Ballymena Observer*, and, to an even greater extent, at the *Down Recorder*. Louis Richardson established the *Lurgan Mail* in 1890 and remained as editor–proprietor for over forty years.[20] John Wier assumed proprietorship of the *Ballymena Observer* in 1870 and served in the position for almost fifty years.[21] William Young (W.Y.) Crichton fulfilled the same role at the *Down Recorder* for sixty-three years.[22] Nonetheless, these exceptionally lengthy tenures were not the only notable features at these newspapers. Louis Richardson founded the *Lurgan Mail* as an unapologetic unionist journal which reflected his own unwavering political allegiance.[23] John Wier of the *Ballymena Observer* was similarly a staunch unionist in addition to being a devout Presbyterian throughout his life.[24] In a slightly different vein, the tendency for prolonged family ownership of provincial papers was again exemplified at the *Down Recorder*. On its 175th anniversary in 2012 its managing director was Marcus Crichton, great-grandson of W.Y. Crichton, who had assumed ownership in 1894. Such traits, whether singularly or collectively, were clearly evident at a variety of Ulster newspapers.

---

[19] *Donegal Democrat: Anniversary Supplement* (27 Aug. 2009).

[20] *Lurgan Mail*, 29 Aug. 1936.

[21] *Ballymena Observer*, 4 Feb. 1927.

[22] *Down Recorder*, 4 Jan. 2012.

[23] *Lurgan Mail*, 29 Aug. 1936.

[24] *Ballymena Observer*, 4 Feb. 1927.

John Edmund Emerson founded the *Banbridge Chronicle* in 1870 and upon his death in 1912 was succeeded by his son Arthur Waldo Emerson, who remained at the helm of the paper until his death in 1951.[25] Another pertinent example of such family ties was at the *Newtownards Chronicle*, where the Henry and Alexander families successively owned the paper for close on one hundred years following its establishment in 1873.[26] At the *Tyrone Courier* such familial links were combined with an undoubted Presbyterian influence. It was acquired by Robert Taylor (R.T.) Simpson, a Presbyterian clergyman, in 1897, and by the time of the paper's centenary in 1980 ownership had passed first to Taylor's son and subsequently his grandson.[27] This religious dimension was perhaps most notable at the *Derry Standard*. This was a tri-weekly publication that claimed a greater circulation than any other unionist title in Ulster apart from the *Belfast Newsletter* and the *Northern Whig*.[28] Established in 1836, the *Derry Standard* became the main public organ of the Presbyterian community in Derry. It developed into a powerful voice in the city and it was stated of many of its readers that 'the bible and the *Standard* were the only literature they read'.[29]

At the *Mid-Ulster Mail*, based in Cookstown, County Tyrone, this significant Presbyterian element was further evident. The paper was founded in 1891 by brothers John and Henry Little (H.L.) Glasgow whose devout Presbyterian faith was matched by their unswerving unionism. H.L. Glasgow edited this steadfast unionist organ for fifty-eight years.[30] James Brown, who was editor–proprietor of the *Newry Telegraph* for close on forty years until his retirement in 1948, also held a firm Presbyterian faith throughout his life. Brown was also active in unionist politics and was a member of the Orange Order.[31] Robert Hill (R.H.) Ritchie, editor–proprietor of the *Fermanagh Times*, was similarly a member of the Orange Order. Described as a 'thorough Protestant and Conservative paper', Ritchie assumed control in 1916 following the death of his father, William Ritchie.[32]

---

25   *Banbridge Chronicle*, 2 May 1951.
26   *Newtownards Chronicle*, 19 July 1973.
27   *Tyrone Courier*, 5 Mar. 1980.
28   *Newspaper press directory and advertisers' guide 1917*, p. 584.
29   Lacy, *Siege city*, pp 179–80.
30   *Irish Times*, 25 Dec. 1950; 9 Apr. 1957.
31   *Newry Reporter*, 17 July 1969; *Newry Telegraph*, 19 July 1969.
32   *Irish Times*, 5 Aug. 1943; *Fermanagh Herald*, 7 Aug. 1943; B.E. Barton, 'The origins and development of unionism in Fermanagh, 1885–1914' in Eileen M. Murphy and William J. Roulston (eds), *Fermanagh: history and society:*

Like-minded manifestations of unionism were further evident at papers such as the *Lisburn Herald*, *Portadown News*, and *Tyrone Constitution*. James McCarrison, who served for forty-seven years as editor of the *Lisburn Herald*, was an unflinching supporter of the unionist cause and a member of the South Antrim battalion of the Ulster Volunteers.[33] John Young, owner of the *Portadown News*, was described in his obituary as 'a staunch unionist and a liberal subscriber to the funds of the Ulster Volunteers'.[34] Support for the Ulster Volunteers evolved into a wholehearted embrace of the British war effort and this was possibly best illustrated at the *Tyrone Constitution*. The paper was acquired by William Johnston in 1904. Johnston was a fervent unionist, as were his sons William and Thomas Ernest, both of whom served in the British army during World War I and later became directors of the paper. Its editor upon the outbreak of war in 1914 was Philip Cruickshank, who was highly involved in the Ulster Volunteers. Cruickshank subsequently enlisted in the Royal Inniskilling Fusiliers and died at the Battle of the Somme in July 1916. His successor as editor of the *Tyrone Constitution* was Robert A. Parke, an equally committed unionist and a devout Presbyterian, whose editorial tenure lasted from 1914 until his retirement in 1968.[35]

Even further instances of such notable support for the unionist cause amongst Ulster's provincial newspapers were clearly apparent at papers such as the *Armagh Guardian* and *Ulster Gazette*. The *Armagh Guardian* was acquired by Samuel Delmege Trimble (a brother of William Copeland Trimble of the *Impartial Reporter*), who was very much a veteran newspaperman by the outbreak of war in 1914 but also an unapologetic unionist.[36] The *Ulster Gazette* (also based in Armagh) was deemed to be an advocate of 'sound evangelical Protestantism' and declared itself 'the official organ of the mid-Armagh Conservative Association and the County Grand Lodge of Armagh'.[37] At the start

---

interdisciplinary essays on the history of an Irish county (Dublin, 2004), p. 310. Despite the totally conflicting political ideologies Ritchie was a close friend of the aforementioned P.A. MacManus, editor of the nationalist *Fermanagh Herald*.

[33] *Lisburn Herald*, 9 Nov. 1940.

[34] *Irish Times*, 15 Dec. 1914.

[35] *The Tyrone Constitution: 150 years in print* (3 Nov. 1994); *Tyrone Constitution*, 5 Apr. 1957; 2 Feb. 1968; 13 Sept. 1974; *Ulster Herald*, 21 Mar. 1942.

[36] *Belfast Telegraph*, 1 Apr. 1947; *Belfast Newsletter*, 2 Apr. 1947; *Irish Independent*, 2 Apr. 1947; Colin Cousins, *Armagh and the Great War* (Dublin, 2011), p. 80.

[37] *Ulster Gazette: 150th Anniversary Supplement* (22 Dec. 1994); *Newspaper press directory and advertisers' guide 1917*, pp 207 and 585.

of World War I its editor was John W. Clarke, who subsequently joined the Royal Irish Fusiliers.[38] Nonetheless, it was at titles such as the *Impartial Reporter* and the *Londonderry Sentinel* that the most uncompromising form of unionism manifested itself and consequently these two publications are profiled in the next two sections. As a counterbalance, two of the province's nationalist titles, the *Anglo-Celt* and the *Donegal Democrat*, are then subjected to detailed scrutiny. The former was a loyal supporter of constitutional nationalism while the latter was launched as an unambiguous proponent of the more militant form of nationalism that supplanted it. The detailed accounts of these four newspapers and the personalities behind them provide a vivid portrayal of how the polarisation of politics in Ulster played out amongst the province's newspapers.

Impartial Reporter

The Trimble family and the *Impartial Reporter*

It is no exaggeration to state that the family association with individual newspapers that is such a distinguishing hallmark of the Irish provincial press is exemplified to the greatest extent by the *Impartial Reporter*. The Trimble family's connection to the paper stretches right back to its foundation in 1825 and although it was sold in 2006 the family still retain a considerable interest right up to the second decade of the twenty-first century.[39] The *Impartial Reporter* was launched by John Gregsten, described as a 'printer and jaunting car proprietor', and its first editor was William Trimble, who assumed proprietorship following Gregsten's death from cholera in 1834.[40] For much of the nineteenth century, the paper was known as the *Fermanagh Reporter*, with William Trimble at the helm for almost fifty years, during which time he became a considerably influential figure in the county. Trimble held a strong Presbyterian faith and was described as a person who fought

---

[38] *Derry People*, 20 Feb. 1915; *Irish Independent*, 25 Mar. 1915; *Freeman's Journal*, 26 Mar. 1915.

[39] 'Impartial Reporter sold to Ulster News Group', *Press Gazette, Fighting for Journalism*, 20 June 2006, available at https://www.pressgazette.co.uk/impartial-reporter-sold-to-ulster-news-group/ (accessed 1 Feb. 2019).

[40] Séamus Mac Annaidh, *Fermanagh books, writers, and newspapers of the nineteenth century* (Enniskillen, 1999), pp 34–5 and 86–7.

his battles 'with his pen in one hand and his bible in the other'.[41] He had eighteen children by his first wife, Jane Beatty, nine of whom died young. Following the death of his first wife, William Trimble married Anne Farrell with whom he fathered a further eight children, six of whom survived.[42]

The third son by William Trimble's second marriage was the aforementioned Samuel Delmege Trimble who ultimately went on to become editor–proprietor of the *Armagh Guardian*. However, it was the eldest son by this marriage, William Copeland Trimble, who inherited control of the *Impartial Reporter*, five years prior to the death of his father in 1888. Like his father before him, William Copeland Trimble married twice, his first wife dying in 1892. He had three sons and two daughters by his first marriage plus two sons and a daughter by his second marriage. Lionel Trimble, one of his sons by his first marriage, died after contracting a chill during a fire that destroyed the paper's printing works in 1901. Noel Trimble, a son by his second marriage, enlisted in the British Army and was killed in France in April 1916. William Copeland Trimble occupied the editorial chair of the *Impartial Reporter* for sixty-six years meaning that for almost the first 110 years of its existence the paper was edited exclusively by father and son.[43]

Following the death of William Copeland Trimble in 1941, the paper passed to his son, William Egbert Trimble, known as 'Master Bertie'. Although he spent some time as a younger man in Dublin and London learning the printing and journalistic trades, he was solely engaged with the *Impartial Reporter* from 1905 until his death in 1967. An accident at the paper's printing works on New Year's Day 1919 left him with a broken thigh and a limp for the rest of his life. His obituary in the nationalist *Fermanagh Herald* noted that William Egbert Trimble 'would constantly write columns of vitriolic stuff about the [Irish] Republic yet he loved Dublin and its attendant cultural and musical circles'. According to the *Herald*, he was also particularly proud of a photograph he had had taken with President Eamon de Valera 'showing both of them smiling and obviously enjoying each other's company'.[44]

---

[41] Ibid., pp 86–7; *Impartial Reporter:150th Anniversary Edition* (22 May 1975).

[42] Desmond McCabe, 'Trimble, William' in McGuire and Quinn, *Dictionary of Irish biography*. Anne Farrell was the widow of John Farrell, a Westport merchant, whose son was the aforementioned J.H. Farrell, founder of the *Portadown News*.

[43] *Impartial Reporter*, 27 Nov. 1941.

[44] *Impartial Reporter*, 16 Feb. 1967; *Fermanagh Herald*, 18 Feb. 1967; *Impartial Reporter:150th Anniversary Edition* (22 May 1975).

William Egbert Trimble was a keen music enthusiast, playing the violin, singing in a local choral society, and arranging the music for morning mass at his local Presbyterian church. His passion for music was inherited by his daughters, Joan and Valerie, who became accomplished concert pianists. They also inherited the reins of the *Impartial Reporter* following the death of their father. Accordingly, the paper faced into the late twentieth century under the fourth generation of the family with whom it had retained an unbroken relationship since its foundation in the early nineteenth century.[45]

William Copeland Trimble

The history of the Irish provincial press during these years is marked by the presence of formidable and imposing personalities such as E.T. Keane (*Kilkenny People*), Patrick Dunne (*Leitrim Observer*), and Jasper Tully (*Roscommon Herald*). However, no figure exemplifies this trait to the same extent as William Copeland Trimble. It is not simply his remarkably long tenure as editor of the *Impartial Reporter* that earns him such a reputation. Rather, it was his response to contemporary developments, whether through his own actions or the columns of his newspaper, which merits such a pre-eminent place in the annals of the Irish provincial print media. Nonetheless, this position of prominence is not altogether surprising for a person described as frequently 'autocratic and egocentric', even by the commemorative edition of his own newspaper.[46]

Trimble's ascension to the helm of the *Impartial Reporter* in the early 1880s coincided with the height of the Irish Land War. His concern for the plight of small farmers in his native county led to his involvement in the formation of the Fermanagh Tenant Farmers Association.[47] His support for land reform resulted in the *Impartial Reporter* depicting the 'landlord class as an historical absurdity which had consistently suppressed the tenantry' to the extent that it 'had generated levels of discontent which threatened revolution'.[48] Accordingly, the Land League

---

[45] *Impartial Reporter*, 16 Feb. 1967; *Fermanagh Herald*, 18 Feb. 1967. The same obituary in the *Fermanagh Herald* also remarked that he was 'bitterly' unionist 'in his loyalties' yet was 'never an Orangeman'.

[46] *Impartial Reporter: 150th Anniversary Edition* (22 May 1975).

[47] Ibid.; *Impartial Reporter*, 27 Nov. 1941.

[48] B.E. Barton, 'The origins and development of unionism in Fermanagh, 1885–1914' in Eileen M. Murphy and William J. Roulston (eds), *Fermanagh: history and society: interdisciplinary essays on the history of an Irish county* (Dublin, 2004), p. 310.

received qualified support from Trimble and his paper and the 1881 Land Act was broadly welcomed. Nevertheless, the strongly nationalist element to the organisation, and its links with Charles Stewart Parnell, meant that such support was never likely to be more than temporary.[49]

As the threat of Home Rule became more serious, the *Impartial Reporter* 'rapidly emerged as an even more strident and extreme vehicle of unionist opinion than its county rival, the *Fermanagh Times*'. Concurrently, the paper developed into 'a veritable quarry of anti-Home Rule invective' while Trimble himself worked tirelessly at propagating the unionist position.[50] With the passing of Home Rule legislation becoming a reality Trimble lent his unequivocal support to Sir Edward Carson's anti-Home Rule campaign. One of the first rallies in this campaign took place in Enniskillen in September 1912 and to mark the occasion William Copeland Trimble set about forming a mounted guard of honour for Carson. This troop of horsemen came to be known as the 'Enniskillen Horse' and ultimately constituted the Ulster Volunteers' only cavalry regiment.[51]

William Copeland Trimble clearly had a strong taste for military etiquette. His personal appearance was described as being 'always of a military style'.[52] One of the circulars sent to those forming the guard of honour for Carson contained precise instructions that 'a pole with the loyal union flag' was 'to be used like a lance, for ornament', 'a red braid' was 'to be wound round the brow band of the bridle' while 'two red, white, and blue rosettes' were 'to be tied at each side of the horse's head' in addition to 'six red, white, and blue ribbons for plaiting the horse's mane'. Trimble's zeal for such militaristic pageantry was further illustrated by the fact that he supplied the flags, rosettes, and ribbons but he also asked that each rider 'come in riding breeches and putties, if he has them, or tight trousers and leggings and spurs'.[53]

In the aftermath of Carson's visit to Enniskillen in September 1912, Trimble forged ahead with his plans for the creation of a cavalry regiment. In November of that year he wrote to the Secretary of War in

---

[49] Frank Thompson, 'The Land War in County Fermanagh' in Murphy and Roulston, *Fermanagh*, p. 299.

[50] Barton, 'The origins and development of unionism in Fermanagh, 1885–1914', pp 313–16.

[51] Peadar Livingstone, *The Fermanagh story: a documented history of the County Fermanagh from the earliest times to the present day* (Enniskillen, 1969), p. 271; *Impartial Reporter: 150th Anniversary Edition* (22 May 1975).

[52] *Impartial Reporter: 150th Anniversary Edition* (22 May 1975).

[53] Ulster Unionists, Drilling or Volunteers-Enniskillen Horse, CO904/27/1-198.

London seeking a supply of lances and in January of the following year he wrote requesting supplies of ammunition.[54] The letters from Trimble sparked a flurry of correspondence between the War Office in London and the Irish Administration in Dublin Castle. Trimble had initially given the impression that his troop of horsemen was formed simply to take its share 'in the defence of his country' and might be incorporated into the territorial system of the army.[55] However, this explanation was given short shrift by the authorities.

The Under-Secretary's office in Dublin Castle concluded that following Carson's visit to Enniskillen 'the idea subsequently appears to have occurred to Mr Trimble to create a permanent drilled force' and that his request was calculated to obtain 'recognition from [a] legal authority so that there might be no evidence of the commission of the offence of illegal training and drilling'.[56] The War Office broadly agreed that 'the communications of this gentleman, who calls himself 'Commander' were couched in language 'to create further difficulty in dealing with practices which are on the border line of illegality'.[57] Effectively, the authorities clearly understood that Trimble's allegiance and that of his aspiring cavalry regiment lay firmly with Edward Carson and the Ulster Unionist Party, despite his protestation that 'we do not touch party colours – our emblem is the Union flag'.[58] Ultimately, Trimble was informed rather curtly that 'the Army Council are not prepared, at the present juncture, to accede to the requests preferred by you'.[59]

William Copeland Trimble was in his early sixties when war broke out in August 1914 and was consequently too old for active service despite his clear ardour for the military lifestyle. He effectively withdrew from any significant form of political activity after 1921 but during the previous two years he had travelled to Australia, Canada, and the USA, and on his travels he frequently addressed meetings regarding the prevailing situation in Ireland.[60] It was during such a series of meetings that Trimble came to the attention of Dáil Éireann's Publicity Department.

Through its contacts in Australia in June 1921 it was learned that 'a man who calls himself William Copeland Trimble' had addressed

[54] Trimble to Seely, 20 Nov. 1912 and 8 Jan. 1913, CO904/27/1-111, CO904/27/1-108.
[55] Trimble to Seely, 20 Nov. 1912 CO904/27/1-111.
[56] Ulster Unionists, Drilling or Volunteers-Enniskillen Horse, CO904/27/1-195.
[57] Ulster Unionists, Drilling or Volunteers-Enniskillen Horse, CO904/27/1-105/6.
[58] Trimble to Seely, 20 Nov. 1912 CO904/27/1-111.
[59] Ulster Unionists, Drilling or Volunteers-Enniskillen Horse, CO904/27/1-93.
[60] *Impartial Reporter: 150th Anniversary Edition* (22 May 1975).

several meetings in New South Wales that had received significant coverage in several newspapers including the *Sydney Morning Herald*. Trimble's speeches at such meetings, some of which were organised by the Protestant Federation of New South Wales, unsurprisingly propagated the Ulster Unionist position in addition to voicing extreme anti-Sinn Féin sentiment. However, it was his address to a meeting held at Parramatta Town Hall that was most notable. Following the standard condemnation of Sinn Féin, Trimble bluntly stated that 'the Irish problem would never be settled as long as there were Irish Celts in Ireland, because they were always a source of trouble'. His ethnically charged condescension preceded his bald assertion that 'there was one man who understood Ireland, and whom Ireland understood'. 'That man', according to Trimble, 'was Oliver Cromwell'. 'What was wanted in Ireland', he concluded, 'was a modern Oliver Cromwell who would deal with outrages on the spot'.[61] Trimble's racial denigration of Irish nationalists and his invocation of a figure so reviled by them was hardly a spontaneous outburst; such sentiment was far from alien to the editorial comment of the *Impartial Reporter* between 1914 and 1921.

Editorial comment, 1914–1921

The *Impartial Reporter* was normally published each Thursday with its masthead proclaiming that in addition to County Fermanagh the paper also served Cavan, Leitrim, North Monaghan, and South Tyrone. It normally comprised eight pages divided into seven columns though the number of pages occasionally dropped during World War I. The front page was predominantly made up of advertisements but also included lists of local property auctions, which, combined with details of auction notices that regularly appeared inside the paper, suggest that the *Impartial Reporter* may have catered for a slightly more affluent cohort of readers than many other provincial newspapers. Frequent advertisements for motor cars, motor cycles, and side cars would appear to lend substance to such an assessment. Further advertisements for a variety of farm supplies and implements plus the publication of several agricultural notices reasonably explain the paper's appended title of *Farmers' Journal*. Other items to be advertised included the standard mix of household items such as flour and soap, plus various medications (most notably Andrews Liver Salt, Beecham's Pills and Beecham's Powders), in addition to notices promoting the paper's own printing business.

[61] 'Ireland today – An Irishman on Sinn Féin', June 1921, P80/185(1) and P80/185(2).

The *Impartial Reporter* made numerous of claims above its editorial column. It asserted that its net sales were 'four times that of any other newspaper published in Enniskillen'. It further asserted that it possessed 'well over double the combined circulation of the other local papers' (presumably in County Fermanagh) and 'five times the combined circulation of other papers in the Clogher Valley'. Such multiple claims can often confuse rather than enlighten, which may explain why by 1921 the *Impartial Reporter* simply stated that its net sales were certified as 6,119 weekly, which equated to 'over six times' the net sales of papers published in the 'districts served by the Great Northern and Sligo Railways'. While such assertions cannot really be verified, the editorial columns over which they appeared were always likely to provide compelling reading with a personality such as William Copeland Trimble at the helm.

Leading articles in the *Impartial Reporter* during the early months of 1914 were understandably preoccupied with the Home Rule issue. From the outset, a highly militant stance was adopted as it stated that Ulster's inclusion under the legislation 'invited Civil War'.[62] Accordingly, the Larne gun-running of April 1914 was enthusiastically lauded as 'a wonderful triumph of organisation'.[63] The arming of the Ulster Volunteers seemed to inspire an emboldened attitude as the paper predicted that there was 'no fear whatever of the Bill being placed on the statute book now'. In a rather smug manner the paper further contended:

> Ulster is too strong. She knows her strength; she smiles at the Prime Minister and the Irish Party; she says nothing; she is peaceful; she is pursuing her ordinary avocations; but the silence is one of tension; she can laugh at political tricksters and the Irish Party; for she is strong in her might, and she knows what she can perform.[64]

It was far from the only time that the paper would endeavour to speak on behalf of the entire province as if the region was an embodiment of political homogeneity and harmony. Nonetheless, the ostensible lack of concern that any Home Rule legislation would be enacted was short-lived. As the reality dawned that the Bill would most likely be passed a slight sense of desperation surfaced as it was suggested that the King should not sign the legislation as 'Ulster will not acknowledge a Dublin parliament'.[65] When it was finally signed into law in September

[62] *Impartial Reporter*, 1 Jan. 1914.
[63] *Impartial Reporter*, 30 Apr. 1914.
[64] *Impartial Reporter*, 14 May 1914.
[65] *Impartial Reporter*, 9 July 1914.

1914 the *Impartial Reporter* once more decided to speak on behalf of the province: 'Ulster said nothing. It remained dumb, though it felt a lot, and girded its teeth all the more'.[66]

The eagerness to speak on Ulster's behalf highlights the paper's somewhat curious interpretation of Ulster's geographic boundaries and indeed its broader attitude to partition. In January 1914, the *Impartial Reporter* emphatically declared that the Home Rule exclusion zone should not simply comprise 'the four north-eastern counties but seven or eight counties of our northern province'.[67] However, by June 1916, the paper had decided that as counties Monaghan, Cavan, and Donegal were predominantly nationalist they did not 'belong to our Ulster'.[68] Accordingly, it decreed 'the new Ulster of the six counties of the Plantation' and had no qualms in admitting that such a revision would ensure a unionist majority in an area that 'will contain two unionists to one nationalist'.[69] Four years later, with the pending establishment of a northern parliament for six of the Ulster counties, the sentiment was restated that the inclusion of the remaining three counties would 'invite trouble' and 'reduce the unionist majority so as to leave it at times in jeopardy'.[70] While the unionist *Cork Constitution* decried partition, the *Impartial Reporter* was quite happy 'to rejoice in being cut off from those with whom she cannot work and with whom no one can work satisfactorily'.[71] As levels of violence grew increasingly protracted during the summer of 1920 the paper seized the opportunity to assert 'the great moral and religious superiority of the North in all relations of life' while the nationalist South had 'become Bolshevik, atheistic, and pagan' and a place where 'the Devil glories in using former followers of the Christ to be his hellish conspirators and manslayers'.[72]

The outbreak of World War I and the attendant issues it generated regarding recruitment and conscription did not pose any difficulties for the *Impartial Reporter*. 'We must back the flag', the paper proclaimed upon

---

[66] *Impartial Reporter*, 1 Oct. 1914.

[67] *Impartial Reporter*, 1 Jan. 1914.

[68] *Impartial Reporter*, 8 June 1916. This was certainly not viewed as a concession to nationalists. The paper simply concluded that 'but for a slice of North Monaghan and a slice of West Cavan, neither of those counties belongs to our Ulster'. It also deemed that 'the same thing applies to three-fourths of County Donegal', with 'the exception of a slice of East Donegal'.

[69] *Impartial Reporter*, 15 June 1916.

[70] *Impartial Reporter*, 18 Mar. 1920.

[71] *Impartial Reporter*, 21 Aug. 1919.

[72] *Impartial Reporter*, 8, 29 July 1920.

the outbreak of war, before warning that 'we have no room in Ireland for traitors'.[73] Commitment to the war effort was notable for its castigation of those it deemed to be 'shirking' their duty, repeated calls for the introduction of conscription, and the excoriation of the Irish Parliamentary Party for its efforts in ensuring that conscription was not extended to Ireland after being introduced in Britain during 1915. 'Ulster's response to the call to the colours has been remarkable', the paper proudly asserted in January 1915.[74] Those who had failed to enlist were deemed 'cowards' who, the paper confidently assured its readers, 'have not proceeded from the homes of Ulster'. That 'disgrace', it continued, 'appertains to the other provinces'.[75] With such a mindset it was hardly surprising that the paper bemoaned that the government's delay 'in introducing compulsory service passes comprehension'.[76] The *Impartial Reporter*'s response to the concerns of nationalist MPs regarding the introduction of conscription was to dismiss them as 'mere parrots' that 'have no minds of their own' and who 'must do as they are told'.[77] Accordingly, such nationalist MPs were denounced for having 'gloried in their shame when they took credit for having had Ireland excluded from the operation of the Compulsory Service Bill'.[78]

To a certain extent the *Impartial Reporter*'s response to the Easter Rising echoed that of the *Cork Constitution* in its outright vilification of both the British Government and the Dublin Castle authorities for its alleged failure to rein in what it considered the more extreme elements of Irish nationalism.[79] In its recognisably unrestrained manner the paper enthusiastically advanced the allegations of 'German gold' while those who took part in the rebellion were denigrated as the 'scum of Ireland's manhood'.[80] The rise of Sinn Féin that began to gather impetus during

---

[73] *Impartial Reporter*, 6 Aug. 1914.

[74] *Impartial Reporter*, 14 Jan. 1915.

[75] *Impartial Reporter*, 11 Nov. 1915.

[76] *Impartial Reporter*, 29 July 1915.

[77] *Impartial Reporter*, 19 Aug. 1915.

[78] *Impartial Reporter*, 21 Sept. 1916.

[79] *Impartial Reporter*, 27 Apr. 1916. According to the paper, 'Mr Henry Asquith and Mr Birrell should be in the same Tower of London (with Roger Casement)' as there had been 'no peace in the country since Mr Asquith became Prime Minister' and 'no trouble in Ireland like that which has occurred during the period of office of Mr Augustine Birrell'.

[80] *Impartial Reporter*, 4 May 1916. Though the tone of *Impartial Reporter* editorials were hardly noted for their moderation, the reaction to Easter 1916 may have

the first half of 1917 afforded the paper fresh opportunity to adopt a condescending attitude towards nationalist Ireland. As Sinn Féin began to assert itself as a serious electoral force its aspiration for an Irish republic was dismissed as 'insane an idea as ever evolved out of the mind of a madman'.[81] The paper's reaction to that party's by-election victory in East Clare in July 1917 prompted a somewhat xenophobic, possibly even racist, response. Following Eamon de Valera's return as MP for the constituency he was described as the 'brown-skinned Spaniard–American, foreign by his father's side, foreign by birth in the United States, and only having connexion with Ireland through his Irish mother'.[82] De Valera's Spanish connections were obviously a source of irritation to the *Impartial Reporter* as it referred to him on several occasions over the next few years in a rather petty manner as 'Senor de Valera'.[83]

All the while the paper maintained its superior stance from within Ulster. 'We in Ulster are not much concerned with the family quarrel', the paper editorialised regarding the struggle within Irish nationalism between the Irish Parliamentary and Sinn Féin. 'In this northern province' (presumably now excluding Monaghan, Cavan, and Donegal) 'we are safe from many of the distractions of the south and west'.[84] Yet it was abundantly clear prior to the East Cavan by-election of June 1918 that the *Impartial Reporter* was far from unconcerned about developments within nationalist politics. The contest between Arthur Griffith of Sinn Féin and John F. O'Hanlon of the Irish Parliamentary Party gave rise to one of the extremely rare instances that the paper voiced any positive sentiment about an Irish nationalist of any creed. In its obvious eagerness for a Sinn Féin defeat the paper described O'Hanlon as 'eminently a nationalist of worth, and a member that the country might be proud of'.[85] This sudden regard for the Irish Parliamentary Party was again visible in the closing stages of the 1918 general election campaign. As the paper conceded that a Sinn Féin victory was virtually certain the Irish electorate was lambasted for having 'rushed to the newest fad' and forgotten 'all that the [Irish] Party has obtained and done for Ireland'.[86]

been even more embittered due to the death of Noel Trimble, a son of William Copeland Trimble, in France in April 1916.

[81] *Impartial Reporter*, 26 Apr. 1917.
[82] *Impartial Reporter*, 19 July 1917.
[83] *Impartial Reporter*, 1 Nov. 1917; 7 Feb. 1918; 6 Feb. 1919; 14 Apr. 1921.
[84] *Impartial Reporter*, 12 July 1917.
[85] *Impartial Reporter*, 19 May 1918.
[86] *Impartial Reporter*, 12 Dec. 1918.

Sinn Féin's sweeping general election victory conveniently removed any perceived necessity to express positive sentiment about any individual strand of Irish nationalism in the pages of the *Impartial Reporter*. Its editorial comment from then until the end of 1921 was marked by almost blanket denigration of Irish nationalism that was frequently quite vitriolic. When it quickly became clear that Sinn Féin would not obtain a hearing at the Paris Peace Conference the paper gleefully saluted the manner in which the US President had 'distinctly snubbed them [Sinn Féin] in an ignominious way which showed profound contempt and disdain'.[87] The proclamation of Sinn Féin in September 1919 was welcomed despite 'years of exasperating forbearance' as was the suppression of Dáil Éireann, 'the so-called assembly of an Irish-speaking parliament'.[88] Terence MacSwiney's death in October 1920 following his prolonged hunger strike was brusquely dismissed as a 'suicide' and a 'theatrical performance' that had been 'going on for weeks'.[89] However, the paper's antipathy towards Irish nationalism appeared to be also inspired by a somewhat racial undertone.

In November 1919, with levels of violence increasing, the paper berated the Dublin Castle administration for being 'ignorant of the mind and way of the Irish Celt'. The same editorial had a very firm view on how to deal with the issue:

> There was one man who did understand them, and there was one man whom they understood – Oliver Cromwell. We do not approve in these days of all that he did do, nor do we at all mean to convey that we need a man of the same unrelenting and Drogheda-ferocious type now – but we do most unhesitatingly assert for the last ten years the country has suffered for the want of such a man of iron resolution, quick execution, firmness of temperament, and exacting in just punishment. *We want a modern Oliver Cromwell.*[90]

The invocation of a figure so loathed by Irish nationalists was certainly no sporadic outburst, as William Copeland Trimble's aforementioned speech in Australia in June 1921 illustrates. Indeed, on no fewer than five separate occasions during 1919 and 1920, the paper called for a modern-day Oliver Cromwell to deal with the situation in Ireland.[91]

---

[87] *Impartial Reporter*, 20 Feb. 1919.
[88] *Impartial Reporter*, 18 Sept. 1919.
[89] *Impartial Reporter*, 28 Oct. 1920.
[90] *Impartial Reporter*, 6 Nov. 1919.
[91] *Impartial Reporter*, 25 Mar., 27 May, 3 June, 2 Dec. 1920.

Castigation of the British Government's lack of resolution was combined with further disparagement of the 'Irish Celt':

> We regret to have to admit it, but we must concede that British Government in Ireland has been a failure by reason of the incapacity of the Englishman (or Welshman) to understand the Irish Celt. Nearly all the politicians imagine that they can wheedle the Celt with soft soap and concessions, promises of Home Rule and the like; and Paddy laughs in his sleeve at the stupid Englishman, and prepares another raid to extract something more. Mr Lloyd George thought he would purchase peace by the doles: Paddy smiled and murdered another man or two; Mr George increased the Old Age Pensions, and Paddy immediately murdered more, and made more raids on women.[92]

With such an extreme and implacable outlook, it was scarcely surprising that the paper was positively seething upon the calling of the truce in July 1921. It was 'humiliating', according to the paper, that England 'has had to confess defeat and surrender and make terms with men whom the Premier and Chief Secretary declared over and over again were murderers and criminals'.[93] In the weeks prior to the signing of the Anglo-Irish Treaty, conflicting opinions were evident as to the status of the six partitioned Ulster counties. In early November, it was confidently predicted that 'the six northern counties are safe' as 'Lloyd George has again affirmed his pledge'.[94] Yet only a week later the paper declared that Lloyd George 'cannot be trusted' as 'there is no knowing what he may do yet'.[95] Nonetheless, the *Impartial Reporter* reacted in near celebratory manner to the agreement reached in London in early December.

This was principally based on the failure to achieve an Irish republic and the necessity to take an oath of allegiance. Any disquiet regarding the possible revision of the boundary of the area over which the Stormont Parliament had administrative control was summarily dismissed.[96] The paper gloated at the unfolding divisions within Sinn Féin and could not

---

[92] *Impartial Reporter*, 29 Jan. 1920.

[93] *Impartial Reporter*, 14 July 1921.

[94] *Impartial Reporter*, 3 Nov. 1921.

[95] *Impartial Reporter*, 10 Nov. 1921.

[96] *Impartial Reporter*, 8 Dec. 1921. Apart from a brief comment that some 'loyalists that live close to the borders of Fermanagh' that 'may find themselves outside the Northern Pale' the paper indicated little concern at any potential boundary changes.

resist the temptation once again condescendingly to question de Valera's Irishness. 'Poor de Valera, the Spaniard, has been outwitted by the crafty Sassenachs', the paper almost joyfully declared.[97] Nor could it resist availing itself of the emerging Treaty split further to deprecate the 'Irish Celt': 'As the Irish Celtic race are by nature fissiparous, a split is almost inevitable'.[98]

However, if many nationalist titles were guilty of underestimating the strength of unionist resolve, the *Impartial Reporter*'s reading of nationalist politics displayed a similar lack of sound judgement. It confidently predicted that De Valera would retire if the Dáil went against his wishes and ratified the Treaty.[99] This was to prove equally lacking in foresight as the suggestion in many nationalist titles that the unionists of Ulster would ultimately feel their interests to be better served under a Dublin parliament. Possibly it provides a salutary lesson to all newspapers that they should restrict themselves to documenting and analysing contemporary developments rather than trying to predict the future.

Conclusion

The *Impartial Reporter* encapsulated so many of the features that hallmarked both unionist and nationalist newspapers across the Irish provincial press in the late nineteenth century and the first half of the twentieth century. Remarkably long editorial tenures, unbroken association with one family over a prolonged period of time, and a highly dominant personality with a deep religious faith at the helm of the newspaper were characteristics that were common to provincial titles across all the four provinces. Nevertheless, no other newspaper embodied these traits to the same extent as the *Impartial Reporter*. Through several generations of the Trimble family dating back to the early 1800s, the paper arguably created a form of template within the provincial print media. However, its editorial comment between 1914 and 1921 was unlikely to have been replicated to any great extent across the country.

The *Impartial Reporter* was a staunchly unionist organ but its editorial output during these years was regularly quite self-serving and frequently strayed well beyond the defence of the unionist position. This most likely reflected the rather dictatorial tendencies of its editor–proprietor, William Copeland Trimble. The self-serving nature of the paper's editorial

---

[97] *Impartial Reporter*, 15 Dec. 1921.
[98] *Impartial Reporter*, 29 Dec. 1921.
[99] *Impartial Reporter*, 15 Dec. 1921.

commentary was best illustrated by its effective redrawing of the map of Ulster to exclude Monaghan, Cavan, and Donegal. While a unionist organ such as the *Cork Constitution* deplored partition the *Impartial Reporter* almost viewed it as cause for celebration. Unionists outside the 'new Ulster' were obviously of no concern to William Copeland Trimble and his paper. The creation of an administrative area in which a unionist majority could be guaranteed was clearly the main priority.

In its advancement of the unionist cause the *Impartial Reporter* did not confine itself to attacking the Irish Parliamentary Party or, in later years, Sinn Féin. It targeted all Irish nationalists, regardless of creed. In the early years of World War I this principally manifested itself in a series of allegations that nationalists were 'shirking' their duty by failing to enlist in the British Army. Yet such disparagement was quite mild in comparison with what was to come. The repeated calls for a 'modern Oliver Cromwell' and the persistent denigration of the 'Irish Celt' (accompanied by the derogatory use of the word 'Paddy') illustrate clearly that the paper had few qualms in engaging in blanket degradation of Irish nationalists. Consequently, it seems almost redundant to conclude that while the *Impartial Reporter* was unquestionably catering for a unionist readership, it displayed no desire to gain any understanding of Irish nationalism, much less come to an accommodation with it. In summary, the paper could justifiably be said to represent what Irish nationalists and others regarded as 'intransigent unionism'.

Londonderry Sentinel

The establishment of the *Londonderry Sentinel* in 1829 coincided with the passing of Catholic emancipation and the two events were certainly not unconnected. Derry historian Brian Lacy notes how the editor of the *Londonderry Journal* at the time, William Wallen, 'vehemently disagreed' with the policy of the paper's new owners in supporting Catholic emancipation. Accordingly, Wallen resigned his post and founded the *Londonderry Sentinel* along with some like-minded friends. The paper first appeared in September 1829, and its opening editorial professed alarm at the 'ill-timed and timid concession'. 'The Protestants have been deceived', it continued, 'by friends and guides in whom we trusted'. However, such people would be held accountable, as it warned that 'if the schoolmaster is abroad, the Protestant Sentinel is at his post'.[100] In the decades that

[100] Lacy, *Siege city*, pp 173–4; *Derry Journal*, 9 June 1972; *Derry Journal: 225th*

followed, the *Sentinel* evolved to become what another local historian has labelled the city's 'chief anti-nationalist thunderer'.[101]

The remarkably lengthy family associations with individual newspapers that were a ubiquitous feature of the Irish provincial press is again in evidence at the *Londonderry Sentinel*. In this case, it was the Colhoun family that fulfilled that role. James Colhoun was a junior member of staff at the time of the paper's foundation in 1829. When William Wallen died in 1843, Colhoun took over the management of the *Sentinel* on behalf of his widow. Upon her death in 1857, James Colhoun assumed proprietorship in conjunction with Thomas Chambers, a Derry solicitor. The partnership with Chambers was amicably terminated about twenty years later leaving Colhoun as sole proprietor. James Colhoun died in October 1897, at which stage the paper passed to his son, William Colhoun.[102]

Like his father before him, William Colhoun was deeply involved in unionist politics in Derry. He was president of the Londonderry Unionist Association and served on the standing committee of the Ulster Unionist Council during the campaign against Home Rule. Upon his death in 1915, the *Irish Times* remarked that 'for almost a quarter of a century past' he 'had been regarded as the leader of Unionism in Londonderry'. At the time of his passing in April of that year, his three sons, James, William, and Jack, were all serving in the British Army.[103] However, it was to his eldest son James that the proprietorship of the *Londonderry Sentinel* passed. James Colhoun served in France for the entirety of World War I with the Inniskilling Fusiliers. He followed in his father's footsteps by becoming president of the city's unionist association. Following his death in September 1945, control of the paper passed to his widow Florence Colhoun, who managed the business until it was sold thirteen years later. The sale of the paper in 1958 marked the end of the Colhoun family's links with the *Londonderry Sentinel*; it was an association that had lasted 129 years.[104]

Anniversary Supplement (6 June 1997). When marking both its centenary and its 150th anniversary, the *Londonderry Sentinel* did not acknowledge that Catholic emancipation was a factor in its establishment but merely stated that William Wallen had resigned the editorship of the *Journal* 'because his convictions were out of harmony with those of the new proprietors'.

[101] Seán McMahon, *A history of County Derry* (Dublin, 2004), p. 115.

[102] *Londonderry Sentinel*, 3 Apr. 1915; 19 Sept. 1929.

[103] *Londonderry Sentinel*, 3 Apr. 1915; *Irish Times*, 2 Apr. 1915.

[104] *Londonderry Sentinel*, 7 Sept. 1945; 19 Sept. 1979; *Irish Independent, Irish Times*, 7 Sept. 1945.

In contrast to the Trimble family at the *Impartial Reporter*, the Colhoun family did not occupy the editorial chair at the *Sentinel*. From 1893 until his retirement in 1931 the paper was edited by John Charles (J.C.) Orr, who served a total of forty-eight years at the paper. Described as 'an exceedingly staunch unionist' with 'a deep-rooted attachment to the cause which he so effectively espoused', Orr was one of the earliest and most enthusiastic recruits to the City of Derry battalion of the Ulster Volunteers.[105] Similarly, one of Orr's senior colleagues at the paper, and indeed his successor as editor, Cecil Davis (C.D.) Milligan, was an equally resolute unionist. He was considered 'a staunch loyalist' with 'a deep-rooted attachment for the cause' and 'a great champion of Ulster and the British way of life'. Milligan was also a member of the Ulster Volunteers, the Orange Order, the City of Londonderry and Foyle Unionist Association, as well as being a devout member of the Church of Ireland.[106] With such a fervently unionist ownership and editorship in place there was little doubt as to where the *Sentinel*'s editorial allegiance lay. Nonetheless, the paper's editorial commentary between 1914 and 1921 is just as compelling as any other Irish provincial title, whether unionist or nationalist.

Editorial comment, 1914–1921

The *Londonderry Sentinel* was a tri-weekly publication (Tuesday, Thursday, and Saturday) usually consisting of eight pages divided into six columns. It carried roughly the same proportion of advertisements as most other provincial newspapers. Nonetheless, many of the individual advertisements that featured strongly indicate a slightly wealthier cohort of readers. This was evidenced by the regular appearance of notices for shipping companies such as the White Star Line, Anchor Line, and Union Castle Line promoting ocean-going liner travel, principally to the USA and Canada but also to South and East Africa. Advertisements for Ford Cars plus a variety of brands of motorcycles and bicycles further strengthens the notion of a somewhat more affluent readership. The regular listing of the London Stock Exchange prices lends further weight to such a conclusion. Apart from this, the advertising space consisted of much of the standard fare of drapery shops, foodstuffs, farm machinery,

---

[105] *Londonderry Sentinel*, 2 Dec. 1941.

[106] *Londonderry Sentinel*, 22 Sept. 1956. Curiously, Milligan was also a founder-member of Derry City Football Club, an institution that predominantly came to be associated with the city's nationalist population.

the paper's own printing works, plus a variety of medications such as Owbridge's Lung Tonic, Mother Siegel's Syrup, and Doan's Backache Kidney Pills.

The *Londonderry Sentinel* advertised itself as 'opposed to Home Rule or any legislation tending to sever the Union between England and Ireland'.[107] In the early months of 1914 this took the form of condemnation of the British government's plan to introduce a measure of Home Rule for Ireland. The plan was regarded as a 'cowardly desertion of the unionists of Ireland' that left it up to 'the unionist manhood of Ulster to emphasise the extent of the outrage by preparing to make all resistance in its power'.[108] Accordingly, the British Army officers involved in the Curragh mutiny of March 1914 were fulsomely praised for having 'manfully offered to resign their commissions rather than do the government's dirty work'.[109] Hostility towards Home Rule took a decidedly more militant tone in the aftermath of the Larne gun-running as the paper predicted 'a death-grapple with whatever forces may be employed to expel them from their birth right in the Empire'. Such a 'death-grapple' would not cease 'until the unionists of Ulster are hopelessly and continually defeated, until the best and bravest are destroyed, until the land has been deluged in blood'.[110]

With the outbreak of war in August 1914, the *Sentinel* promptly expressed its loyalty to the British cause while John Redmond's offer of nationalist assistance was instantly dismissed as a 'put-up job'.[111] Thereafter the paper frequently mirrored the *Impartial Reporter*'s sentiments regarding recruitment, if not with the same strength of language, alleging minimal levels of enlistment across nationalist Ireland in contrast with what it claimed was the highly enthusiastic response from the unionist community in Ulster. Indeed, the supposed failure of nationalists to enlist was a constantly recurring theme throughout the war. Cabinet ministers were lambasted for their failure to acknowledge 'the extraordinary disparity between the enlistment figures of the purely nationalist parts of Ireland and those of the area which includes Ulster'.[112] Similarly, the government was warned of the necessity to act 'to prevent the wholesale flight to America of shirkers from the western counties

---

[107] *Newspaper press directory and advertisers' guide 1917*, p. 584.
[108] *Londonderry Sentinel*, 17 Jan. 1914.
[109] *Londonderry Sentinel*, 24 Mar. 1914.
[110] *Londonderry Sentinel*, 11 June 1914.
[111] *Londonderry Sentinel*, 4 Aug. 1914.
[112] *Londonderry Sentinel*, 9 Jan. 1915.

of Ireland'.[113] Yet when a report published by the Lord Lieutenant in February 1915 contradicted the *Sentinel*'s claims regarding recruitment, the figures were dismissed as being 'ridiculously astray' and 'bogus'.[114] Undeterred, the paper proceeded to call for conscription to be introduced in Ireland but claimed the government 'may be too greatly afraid of Mr Redmond and Mr Devlin'.[115]

In the immediate aftermath of Easter 1916 the *Sentinel* echoed the response of many provincial papers, both unionist and nationalist, in alleging German involvement in the rebellion. It claimed that 'a German auxiliary vessel disguised as a neutral and working in conjunction with a German submarine' had unsuccessfully attempted to land arms in the country.[116] Although the rebels were labelled 'the Dublin mobsmen', the *Sentinel* appeared to express a grudging admiration for their ability to capture several buildings in Dublin that represented 'a fairly substantial achievement'.[117] Nonetheless, it agreed that 'it was absolutely necessary to make a speedy example of the ringleaders' in order to discourage 'certain people suspected of, shall we say, a sneaking sympathy with the movement for clearing the hated English garrison out of Ireland'.[118]

The rise of Sinn Féin that ensued was greeted by the *Sentinel* with understandable antipathy. However, it did not engage to any noticeable extent, in the broad denigration of Irish nationalists so typical of the *Impartial Reporter*. Indeed, the paper displayed a significant degree of foresight in its response to Sinn Féin's early electoral successes. Shortly after Count Plunkett's election as MP for North Roscommon in February 1917 it presciently articulated the fears of the Irish Parliamentary Party when commenting that 'the Plunkett poison may spread' and later acknowledged that party's dread of a general election as it would result in its 'political extinction'.[119] Éamon de Valera's victory in East Clare a few months later provided further confirmation, if it were needed, that 'the Sinn Féiners will sweep the decks as soon as they are given a chance'.[120] Despite its accurate assessment of Sinn Féin's electoral prospects the paper clearly harboured fears of its burgeoning influence.

[113] *Londonderry Sentinel*, 6 Nov. 1915.
[114] *Londonderry Sentinel*, 3 Feb. 1916.
[115] *Londonderry Sentinel*, 7 Oct. 1916.
[116] *Londonderry Sentinel*, 25 Apr. 1916.
[117] *Londonderry Sentinel*, 27 Apr. 1916.
[118] *Londonderry Sentinel*, 9 May 1916.
[119] *Londonderry Sentinel*, 17 Feb., 15 Mar. 1917.
[120] *Londonderry Sentinel*, 12 July 1917.

This was quite evident following the South Armagh by-election early in 1918 when it welcomed the Irish Parliamentary Party's victory over Sinn Féin and gladly admitted that 'South Armagh unionists' had 'helped the Redmondite candidate to beat the Sinn Féiner'.[121] The paper was guilty of considerable misreading of Sinn Féin tactics when it declared, in anticipation of that party's general election success, that its abstentionist policy could be abandoned in the face of pressure from the Catholic Church.[122]

The *Sentinel*'s hostility towards Sinn Féin generally did not manifest itself in the supercilious and partitionist tones that hallmarked the *Impartial Reporter*'s editorial commentary. Equally, it did not overtly purport to speak on behalf of the broader province of Ulster. Initially the paper objected to the entire island of Ireland being governed by a Home Rule parliament but ultimately it simply sought the exclusion of the six Ulster counties from any such measure. With the passing of the Home Rule bill in 1914 it defiantly proclaimed that 'a Dublin parliament will never rule over the northern province'.[123] Unionists from the south of Ireland were censured for their participation in the Irish Convention of 1917 and accused of not being representative of 'southern unionists generally'.[124] The establishment of the Stormont parliament four years later was welcomed as a 'measure of self-government' that was 'compatible with the security of Britain and the inalienable liberties of the North'.[125]

Throughout the three years leading up to the establishment of the Stormont parliament, the *Londonderry Sentinel* had been a persistent critic of Sinn Féin for what it perceived as the party's inextricable links to the more violent elements of militant republicanism. Unlike the unionist *Cork Constitution* there was never any suggestion that the Sinn Féin leadership may simply have been unable to control such elements. The first meeting of Dáil Éireann in January 1919 was considered 'an incitement to crime' while Sinn Féin was later accused of possessing 'a great secret army, whose business it is to murder police and soldiers, and who succeed in frightening the population into screening the murderers'.[126]

---

[121] *Londonderry Sentinel*, 5 Feb. 1918. This effectively confirms the assertion of the *Meath Chronicle* (referred to in Chapter 3) that the Irish Parliamentary Party victory was only achieved with unionist support.

[122] *Londonderry Sentinel*, 21 Dec. 1918.

[123] *Londonderry Sentinel*, 17 Sept. 1914.

[124] *Londonderry Sentinel*, 5 Mar. 1918.

[125] *Londonderry Sentinel*, 14 June 1921.

[126] *Londonderry Sentinel*, 23 Jan., 23 Oct. 1919.

As the likelihood of some form of Irish self-government was being considered during 1920, the paper expressed its horror at the possibility that 'control of three parts of the country' would pass 'into the hands of men whose political creed consists of hatred both of England and the majority of the people in the remaining quarter'.[127] Indeed, the concern at what it considered the government's leniency in 'allowing the unhindered development of the Sinn Féin programme' was so great that it believed there would be 'no alternative but for the Ulster Volunteers to reorganise their force and take steps to stem an invasion which would result in reducing Ulster to the deplorable condition of the South and West'.[128] Yet despite its antagonism towards Sinn Féin the *Sentinel* was willing to afford some degree of respect to Irish nationalists.

This was most evident at the time of the hunger strike of Terence MacSwiney during September and October 1920. While the *Impartial Reporter* rather cruelly dismissed MacSwiney's death as a 'suicide', the *Londonderry Sentinel* adopted quite a different view. Even prior to his death it expressed its clear admiration at the 'remarkable struggle' of a man displaying a 'firmness of will throughout' and a 'wonderful reserve of vitality'.[129] Upon his death the paper seemed genuinely moved by 'the remarkable courage of the man' and lauded his bravery in his 'desire to die for Ireland' that was 'strong enough to sustain him against the horrible pangs of starvation'.[130] The *Sentinel* also accorded Eamon de Valera a certain amount of credit several months later when it acknowledged that the recent Sinn Féin election manifesto 'was marked by a moderation of expression not observed in many of his [de Valera's] earlier pronouncements'.[131] Nonetheless, the reaction to the truce of July 1921 was one of anger and suspicion.

In a manner not entirely dissimilar to that of the *Impartial Reporter*, the *Sentinel* accused Lloyd George of maintaining a silence as to 'the extent of the surrender which has been extorted from the British Government'.[132] Later editorials decried the government for consulting 'with the conspirators against the lives of the King's soldiers and police' while it was additionally asserted that 'there is no knowing to what lengths Mr Lloyd George will go in the attempt to placate the

[127]   *Londonderry Sentinel*, 2 Mar. 1920.
[128]   *Londonderry Sentinel*, 13 July 1920.
[129]   *Londonderry Sentinel*, 11 Sept. 1920.
[130]   *Londonderry Sentinel*, 26 Oct. 1920.
[131]   *Londonderry Sentinel*, 7 May 1921.
[132]   *Londonderry Sentinel*, 23 July 1921.

rebels'.[133] Accordingly, when rumours surfaced in late November that deliberations had broken down, the paper happily speculated that the talks had 'gone to pieces' and that 'the farewells may have been already said'.[134]

Upon the completion of negotiations in London the reaction of the *Londonderry Sentinel* differed somewhat to that of the *Impartial Reporter* in that it did not focus to any great extent on Sinn Féin's failure to secure an Irish republic. In the immediate aftermath of the talks the most notable aspect of its response was what it regarded as the 'treachery' of Lloyd George in breaking 'his distinct pledge to Sir James Craig that nothing would be done to the prejudice of the rights of the northern parliament behind the back of the northern premier'.[135] While this was clearly a reference to a potential boundary revision the paper curiously did not express any further concerns in this regard. Instead, the *Sentinel* turned its attention to the emerging divisions within Sinn Féin and appeared to take a certain pleasure in labelling Dáil Éireann a 'laughable farce' that was 'leisurely making up its mind' whether to accept or reject the Treaty.[136]

Conclusion

The *Londonderry Sentinel* displayed assorted traits that were common to many other Irish provincial newspapers. Easily the most visible of these was the association with the Colhoun family that lasted well over a century. Allied to this was the lengthy editorial tenure of J.C. Orr that lasted close on four decades. The involvement of three generations of the Colhoun family in the unionist politics of the city, and indeed that of successive editors J.C. Orr and C.D. Milligan, provides further examples of senior newspapermen playing a highly active role in local politics.

From an editorial perspective, the *Londonderry Sentinel* articulated many of the sentiments that might be expected of a solidly unionist newspaper. These included a militant assertion of Ulster's right to be excluded from Home Rule, outright condemnation of the 1916 Rising, castigation of the Sinn Féin party for its assumed involvement in attacks on Crown forces, and, perhaps most notably, a suspicion and distrust of the British Government for supposedly acceding to nationalist demands.

---

[133] *Londonderry Sentinel*, 11 Oct., 19 Nov. 1921.
[134] *Londonderry Sentinel*, 26 Nov. 1921.
[135] *Londonderry Sentinel*, 13, 17 Dec. 1921.
[136] *Londonderry Sentinel*, 20, 22 Dec. 1921.

Yet the *Sentinel* never descended to the racial denigration of the 'Irish Celt' nor the name-calling (e.g. 'Senor de Valera') that so typified the editorial commentary of the *Impartial Reporter*. Indeed, its reaction to the hunger strike and subsequent death of Terence MacSwiney indicated a clear acceptance that it was not only unionists who could be possessed of honour and integrity: quite an admission for a staunchly unionist organ. Ultimately, however, the *Sentinel* retreated to a more recognisably unionist position in appearing to derive particular enjoyment in witnessing emerging nationalist divisions over the Treaty.

Anglo-Celt

The *Anglo-Celt* was founded in 1846 by Sir John Young (who later held the office of Chief Secretary for Ireland) of Bailieborough, with Gustavus Tuite D'Alton serving as the first editor. The paper was launched with the specific purpose of supporting Sir Robert Peel's campaign for the repeal of the Corn Laws. The realisation of this goal the following year resulted in a change of ownership of the paper.[137] In 1847, the *Anglo-Celt* was acquired by twenty-four-year-old Zacariah Wallace of Coolock in Dublin. Wallace, who also fulfilled the role of editor, is described by the paper's 150th anniversary edition as a 'liberal, constitutional, and utilitarian nationalist'. He had been deeply shocked by the horrors of the Great Famine for which he believed the landlord system to be the principal cause and was consequently a strong proponent of land reform. In 1852, he was convicted of seditious libel relating to an editorial he had penned regarding a land dispute in County Clare. Wallace received a six-month prison sentence and a £50 fine and although there were strong appeals for his release on health grounds none was successful. His health broken from the ordeal, Zacariah Wallace died in February 1857 at the early age of thirty-five.[138]

Following Wallace's death, his sister-in-law Charlotte Bournes (also guardian of his two children) assumed the reins of the *Anglo-Celt*. However, Wallace's father Joseph soon gained control of the paper. Joseph Wallace was a conservative whose political views differed considerably from those of his late son, with the result that the paper ceased publication in 1858. In the meantime, Charlotte Bournes, whose political sympathies were very much in harmony with those of her deceased

---

[137] *Anglo-Celt: Souvenir Supplement 1846–1996* (30 May 1996).
[138] Ibid.

brother-in-law, founded the *Cavan Observer*. This title first appeared in 1857 and remained in print until her death seven years later. By this time, the *Anglo-Celt* was just about to resume publication.[139]

The reappearance of the *Anglo-Celt* in 1864 provides yet another instance of the highly significant role of the Catholic Church in the history of the Irish provincial press. At the initiation of the Roman Catholic Bishop of Kilmore, Dr Nicholas Conaty, John F. O'Hanlon, then the chief reporter with the *Evening Mail* in Dublin, was approached with a view to taking over the ownership and editorship of the *Anglo-Celt*. O'Hanlon's subsequent assumption of the dual role marked the beginning of a family association with the paper that still existed over 150 years later.[140]

John F. O'Hanlon was a supporter of Isaac Butt and the nascent Home Rule movement, and played a significant role in the campaign of Joseph Biggar when the latter was returned as an MP at the 1874 general election.[141] He was also active in the campaign for land reform and was a leading member of the Cavan Farmers Defence League.[142] Following his death in 1885 ownership of the paper passed to his wife Kate, who hailed from a significant journalistic family and who remained in control of the paper until her death in 1908.[143] Upon her passing, her two sons, John F. (J.F.) O'Hanlon and Edward T. (E.T.) O'Hanlon, assumed control of the *Anglo-Celt* and were jointly to remain at the helm of the paper until the middle of the twentieth century.[144]

E.T. O'Hanlon succeeded to the editorial chair when he was only eighteen years of age, following the death of his father. He served in that position for a remarkable sixty-one years. His nephew, Edward (Ned) O'Hanlon, who succeeded him as editor, remembered him as 'a quiet undemonstrative man'.[145] E.T. O'Hanlon was a devout Catholic and a

[139] Ibid.
[140] Ibid.
[141] Ibid.
[142] Gerard Moran, 'The emergence and consolidation of the Home Rule movement in County Cavan, 1870–86' in Raymond Gillespie (ed.), *Cavan: essays on the history of an Irish county* (Dublin, 1995), p. 162.
[143] *Anglo-Celt: Souvenir Supplement 1846–1996* (30 May 1996). Kate O'Hanlon's father was Edward O'Farrell, proprietor of the *Evening Post* in Dublin, while her brother was Edward French O'Farrell, chief sub-editor of the *Daily Telegraph* in London.
[144] Ibid.
[145] Ibid.

keen supporter of the GAA as well as being a very active member of local tennis and golf clubs. He was also closely associated with Sir Horace Plunkett and the cooperative movement and indeed the *Anglo-Celt* devoted considerable attention to agricultural affairs.[146] His brother, J.F. O'Hanlon, had a somewhat more prominent public persona.

J.F. O'Hanlon was managing-director of the *Anglo-Celt* newspaper for over sixty years. In addition to sharing his brother's wholehearted Catholicism he was also an energetic advocate of the GAA and was the first chairman of the organisation in County Cavan. He was also a member of the Irish Parliamentary Party which brought him into close contact with senior figures such as John Redmond, Joseph Devlin, and John Dillon. J.F. O'Hanlon also played a significant role in local politics: he was initially a member of the Cavan Board of Guardians and later the Cavan Urban Council where he served as chairman for a number of years. Most notably, however, J.F. O'Hanlon was the Irish Parliamentary Party candidate in opposition to Arthur Griffith of Sinn Féin in the East Cavan by-election of June 1918.[147]

Hugh Oram comments that the *Anglo-Celt* granted fair coverage to both sides during the by-election campaign.[148] This is quite a valid observation as the paper principally assumed an anti-conscription stance rather than engaging in any denigration of Sinn Féin. Although J.F. O'Hanlon lost the contest, his defeat was more likely due to the heightened political atmosphere of the time rather than any lack of personal popularity. Clear evidence of such an assertion was provided only nine years later when O'Hanlon headed the poll at the 1927 general election to take a seat as an independent TD. He held the seat until 1933 and was principally an advocate of the farmer's cause during his time in Dáil Éireann.[149]

During the by-election campaign in 1918 the *Meath Chronicle* had very unfairly referred to J.F. O'Hanlon as 'a pro-Britisher' and 'England's candidate' (as detailed in Chapter 2).[150] It was not the only time a degree of conflict would arise between the two papers. In the prelude to the general

---

[146] *Anglo-Celt*, 24 May 1947. Although J.F. O'Hanlon has been referred to as editor of the *Anglo-Celt* in some local history texts, the obituaries of both E.T. O'Hanlon and J.F. O'Hanlon, and indeed the paper's 150th anniversary edition, record E.T. O'Hanlon as the long-time editor of the paper.

[147] *Anglo-Celt*, 29 Dec. 1956.

[148] Oram, *The newspaper book*, p. 136.

[149] *Anglo-Celt*, 29 Dec. 1956.

[150] *Meath Chronicle*, 15 June 1918.

election of December 1918, an article appeared in the Navan-based paper implying that the delay in the release of voters' lists for East Cavan was attributable to the *Anglo-Celt*, which held the printing contract for the publication of such voter records.[151] The *Anglo-Celt* duly sued the *Meath Chronicle* for libel which ultimately resulted in James Davis, proprietor of the *Meath Chronicle*, being required to issue an apology (published in a number of local and national newspapers) to the effect that their initial claim was completely without foundation.[152]

Regardless of this implied assertion of bias by the *Meath Chronicle*, such a notion could have easily been dispelled by the fact that there was a significant Sinn Féin presence at the *Anglo-Celt*. Thomas K. Walsh, who joined the paper in 1903 and subsequently spent forty-seven years on the editorial staff, was highly involved in the establishment of the Sinn Féin party in County Cavan. He later took an active part in the War of Independence as a result of which he was interned at both Ballykinlar Camp in County Down and Crumlin Road Gaol in Belfast. While Walsh's brand of nationalism clashed with that of the O'Hanlon brothers, he shared their steadfast Catholic faith. Another common characteristic was his enthusiasm for the GAA and Thomas K. Walsh was central to the foundation of one of the first hurling clubs in County Cavan in 1904.[153]

Editorial comment, 1914–1921

The listing for the *Anglo-Celt* in the *Newspaper press directory* described the paper as circulating in as many as ten adjoining counties in Ulster and Leinster, and extensively in the USA and Canada. It is open to question whether such a remarkable geographical spread of readers could be verified but the additional information that the paper devoted particular attention to agriculture was quite evident in the pages of the *Anglo-Celt* between 1914 and 1921.[154] The paper normally comprised twelve pages divided into seven columns and regularly featured agricultural announcements such as notices of upcoming fairs and shows, plus frequent items concerning the

---

[151] *Meath Chronicle*, 7 Sept. 1918.
[152] *Irish Independent*, 19, 28 June 1919.
[153] *Anglo-Celt*, 15 Apr. 1950. Walsh was a native of Westport where he had commenced his journalistic career working under the Doris brothers at the *Mayo News*. He also worked at the *Connaught Telegraph* prior to moving to the *Anglo-Celt*.
[154] *Newspaper press directory and advertisers' guide 1917*, p. 209.

care of livestock and crops. Accordingly, many of the advertisements that appeared were of a related nature. Goods advertised included farm implements and machinery, seeds, rick covers and tarpaulins, plus details of veterinary care for animals.

In addition to the numerous farming-related advertisements, the paper also carried the standard advertising fare promoting local grocery stores and drapery shops plus various foodstuffs (most notably several different brands of flour). Like many other provincial newspapers, medications also featured strongly. Amongst those appearing regularly in the advertising columns of the *Anglo-Celt* were Angier's Emulsion (for bronchitis and coughs), Sloan's Liniment (for throat and chest), and Zam-Buk embrocation (for sore and tender skin). Other items to feature strongly in these columns included Locke's Whiskey, Velvan Plug pipe tobacco, Ford Cars, and Raleigh Bicycles.

Despite its significant ties with the Irish Parliamentary Party the *Anglo-Celt* tended to devote considerably less editorial attention to ongoing political developments than many other provincial titles. As the Home Rule issue, but more specifically unionist opposition to it, came to the fore in the early months of 1914, it refrained from making any major editorial pronouncements though it did voice its disapproval of the prevailing situation in the 'Unionist North' where 'no Catholic has the remotest chance of receiving ordinary fair play'.[155] Such comments, however, were notable for their infrequency. With the outbreak of war several months later the paper focused on the necessity for Irishmen to play their part in defeating 'the Army which has deliberately butchered little children and old women in its march through Belgium'.[156] While the *Anglo-Celt* unequivocally articulated Irish support for the war effort its attitude towards conscription was rather different.

To a certain extent, the paper echoed the stance of the *Tuam Herald* in wholeheartedly promoting recruitment but vehemently opposing conscription. The *Anglo-Celt*, however, made certain claims in this regard that would not have been appreciated by unionists in Ulster. As early as September 1914, the paper asserted that the response of the Ulster Volunteers to Lord Kitchener's appeal for recruits was greatly overstated by the unionist leadership.[157] As the possibility of conscription became a live issue during the course of the war the paper declared that Sir Edward Carson 'knows in his heart that the unionist farmers are as bitterly opposed

[155] *Anglo-Celt*, 21 Mar. 1914.
[156] *Anglo-Celt*, 10 Oct. 1914.
[157] *Anglo-Celt*, 19 Sept. 1914.

to their sons being taken off the land as are the nationalists'.[158] The notion of unionist aversion to compulsory recruitment was a theme the paper continued to pursue. As the measure was just about to be introduced in Ireland the *Anglo-Celt* speculated that it was not only unionists drawn from the farming community that would not welcome conscription. In an editorial from April 1918, the paper claimed that 'many of Sir Edward Carson's followers' were happily avoiding conscription having gained employment in 'the northern shipyards and other Belfast industries' that were essential to 'the prosecution of the war'.[159]

It was this same issue that principally dominated the *Anglo-Celt*'s editorial commentary in the weeks leading up to the East Cavan by-election of June 1918. In the contest that pitted its managing-director, J.F. O'Hanlon, against Sinn Féin's Arthur Griffith, the paper refrained from engaging in any significant criticism of Sinn Féin and instead expressed the desire for 'unity in the face of the menace of conscription'.[160] In this respect, much significance was afforded to O'Hanlon's offer to stand aside, 'if his opponent did likewise', so that the seat could 'be handed over to a prominent Irishman, who would hold it until the danger of conscription had passed'.[161] The proposal was never likely to garner any major consideration within Sinn Féin, which was seeking to re-establish its authority following electoral defeats in South Armagh, East Tyrone, and Waterford in the previous six months. The arrest of Arthur Griffith and many of his party colleagues a short time before polling day was viewed by the *Anglo-Celt* as having 'no other effect than to gain momentary adherents to the cause of Sinn Féin' and consequently decided the contest in Griffith's favour.[162]

Prior to this time, the *Anglo-Celt* had not really voiced any great antipathy towards Sinn Féin or any strand of militant nationalism. Following the Easter Rising it did not allege any collusion with Germany

---

[158] *Anglo-Celt*, 9 Dec. 1916.

[159] *Anglo-Celt*, 20 Apr. 1918.

[160] *Anglo-Celt*, 4 May 1918.

[161] *Anglo-Celt*, 11, 18, 25 May 1918. Thomas J. Morrissey, 'O'Neill, Laurence' in McGuire and Quinn, *Dictionary of Irish biography*. This offer was repeated a number of times in the weeks leading up to the poll. Initially, it was suggested that the Lord Mayor of Dublin, Laurence O'Neill, could be the compromise candidate. O'Neill had convened and chaired an anti-conscription conference at Dublin's Mansion House that brought together several divergent nationalist groups opposed to the measure.

[162] *Anglo-Celt*, 29 June 1918.

but protested at the severity of the response of the authorities. Such a response could only be justified, the paper argued, 'if anywhere in Ireland there was anything but an impotent minority that approved the insanity of the insurrection'.[163] The rise of Sinn Féin that ensued during 1917 drew minimal editorial response. However, the Irish Parliamentary Party's defeat to that party at the South Longford by-election in May 1917 highlighted the need for John Redmond 'to make it perfectly plain to Mr Lloyd George that no measure of Home Rule will be accepted by this country which is not complete'. Basically, this meant that a Dublin parliament 'for three-fourths or nine-tenths of the country would not be an Irish representative assembly, and could be productive of nothing but harm'.[164]

As a nationalist newspaper in Ulster, the *Anglo-Celt*'s opposition to partition was more pronounced than its nationalist counterparts elsewhere. There was little evidence of any fear that Cavan, or any part of it, might ultimately come under the administration of a Belfast parliament. Yet this did not diminish the distaste for partition to any extent. Much of the initial opposition was based on the straightforward argument that it was not economically feasible as Ulster depended heavily on trade from the rest of Ireland.[165] While this was a recurring theme whenever the paper editorialised on the matter, much of its ire was directed at Sir Edward Carson. He was the person that had 'lunched with the Kaiser' and 'by his introduction of German guns into this country he gave to other minds the idea of recoursing to arms'.[166] In a similar vein, Carson was effectively accused of hypocrisy for having 'reluctantly agreed to the six county arrangement' and how 'it wrings his heart strings that the unionists of Cavan, Monaghan, and Donegal have been cut off from their brethren in the North-East'.[167] The establishment of the Stormont parliament in 1921 was met with outright cynicism by the *Anglo-Celt*. It was an assembly, the paper believed, with little power to legislate 'beyond what the County Councils undertake at present' and its members would soon 'become fully conscious as to how impotent they are to achieve anything worthwhile'.[168]

Although the *Anglo-Celt* clearly held strong views on issues such as Irish support for the war effort, conscription, and partition, it should not mask the fact that agricultural matters accounted for the majority

[163] *Anglo-Celt*, 13 May 1916.
[164] *Anglo-Celt*, 12 May 1917.
[165] *Anglo-Celt*, 11 July, 1 Aug. 1914.
[166] *Anglo-Celt*, 23 Nov. 1918.
[167] *Anglo-Celt*, 8 May 1920.
[168] *Anglo-Celt*, 25 June 1921.

of editorial attention between 1914 and 1921. This is a point well noted by local historian Eileen Reilly, who comments that 'the editorials of the *Anglo-Celt* reflect as much a preoccupation with agriculture' during World War I as with the progress of the war.[169] It was a preoccupation that did not diminish in subsequent years. During 1917, a total of twenty-three of the paper's weekly editorials related to agriculture while in 1918 the figure was seventeen. The trend lessened somewhat during 1919 and 1920 but in 1921 a remarkable total of twenty-eight editorials were agriculture-related. Leading articles with headings such as 'Get in the Food Crops', 'The Outrageous Prices of Artificial Manures', 'Butter and Eggs', 'The Wool Swindle – and How to End It', and 'The Lessons Denmark Teaches Our Farmers', provide some indication of where the editorial priorities of the *Anglo-Celt* lay.[170]

In mid-December 1921, at the height of the debate on the Anglo-Irish Treaty, a leading article of the *Anglo-Celt* was headed, 'How to Prevent Factory Butter from Injuring the Name of Our Choicest Product'.[171] Nonetheless, it was not the case that the paper refrained from editorial comment on the Treaty. The agreement was warmly welcomed for opening up 'that vista which the country has been longing for down the centuries' that provided the 'possibility of development to which no limits can be placed'.[172] It was confidently stated that 'so far as the rural population in the country is concerned there is practical unanimity in favour of confirming the agreement'.[173] However, the strength of opposition to the Treaty within Dáil Éireann was somewhat underestimated as it predicted that those members arguing against endorsement would ultimately 'submit to its ratification in obedience to the wishes of their constituents'.[174] Despite the *Anglo-Celt*'s vehement opposition to partition the issue did not really feature in its editorial response to the Treaty.

Conclusion

Many of the highly discernible traits within the Irish provincial print media during this era were very much in evidence at the *Anglo-Celt*. The

---

[169] Eileen Reilly, 'Cavan in the era of the Great War, 1914–18' in Gillespie, *Cavan*, p. 186.

[170] *Anglo-Celt*, 22 Jan., 19 Feb., 11, 18 June, 20 Aug. 1921.

[171] *Anglo-Celt*, 17 Dec. 1921.

[172] *Anglo-Celt*, 10 Dec. 1921.

[173] *Anglo-Celt*, 31 Dec. 1921.

[174] Ibid.

remarkably lengthy association with the O'Hanlon family, the prolonged tenures of both E.T. and J.F. O'Hanlon, and strong support for the GAA meant that the paper held much in common with its nationalist counterparts. Despite its close links with the Irish Parliamentary Party it rarely adopted a condemnatory attitude towards Sinn Féin. Equally, it did not engage in the stinging criticism of the British Government that, particularly from 1920 onwards, was such a feature of many nationalist titles. This was not because the *Anglo-Celt* assumed the role of a disinterested bystander in the manner of the *Clonmel Chronicle*. Rather it was because agriculture and related matters were accorded editorial priority to a considerable extent between 1914 and 1921. Nonetheless, the paper displayed one other tendency that was common to many nationalist publications. In casting doubt over the staying power of the Stormont parliament the *Anglo-Celt* clearly underestimated unionist resolve. It was hardly alone, though, in making such an error.

Donegal Democrat

John Downey was the main personality behind the establishment of the *Donegal* Democrat in 1919. Downey was foreman at the printing works of the *Donegal Vindicator*, the main title serving County Donegal at the time, but he clearly felt that the county needed a newspaper that reflected the form of nationalism that had swept Sinn Féin to general election victory in December 1918. With this in mind he resigned his position at the *Vindicator* to establish the *Donegal Democrat* in conjunction with Cecil A. Stephens, and the paper made its first appearance in June 1919.[175] John Downey was a devout Catholic and was also an enthusiastic supporter of both the GAA and the Gaelic League. As early as 1909, he played hurling for the Aodh Ruadh club and remained a regular attendee at GAA matches throughout his life. Equally, his efforts to promote the Gaelic League were described as 'lifelong and legion'.[176] Downey fulfilled the role of editor–proprietor of the *Donegal Democrat* from its foundation in 1919 until his death in 1947. The paper's co-founder, Cecil A. Stephens, shared several of Downey's most notable attributes. He was also a GAA enthusiast and acted as secretary of the first GAA club formed in Ballyshannon, a position he also filled at the branch of the Gaelic League in the town. During the 1918 general election campaign

[175] *Donegal Democrat*, 24 May 1947, 15 Jan. 1971.
[176] *Donegal Vindicator*, 24 May 1947.

Stephens canvassed for the Sinn Féin party and was also an intelligence officer in the IRA.[177]

The ninetieth anniversary edition of the *Donegal Democrat* credits the famed Donegal republican Peadar O'Donnell as playing a role in the foundation of the paper. It is claimed that during 1918, while O'Donnell was working as a full-time trade union official, he was approached by three printers working at the *Donegal Vindicator* who were in dispute with their employer. According to the story, the three workers were advised by O'Donnell that they stood little chance of success in their dispute and should start their own newspaper instead, which subsequently led to the establishment of the *Donegal Democrat*.[178] The veracity of this account is rather questionable as it is not even suggested that John Downey was one of these printers. Nonetheless, there is little doubt that the newly established paper strongly sympathised with O'Donnell's republican ideals, which renders its editorial comment all the worthier of scrutiny.

Editorial comment, 1919–1921

From the time of its launch, the *Donegal Democrat* claimed circulation not only in County Donegal but also in Tyrone, Fermanagh, Leitrim, and Sligo. It usually comprised six or eight pages and during most of its first year of publication it took what is possibly best described as the latter-day tabloid appearance. The front page was noticeable for a complete absence of advertisements though a wide variety of goods and services were advertised within the paper. These included items such as motor cars, bicycles, and clothing, plus various groceries and provisions, while the many services promoted included dressmaking, hairdressers, undertakers, dentistry, and optometry.

Key events and developments such as the outbreak of World War I, the Easter Rising, the conscription crisis, and the rise of the Sinn Féin party cannot be considered in the case of the *Donegal Democrat* as it did not commence publication until 1919. Nonetheless, as the last extant provincial newspaper to be established prior to independence its editorial output is no less deserving of careful consideration. Although it was generally considered a broadly republican organ much of its editorial space was devoted to local matters in a manner similar to the *Midland Tribune* and *Leitrim Observer*. However, when its lead articles turned their attention to political developments it was abundantly clear that the

---

[177]   *Donegal Democrat*, 15 Jan. 1971.
[178]   *Donegal Democrat: Anniversary Supplement* (27 Aug. 2009).

Democrat was a highly enthusiastic proponent of the form of nationalism that had dramatically risen to the fore in the two years preceding its own birth.

In its very first issue the *Donegal Democrat* claimed that it would publish the 'unbiased truth, without regard to class, creed, or politics', hardly a new departure for any fledgling newspaper. It also claimed that it would be an 'independent newspaper' and 'a non-political paper in a world of politics'.[179] Yet within a few months it was quite clear where its political sympathies lay. Upon the proclamation of Dáil Éireann in September 1919 the paper protested at 'this latest act of repression' and proposed that Ireland's case be brought 'before the nations of the world for a fair hearing'. Failing that, England should 'quit this country and let us manage our own affairs'.[180]

The amount of newspaper suppressions that had taken place in the few years before its launch meant that the *Democrat* was clearly aware that expressing such sentiments ran a similar risk in its own case. In January 1920, it complained that if 'DORA [Defence of the Realm Act] does not approve of our opinions or those of our correspondents, we are suppressed without warning'.[181] The paper's ninetieth anniversary edition states that its offices were raided by police and military on several occasions during the War of Independence.[182] However, there is little evidence of the *Donegal Democrat* being suppressed or missing any issues due to enforced closure. Nevertheless, this is not to suggest that the paper was less than forceful in expressing its disapproval of British policy in Ireland.

As levels of violence increased during 1920 the *Democrat* accused the British Government of 'every day pouring fresh troops and all kinds of weapons of modern warfare into the country'.[183] Condemnation of British tactics in Ireland was not as frequent or as vociferous as in papers such as the *Enniscorthy Echo* and *Kilkenny People* but it was certainly not restrained. This was particularly evident upon the death of Terence MacSwiney in October 1920:

> The brutality of his [Terence MacSwiney's] unchivalrous captors was so excessive that even the decent portion of their own bought press cried shame in their deeds. For whilst the agony of death was watched

---

[179] *Donegal Democrat*, 6 June 1919.

[180] *Donegal Democrat*, 19 Sept. 1919.

[181] *Donegal Democrat*, 23 Jan. 1920.

[182] *Donegal Democrat: Anniversary Supplement* (27 Aug. 2009).

[183] *Donegal Democrat*, 18 June 1920.

by an outraged world, the Huns of the British House of Commons laughed at their handiwork, and the pigs that form the British Government grunted their satisfaction at the torture endured by one whose nobility they were too ignorant to understand.[184]

Just over a month later, the paper defiantly asserted that 'the reprisal policy may go some way towards quelling the spirit of revolt, but unless the root cause be removed, the spirit of revolt is but driven underground'.[185] By April 1921, it rather presciently remarked that even 'Lloyd George himself confesses that he recognises that force is not a remedy'.[186]

In common with many other nationalist titles, the *Donegal Democrat* felt a deep sense of bitterness that 'the policy of physical resistance', sponsored by Sir Edward Carson at the time of the Home Rule crisis and 'preached by his followers from every platform in Ulster', appeared to have been rewarded. Accordingly, the *Democrat* considered the Government of Ireland Act (disparagingly referred to as the 'Partition Act') 'a complete surrender to Ulster's physical resistance campaign'.[187] The opening of the Stormont parliament in June 1921 by King George prompted the paper to question why £40,000 was spent on preparations for the royal visit when 'unemployment is rife in Belfast' with 'the majority of those at work' on 'half-time', while simultaneously 'the army of expelled workers is not decreasing'.[188] Such comments may also have been intended to cast doubt on the economic viability of the new Northern Ireland state and its prospects for survival. If so, then the *Donegal Democrat* was not unlike many other nationalist titles in underestimating unionist resistance to any notion of participation in a Dublin parliament.

The truce of July 1921 was greeted with extreme caution, but the paper believed that 'no avenue to peace should be left unexplored'.[189] Reaction to the agreement reached in London six months later was somewhat muted. It was conceded that 'in no previous attempt at settlement were such favourable terms proposed much less agreed upon'. It was further acknowledged that the main negotiators had 'suffered much for the cause which they advocated' and accordingly were fully aware of the possibilities

---

[184]   *Donegal Democrat*, 29 Oct. 1920.
[185]   *Donegal Democrat*, 10 Dec. 1921.
[186]   *Donegal Democrat*, 29 Apr. 1921.
[187]   *Donegal Democrat*, 27 May 1921.
[188]   *Donegal Democrat*, 24 June 1921.
[189]   *Donegal Democrat*, 1 July 1921.

of achieving their objectives.[190] There was little further editorial discussion of the Treaty which provokes a suspicion that the paper did not wholly approve. This may have been because editor–proprietor John Downey was a strong supporter of Eamon de Valera (and, indeed, Downey was later an enthusiastic Fianna Fáil supporter) and did not wish to appear as solidly pro-Treaty.[191] Regrettably, this is only speculation, so it is perhaps best simply to conclude that the *Donegal Democrat* welcomed the Anglo-Irish Treaty without wholeheartedly endorsing it.

Conclusion

To a certain extent this case study of the *Donegal Democrat* neatly bookends one of the principal journalistic developments considered in this study of the Irish provincial press. The emergence of a distinctly nationalist bloc within the Irish provincial press that began in the early 1880s with the launch of titles such as the *Leinster Leader* and *Midland Tribune* was effectively concluded with the foundation of the *Donegal Democrat* in 1919. The most noteworthy features that characterised so many of these newspapers, such as a strong Catholic dimension and wholehearted support for sporting and cultural organisations such as the Gaelic League and GAA, were just as evident at the *Democrat* as they were in those nationalist titles that were launched from 1880 onwards. Both co-founders of the paper, editor–proprietor John Downey and Cecil A. Stephens, personified these attributes that were so prevalent across the nationalist print media.

The *Democrat*'s editorial commentary on the final two years prior to Irish independence somewhat mirrored that of the *Midland Tribune* and *Leitrim Observer* in shying away from political developments at certain times and concentrating on local issues instead. However, when leading articles shifted their focus to politics, they tended to reflect the form of nationalism that had replaced that endorsed by those provincial publications established in the 1880s and 1890s. The *Donegal Democrat* was clearly supportive of the republican agenda though perhaps not as strongly as claimed by some local historians. Nonetheless, the slightly veiled under-estimation of unionist resolve that was articulated in the paper was a feature it shared with most other nationalist titles. Ultimately, the *Donegal Democrat* welcomed the Anglo-Irish Treaty, though its rather lukewarm response was possibly a portent of what was to follow.

[190]   *Donegal Democrat*, 9 Dec. 1921.
[191]   *Donegal Democrat: Anniversary Supplement* (27 Aug. 2009).

Summary: Ulster newspapers

The political and religious demographics of the province of Ulster meant that the structure of the print media within the province differed from that of the rest of Ireland. The greater number of unionist titles was obviously the most visible difference but the predominance of these titles within the six counties that ultimately comprised the Northern Ireland state was quite remarkable. Other factors also distinguished the composition of the provincial press in Ulster from the other three provinces. The most notable of these factors was the concentration of local titles in counties Antrim and Down. However, it is not simply the high number of titles in these counties that is noteworthy. The eighteen local titles located in these two counties were spread across eleven different towns, all within close proximity of Belfast. This concentration and internal spread of local newspapers was not replicated anywhere else in Ireland. Nonetheless, this was not the only way in which the composition of the provincial press in Ulster differed from the other three provinces.

The unionist titles that constituted the greater part of the provincial print media in the province were established throughout the nineteenth century. These ranged from the two publications launched in the early part of the century that are scrutinised in this chapter, the *Impartial Reporter* (1825) and the *Londonderry Sentinel* (1829), to titles established in the later 1800s such as the *Tyrone Courier* (1880), *Lurgan Mail* (1890), and *Mid-Ulster Mail* (1891). By contrast, almost all the nationalist papers only emerged after 1900. The exception was the *Derry Journal*, which, ironically, was the oldest provincial paper in Ulster but did not develop a specifically nationalist outlook until the latter part of the nineteenth century. Prior to 1900, it was one of only two nationalist organs (the other being the *Irish News*, established in 1891) published in the six-county area that came under the authority of the Stormont parliament. Across the entire province, the only other nationalist titles in operation at the turn of the twentieth century were the *Donegal Vindicator* and the *Anglo-Celt*.

Despite the markedly divergent political outlook of many of Ulster's provincial papers there were still a number of traits they held in common with their nationalist counterparts throughout Ireland. Family ties to individual newspapers and remarkably lengthy editorial reigns were just as prevalent within the print media in Ulster. The Trimble family's association with the *Impartial Reporter* is doubtless the most pertinent example of the former but it was also in evidence at several other titles. The *Londonderry Sentinel* (Colhoun family), *Down Recorder* (Crichton family), and *Tyrone Courier* (Simpson family) all exemplify this characteristic, if not to the same extent as the *Impartial Reporter*. In a similar vein, the exceptionally lengthy editorial tenures of, amongst others, James McCarrison (forty-seven years at the *Lisburn Herald*), W.Y. Crichton (sixty-three years at the *Down Recorder*), and H.L. Glasgow (fifty-eight years at the *Mid-Ulster Mail*), clearly demonstrate that such editorial longevity was not the sole preserve of nationalist journalists.

Editors and proprietors of unionist papers were equally noted for their participation in politics as their nationalist peers. Although they were never elected to public office, the involvement of newspapermen such as William Copeland Trimble and William Colhoun in the campaign against Home Rule was considerable. Many of their like-minded fellow-journalists in Ulster either became members of the Ulster Volunteers or were highly supportive of the organisation. J.C. Orr, the editor under William Colhoun at the *Londonderry Sentinel*, was one such figure, while others noted for their staunch unionism included John Young (*Portadown News*), Louis Richardson (*Lurgan Mail*), and Thomas Johnston (*Tyrone Constitution*). Additionally, and again in common with several of their nationalist counterparts, many senior newspapermen in Ulster held a deep religious faith. In this respect, it was the Presbyterian faith that predominated. Exemplifying this attribute were journalists such as John Weir (*Ballymena Observer*), James Brown (*Newry Telegraph*), and R.T. Simpson (*Tyrone Courier*).

Although nationalist titles were very much in a minority in Ulster, they still displayed similar characteristics to those in the other three provinces. The devout Catholic faith of so many provincial newspapermen elsewhere in the country was mirrored in Ulster by Michael Lynch (*Ulster Herald*), P.A. MacManus (*Fermanagh Herald*), J.J. McCarroll (*Derry Journal*), and John Downey (*Donegal Democrat*). Their newspapers were similarly strong supporters of both the Gaelic League and the GAA. Other nationalist titles such as the *Donegal Vindicator*, *Frontier Sentinel*, and *Anglo-Celt* were equally supportive of both organisations. Nationalist newspapers in Ulster were also noted for their lengthy family associations, most notably the O'Hanlon family at the *Anglo-Celt*, where E.T. O'Hanlon served as editor for over sixty years. Similarly, Joseph Connellan served for almost the same length of time in the editorial chair of the *Frontier Sentinel*, proving that prolonged editorial tenures were unquestionably a countrywide phenomenon, regardless of political creed. The editorial commentary of Ulster newspapers, however, cannot be so easily summarised.

The *Impartial Reporter* of Enniskillen was quite unique in this respect. Doubtless, the paper displayed traits that were common to organs professing the conflicting political ideologies in Ireland at the time. Nonetheless, it is still almost impossible to identify a nationalist publication whose nationalism was of an equivalent extreme to the unionism of the *Impartial Reporter*. Uncompromising and diehard may be the kindest descriptions of its editorial commentary though it also could be considered rabid and sectarian. The *Londonderry Sentinel* was an equally staunch unionist organ though its antipathy towards Irish nationalists rarely reached the vituperative levels of the *Impartial Reporter*. Indeed, the *Londonderry Sentinel* was occasionally willing to afford some degree of merit to Irish nationalists (most notably upon the death of Terence MacSwiney), an occurrence that was never likely to be replicated within the pages of the *Impartial Reporter*.

Despite the *Anglo-Celt*'s close links to the Irish Parliamentary Party and the *Donegal Democrat*'s clear republican sympathies, neither paper tended to focus on political developments to the same extent as the two unionist titles. In the case of the *Anglo-Celt*, agricultural matters commanded considerable editorial attention while the leading articles of the *Donegal Democrat* focused on local matters to a notable extent during the first two years of its existence. Both papers obviously opposed partition but afforded the matter scant attention upon the conclusion of the Anglo-Irish Treaty in December 1921. Furthermore, despite some indications that the *Donegal Democrat* was the recipient of some unwanted attention from Crown forces, there is little evidence of nationalist titles in Ulster being suppressed or subjected to enforced closure during these years. Nonetheless, such an assertion may be slightly misleading considering the significantly lower number of nationalist titles in the province.

In the final analysis, it can be justifiably stated that the provincial print media in Ulster exhibited many contrasting features with the rest of Ireland while simultaneously displaying much that was common. Wholehearted nationalism elsewhere was matched by staunch unionism in Ulster. Devout Catholicism in the other three provinces was counter-balanced by God-fearing Presbyterianism in Ulster. The characteristics of nationalist titles in the province mirrored those in Leinster, Connacht, and Munster but they were very much in a minority and most were only launched early in the twentieth century. In many ways, the composition of the provincial print media in Ulster could unfortunately be viewed as a microcosm of the problem that was to affect the region for years to come.

Conclusion

The introduction to this study refers to the limited amount of texts that constitute Ireland's newspaper historiography. It is also noted how the gap is even more pronounced in the case of Irish regional newspapers and is particularly conspicuous in relation to the 1914–21 period. Such a gap is highlighted by Maurice Walsh who notes the willingness of historians to draw upon newspapers as a source though it is not accompanied by any inclination towards investigation or detailed scrutiny of such popular source material. As Walsh further notes, 'newspaper evidence is often cited but rarely analysed'.[1] The example, that is referred to in the introduction, of J.J. Lee's liberal citation of the response of Irish provincial papers to the Easter Rising is a case in point.

This book does not consist entirely of the analysis alluded to by Walsh. Nonetheless, it constitutes one of the steps that is required to start addressing this imbalance. In order to tackle the challenge of such a considerable task this study posed four primary research questions. The first of these questions sought to determine the nature of the relationship between provincial press and society. In this respect, probably the most dominant feature was the remarkably strong religious dimension to this relationship that manifested itself in the deep religious faith of most editors and proprietors.

Amongst unionist titles in Ulster it was the Presbyterian faith that was most prevalent. Devout Catholicism predominated amongst the editors and proprietors of nationalist publications. When P.J. Doris of the *Mayo News* died in 1937 his obituary extolled his 'virtuous piety' and proudly referred to the fact that during his months of incarceration

---

[1] Walsh, *The news from Ireland*, pp 3–6.

in England after the Easter Rising 'he never missed morning mass and communion'.[2] With very few exceptions the obituaries of such newspapermen are similarly notable for their references to the steadfast Catholic faith of the deceased. As local newspapers played a key role in the lives of their readers this considerable Catholic influence within the regional print media may well have contributed to the powerful position occupied by the Catholic Church in Ireland over such a long period of time. Such a position was swiftly becoming evident in the emergent Irish Free State where, as M.P. McCabe observes, the fledgling Fianna Fáil party sought 'to demonstrate their greater commitment to Catholic principles than Cumann na nGaedheal'.[3] The role of the provincial press in this regard was certainly acknowledged by Archbishop Neil Farren of Derry when he was guest of honour at the golden jubilee dinner of the *Ulster Herald* in 1952. At a function in Omagh that was also attended by several members of the local Catholic clergy, Archbishop Farren paid tribute 'to the work of our Catholic and Irish newspapers generally'.[4] Yet any role the provincial press may have played in this regard has received virtually no acknowledgement from those who have documented the history of the Catholic Church in Ireland.

The late Emmet Larkin was arguably the foremost historian of the Catholic Church in Ireland. Yet in his eight volumes of work charting the history of the Irish Catholic Church in the second half of the nineteenth century there is absolutely minimal reference to the provincial press. This situation is much the same regarding other historians of the Irish Catholic Church. These include Tom Inglis, Mary Harris, John Henry Whyte, Patrick J. Corish, Desmond Fennell, Oliver Rafferty, Kevin Collins, and Desmond J. Keenan. Some of the related texts by these authors occasionally cite provincial newspapers but none credits the provincial press with playing any role in the history of the Catholic Church in Ireland. Likewise, Patrick Murray does not acknowledge the provincial print media in his book, *Oracles of God: the Roman Catholic Church and Irish politics, 1922–37*, but draws heavily on provincial newspapers as a source throughout. However, if the role of the provincial press has been largely overlooked in the historiography of the Irish Catholic Church then one other somewhat darker element of this inter-relationship has also been highly neglected by most historians.

---

[2] *Mayo News*, 27 Feb. 1937.
[3] M.P. McCabe, *For God and Ireland: the fight for moral superiority in Ireland, 1922–1932* (Dublin, 2013), p. 243.
[4] *Derry People, Ulster Herald*, 20 Dec. 1952.

In his study of sexual crime in the Irish Free State between 1922 and 1933, Anthony Keating clearly illustrates that 'the vast majority of sexual crime cases brought to court were never reported.[5] Those that were reported, as Keating further points out, were described in rather oblique and coded terms and frequently endeavoured to distance the perpetrator or the nature of the crime from the area in which it took place.[6] Those newspapers that adopted such an evasive stance on this matter were, by and large, still edited by the same personalities that have been depicted in this study. This cohort of senior newspapermen were products of the dramatic political developments that took place in Ireland from the 1880s onwards and, for the most part, were devout Catholics and ardent nationalists. Consequently, there was little appetite to reveal these 'unpalatable aspects of Irish life' which would cast a deep shadow on the desired portrayal of 'the social and moral health of the Free State'.[7] However, it would be unfair to accuse the provincial press of complicity in a cover-up of these sexual crimes that came back to haunt Irish society so many decades later. Nevertheless, 'the timidity of Irish journalistic culture in this regard' can only be viewed as a contributory factor in 'ensuring a paucity of action regarding these issues' that led to 'a failure to adequately protect the victims of sexual crime for generations to come'.[8]

The relationship between the provincial press and another major institution of Irish society, the Gaelic Athletic Association, is understandably not coloured by such darker features. Nevertheless, the historical link between the two bodies is undeniable and is one of the most distinctive aspects of the relationship between the provincial print media and broader Irish society. Throughout this study the support of various newspaper editors and proprietors for the GAA has been repeatedly cited. It was unquestionably a distinguishing feature of the provincial press across all four provinces and was epitomised by senior pressmen such as James Reddy (*Nationalist and Leinster Times*), Terence Devere

---

[5] Anthony Keating, 'Sexual crime in the Irish Free State 1922–33: its nature, extent and reporting' in *Irish Studies Review*, 20, no. 2 (May 2012), p. 149.

[6] Ibid., p. 147. Keating outlines in detail how a variety of provincial newspapers used terms such as 'terrible and very deplorable' or a 'case of a bad and loathsome type' to describe the court proceedings while frequently it was reported that the convicted person was a 'stranger' or a 'gypsy'.

[7] Ibid., p. 139.

[8] Ibid., p. 149; Anthony Keating, 'Setting the agenda for the press: the 1929 case against the *Waterford Standard*' in *New Hibernia Review*, 1, no. 2 (Summer 2012), p. 32.

(*Western People*), Brandon J. Long (*Clonmel Nationalist*), and Joseph Connellan (*Frontier Sentinel*). The key role played by local newspapers was recognised by Liam Mulvihill, who served as director-general of the GAA for twenty-nine years (1979–2008). At an award ceremony in 1980 organised by the Connacht Council of the GAA, Mulvihill acknowledged that 'the provincial press and the GAA grew up together' and further added that 'there has always been a close link between the GAA and the local press and through this it has made our association such as it is'.[9] This extremely close relationship was also recognised by Tomás Ó Duinn in 'An Irishman's Diary' in the *Irish Times* in 1992. Noting the generous coverage allotted to Gaelic games over the years by 'virtually all provincial editors', Ó Duinn observed that 'no organisation is more indebted to provincial newspapers than the GAA'.[10] Yet, much like the case of the Catholic Church, historians of the organisation have afforded scant attention to any part played by the provincial press.

The historiography of the GAA is, perhaps understandably, not as substantial as that of the Catholic Church. Nonetheless, numerous texts have been published that chart the history of the association. Foremost amongst these works is arguably Marcus de Búrca's, *The GAA: a history*. This is undoubtedly a comprehensive work though the only provincial journalist mentioned is John Wyse Power, who was a journalist at the *Leinster Leader* when he attended the inaugural meeting of the GAA in Thurles in 1884.[11] Power, who is probably better known for his IRB connections, is also referred to in *Michael Cusack and the GAA*, another of de Búrca's works on the subject, and also in Séamus Ó Riain's, *Maurice Davin (1842–1927): first president of the GAA*. However, Wyse Power, who served as general secretary of the organisation, is rarely mentioned in his capacity as a journalist in either of these texts. Several provincial newspapers are sourced in the latter publication, but it does not credit the provincial press with any role in the early development of the GAA. Further works by Mike Cronin and Paul Rouse contain minimal reference to the provincial print media. As if to emphasise this oversight, the fourteen essays documenting various aspects of the history of the association contained in *The Gaelic Athletic Association 1884–2009*,

---

[9] *Western People*, 3 Dec. 1980. By coincidence, the ceremony at which Mulvihill made these remarks was held at the clubhouse of the Ballina Stephenites club, one of whose founder members, Terence de Vere, was also involved in the foundation of the *Western People* and later became proprietor of the paper.

[10] *Irish Times*, 16 Jan. 1992.

[11] Marcus de Búrca, *The GAA: a history* (2nd ed., Dublin, 1999), p. 17.

make no reference to the provincial press, though local papers are occasionally cited.

The Gaelic League was another organisation with extremely strong links to the provincial press. One of the primary aims of the Gaelic League was the promotion of the Irish language and in this regard many local titles lent their wholehearted support. However, in contrast to the GAA, the Irish language did not become an intrinsic part of Irish society. The reasons for this are not so easily explained and it is certainly a subject that requires further research. Consequently, unlike the GAA and the Catholic Church, there is no substantial historiography of this somewhat complex aspect of Irish society. Nonetheless, there is little doubt that the Gaelic League, and in turn the Irish language, had a staunch ally in the Irish provincial press. Many of those journalists already noted for their strong Catholic faith and their affinity to the GAA were equally supportive of the Irish language movement. In this regard, they were joined by journalists such as Seán Etchingham (*Enniscorthy Echo*), John Burke (*Tuam Herald*), Peadar O'hAnnracháin (*Southern Star*), Edward Long (*Tipperary Star*), and P.J. Flanagan (*Derry People*).

The support of these senior pressmen for organisations such as the Gaelic League and the GAA hallmarked the relationship between the provincial press and Irish society. To a significant extent these defining traits equally contribute to answering the second major research question of this book which aimed to establish the characteristics of the proprietors, editors, and reporters who constituted the senior ranks of the provincial print media. In this respect, possibly one of the striking features of the Irish provincial press during these years is that it produced its own cast of characters that, to a certain extent, mirrored some of the aspects of the broader political arena.

This revolutionary period in Ireland was notable for the prominence of individual personalities such as Arthur Griffith, Eamon de Valera, Michael Collins, and Edward Carson. On a microcosmic level this was reflected within the ranks of the Irish provincial press by the presence of such unique and distinctive figures as E.T. Keane, Jasper Tully, and William Copeland Trimble. The eventual split between de Valera and Collins was even replicated to a certain extent in the provincial press by the estrangement of the Doris brothers at the *Mayo News*. Indeed, the separation of Irish nationalism into constitutional and republican camps that began to manifest itself most acutely after the 1916 Rising was personified at a number of provincial publications.

The case of the Doris brothers is probably the most fitting example of this, but it was also evident at several other newspapers. In the case of the *Enniscorthy Echo*, where Sir Thomas Esmonde and William Sears were co-founders of the paper, Esmonde's ultimate allegiance to the Irish Parliamentary Party was counterbalanced by the complete transfer of loyalty of William Sears to the Sinn Féin cause. Similarly, the unswerving loyalty to John Redmond of T.F. McGahon, long-time editor of the *Dundalk Democrat*, contrasted with the ardent republicanism of Frank Necy, a journalist at the same paper for almost fifty years (including twenty as editor). The *Tuam Herald* provided another example of the opposing strands of Irish nationalism co-existing at the same paper. R.J. Kelly, editor–proprietor of the paper for almost fifty years, had little time for Irish republicanism. Yet John Burke, whom Kelly employed as manager at the *Herald* (and who later assumed control of the paper), became an elected Sinn Féin representative. At the *Anglo-Celt* in Cavan the close links of the O'Hanlon brothers to the Irish Parliamentary Party did not prevent Thomas K. Walsh, an early Sinn Féin activist in the county, from serving on the paper's editorial staff for close on half a century. However, those newspapers and newspapermen that constituted the provincial print media provided far more than a simple mirror image of broader Irish society.

It was stated in the introduction to this study that it would not be merely an assessment of Irish provincial newspapers as faceless entities. The ensuing examination of local newspapers in all four Irish provinces has illustrated that a substantial number of these publications featured highly dominant and distinctive personalities at the helm. The aforementioned Keane, Tully, and Trimble were far from the only figures to fall into this category, though their highly individualistic and abrasive natures possibly set them apart amongst this cohort of newspaper editors and proprietors. Yet the regional press in Ireland was equally notable for other highly distinctive figures whose names became synonymous with the publication at which they spent the greater part of their journalistic careers.

This is very much the case with respect to several of the individual case studies contained in this work. In Leinster, James Pike of the *Midland Tribune* and William Sears of the *Enniscorthy Echo* certainly fall into this category. Patrick Dunne of the *Leitrim Observer* in Connacht is another fitting example of such a newspaperman. In Munster, the trio of Maurice Griffin, Daniel Nolan, and Thomas Nolan are indelibly linked to the history of the *Kerryman* newspaper. The case studies of Ulster newspapers provide equally pertinent examples in this regard. Aside from the obvious example of William Copeland Trimble at the *Impartial Reporter*, this extremely strong link between specific personalities and their newspaper is further illustrated by the O'Hanlon brothers at the *Anglo-Celt* and John Downey of the *Donegal Democrat*. It was an attribute that was far from limited to those newspapers examined in these case studies. Further examples of this trait include journalists such as Michael A. Casey (*Drogheda Independent*), P.A. McHugh (*Sligo Champion*), J.P. Farrell (*Longford Leader*), Edward Walsh (*Munster Express*), and Michael Lynch (*Ulster Herald*).

This undeniable bond between individual personalities and their newspapers was undoubtedly burgeoned by the remarkable length of time that several of these figures spent at the helm of their respective publications. E.T. Keane, Jasper Tully, and William Copeland Trimble have been cited as some of the most dominant personalities of the provincial print media but all three served remarkably lengthy tenures directing the fortunes of their papers. Keane spent over fifty years as editor–proprietor of the *Kilkenny People*; Tully fulfilled the same role at the *Roscommon Herald* for fifty-seven years, while Trimble's term as editor–proprietor of the *Impartial Reporter* lasted sixty-six years. These three newspapermen were far from unique in remaining in the editorial chair for such prolonged periods.

The most pronounced example of this striking feature of the Irish provincial press was, without doubt, J.P. Hayden, who spent seventy-two years as editor–proprietor of the *Westmeath Examiner*. Nonetheless, there were numerous other examples of this editorial longevity and it embraced both nationalist and unionist titles. In the nationalist camp it was exemplified by figures such as Patrick Dunne (editor–proprietor of the *Leitrim Observer* for close on sixty years), Joseph Connellan (editor of the *Frontier* Sentinel for just under sixty years), Con Cregan (editor of the *Limerick Leader* for almost fifty years), and William Myles (editor of the *Tipperary Star* from 1925 until 1975). This trait was equally exemplified at unionist organs by journalists such as W.Y. Crichton (editor of the *Down Recorder* for over sixty years), H.L. Glasgow (editor of the *Mid-Ulster Mail* for fifty-eight years), and Robert A. Parke (editor of the *Tyrone Constitution* for over fifty years). Indeed, editorial tenures ranging from thirty to fifty years were decidedly common across the Irish provincial press if not even the norm.

This editorial longevity within the regional print media was accompanied by a distinct element of continuity that existed due to so many titles remaining under family ownership for extended periods of time. Again, this was a feature that was evident across all four provinces and applied to both nationalist and unionist papers. In Leinster, the Davis and Powell families at the *Meath Chronicle* and *Midland Tribune* respectively typified this trait. The Gillespie family at the *Connaught Telegraph* and both the Kelly and Burke families at the *Tuam Herald* in Connacht provide further examples of this recurring trend. Prolonged family connections to provincial newspapers was epitomised in Munster by the Galvin family at the *Clare Champion* and the Walsh family at the *Munster Express*. Ulster was equally no exception to such familial ties. The Trimble family connection to the *Impartial Reporter* was the most extraordinary instance of family ownership but it also existed at other unionist titles such as the *Londonderry Sentinel* and *Down Recorder*, which were synonymous with the names of the Colhoun and Crichton families respectively. Even the limited number of nationalist titles in the province also displayed such a trait; the O'Hanlon family's connection to the *Anglo-Celt* and the Lynch family's ties to the *Ulster Herald* being equally pertinent examples.

This element of continuity had probably not yet been established at several nationalist titles by 1914, many having only been launched in the previous two or three decades. Consequently, the dramatic developments that took place in the following seven years came at a relatively early stage of their development. Many of them had to operate in circumstances under which they had not previously experienced. This leads to the third research question outlined at the outset of this study: how the relationship between the provincial press and the British authorities manifested itself. Between 1914 and 1921, the environment in which provincial journalists were forced to operate presented far greater dangers than anything that had been experienced theretofore. During this time the British authorities sought to exert control over the output of newspapers to an extent that had not previously been encountered. It was a period that commenced upon the outbreak of war in August 1914.

The Defence of the Realm Act was the tool utilised by the British Government in its endeavours to exercise such control. This was superseded by the Restoration of Order in Ireland Act which came into force as hostilities intensified in Ireland. Prior to Easter 1916, very few provincial papers had been affected by such legislation, but this changed significantly thereafter. Many papers were suppressed over the course of the next few years, with the *Enniscorthy Echo*, *Kilkenny People*, *Clare Champion*, and *Southern Star* enduring the lengthiest terms of suppression. Newspaper owners such as P.J. Doris (*Mayo News*), William Sears (*Enniscorthy Echo*), Maurice Griffin (*Kerryman*), and Patrick Dunne (*Leitrim Observer*) were imprisoned due to their Sinn Féin links. Provincial titles such as the *Westmeath Independent*, *Kerryman*, *Leitrim Observer*, and *Galway Express* suffered attacks on their premises by Crown forces that resulted in their non-publication for prolonged periods, with the *Galway Express* actually ceasing operations a few months later. Attacks on newspaper offices were not the sole preserve of Crown forces as the IRA targeted the *Cork Examiner, Cork Constitution*, and *Skibbereen Eagle*.

In general, unionist titles did not have to operate in fear of suppression. Initially, this may seem a rather redundant observation. However, it is worth recalling some of the editorial commentary of unionist newspapers from 1914 that has been considered in this study. With the imminent passing of the Home Rule bill the leading articles of the *Cork Constitution, Impartial Reporter*, and *Londonderry Sentinel* spoke of civil war, championed the cause of the Ulster Volunteers, and expressed tacit approval for the Larne gun-running of April 1914. Not only was open defiance of the British Government loudly voiced, particularly in the two Ulster titles, but the *Londonderry Sentinel* spoke of the land being 'deluged in blood' should there be any attempt to enforce Home Rule in Ulster.[12] Yet such newspapers drew no censure from the authorities. Accordingly, it is understandable that many nationalist titles may well have felt aggrieved at the rather inconsistent application of censorship and the frequently innocuous reasons for the suppression of newspapers that occurred with regularity in the wake of the Easter Rising. The fact that so many provincial titles came into varying degrees of conflict with the British authorities leads to the obvious question as to the nature of the sentiment being articulated by such publications. Accordingly, this explains the necessity for the fourth and final question posed in this book. This question sought to determine how the provincial press responded to the numerous critical developments that took place in Ireland between 1914 and 1921.

This study does not purport to be a definitive analysis of the response of the provincial press in Ireland to events that occurred during these years. Nevertheless, the close scrutiny of seventeen different titles across all four provinces provides a highly valuable insight into how such events were perceived across the country. Possibly the most marked feature of the editorial commentary is the criticism of the events of Easter 1916 that was expressed in many nationalist titles. However, this criticism was significantly tempered by a distinct sense of anger with the British government, which, many of these papers claimed, created the environment for rebellion. This environment, according to many of these publications, was brought about by the government's toleration of the actions of Edward Carson and the Ulster Volunteers and the attendant arming and drilling of the

---

[12] *Londonderry Sentinel*, 11 June 1914.

latter body. The other most discernible feature of the editorial commentary of nationalist papers was the enthusiastic response to the Anglo-Irish Treaty of 1921. Notably, titles that had come to be regarded as Sinn Féin organs, such as the *Meath Chronicle, Enniscorthy Echo, Kilkenny People*, and *Southern Star* expressed warm approval for the agreement. Crucially though, most nationalist titles expressed relatively little concern regarding partition, mistakenly assuming that northern unionists would eventually come to believe that their interests would be better served under a Dublin parliament. However, it would not be correct to assume that there was a relatively uniform response to events during the 1914–21 period from either the nationalist or unionist sections of the Irish provincial press.

As this study has clearly demonstrated, the editorial output of papers such as the *Kilkenny People* and the *Kerryman* differed markedly from fellow-nationalist titles such as the *Tuam Herald* and *Anglo-Celt*. Equally, amongst unionist titles, clear differences were evident. The most pronounced example of this was the *Cork Constitution*'s utter distaste for partition while the *Impartial Reporter* welcomed it in an almost celebratory manner. In many cases, editorial commentary was of a distinctly impassioned and intense nature, which, in the case of nationalist papers, incurred the wrath of the Press Censor. In some instances, the fervid nature of leading articles was due to the editor's commitment to either the republican or unionist cause while in other instances it was attributable to the forceful personality of the person occupying the editorial chair. Quite often it was a combination of both these factors. Regardless of the personalities of individual editors there is little doubt that editorial responses to events in Ireland between 1914 and 1921 are not easily categorised and were certainly not uniform.

This lack of uniformity was discernible amongst nationalist papers in the provinces and even amongst those that came to be regarded as Sinn Féin organs. While there is clear evidence of support for a more separatist form of nationalism prior to 1916 at the *Meath Chronicle, Enniscorthy Echo*, and most notably the *Mayo News* and *Kerryman*, the same could hardly be said for the *Midland Tribune* or *Kilkenny People*. It could be suspected that the shift in attitude of the latter two titles may have had as much to do with the changing public mood as with an altered political philosophy. Nonetheless, their change of allegiance at least began to manifest itself before Sinn Féin began to achieve any major electoral success. The same could not be said for the *Tuam Herald*, a solidly nationalist organ but certainly not a Sinn Féin supporter. Nonetheless, its antagonism towards the party dissipated almost overnight following Sinn Féin's resounding victory at the 1918 general election.

It is rather ironic that Sinn Féin's ascension to such a position appears to have been anticipated to a more significant extent by the unionist titles profiled in this study than by their nationalist contemporaries. This is clear from the editorials of the *Cork Constitution* and *Londonderry Sentinel* in the months following the Easter Rising leading up to Sinn Féin's first by-election victory. Indeed, the *Cork Constitution*'s editorial commentary during these years frequently demonstrated an appreciation of certain aspects of Irish nationalism that might not have been expected of a unionist title. This was evident in its acceptance of the impartiality of the Dáil courts and a recognition that not all elements of Sinn Féin were connected to republican violence.

Such appreciation was understandably less visible in the two unionist papers in Ulster. Nonetheless, the *Londonderry Sentinel*'s heartfelt admiration for the hunger strike of Terence MacSwiney contrasted sharply with the *Impartial Reporter*'s harsh dismissal of MacSwiney's death as a suicide. Indeed, the *Impartial Reporter*'s rather disingenuous endorsement of the Irish Parliamentary candidate at the East Cavan by-election of 1918 was the only instance of it even bordering on displaying a modicum of respect for Irish nationalism. Aside from these isolated examples neither paper indicated any sense of reappraisal of Irish nationalism during these years nor any fear that the British Government might yield to nationalist demands. The only indication of any anxiety in this regard came in July 1921 with the calling of a truce by the British Government. However, such anxiety appears to have been allayed following the Anglo-Irish Treaty and the emergent split in republican ranks.

This split in Sinn Féin was to be the dominant feature of the early years of the Irish Free State and the subsequent civil war was to have a lasting and divisive effect on Irish politics. Without doubt, the editors of nationalist newspapers did not envision an independent state as being hallmarked by such bitter division. This is hardly surprising as most provincial editors devoted scant attention to what might result in the aftermath of the autonomy they sought. Many of them were highly vocal in asserting the absolute validity of claims for Irish self-government and displayed little hesitation in criticising the British Government for preventing or delaying the realisation of such claims. Yet the same provincial editors rarely elaborated as to how Irish society would benefit under this new scenario to which they so aspired. Apart from the occasional economic argument there is minimal evidence of any attempt to explain how the lives of ordinary Irish citizens would improve once some form of self-government was achieved.

It can only be concluded that the provincial press shared the sentiments of both Sinn Féin and the IRA, who, as claimed by Michael Laffan, 'had no interest in digging down to the roots of Irish society'. The primary aim was 'to sweep away the King, Westminster and the Dublin Castle system rather than to improve the lot of the poor or curb the power of the rich'.[13] Laffan further contends that 'Sinn Féin was an establishment-in-waiting'.[14] Ireland's regional newspapers, with their traditions of prolonged editorial reigns and extended periods of family ownership, slotted conveniently into such a niche. The newly independent state, so yearned for by provincial editors and proprietors, was highly conservative in nature. As Tom Garvin notes, the Free State was founded 'with effective legal and institutional continuity by a conservative, if democratic, nationalist elite in 1922'.[15] Indeed, Garvin traces the origins of the new state back to the late 1800s and notes 'the rise of a cheap, popular, mainly nationalist provincial press' as one of the significant factors that aided its emergence.[16] Laffan's and Garvin's assertions as to the absence of any real change with the establishment of the Free State are supported by John M. Regan, who similarly argues that, following independence from Britain, 'Irish institutions much as Irish society remained the same as what went before'.[17]

Such commentary by Laffan, Garvin, and Regan are broadly representative of the views of historians that Ireland experienced a political and military transformation during the 1914–21 period. Similar to the Irish Parliamentary Party and Sinn Féin, the provincial press articulated little interest in any form of social revolution. This may seem slightly peculiar considering how frequently so many of these newspapers had vehemently stated the need for change in the manner in which Ireland was governed. Indeed, many of them, as detailed during the course of this study, had been on the receiving end of much undesired attention for advocating such views. Nevertheless, even if the provincial

---

[13] Michael Laffan, 'Labour must wait': Ireland's conservative revolution' in Ciaran Brady and Patrick J. Corish (eds), *Radicals, rebels, and establishments: papers read before the Irish Conference of Historians, Maynooth, 16–19 June 1983* (Maynooth, 1983), p. 203.

[14] Ibid., p. 219.

[15] Tom Garvin, *Preventing the future: why was Ireland so poor for so long?* (Dublin, 2004), p. 26.

[16] Ibid., p. 31.

[17] John M. Regan, *The Irish counter-revolution, 1921–1936: Treatyite politics and settlement in independent Ireland* (Dublin, 2001), p. 378.

press of this period was highly conservative in nature its development as a fundamental element of Ireland's print media cannot be ignored.

Those newspapers and their staff that had to operate under the threat of forcible closure and possibly violent attack contributed significantly to the role and influence of the Irish provincial press. It is a contribution that has rarely merited consideration, whether in pre-independence or post-independence Ireland. The more dramatic cases of the suppression of nationalist titles or attacks by Crown forces has been the focus of the limited historical recognition it has received up to now. Many nationalist titles avoided such experiences, but it is these clashes with the British authorities that hallmark the experience of Irish provincial newspapers during these years. Yet such clashes could hardly be considered extraordinary in what was one of the most turbulent periods of Irish history. It is a period that has given rise to a multitude of texts documenting various other aspects of Irish society. These include biographies of political and military leaders, detailed depictions of key events, as well as numerous volumes of local history. Up to now newspapers have rarely been the focus of any of the substantial number of publications relating to the 1914–21 period. At least the experience of national titles has been documented to some extent by Ian Kenneally (as detailed in the introduction). There has been minimal research into their counterparts in the provinces which has been a somewhat glaring omission.

The provincial press has been cited with regularity in many of these works documenting various facets of this critical period of Irish history. It is a source that, up to now, has remained largely unresearched and unanalysed without any evident consideration as to political sympathy or possible prejudice. The structure of this book, each case study providing a brief history of the newspaper in addition to profiling its key personalities, contributes significantly in redressing this imbalance. Consequently, this study fulfils the dual function of providing a thorough assessment of such popular source material and filling a rather critical gap in the history of the Irish print media. Yet this study does more than simply fill a historiographical void.

The history of the Irish provincial press between 1914 and 1921 fully merits such scrutiny in its own right. Not alone did it produce a range of memorable characters, but it also featured a range of personalities that played an active and important part in both the political and military campaign that ultimately resulted in the establishment of the Irish Free State. Provincial newspapers were required to deal with the uncertainty and ambiguity of censorship allied to the attendant threat of suppression in a rapidly changing political atmosphere. This precarious environment in which these papers were forced to operate only worsened during the War of Independence when many of them were subjected to attacks on their premises and intimidation of their staff. Titles that were only in their infancy, but went on to be become pillars of the provincial press, such as the *Clare Champion* and the *Kerryman*, endured prolonged periods of suppression and enforced closure. Additionally, many newspapermen were arrested and imprisoned. All the while such newspapers strived to survive as financial entities. Ultimately, however, the provincial press emerged as a rather conservative force in the newly independent state for which it had strongly agitated.

Despite these ordeals in the midst of such a well-documented period of Irish history, and the undoubted position of influence it came to assume, the provincial press has, as John Horgan points out, 'rarely, if ever' been 'the subject of intensive discussion or research' and has tended 'to be taken for granted'.[18] The experiences of provincial newspapers and their personnel documented in this study clearly illustrate just how much of an anomaly this has been. It also highlights the disservice it has equally been, not only to Irish journalistic historiography, but also to the broader history of Ireland during this period.

---

[18] John Horgan, 'The provincial papers of Ireland: ownership and control and the representation of "community"' in Desmond Bell (ed.), *Is the Irish Press independent? essays on ownership and control of the provincial, national, and international press in Ireland* (Dublin, 1986), p. 11.

Appendices

Appendix A
Map of Ireland Detailing Newspaper Titles
in Each County between 1914 and 1921

Northern Ireland

1 **Fermanagh** – *Fermanagh Herald, Fermanagh Times, Impartial Reporter*
2 **Tyrone** – *Dungannon Democrat, Mid-Ulster Mail, Strabane Chronicle, Strabane Weekly News, Tyrone Constitution, Tyrone Courier, Ulster Herald*
3 **Derry** – *Coleraine Chronicle, Derry Journal, Derry People, Derry Standard, Derry Weekly News, Irish Daily Telegraph, Londonderry Sentinel, Northern Constitution*
4 **Antrim** – *Ballymena Observer, Ballymena Weekly Telegraph, Ballymoney Free Press, Carrickfergus Advertiser, Larne Times, Lisburn Herald, Lisburn Standard, North Antrim Standard*
5 **Down** – *Banbridge Chronicle, County Down Spectator/Newtownards Spectator, Down Recorder, Dromore Leader, Dromore Weekly Times, Frontier Sentinel, Newry Reporter, Newry Telegraph, Newtownards Chronicle, North Down Herald/Newtownards Herald*
6 **Armagh** – *Armagh Guardian, Lurgan Mail, Portadown Express, Portadown News, Ulster Gazette*

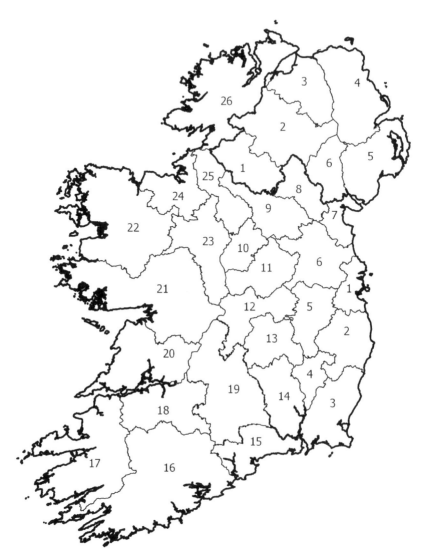

Source: Dr Susan Hegarty, School of History and Geography,
Dublin City University

Republic of Ireland

1 **Dublin** – Newspapers based in Dublin are not included in this study as
   they do not constitute part of the provincial press
2 **Wicklow** – *Bray and South Dublin Herald, Wicklow Newsletter,
   Wicklow People, Wicklow Press*

3 **Wexford** – *Enniscorthy Echo, Enniscorthy Guardian, New Ross Standard, Wexford Free Press, Wexford People*

4 **Carlow** – *Carlow Sentinel, Nationalist and Leinster Times*

5 **Kildare** – *Kildare Observer, Leinster Leader*

6 **Meath** – *Meath Chronicle, Meath Herald*

7 **Louth** – *Drogheda Advertiser, Drogheda Argus, Drogheda Independent, Dundalk Democrat, Dundalk Examiner, Dundalk Herald*

8 **Monaghan** – *Northern Standard*

9 **Cavan** – *Anglo-Celt, Irish Post*

10 **Longford** – *Longford Independent, Longford Journal, Longford Leader*

11 **Westmeath** – *Westmeath Examiner, Westmeath Guardian, Westmeath Independent, Westmeath Nationalist and Midland Reporter*

12 **Offaly** – *King's County Chronicle/Leinster Reporter, King's County Independent, Midland Tribune*

13 **Laois** – *Leinster Express*

14 **Kilkenny** – *Kilkenny Journal, Kilkenny Moderator, Kilkenny People*

15 **Waterford** – *Dungarvan Observer, Munster Express, Waterford News/Waterford Evening News, Waterford Standard, Waterford Star/Waterford Evening Star*

16 **Cork** – *Cork Constitution, Cork Weekly News, Skibbereen Eagle, Southern Star* (for the purposes of this study the *Cork Examiner* is not included as it had a broad readership across the province of Munster and its experiences are comprehensively documented by Ian Kenneally in *The paper wall: newspapers and propaganda in Ireland 1919–1921*)

17 **Kerry** – *Kerry Advocate, Kerry Evening Post, Kerryman/Liberator, Kerry News, Kerry People, Kerry Press, Kerry Sentinel, Kerry Weekly Reporter, Killarney Echo*

18 **Limerick** – *Limerick Chronicle, Limerick Echo, Limerick Leader, Munster News, Weekly Observer*

19 **Tipperary** – *Clonmel Chronicle, Clonmel Nationalist, Nenagh Guardian, Nenagh News, Tipperary People/Tipperaryman, Tipperary Star*

20 **Clare** – *Clare Champion, Clare Journal/Saturday Record, Kilrush Herald*

21 **Galway** – *Connacht Tribune, East Galway Democrat, Galway Express, Galway Observer, Galway Pilot, Tuam Herald, Western News/Galway Leader/Loughrea Guardian/Tuam People*

22 **Mayo** – *Ballina Herald, Connaught Telegraph, Mayoman, Mayo News, Western People*

23 **Roscommon** – *Roscommon Herald, Roscommon Journal, Roscommon Weekly Messenger, Strokestown Democrat, Western Nationalist*

24 **Sligo** – *Sligo Champion, Sligo Independent, Sligo Nationalist/Connachtman*

25 **Leitrim** – *Leitrim Advertiser, Leitrim Observer*

26 **Donegal** – *Donegal Democrat, Donegal Vindicator/Donegal Independent*

Appendix B
Irish Regional Newspapers, 1914–1921

Title	Publication dates	Political leaning/ orientation	Key figures	Censored	Suppressed
Anglo–Celt	1847–	Nationalist	E.T. O'Hanlon, J.F. O'Hanlon	No	No
Armagh Guardian	1844–1982	Unionist	S.D. Trimble	No	No
Ballina Herald	1844–1962	Neutral	J. Duncan	Yes	Yes
Ballymena Observer	1855–	Unionist	J. Wier	No	No
Ballymena Weekly Telegraph	1867–1970	Neutral	T. Boyd	No	No
Ballymoney Free Press	1863–1934	Unionist	J. Shannon	No	No
Banbridge Chronicle	1870	Independent	A.W. Emerson	No	No
Bray and South Dublin Herald	1876–1927	Unstated	F. McPhail	No	No
Carlow Sentinel	1831–1920	Unionist	G. Langran	No	No
Carrickfergus Advertiser	1883–	Neutral	J. Bell	No	No
Clare Champion	1903–	Nationalist	T. Galvin, J. Maguire, S. Maguire	Yes	Yes
Clare Journal/Saturday Record	1776–1936	Unstated	O. Tuohy	No	No
Clonmel Chronicle	1848–1935	Independent	A.R. Burns	No	No
Clonmel Nationalist	1890–	Nationalist	B.J. Long	No	No

Title	Publication dates	Political leaning/ orientation	Key figures	Censored	Suppressed
Coleraine Chronicle	1844–	Unionist	J. Shannon	No	No
Connacht Tribune	1909–	Nationalist	T.J.W. Kenny	Yes	No
Connaught Telegraph	1828–	Nationalist	T.H. Gillespie	No	No
Cork Constitution	1822–1924	Unionist	H.L. Tivy, W.J. Ludgate	No	No
Cork Weekly News	1883–1925	Unstated		No	No
County Down Spectator/ Newtownards Spectator	1904–	Unionist	D.E. Alexander	No	No
Derry Journal	1772–	Nationalist	J.J. McCarroll	No	No
Derry People	1902–	Nationalist	P.J. Flanagan	No	No
Derry Standard	1836–1964	Unionist	J.C. Glendenning	No	No
Derry Weekly News	1892–1956	Unstated	Owned by North of Ireland Publishing Co.	No	No
Donegal Democrat	1919–	Nationalist	J. Downey, C.A. Stephens	No	No
Donegal Vindicator/Donegal Independent	1831–1956	Nationalist	J. McAdam	No	No
Down Recorder	1836–	Unionist	W.Y. Crichton	No	No
Drogheda Advertiser	1837–1929	Unionist	R.H. Taylor	No	No
Drogheda Argus	1835–	Nationalist	M. McKeown	No	No
Drogheda Independent	1884–	Nationalist	M.A. Casey	No	No
Dromore Leader	1916–	Unionist	J. Lindsay	No	No
Dromore Weekly Times	1900–52	Neutral	R.J. Hunter	No	No

Title	Publication dates	Political leaning/ orientation	Key figures	Censored	Suppressed
Dundalk Democrat	1849–	Nationalist	T.F. McGahon	No	No
Dundalk Examiner	1830–1960	Nationalist	J. Mathews	Yes	Yes
Dundalk Herald	1868–1921	Unionist		No	No
Dungannon Democrat	1913–23	Nationalist	B. Conway	No	No
Dungarvan Observer	1912–	Unstated	J.A. Lynch	No	No
East Galway Democrat	1910–49	Nationalist	N.E. O'Carroll	No	No
Enniscorthy Echo	1902–	Nationalist	William Sears	Yes	Yes
Enniscorthy Guardian	1889–	Nationalist	Owned by *Wexford People*	No	No
Fermanagh Herald	1902–	Nationalist	P.A. MacManus	No	No
Fermanagh Times	1880–1949	Unionist	R.H. Ritchie	No	No
Frontier Sentinel	1904–72	Nationalist	J. Connellan	No	No
Galway Express	1853–1920	Unionist up to 1917	H.D. Fisher, T. Walshe	Yes	Yes
Galway Observer	1881–1966	Nationalist	A.G. Scott	No	No
Galway Pilot	1883–1918	Independent	J.N. Sleator	No	No
Impartial Reporter	1825–	Unionist	W.C. Trimble	No	No
Irish Daily Telegraph	1904–52	Neutral	W&G Baird Ltd (owners of *Belfast Telegraph*)	No	No
Irish Post	1910–20	Unionist	W&G Baird Ltd (owners of *Belfast Telegraph*)	No	No
Kerry Advocate	1914–1916	Nationalist	M.P. Ryle, T. O'Donnell	No	No
Kerry Evening Post	1774–1917	Unionist	G. Raymond	No	No

Title	Publication dates	Political leaning/ orientation	Key figures	Censored	Suppressed
Kerryman/Liberator	1904–	Nationalist	M. Griffin, T. Nolan, D. Nolan	Yes	Yes
Kerry News	1894–1941	Nationalist	C. O'Mahony	Yes	Yes
Kerry People	1902–28	Nationalist	M.P. Ryle	No	No
Kerry Press	1914–16	Nationalist	J. Savage	No	No
Kerry Sentinel	1878–1918	Nationalist	E. Harrington	No	No
Kerry Weekly Reporter	1883–1936	Nationalist	C. O'Mahony	Yes	Yes
Kildare Observer	1879–1935	Independent	J. Gray	No	No
Kilkenny Journal	1766–1965	Nationalist	Kenealy family, J. Upton	No	No
Kilkenny Moderator	1814–1925	Unionist	I.B. Lalor	No	No
Kilkenny People	1893–	Nationalist	E.T. Keane	Yes	Yes
Killarney Echo	1899–1920	Nationalist		Yes	Yes
Kilrush Herald	1877–1922	Independent	P.J. Boyle	No	No
King's County Chronicle/Leinster Reporter	1845–1963	Unionist	J. Wright, A. Wright	No	No
King's County Independent	1894–	Nationalist	Owned by *Westmeath Independent*	No	No
Larne Times	1891–1983	Unstated	W&G Baird Ltd (owners of *Belfast Telegraph*)	No	No
Leinster Express	1831–	Independent	M.C. Carey	No	No
Leinster Leader	1880–	Nationalist	J.L. Carew, M. O'Kelly	Yes	No

Title	Publication dates	Political leaning/ orientation	Key figures	Censored	Suppressed
Leitrim Advertiser	1856–1924	Independent	B. McKiernan	No	No
Leitrim Observer	1890–	Nationalist	P. Dunne	No	Yes
Limerick Chronicle	1766–1953	Unionist	J.A. Baldwin	No	No
Limerick Echo	1898–1947	Nationalist	C. O'Sullivan	Yes	Yes
Limerick Leader	1889–	Nationalist	J. Buckley, C. Cregan	Yes	Yes
Lisburn Herald	1891–1969	Unionist	R. McMullen, J. McCarrison	No	No
Lisburn Standard	1876–1959	Unionist	V. McMurray, J. Kennedy	No	No
Londonderry Sentinel	1829–	Unionist	W. Colhoun, J. Colhoun, J.C. Orr	No	No
Longford Independent	1868–1925	Independent	J.H. Turner	No	No
Longford Journal	1839–1937	Unionist	W.T. Dann	No	No
Longford Leader	1897–	Nationalist	J.P. Farrell	No	No
Lurgan Mail	1890–	Unionist	L. Richardson	No	No
Mayo News	1892–	Nationalist	P.J. Doris, W. Doris	Yes	Yes
Mayoman	1919–21	Nationalist	J.J. Collins	No	No
Meath Chronicle	1897–	Nationalist	T. Daly, J. Davis, H.G. Smith, P. Quilty	Yes	Yes
Meath Herald	1845–1936	Unionist	W.A. McDougall	No	No
Midland Tribune	1881–	Nationalist	J. Pike, M. Powell	Yes	Yes
Mid–Ulster Mail	1891–	Unionist	John & H.L. Glasgow	No	No
Munster Express	1860–1935	Nationalist	E. Walsh	No	No

Title	Publication dates	Political leaning/ orientation	Key figures	Censored	Suppressed
Munster News	1851–1935	Nationalist	F. Counihan & Sons	Yes	Yes
Nationalist and Leinster Times	1883–	Nationalist	J. Reddy	Yes	No
Nenagh Guardian	1838–	Unionist up to 1916	Prior family, J. Ryan	No	No
Nenagh News	1894–1926	Nationalist	J.F. Power	No	No
New Ross Standard	1879–	Nationalist	Owned by *Wexford People*	No	No
Newry Reporter	1867–	Independent	J.A. Bell	No	No
Newry Telegraph	1812–1970	Unionist	J. Brown	No	No
Newtownards Chronicle	1873–	Unionist	Henry family	No	No
North Antrim Standard	1887–1922	Unionist	J.M. Russell	No	No
North Down Herald/ Newtownards Herald	1871–1957	Unionist	R.D. Montgomery	No	No
Northern Constitution	1875–	Unionist	J.M. Russell	No	No
Northern Standard	1839–	Unionist	P. McMinn, J.J. Turley	No	No
Portadown Express	1906–20	Unionist	A. Shannon	No	No
Portadown News	1859–1982	Unionist	J. Young, J. Campbell	No	No
Roscommon Herald	1859–	Nationalist	J. Tully	No	No
Roscommon Journal	1828–1927	Independent	W. Tully	No	No
Roscommon Messenger	1848–1935	Nationalist	J.P. Hayden	No	No
Skibbereen Eagle	1857–1922	Independent	J.T. Wolfe, P. Sheehy	No	No
Sligo Champion	1836–	Nationalist	P.A. McHugh, A. McHugh	Yes	No
Sligo Independent	1855–1961	Unionist	W.D. Peebles	No	No

Title	Publication dates	Political leaning/orientation	Key figures	Censored	Suppressed
Sligo Nationalist/Connachtman	1910–20	Nationalist	B. McTernan, R.G. Bradshaw	Yes	Yes
Southern Star	1890–	Nationalist	J.M. Burke, P. O'Hourihane, S. Buckley, S. Hales	Yes	Yes
Strabane Chronicle	1896–	Independent	North-West of Ireland Printing & Publishing Co.	No	No
Strabane Weekly News	1908–	Unionist	Owned by *Tyrone Constitution*	No	No
Strokestown Democrat	1913–48	Nationalist	P. Morahan	No	No
Tipperary People/Tipperaryman	1921–34	Nationalist	J.R. & E. McCormack	No	No
Tipperary Star	1909–	Nationalist	E. Long	Yes	No
Tuam Herald	1837–	Nationalist	R.J. Kelly, J. Burke	No	No
Tyrone Constitution	1844–	Unionist	T. Johnston, R.A. Parke	No	No
Tyrone Courier	1880–	Unionist	R.T. Simpson	No	No
Ulster Gazette	1844–	Unionist	W.J. Greer, J.W. Clarke	No	No
Ulster Herald	1901–	Nationalist	M. Lynch, A. Mulvey	Yes	No
Waterford News	1848–	Nationalist	E. Downey	Yes	Yes
Waterford Standard	1863–1953	Unionist	R. Whalley, D.C. Boyd	No	No
Waterford Star	1891–	Nationalist	C. O'Mahony	No	No
Weekly Observer	1914–27	Nationalist	A.J. Byrnes, S. Brouder	Yes	Yes
Western Nationalist	1907–20	Nationalist	J. Flanagan	No	No
Western News	1876–1926	Nationalist	W. Hastings	No	No
Western People	1883–	Nationalist	T. Devere, T.A. Walsh	No	No

Title	Publication dates	Political leaning/ orientation	Key figures	Censored	Suppressed
Westmeath Examiner	1882–	Nationalist	J.P. Hayden	No	No
Westmeath Guardian	1835–1928	Unionist	F.J. Farrell	No	No
Westmeath Independent	1846–	Nationalist	T. Chapman, M. McDermott-Hayes	Yes	Yes
Westmeath Nationalist/Midland Reporter	1891–1939	Nationalist	G.W. Tully	No	No
Wexford Free Press	1888–1971	Nationalist	M.A. Corcoran, W. Corcoran	No	No
Wexford People	1853–	Nationalist	E. O'Cullen	Yes	No
Wicklow Newsletter	1858–1927	Unionist	F. McPhail, R. Egan	No	No
Wicklow People	1882–	Nationalist	Owned by *Wexford People*	No	No
Wicklow Press	1905–16	Nationalist	M.A. Corcoran, W. Corcoran	No	No

Appendix C
Newspaper Timelines

Chapter 2 The Pale and Beyond: Leinster

Meath Chronicle
1897 Founded by Tom Daly with the assistance of his brother Michael.
1907 Printing operation moves from Kells to Navan.
1917 Acquired by James Davis following the death of the Daly brothers.
1897–1919 Edited successively by Tom Daly, Michael Daly, Michael Judge, and Hugh G. Smith.
1918 Printing machinery seized by Crown forces.
1919–60 Edited by Patrick Quilty.

Enniscorthy Echo
1902 Founded by group led by William Sears but also including Sir Thomas Esmonde, sitting MP for North Wexford, as financial backer.
1905 William Sears unsuccessfully seeks nomination as Irish Parliamentary Party candidate for South Mayo constituency. Sears transfers allegiance to Sinn Féin soon afterwards.
1907–9 Sir Thomas Esmonde leaves Irish Parliamentary Party to join Sinn Féin. On his return to the Irish Parliamentary Party Esmonde begins to sever his links with the paper.
1914 Paper comes to the attention of police authorities for the first time.
1916 Suppressed following Easter Rising and does not reappear until February 1917.
1918 William Sears elected as Sinn Féin MP for South Mayo.
1916–21 William Sears serves various terms of imprisonment along with other journalists from the paper.
1929 Death of William Sears.

Kilkenny People
1893 Founded by E.T. Keane and P.J. O'Keefe.
1916 Paper comes to the attention of the Press Censor in the aftermath of the Easter Rising.
1917 Keane arrested for making a seditious speech. Paper suppressed from July until October for infringing Defence of the Realm regulations.
1919 Paper suppressed from early August until mid-September for breaching Defence of the Realm regulations. Keane subsequently receives twenty-eight-day prison sentence for possession of firearms.
1893–1945 E.T. Keane, editor–proprietor.

Midland Tribune

1881 Founded by three Catholic priests: Robert Little, Denis Sheehan, and Patrick Brennan.

1888 John Powell assumes proprietorship.

1892 Margaret Powell (wife of John) assumes legal ownership.

1901 Death of John Powell.

1912 James Pike appointed editor.

1919 Paper suppressed for one week in September for publishing advertisement for Dáil Éireann loan.

1892–1931 Margaret Powell, proprietor.

1912–48 James Pike, editor.

Chapter 3 West of the Shannon: Connacht

Tuam Herald

1837 Founded by Richard Kelly.

1884 R.J. Kelly assumes ownership.

1901 John Burke joins paper.

1884–1930 R.J. Kelly, editor–proprietor.

1930 R.J. Kelly sells paper.

1931 Death of R.J. Kelly, John Burke acquires paper.

Roscommon Herald

1859 Founded by George Tully.

1881 Jasper Tully inherits ownership.

1892–1906 Tully serves as Irish Parliamentary Party MP for South Leitrim.

1917 Tully unsuccessfully contests North Roscommon by-election.

1881–1938 Jasper Tully, editor–proprietor though Tully resigns editorship a few years prior to his death in 1938.

Mayo News

1892 Founded by brothers William and P.J. Doris.

1898 William Doris elected to Mayo County Council.

1910 William Doris elected Irish Parliamentary MP for West Mayo marking permanent estrangement with P.J. who ultimately supports Sinn Féin.

1910–18 William Doris serves as MP for West Mayo.

1916 P.J. Doris arrested following Easter Rising and detained in Reading Gaol until December.

1918 Paper suppressed from early April until mid-May.

1926 Death of William Doris.

1937 Death of P.J. Doris.

1910–37 P.J. Doris, editor–proprietor.

Leitrim Observer
1890 Founded by Mulvey family.
1904/10 Patrick Dunne acquires paper.
1920 Premises attacked and destroyed by Crown forces in November,
     forcing paper out of publication until January 1923. Patrick Dunne
     subsequently arrested and detained.
1904/10–1968 Patrick Dunne, editor–proprietor.

Chapter 4 Southern Exposure: Munster

Cork Constitution
1822 Launched as a bi-weekly paper, becoming a daily in 1867.
1882 Purchased by H.L. Tivy from the Savage family who had owned the
     paper for several years.
1879–1919 Edited by William J. Ludgate.
1919–21 Presses attacked by IRA, threats issued to H.L. Tivy.
1920 H.L. Tivy assumes editorial control.
1922 Machinery wrecked by anti-Treaty forces, publication suspended.
1924 Ceases publication for good.

Skibbereen Eagle
1858 Founded by John William Potter.
1874 Fred Potter assumes full control.
1898 Publication of editorial stating the paper was 'keeping its eye on the
     Tsar of Russia'.
1906 Death of Fred Potter, paper inherited by Eldon Potter.
1908 Jasper Wolfe becomes director.
1915 Patrick Sheehy becomes editor.
1917 Printing machinery vandalised following break-in at offices.
1920 Patrick Sheehy attacked in his home.
1922 Ceases publication for good.
1858–1922 Variously published as the *Skibbereen and West Carbery Eagle*, *West
     Cork Eagle*, and the *Cork County Eagle*.

Southern Star
1890 Founded by John O'Sullivan with the aid of his brother Florence
     O'Sullivan.
1892 Acquired by consortium headed by Monsignor John O'Leary.
1890–1917 Edited by several different journalists including Florence
     O'Sullivan, J.J. Comerford, Michael J. Flynn, Patrick O'Driscoll,
     Seumas O'Kelly, D.D. Sheehan, and J.M. Burke.
1916 Printing machinery seized by police and paper suppressed for one month.
1917 Purchased by Sinn Féin interests led by Peadar O'Hourihane and
     including Michael Collins.

1918 Ernest Blythe appointed editor but arrested shortly afterwards.

1918–19 Suppressed on three separate occasions, the lengthiest suppression lasting from August 1918 to April 1919.

1916–21 Editors during this time, in addition to Ernest Blythe, include Peadar O'Hourihane, Seán Hayes, Dick Connolly, Arthur Nix, Eoin Sharkey, and J.M. Burke (for the second time).

Clonmel Chronicle

1848 Founded by group headed by Joseph Napier Higgins and later acquired by Edmond Woods.

1893 Acquired by trio of journalists led by David Montgomery.

1909 Arthur Ross Burns becomes editor.

1910 New board of directors appointed.

1909–27 Arthur Ross Burns, editor.

1935 Ceased publication following acquisition by *Clonmel Nationalist*.

Kerryman

1904 Founded by Maurice Griffin, Thomas Nolan, and Daniel Nolan.

1908 Maurice Griffin becomes a member of Sinn Féin.

1916 Maurice Griffin arrested and detained following Easter Rising. Paper suppressed from mid-August until early October.

1919 Briefly suppressed for publishing advertisement for Dáil Éireann loan.

1920 Publication suspended for two weeks due to high level of violence in Tralee area.

1921 Printing works and offices wrecked by Crown forces resulting in cessation of publication until August 1923.

Chapter 5 Northern Drumbeats: Ulster

Impartial Reporter

1825 Founded by John Gregsten with William Trimble as first editor.

1834 William Trimble assumes proprietorship following death of John Gregsten.

1883 William Copeland Trimble assumes control of paper.

1888 Death of William Trimble.

1912 William Copeland Trimble forms guard of honour, known as the 'Enniskillen Horse', for Edward Carson's visit to the town and subsequently endeavours to establish permanent cavalry regiment.

1916 Death of Noel Trimble, son of William Copeland Trimble, while serving in the British Army in France during World War I.

1919–21 William Copeland Trimble tours Australia, USA, and Canada.

1941 Death of William Copeland Trimble.

1883–1941 William Copeland Trimble, editor–proprietor.

Londonderry Sentinel

1829 Founded by William Wallen.

1843 Death of William Wallen.

1857 James Colhoun assumes joint proprietorship with Thomas Chambers.

1877/8 James Colhoun assumes sole proprietorship.

1893–1931 J.C. Orr, editor.

1897 Death of James Colhoun following which control of paper passes to
     William Colhoun.

1915 Death of William Colhoun following which control of paper passes to
     his son James.

1945 Death of James Colhoun.

Anglo-Celt

1846 Founded by Sir John Young with Gustavus Tuite D'Alton as first
     editor.

1847 Acquired by Zacariah Wallace.

1852 Conviction and imprisonment of Zacariah Wallace.

1857 Death of Zacariah Wallace.

1858–64 Paper ceases publication.

1864 John F. O'Hanlon becomes owner and editor.

1885 Death of John F. O'Hanlon.

1908 E.T. O'Hanlon and J.F. O'Hanlon assume joint control.

1918 J.F. O'Hanlon stands as Irish Parliamentary Party candidate at East
     Cavan by-election in opposition to Sinn Féin's Arthur Griffith.

1927 J.F. O'Hanlon elected to Dáil Éireann.

1947 Death of E.T. O'Hanlon, editor for sixty-one years.

1956 Death of J.F. O'Hanlon, managing-director for sixty years.

Donegal Democrat

1919 Founded by John Downey and C.A. Stephens.

1919–47 John Downey, editor.

1947 Death of John Downey.

1971 Death of C.A. Stephens.

Bibliography

Primary sources

Contemporary publications
Newspaper press directory and advertisers' guide 1917
Newspaper press directory and advertisers' guide 1918
Newspaper press directory and advertisers' guide 1922

State documents
National Archives of Ireland
Census of Ireland 1901/1911 (www.census.nationalarchives.ie/)
Press Censorship Records 1916–1919

The National Archives (United Kingdom), Kew
Colonial Office files

Parliamentary publications
Dáil Éireann, Official Report of the Parliamentary Debates of the Houses of
    the Oireachtas, January 1919 to the present
    (https://www.oireachtas.ie/en/debates/find/)

Personal papers
Bureau of Military History, Dublin
Ernest Blythe (WS939)
Seán Brouder (WS1236)
Mary Alden Childers collection (CD6)
William Myles (WS795)

National Library of Ireland
Piaras Béaslaí papers
Florence O'Donoghue papers
John Redmond papers

University College Dublin
Ernest Blythe papers
Desmond Fitzgerald papers
Irish Volunteers papers

Newspapers and periodicals

Anglo-Celt	*Killarney Echo*
Ballymena Observer	*Leinster Express*
Banbridge Chronicle	*Leitrim Observer*
Belfast Newsletter	*Limerick Leader*
Belfast Telegraph	*Lisburn Herald*
Clare Champion	*Londonderry Sentinel*
Clonmel Chronicle	*Lurgan Mail*
Clonmel Nationalist	*Mayo News*
Connacht Sentinel	*Meath Chronicle*
Connacht Tribune	*Midland Tribune*
Connaught Telegraph	*Munster Express*
Cork Constitution	*Nationalist and Leinster Times*
Cork Examiner	*Nenagh Guardian*
Daily News	*Newry Reporter*
Derry Journal	*Newry Telegraph*
Derry People	*Newtownards Chronicle*
Donegal Democrat	*Northern Standard*
Donegal Vindicator	*Offaly Independent*
Down Recorder	*Roscommon Herald*
Drogheda Independent	*Skibbereen Eagle*
Dundalk Democrat	*Sligo Champion*
Enniscorthy Echo	*Sligo Nationalist*
Fermanagh Herald	*Southern Star*
Freeman's Journal	*Tipperary Star*
Frontier Sentinel	*Tuam Herald*
Impartial Reporter	*Tyrone Constitution*
Irish Bulletin	*Tyrone Courier*
Irish Independent	*Ulster Herald*
Irish Journalist	*Western People*
Irish Press	*Westmeath Examiner*
Irish Times	*Westmeath Independent*
Kerryman	*Wexford People*
Kilkenny People	

Books

Barry, Tom, *Guerrilla days in Ireland* (Dublin, 1981).

Breen, Dan, *My fight for Irish freedom* (Dublin, 1981).

Brennan, Robert, *Allegiance* (Dublin, 1950).

Comerford, J.J., *My Kilkenny IRA days: 1916–22* (Kilkenny, 1978).

Deasy, Liam, *Towards Ireland free: the West Cork brigade in the War of Independence, 1917–1921* (Dublin, 1973).

Escott, T.H.S., *Masters of English journalism: a study of personal forces* (London, 1911).

Secondary sources

Books and essays

Augusteijn, Joost, *From public defiance to guerrilla warfare: the experience of ordinary volunteers in the Irish War of Independence, 1916–1921* (Dublin, 1996).

Barton, B.E., 'The origins and development of unionism in Fermanagh, 1885–1914' in Eileen M. Murphy and William J. Roulston (eds), *Tyrone: history and society: interdisciplinary essays on the history of an Irish county* (Dublin, 2004), pp 307–37.

Bew, Paul, *Conflict and conciliation in Ireland 1890–1910: Parnellites and radical agrarians* (Oxford, 1987).

Bingham, Adrian, and Conboy, Martin, *Tabloid century: the popular press in Britain, 1896 to the present* (Oxford, 2015).

Borgonovo, John, *Spies, informers and the 'Anti-Sinn Féin Society': the intelligence war in Cork city, 1919–1921* (Dublin, 2007).

—— *The dynamics of war and revolution: Cork City, 1916–1918* (Cork, 2013).

Boyce, D. George, *Nationalism in Ireland* (3rd ed., London, 1995).

—— *Nineteenth-century Ireland: the search for stability* (rev. ed., Dublin, 2005).

Buckley, Patrick, 'Blythe, Ernest (de Blaghd, Earnán)' in James McGuire and James Quinn (eds), *Dictionary of Irish biography* (Cambridge, 2009).

Burke, John, 'Evolving nationalism: Michael McDermott-Hayes and the *Westmeath Independent*, 1900–20' in Ian Kenneally and James T. O'Donnell (eds), *The Irish regional press, 1892–2018: revival, revolution and republic* (Dublin, 2018), pp 29–40.

Burke, William P., *History of Clonmel* (2nd ed., Kilkenny, 1983).

Cadogan, Tim, and Falvey, Jeremiah, *A biographical dictionary of Cork* (Dublin, 2001).

Callanan, Frank, *The Parnell split, 1890–91* (Cork, 1992).

Clark, Gemma M., *Everyday violence in the Irish Civil War* (Cambridge, 2014).

Coleman, Marie, *County Longford and the Irish Revolution, 1910–1923* (Dublin, 2003).

—— 'Keane, Edward Thomas ('E.T.')' in James McGuire and James Quinn (eds), *Dictionary of Irish biography* (Cambridge, 2009).

Conboy, Martin, *Journalism: a critical history* (London, 2004).

Coogan, Oliver, *Politics and war in Meath, 1913–23* (Dunshaughlin, 1983).

Coogan, Tim Pat, *Michael Collins: a biography* (London, 1990).

Costello, Francis, *The Irish Revolution and its aftermath, 1916–1923: years of revolt* (Dublin, 2003).

Cousins, Colin, *Armagh and the Great War* (Dublin, 2011).

Craig, Maurice, *The personality of Leinster* (Dublin, 1961).

Cronin, Maurice, 'Hales, Seán' in James McGuire and James Quinn (eds), *Dictionary of Irish biography* (Cambridge, 2009).

Cronin, Mike, Rouse, Paul, and Duncan, Mark, *The GAA: county by county* (Cork, 2011).

Curry, James, '*The Worker*: James Connolly's organ of the Irish working class' in Mark O'Brien and Felix M. Larkin (eds), *Periodicals and journalism in twentieth century Ireland: writing against the grain* (Dublin, 2014), pp 75–88.

Davis, Richard P., *Arthur Griffith and non-violent Sinn Féin* (Dublin, 1974).

De Búrca, Marcus, *The GAA: a history* (Dublin, 1980).

Deignan, Padraig, *The Protestant community in Sligo, 1914–49* (Dublin, 2010).

Dempsey, Pauric J. and Hawkins, Richard, 'Chartres, John Smith' in James McGuire and James Quinn (eds), *Dictionary of Irish biography* (Cambridge, 2009).

Elliot, Marianne, *The Catholics of Ulster* (London, 2000).

Farry, Michael, *The aftermath of revolution: Sligo, 1921–23* (Dublin, 2000).

—— *The Irish revolution, 1912–23: Sligo* (Dublin, 2012).

Ferguson, Niall, *The pity of war* (London, 1998).

Ferriter, Diarmaid, *The transformation of Ireland, 1900–2000* (London, 2004).

Fitzpatrick, David, *Politics and Irish life, 1913–1921: provincial experience of war and revolution* (Cork, 1998).

Foley, Michael, 'How journalism became a profession' in Kevin Rafter (ed.), *Irish journalism before independence: more a disease than a profession* (Manchester, 2011), pp 22–35.

Foster, R.F., *Charles Stewart Parnell: the man and his family* (Atlantic Highlands, NJ, 1976).

Fussell, Paul, *The Great War and modern memory* (London, 1981).

Garvin, Tom, *Preventing the future: why was Ireland so poor for so long?* (Dublin, 2004).

Gaughan, J. Anthony, *A political odyssey: Thomas O'Donnell, M.P. for West Kerry, 1900–1918* (Dublin, 1983).

Glandon, Virginia E., *Arthur Griffith and the advanced-nationalist press, Ireland, 1900–1922* (New York, 1985).

Greene, Ted, *Drogheda, its place in Ireland's history* (Julianstown, 2006).

Hart, Peter, *The IRA and its enemies: violence and community in Cork, 1916–1923* (Oxford, 1998).

—— *Mick: the real Michael Collins* (London, 2005).

Hayes, Joseph C., *Guide to Tipperary newspapers, 1770–1989* (Tipperary, 1989).

Hayward, Richard, *Munster and the city of Cork* (London, 1964).

Hickey, D.J. and Doherty, J.E., *A new dictionary of Irish history from 1800* (Dublin, 2005).

Hochschild, Adam, *To end all wars: a story of protest and patriotism in the First World War* (London, 2012).

Hopkinson, Michael, *The Irish War of Independence* (Dublin, 2002).

Horgan, John, 'The provincial papers of Ireland: ownership and control and the representation of "community"' in Desmond Bell (ed.), *Is the Irish Press independent? essays on ownership and control of the provincial, national, and international press in Ireland* (Dublin, 1986), pp 10–13.

Howard, Philip E.N., Rainie, Lee, and Jones, Steve, 'Days and nights on the Internet' in Barry Wellman and Caroline Haythornwaite (eds), *The internet in everyday life* (Oxford, 2002), pp 45–73.

Hunt, Tom, 'County Longford: sport and society, 1850–1905' in Martin Morris, James Kelly, and Fergus O'Ferrall (eds), *Longford: history and society: interdisciplinary essays on the history of an Irish county* (Dublin, 2010), pp 511–38.

Inoue, Keiko, 'Propaganda II: propaganda of Dáil Éireann, 1919–21' in Joost Augusteijn (ed.), *The Irish Revolution, 1913–1923* (London, 2002), pp 87–102.

James, Dermot, *From the margins to the centre: a history of the Irish Times* (Dublin, 2008).

Jordan, Donald E. Jr, *Land and popular politics in Ireland: County Mayo from the Plantation to the Land War* (New York, 1994).

Keating, Anthony, 'Criminal libel, censorship and contempt of court: D.C. Boyd's editorship of the *Waterford Standard*' in Kevin Rafter and Mark O'Brien (eds), *The state in transition: essays in honour of John Horgan* (Dublin, 2015), pp 213–34.

Kenneally, Ian, *The paper wall: newspapers and propaganda in Ireland, 1919–1921* (Cork, 2008).

—— 'Truce to treaty: Irish journalists and the 1920–21 peace process' in Kevin Rafter (ed.), *Irish journalism before independence: more a disease than a profession* (Manchester, 2011), pp 213–25.

—— 'A tainted source'? The *Irish Bulletin*, 1919–21' in Mark O'Brien and Felix M. Larkin (eds), *Periodicals and journalism in twentieth century Ireland: writing against the grain* (Dublin, 2014), pp 89–101.

Kennedy, Michael, 'Brennan, Robert' and 'Lester, Seán (John Ernest)' in James McGuire and James Quinn (eds), *Dictionary of Irish biography* (Cambridge, 2009).

Knightley, Phillip, *The first casualty; from the Crimea to Vietnam: the war correspondent as hero, propagandist, and myth maker* (rev. ed., London, 1982).

Lacy, Brian, *Siege city: the story of Derry and Londonderry* (Belfast, 1990).

Laffan Michael, 'Labour must wait: Ireland's conservative revolution' in Ciaran Brady and Patrick J. Corish (eds), *Radicals, rebels, and establishments: papers read before the Irish Conference of Historians, Maynooth, 16–19 June 1983* (Maynooth, 1983), pp 203–22.

Larkin, Felix M., 'Gray, Edmund William Dwyer' in James McGuire and James Quinn (eds), *Dictionary of Irish biography* (Cambridge, 2009).

—— 'Double helix: two elites in politics and journalism in Ireland, 1870–1918' in Ciaran O'Neill (ed.), *Irish elites in the nineteenth century* (Dublin, 2012), pp 125–36.

—— 'Parnell, politics and the press in Ireland 1875–1924' in Pauric Travers and Donal McCartney (eds), *Parnell reconsidered* (Dublin, 2013), pp 76–91.

—— 'Green shoots of the new journalism in the *Freeman's Journal*, 1877–1890' in Karen Steele and Michael de Nie (eds), *Ireland and the new journalism* (New York, 2014), pp 35–55.

Lee, J.J., *Ireland 1912–1985: politics and society* (Cambridge, 1989).

Legg, Marie-Louise, *Newspapers and nationalism: the Irish provincial press, 1850–1922* (Dublin, 1998).

Li, Xigen (ed.), *Internet newspapers: the making of a mainstream medium* (Mahwah, NJ, 2005).

Livingstone, Peadar, *The Fermanagh story: a documented history of the County Fermanagh from the earliest times to the present day* (Enniskillen, 1969).

—— *The Monaghan story: a documented history of the County Monaghan from the earliest times to 1976* (Enniskillen, 1980).

Lyons, F.S.L., *The fall of Parnell, 1890–91* (London, 1960).

MacAnnaidh, Séamus, *Fermanagh books, writers, and newspapers of the nineteenth century* (Enniskillen, 1999).

McCabe, Desmond, 'Trimble, William' in James McGuire and James Quinn (eds), *Dictionary of Irish biography* (Cambridge, 2009).

McCabe, M.P., *For God and Ireland: the fight for moral superiority in Ireland, 1922–1932* (Dublin, 2013).

McGee, Owen, 'Doris, William' and 'McHugh, Patrick Aloysius' in James McGuire and James Quinn (eds), *Dictionary of Irish biography* (Cambridge, 2009).

McMahon, Seán, *A history of County Derry* (Dublin, 2004).

Margach, James, *The abuse of power: the war between Downing Street and the media from Lloyd George to Callaghan* (London, 1978).

Mattimoe, Cyril, *North Roscommon: its people and past* (Boyle, 1992).

Martin, Shannon E., 'Newspaper history traditions' in Shannon E. Martin and David A. Copeland (eds), *The function of newspapers in society: a global perspective* (Westport, Conn., 2003), pp 1–11.

Maume, Patrick, *The long gestation: Irish nationalist life, 1891–1928* (Dublin, 1999).

—— 'Esmonde, Sir Thomas Henry Grattan' and 'Ryle, Maurice P.' in James McGuire and James Quinn (eds), *Dictionary of Irish biography* (Cambridge, 2009).

—— 'Irish Ireland and Catholic Whiggery: D.P. Moran and *The Leader*' in Mark O'Brien and Felix M. Larkin (eds), *Periodicals and journalism in twentieth century Ireland: writing against the grain* (Dublin, 2014), pp 47–60.

Meehan, Ciara, '"The prose of logic and scorn": Arthur Griffith and Sinn Féin, 1906–1914' in Kevin Rafter (ed.), *Irish journalism before independence: more a disease than a profession* (Manchester, 2011), pp 186–99.

Meehan, Rosa, *The story of Mayo* (Castlebar, 2003).

Moran, Gerard, 'The emergence and consolidation of the Home Rule movement in County Cavan, 1870–86' in Raymond Gillespie (ed.), *Cavan: essays on the history of an Irish county* (Dublin, 1995), pp 159–76.

Morgan, Gerard, 'The Ancient Order of Hibernians in County Longford' in Martin Morris, James Kelly, and Fergus O'Ferrall (eds), *Longford: history and society: interdisciplinary essays on the history of an Irish county* (Dublin, 2010), pp 577–600.

Morrissey, Thomas J., 'O'Neill, Laurence' in James McGuire and James Quinn (eds), *Dictionary of Irish biography* (Cambridge, 2009).

Murphy, Brian P., *The origins and organisation of British propaganda in Ireland, 1920* (Cork, 2006).

Murphy, Gerard, *The year of disappearances: political killings in Cork, 1920–1921* (Dublin, 2010).

Murphy, William, 'Enniscorthy's Revolution' in Colm Tóibín (ed.), *Enniscorthy: a history* (Wexford, 2010), pp 399–426.

Novick, Benjamin Z., *Conceiving revolution: Irish nationalist propaganda during the First World War* (Dublin, 2001).

—— 'Propaganda I: advanced nationalist propaganda and moralistic revolution, 1914–18' in Joost Augusteijn (ed.), *The Irish Revolution, 1913–1923* (London, 2002), pp 32–48.

Ó Baoighill, Pádraig, 'The Irish language in Tyrone' in Charles Dillon and Henry A. Jefferies (eds), *Tyrone: history and society* (Dublin, 2000), pp 665–96.

O'Brien, Mark, *De Valera, Fianna Fáil and the Irish Press: the truth in news?* (Dublin, 2001).

—— *The Irish Times: a history* (Dublin, 2008).

—— 'Journalism in Ireland: the evolution of a discipline' in Kevin Rafter (ed.), *Irish journalism before independence: more a disease than a profession* (Manchester, 2011), pp 9–21.

O'Brien, Mark and Rafter, Kevin (eds), *Independent newspapers: a history* (Dublin, 2012).

O'Callaghan, M., 'The GAA in County Roscommon' in Martin F. Coffey (ed.), *Roscommon, past and present* (Dublin, 1961), pp 87–110.

O'Donnell, Seán, *Clonmel 1900–1932: a history* (Clonmel, 2010).

O'Driscoll, Des, *Irish Examiner: 100 years of news* (Dublin, 2005).

O'Dwyer, Martin, *A biographical dictionary of Tipperary* (Cashel, 1999).

O'Dwyer, Michael, 'A history of Kilkenny newspapers, 1767–2009' in John Bradley (ed.), *Kilkenny through the centuries: chapters in the history of an Irish city* (Kilkenny, 2009), pp 382–94.

Oram, Hugh, *The newspaper book: a history of newspapers in Ireland, 1649–1983* (Dublin, 1983).

Phoenix, Éamon, 'Nationalism in Tyrone, 1880–1972' in Charles Dillon and Henry A. Jefferies (eds), *Tyrone: history and society* (Dublin, 2000), pp 765–808.

Potter, Matthew, 'Keeping an eye on the Tsar: Frederick Potter and the *Skibbereen Eagle*' in Kevin Rafter (ed.), *Irish journalism before independence: more a disease than a profession* (Manchester, 2011), pp 49–61.

Price, Dominic, *The flame and the candle: war in Mayo 1919–1924* (Cork, 2012).

Read, Donald, *The power of news: the history of Reuters* (2nd ed., Oxford, 1999).

Regan, John M., *The Irish counter-revolution, 1921–1936: treatyite politics and settlement in independent Ireland* (Dublin, 2001).

Reilly, Eileen, 'Cavan in the era of the Great War, 1914–18' in Raymond Gillespie (ed.), *Cavan: essays on the history of an Irish county* (Dublin, 1995), pp 177–95.

Sheehan, Jeremiah, *Worthies of Westmeath: a biographical dictionary with brief lives of famous Westmeath people* (Moate, 1987).

Smith, Gus, *Tommy O'Brien, good evening listeners* (Dublin, 1987).

Steele, Karen, *Women, press, and politics during the Irish revival* (New York, 2007).

Steele, Karen, and de Nie, Michael (eds), *Ireland and the new journalism* (New York, 2014).

Taylor, Philip M., *Munitions of the mind: a history of propaganda from the ancient world to the present era* (3rd ed., New York, 2003).

Thompson, Frank, 'The Land War in County Fermanagh' in Eileen M. Murphy and William J. Roulston (eds), *Fermanagh: history and society: interdisciplinary essays on the history of an Irish county* (Dublin, 2004), pp 287–305.

Tiernan, Sonja, '"Challenging the headship of man": militant suffragism and the *Irish Citizen*' in Mark O'Brien and Felix M. Larkin (eds), *Periodicals and journalism in twentieth century Ireland: writing against the grain* (Dublin, 2014), pp 61–74.

Uí Chollatáin, Regina, *'An Claidheamh Soluis agus Fáinne an Lae*: the turning of the tide' in Mark O'Brien and Felix M. Larkin (eds), *Periodicals and journalism in twentieth-century Ireland: writing against the grain* (Dublin, 2014), pp 31–46.

Ungoed-Thomas, Jasper, *Jasper Wolfe of Skibbereen* (Cork, 2008).

Vaughan, W.E. and Fitzpatrick, A.J., *Irish historical statistics: population, 1821–1971* (Dublin, 1978).

Walsh, Maurice, *The news from Ireland: foreign correspondents and the Irish Revolution* (London, 2008).

Wheatley, Michael, *Nationalism and the Irish Party: provincial Ireland, 1910–1916* (Oxford, 2005).

White, Lawrence William, 'Dolan, Charles Joseph' and 'O'Brien, Nora Connolly' in James McGuire and James Quinn (eds), *Dictionary of Irish biography* (Cambridge, 2009).

Wiener, Joel H., *The Americanization of the British press, 1830s-1914: speed in the age of transatlantic journalism* (New York, 2011).

Williams, Kevin, *International journalism* (London, 2011).

Commemorative editions

75 years of Longford: The Longford Leader 1897–1972 (29 Sept. 1972).

Anglo-Celt: Souvenir Supplement 1846–1996 (30 May 1996).

Connacht Tribune: 100th Anniversary: Souvenir Centenary Supplement (22 May 2009).

Connaught Telegraph: Commemorative Issue (Apr. 1996).

Derry Journal: 225th Anniversary Supplement (6 June 1997).

Donegal Democrat: Anniversary Supplement (27 Aug. 2009).

Drogheda Independent: Centenary Supplement (11 May 1984).

Impartial Reporter: 150th Anniversary Edition (22 May 1975).

The Kerryman: 1904–2004 (5 Aug. 2004).

Leinster Leader: Centenary Supplement (15 Nov. 1980).

Leitrim Observer: 1890–1990: One hundred years of history in the making (28 Nov. 1990).

Mayo News: Centenary Supplement (2 Mar. 1994).

Midland Tribune: 1881–1981: 100 years of a family newspaper (7 Nov. 1981).

Munster Express: Waterford through the ages, 1860–2010 (8 Oct. 2010).

The Nationalist [Clonmel]: *Centenary Supplement 1890–1990* (29 Dec. 1990).

Nationalist and Leinster Times: Centenary Issue 1883–1983 (23 Sept. 1983).

One hundred years of life and times in North Leinster: A Meath Chronicle Centenary publication (30 Aug. 1997).

Roscommon Herald: Centenary Supplement (5 Dec. 1959).

Sligo Champion: Sesquicentenary Issue 1836–1986 (5 Dec. 1986).

Southern Star 1889–1989: Centenary Supplement (11 Nov. 1989).

Tuam Herald: 150th Anniversary Supplement (21 May 1988).

The Tyrone Constitution: 150 years in print (3 Nov. 1994).

Ulster Gazette: 150th Anniversary Supplement (22 Dec. 1994).

Waterford News & Star: 150th Anniversary Supplement (6 Nov. 1998).

Western People, 125th Anniversary 1883–2008 (18 Nov. 2008).
Westmeath Independent: 150th Anniversary Special Supplement (July 1996).

Journal articles

Beaumont, Jacqueline, 'The British press and censorship during the South African War 1899–1902' in *South African Historical Journal*, 41, no. 1 (1999), pp 267–89.

Bingham, Adrian, 'The digitization of newspaper archives: opportunities and challenges for historians' in *Twentieth Century British History*, 21, no. 2 (2010), pp 225–31.

Costello, Francis J., 'The role of propaganda in the Anglo-Irish War 1919–1921' in *The Canadian Journal of Irish Studies*, 14, no. 2 (1989), pp 5–24.

Fitzgerald, Patrick, 'The keys to the Kingdom: the *Kerry Sentinel*, its commercial and political rivals' in *Journal of the Kerry Archaeological and Historical Society*, 2, no. 15 (2015), pp 103–20.

Goldfarb, Alice, 'Words as weapons: propaganda in Britain and Germany during the First World War' in *Journal of Contemporary History*, 13, no. 3 (1978), pp 467–98.

Keating, Anthony, 'Setting the agenda for the press: the 1929 case against the *Waterford Standard*' in *New Hibernia Review*, 1, no. 2 (2012), pp 17–32.

—— 'Sexual crime in the Irish Free State 1922–33: its nature, extent and reporting' in *Irish Studies Review*, 20, no. 2 (2012), pp 135–55.

Larkin, Felix M., 'A great daily organ: the *Freeman's Journal*, 1763–1924 in *History Ireland*, 14, no. 3 (2006), pp 44–9.

—— 'Keeping an eye on Youghal: The *Freeman's Journal* and the Plan of Campaign in East Cork 1886–1892' in *Irish Communications Review*, vol. 13 (2012), pp 19–30.

Moran, Gerard, 'James Daly and the rise and fall of the Land League in the West of Ireland, 1879–82' in *Irish Historical Studies*, 29, no. 114 (1994), pp 189–207.

Novick, Benjamin Z., 'DORA, suppression, and nationalist propaganda in Ireland, 1914–1915' in *New Hibernia Review/Iris Éireannach Nua*, 1, no. 4 (1997), pp 34–52.

O'Brien, Mark, 'Journalism and emerging professionalism in Ireland' in *Journalism practice*, 10, no. 1 (2016), pp 109–22.

—— 'With the Irish in France: the national press and recruitment in Ireland, 1914–1916' in *Media History*, 22, no. 2 (2016), pp 1–15.

Ó'Drisceoil, Donal, 'Keeping disloyalty within bounds? British media control in Ireland, 1914–19' in *Irish Historical Studies*, 38, no. 149 (2012), pp 52–69.

Rynne, Frank, 'This extra parliamentary propaganda: Land League posters' in *History Ireland*, 16, no. 6 (2008), pp 38–41.

Unpublished theses

Doughan, Christopher, 'What the papers said: portrayals of the Irish War of Independence in the British and Irish print media' (MA; NUI Maynooth, 2011).

Reynolds, Shane, 'Fr Michael O'Flanagan and the North Roscommon by-election of 1917: sowing the seeds of republican constitutionalism' (MA; St Patricks College, 2010).

Online sources

'Bill O'Herlihy bids farewell after 49 years on RTÉ', RTÉ World Cup Final coverage, 13 July 2014, available at https://www.youtube.com/watch?v=WEYBSz79ZJM (accessed 1 Feb. 2019).

'*Impartial Reporter* sold to Ulster News Group', *Press Gazette, Fighting for Journalism*, 20 June 2006, available at https://www.pressgazette.co.uk/impartial-reporter-sold-to-ulster-news-group/ (accessed 1 Feb. 2019).

Index

Withdrawn from Stock
Dublin City Public Libraries